With Power Comes Responsibility

ALSO AVAILABLE FROM BLOOMSBURY

A Philosophy of Struggle, Leonard Harris
On Resistance, Howard Caygill
Challenging Power, Cynthia Kaufman

With Power Comes Responsibility

The Politics of Structural Injustice

Maeve McKeown

BLOOMSBURY ACADEMIC
LONDON • NEW YORK • OXFORD • NEW DELHI • SYDNEY

BLOOMSBURY ACADEMIC
Bloomsbury Publishing Plc
50 Bedford Square, London, WC1B 3DP, UK
1385 Broadway, New York, NY 10018, USA
29 Earlsfort Terrace, Dublin 2, Ireland

BLOOMSBURY, BLOOMSBURY ACADEMIC and the Diana logo are trademarks of
Bloomsbury Publishing Plc

First published in Great Britain 2024
Copyright © Maeve McKeown, 2024

Maeve McKeown has asserted her right under the Copyright, Designs and Patents Act,
1988, to be identified as Author of this work.

For legal purposes the Acknowledgements on pp. ix–xiii constitute
an extension of this copyright page.

Cover design by Ben Anslow

Bloomsbury Publishing Plc does not have any control over, or responsibility for, any
third-party websites referred to or in this book. All internet addresses given in this
book were correct at the time of going to press. The author and publisher regret any
inconvenience caused if addresses have changed or sites have ceased to exist,
but can accept no responsibility for any such changes.

A catalogue record for this book is available from the British Library.

A catalog record for this book is available from the Library of Congress.

ISBN: HB: 978-1-3501-9577-6
PB: 978-1-3501-9578-3
ePDF: 978-1-3501-9579-0
eBook: 978-1-3501-9580-6

Typeset by Newgen KnowledgeWorks Pvt. Ltd., Chennai, India
Printed and bound in Great Britain

To find out more about our authors and books visit www.bloomsbury.com
and sign up for our newsletters.

For my parents

Contents

Figure

Acknowledgements

This book began as my PhD dissertation at the School of Public Policy, University College London, completed in 2015. Turning the thesis into a book has taken a lot longer than I had wanted or anticipated. Lots of factors got in the way: mostly ill-health. I have epilepsy, and during the course of my PhD, postdocs and academic work, I've had six seizures, five of which led to hospitalization. Apart from the immediate fallout, a lot of my time and energy goes into preventing seizures, including prioritizing nutrition, fitness and rest. I also have to deal with the side effects of powerful medications that cause fatigue. Some days I wake up and I just can't work. I'm mentioning this because I think it is important to point out just how time-consuming and draining it is to manage a disability. Productivity on the level universities and competitive peers have come to expect is not possible for many people with disabilities. This leaves us at a significant disadvantage in the job market, which is my next point.

Another factor has been job insecurity. I have jumped from job to job, city to city, with all the time and emotional drains that this involves. I've applied for over three hundred jobs and had sixteen job interviews in the course of writing this book. I can't bring myself to total up the hours spent on this labour. It has been relentless. Not to mention the emotional roller coaster of getting my hopes up and having them repeatedly dashed. There have been periods when my inbox contains a daily rejection. None of this is conducive to good research.

When I have found employment, the teaching loads have been excessive, meaning I have had to squeeze research into evenings and weekends. It is only finally, now, in my second year of a tenure track post that I have had the headspace to sit down and finish this book. To that extent, I would like to thank Campus Fryslân at the University of Groningen, who have given me this job security, and whose students on the 'Global Responsibility and Leadership' programme have given me the inspiration and impetus to persist in finishing this book project.

Really, the conditions in academia right now are awful. It is structurally unjust. As a disabled woman, I have been structurally disadvantaged in relation to my male and able-bodied colleagues. The same goes for people of colour. The academy was not built for us, built as it was for white, propertied, able-bodied men. Thus, I am reluctant to perform gratitude to any other academic institutions since they have actively hindered this project. I guess this has been fuel to the fire of writing a book on structural injustice, but it would have been much nicer to have had an easier ride.

Of course, these working conditions seem relatively good when considering the kinds of structural injustices addressed in this book, and to that extent these comments may appear as insignificant gripes in the context of global poverty, labour exploitation and climate crisis. However, I would respond that these working conditions are inhibiting critical research into structural injustices and their solutions. If critical research is one pillar in the fight against structural injustice, then the erosion of working conditions in academia is worth caring about. And, ultimately, if we want a world where everyone has access to quality education, then considering who gets to be part of the academy as a student or staff member is also worthy of attention.

Who I will thank are the colleagues who have put their necks on the line and campaigned for equality and job security in academia. They deserve thanks for their ongoing campaigns to make the academy a friendlier place for people from minority backgrounds.

I realize it is unorthodox to include comments like this in an acknowledgements section, which is usually dedicated to expressing gratitude, but I include this section because I believe we have to stop being so deferential to powerful agents in the name of professionalism. The current conditions in academia are preventing many people from achieving their full potential. I wrote this book in spite of, not because of, the institutional frameworks in which I have been working. Unless we call out the agents that hold us back, nothing will change. I also suspect that many precarious academics will recognize and empathize with these comments.

Having said all this, I am, of course, immensely grateful for many people who have supported me. The process of writing this book went through multiple phases. At each phase, many people have been involved in helping shape the research or talk it through with me. My PhD supervisor, Cécile Laborde, was gracious in letting me explore different possibilities in my engagement with the topics of structural injustice and responsibility. She gave me the autonomy to pursue my research in my own way and at my own pace, as well as providing excellent, rigorous feedback on the content and unparalleled intellectual guidance. Cécile remains a great friend and inspiration. My second supervisor, Albert Weale, helped reign in my more extravagant tendencies and opened my eyes to literature and ideas I might not otherwise have explored. Even though Jonathan Wolff was not an official supervisor of my thesis, he has over the years become an invaluable source of ongoing mentorship and support, critically engaging with my take on structural injustice, but always with kindness and good humour. I am hugely grateful for his wisdom and comradeship. Also, thanks to my PhD cohort, who I spent many happy hours with debating about all their research topics and discussing the trials and tribulations of PhD life.

During the first year of my PhD, I occupied UCL alongside dozens of my fellow students. UCL Occupation stood against the tripling of UK university fees, advocating free education for all. We occupied the university three times, eventually resulting in an injunction being taken out against the UCL13, including me. While these were sometimes testing times, they were also glorious times where I honed insights into activism that I had experienced in earlier life from the anti-sweatshop movement, anti-Iraq war protests and various instances of feminist activism, and learned all sorts of new skills and strategies. This was an immensely productive time for shaping my ideas and knowledge of political responsibility and I would like to thank everyone involved. It was also here that I met David Wearing who invited me to join New Left Project (NLP), an editorial collective dedicated to making left-wing theory and practice more accessible to a general audience. I was an editor at NLP for three years, during which time I met many wonderful comrades, got involved in lots of spats, and ultimately learned loads about structural injustice and responsibility. Thanks Dave for including me, and for your ongoing friendship and support, and to Rhian E. Jones, as the three of us keep the NLP spirit alive.

The intellectual guiding light of this project is Iris Marion Young. Sadly, I never met her, as she passed away before I began my graduate studies. I hope she would appreciate this text, even though I'm sure she would have disagreed with some of it. When I first encountered political theory, I thought it was hopelessly boring and irrelevant; it was reading Iris Marion Young that converted me to this field. I love her work and, from everything I have heard about her, I'm sure I would have loved her as a person too.

I must thank my fellow Iris Marion Young fans who have engaged in countless conversations with me over the years about the themes of this book, including Alasia Nuti, Robin Zheng, Melanie Brazzell, Mara Marin and Mirjam Müller. Alison Jagger, herself a friend and collaborator with Iris, has been a wonderful interlocuter, with great anecdotes about Iris, as well as brilliant insights into her and my work. In more recent years, Jude Browne has become a close collaborator and friend, as we have worked on our edited volume *What Is Structural Injustice?* I am very grateful for Jude's belief in me and mentorship in navigating academic publishing and the job market. Thanks to the contributors to that book, all of whose work has contributed to my own thinking on this topic.

While I have been critical of academic institutions above, I was given the opportunity by Rainer Forst to do a one-year research postdoc at *Justitia Amplificata*. It was a fantastic experience to work in Frankfurt, the home of critical theory, and to spend two months in Berlin under the stewardship of Stefan Gosepath at the Frei Universität. I met many wonderful people in Frankfurt and Berlin, including my fellow postdoc Antoinette Scherz, and it was here in particular that I developed the research strand on historical injustice.

At Oxford University, I met Sarah Bufkin with whom I established a Critical Theory reading group. The conversations there stimulated many thoughts that eventually made their way into these pages. Also at Oxford, I set up the St Hilda's Feminist Salon, where I invited feminist academics, activists and artists to discuss their life and work. I would like to thank all the salon guests, who were exemplars of political-responsibility-taking, as well as the students who helped organize the salons. Special thanks to Laura Paterson who went above and beyond in supporting the salon and being an exceptional source of emotional support; as two provincial girls, we navigated the rarefied world of Oxford University together. At Cambridge, I was grateful to meet wonderful scholars who read drafts of my work and provided invaluable feedback, including Duncan Bell, Rae Langton, Richard Holton and John Filling.

The move to the Netherlands during a pandemic was a bit of a nightmare. So I cannot express my gratitude enough for Élise Rouméas, who has been a pillar of strength in the storm both professionally and personally. Immense thanks also to Charlotte Knowles who became an instant friend for life on our first meeting. She and her husband Richard's friendship (and DIY skills) have meant more to me than they could know.

Many thanks to Liza Thompson, my editor at Bloomsbury, who took a chance on me and this book, as well as the editorial assistants Lucy Harper, Katrina Calsado and Ben Piggott. Also thanks to the anonymous reviewer whose insights helped sharpen the final text.

Versions of draft chapters of this book have been presented at numerous conferences and invited talks: 'Structural Injustice, Historical Injustice, and Reparations' (Duisburg-Essen, 2022), 'The Politics of Poverty' (Groningen, 2022), 'The Corporation in Society' (Utrecht, 2022), 'Structural Injustice and the Law' (UCL, 2022), 'Responsibility for Global Structural Injustice' (Paris-Sorbonne, 2021), 'Structural Injustice' (Cambridge, 2021), Political Philosophy Seminar (Cambridge, 2021), 'Poverty and Feasibility' (ANU, 2019), 'Ethics and Public Policy' (Blavatnik School of Government, 2019), Nuffield Workshop (Oxford, 2019), Philosophy Colloquium (St Gallen, 2018), Open Minds (Manchester, 2018), Philosophy Colloquium (Birmingham, 2018), Birkbeck Study Day (2018), 'Priority in Practice' (Blavatnik School of Government, 2017), 'Colloque Iris Marion Young' (Paris-Sorbonne, 2017), 'Radical Perspectives on Exploitation' (Humboldt, 2016), 'Exploring the Influence of Iris Marion Young' (LMU, 2016), 'From the Transatlantic Slave Trade to Engaging the *Maangamizi*' (QUB, 2016), 'Intergenerational Justice: Historical Perspectives' (Exeter, 2016), 'The Ethics of International Institutions' (Manchester, 2016), CSSJ (Oxford, 2016), The Social Justice Seminar Series (Newcastle, 2015), University of Brighton Philosophy Society (2015), 'Repairing the Past, Imagining the Future' (Edinburgh, 2015),

ECPR (Montreal, 2015), 'Collective Responsibility for the Future' (UCD, 2015), 'Frontiers of Responsibility' (Paris–Sorbonne, 2014), as well as several graduate conferences, notably the Yaoundé PhD seminar. Thanks to the conference organizers for the invitations, and the participants for their comments and suggestions, which have strengthened the book enormously.

Some of the text has appeared in my thesis 'Responsibility without Guilt: A Youngian Approach to Responsibility for Global Injustice' (UCL, 2015) and previously published articles, including 'Backward-Looking Reparations and Structural Injustice', *Contemporary Political Theory* 20, no. 4 (2021): 771–94; 'Iris Marion Young's "Social Connection Model of Responsibility": Clarifying the Meaning of Connection', *Journal of Social Philosophy* 49, no. 3 (Fall 2018): 484–502; 'Sweatshop Labour as Global Structural Exploitation'. In *Exploitation: From Practice to Theory*, ed. Monique Deveaux and Vida Panitch. London: Rowman & Littlefield International, 2017, 35–57; 'Global Structural Exploitation: Towards an Intersectional Definition', *Global Justice: Theory Practice Rhetoric* 9, no. 2 (2016): 155–77.

Finally, I would like to thank my parents. My mother, Stephanie, a research scientist in the fight against cancer, and my father, James, a trade union official, for instilling in me a sense of social justice and the need to fight for a better world. They, in fact, met on a civil rights protest. To my sister Siobhan, her husband Darren, and their children Benjy and Florence, for being my safe haven in Whitley Bay. To my oldest and dearest Belfast friends, Deborah Hughes and Derek Irwin, who know me better than anybody. My Belfast friends Clare Caldwell and Anja McLoughlin, who also relocated to London and keep me grounded. My dear friend Stephen Jeffreys who employed me when I had to take time out of my PhD, without which my academic career might have ended there, and who is sadly no longer with us. My London flatmate Jennie Wightman, who endured the PhD with me with inimitable patience and kindness. My London and festival gang, Florian Fischer, Jon Bradfield, James Woor and Jose Leonardo Castejón, for being the most fun, cultured and lovely bunch imaginable. Liz Nash who always helps me out when needed. Plus all my friends around the world – too many to mention – you know who you are and thank you. And I would like to thank my adorable cat, Magnus Wolfe Tone McKeown, for being a constant source of cuteness, diversion and cuddles throughout the writing of this book.

Chapter 1

From global justice to structural injustice

Power concedes nothing without a demand.
It never did and it never will.

FREDERICK DOUGLASS

Structural injustice is the ordinary injustice that characterizes our world in the early twenty-first century. There are close to eight billion people in the world today, most of whom are living their lives in morally unobjectionable ways, and yet the cumulative outcome of individuals' daily activities is the marginalization and exploitation of the world's poorest people, and climate crisis. While there are egregious instances of deliberate repression in the world today, including mass human rights violations, genocide and authoritarianism, a lot of the injustice we are grappling with is structural. It seems impossible to participate in everyday life without somehow contributing to structural injustice. Responsibility for structural injustice is, therefore, not moral but political, and shared among all agents connected to it.

At least, this is the story we have been told about structural injustice so far. On this view, structural injustice is the unintended, cumulative outcome of individuals' and other agents' quotidian actions. In this book, I tell a different story. Sometimes structural injustice is a mere unintended accumulation of disparate activities, and it will require wholesale systemic change to overcome. However, there are also cases where the injustice *could be ameliorated* without wholesale structural change, but the agents with the capacity to make these changes fail to do it. In yet other cases, even though structural injustice emerges from the accumulation of multiple processes and activities, there are *powerful* agents that *deliberately* perpetuate the injustice because they benefit from it. I call these different types of structural injustice pure, avoidable and deliberate, respectively. In distinguishing different types of structural injustice in this way, I argue further that not all agents are equally responsible for it or responsible in the same way.

My main thesis is that a critical theory of structural injustice should incorporate *power*. With that in mind, in this book I address the questions: what does it mean for injustice to be structural, or what is structural injustice? What is the relationship between power and structural injustice? Who bears responsibility for structural injustice? And if, as Frederick Douglass argued, power concedes nothing without a demand, what can ordinary individuals like you and me do about it? To get started, in this introduction I put structural injustice theory in the context of the global justice debate before looking at its advantages and disadvantages, then I provide a plan of the book.

Responsibility for global justice

The idea of structural injustice is not new. Its origins can be traced back to Marx but perhaps even further.[1] Marx famously argued that exploitation is built into the capitalist economy – exploitation being the extraction of surplus value from the work of the proletariat. Feminists and critical race theorists have highlighted the ways in which sexism and racism are also built into institutions, social norms and social structures.

But the concept of 'structural injustice' has found itself in the philosophical spotlight over the past decade due to the pioneering work of feminist critical theorist Iris Marion Young. She drew attention to the concept by engaging with and critiquing a long-standing debate in philosophy, the 'Global Justice' debate. The global justice debate started with the question 'What do we owe to distant others: the poor, the hungry, the needy?' This was addressed by Peter Singer in his 1972 article 'Famine, Affluence and Morality' and it sparked a philosophical debate that persists to this day.

Singer introduced the famous thought experiment of a small child drowning in a pond. Obviously if a person walks past a pond and sees a small child drowning, they ought to save the child. According to Singer, the underlying principle is this: 'if it is in our power to prevent something bad from happening, without thereby sacrificing anything morally significant, we ought, morally, to do it.'[2] Singer extends this principle to children dying from famine and extreme poverty: if you can save a child's life by donating some spare cash that would

---

[1]Lewis Gordon points out that structural analysis is integral to critical race theories dating back to eighteenth-century critiques of slavery, W. E. B. Du Bois's work on race and even back to antiquity in discussions of *Ma'at* in the *Sekhti-nefer-medu* (1850 BCE). Lewis R. Gordon, 'Decolonizing Structural Justice and Political Responsibility', in *What Is Structural Injustice?*, ed. Jude Browne and Maeve McKeown (Oxford: Oxford University Press, 2024).

[2]Peter Singer, 'Famine, Affluence and Morality', in *The Global Justice Reader*, ed. Thom Brooks (Oxford: Blackwell, 2008), 388.

otherwise be spent on non-essential items (new clothes, a cinema ticket, a bottle of water, etc.), then you ought to.

This seems plausible, but on closer inspection, Singer's starting question is flawed. 'We' implicitly refers to we Northern, rich, (predominantly) white people. But not everyone in the Global North is rich (or white).[3] 'Distant others' refers to Black and Brown people in far-off places who cannot help themselves (like the child drowning in a pond). Implicitly, these people have no agency. What we 'owe' is based on abstract moral reasoning; what looks like a straightforward and unobjectionable moral principle – if we can prevent suffering and death with minimal sacrifice, we should – covers up a web of institutional relationships and power structures that create and sustain global poverty.

'We' rich, white Westerners are not social atoms, unconnected to distant people. We are connected by trade, markets, international laws and institutions. There is no suggestion in Singer's approach that our countries, and not merely us as individuals, 'owe' their countries on the basis that our countries colonized them, expropriated their resources, enslaved their people and carved up their territory in arbitrary ways generating decades of conflict; that the Global North continues to extract materials from the South at an unsustainable rate against a background of international trade rules and an international economic-political order that continues to marginalize them. No suggestion that 'our' wealth depends on their immiseration.

Looking back now, Singer's question seems hopelessly naïve at best, downright obstructive and colonial at worst, a restatement of the white man's burden. But the limitations of Singer's approach were recognized at the time. This was the period of decolonization after all, when collective self-determination of the Global South was becoming a reality and the 'Third World' bloc was pushing for a new relationship with the First and Second World blocs based on 'Trade Not Aid'.[4] The Argentine economist Raúl Prebisch argued for a 'New International Economic Order' (NIEO) in 1963, which was adopted in a UN

---

[3]Of course, on the utilitarian framework, the people who should transfer money are any individuals who have disposable income or wealth, not merely white Westerners. But the way Singer addresses his argument to this day is towards this audience, specifically 'the average family in the United States' (Peter Singer, 'The Singer Solution to World Poverty', *New York Times*, 1999). At the time of writing, 60 per cent of the US population is non-Hispanic white, therefore, the average. The whiteness of the 'effective altruism' movement, which is inspired by Singer's theory, has been noted by others, for instance, Amia Srinivasan describes it as a 'rather homogenous movement of middle-class white men', Amia Srinivasan, 'Stop the Robot Apocalypse', *London Review of Books* 37, no. 18 (2015): 3–6. This is also borne out in practice. 'The Giving Pledge' is an effective altruism project for billionaires started by Bill and Melinda Gates and Warren Buffet in 2010. A study of the demography of the participants found that 'The Giving Pledge population is predominantly male, white, and based in the USA' (Hans Peter Schmitz and Elena M. McCollim, 'Billionaires in Global Philanthropy: A Decade of the Giving Pledge', *Society* 58 (2021): 121).
[4]Katrina Forrester, *In the Shadow of Justice: Postwar Liberalism and the Remaking of Political Philosophy* (Princeton, NJ: Princeton University Press, 2019), 144.

General Assembly resolution in 1974. This radical (and unfulfilled) resolution included proposals for sovereign control over natural resources, equitable trade relationships, debt forgiveness and regulation of corporations, among other reforms of the international legal and political order.[5]

One of the problems with Singer's approach was that the question was framed within the discipline of Western ethics. Ethics asks what *individuals* owe to each other. Its narrow focus on the individual and how the individual ought to relate to other individuals excludes questions about institutional relationships, power and politics. As Katrina Forrester has pointed out, Singer responded to critics at the time by saying that he wanted to focus on the humanitarian crisis afoot, abstracted from international politics.[6] But it is not possible to abstract humanitarian crises from politics, because a humanitarian crisis like a famine is parasitic on existing structural injustice. Structural injustice cannot be alleviated by mere transfers of money from rich individuals to poor individuals, because as long as the underlying structures remain, people will be vulnerable to crises like famine and the persistent, ongoing structural injustice of poverty.

The global justice debate did quickly move to the adjacent discipline of political philosophy. But in political philosophy, the issue was framed in an even less helpful way. At that time, the field was dominated by one book – John Rawls's *A Theory of Justice* (1971). Rawls was interested in distributive justice within a closed society (specifically a post-Second World War liberal democracy). He focused on the principles by which state institutions should distribute collective resources, or, as Rawls puts it, 'the benefits and burdens of social cooperation'.[7] Political philosophers, notably Charles Beitz, then asked whether Rawls was right to restrict his conception of justice to a closed society, or whether it should apply globally.[8]

Rawls was primarily interested in 'ideal theory': what justice would look like under ideal conditions. He set aside questions of 'non-ideal theory', arguing that we need to know what constitutes justice in the ideal in order to know what to do about injustice in the present. This argumentative strategy meant that questions of real-world injustice were neglected not only by Rawls but also by most political philosophers that came after and operated 'in the shadow of justice', as Katrina Forrester puts it. From the 1980s onwards, political philosophers concentrated on how Rawls's ideal theory of justice could contribute to thinking about global justice. In the global justice debate, the

---

[5]United Nations General Assembly, 'Declaration on the Establishment of a New International Economic Order' (Geneva, 1974), http://www.un-documents.net/s6r3201.htm.
[6]Forrester, *In the Shadow of Justice*, 144.
[7]John Rawls, *A Theory of Justice*, revised edn (Cambridge, MA: Belknap Press of Harvard University Press, 1971), 4.
[8]Charles R. Beitz, *Political Theory and International Relations*, 2nd edn (Princeton, NJ: Princeton University Press, 1999).

core question was: is Rawlsian justice global or domestic in scope? From the 1990s, political philosophers broadened their range of questions related to global justice, but hangovers from the Rawlsian debate remained. Debate still rested on whether distributive justice is global in scope (cosmopolitanism) or domestic in scope (nationalism, statism).

Cosmopolitanism as a concept has its origins in Ancient Greece when Diogenes the Cynic described himself as a 'citizen of the world' and it crops up time and again over the course of the discipline's history. Over the past three decades, it has developed as a distinct moral and political position. For cosmopolitans, all human beings count as moral equals, individuals not groups (like states or nations) are the primary units of moral concern, and moral obligations towards fellow human beings apply to all people everywhere.[9] This basic moral tenet can have many implications depending on other theoretical commitments. Cosmopolitanism has formed the basis of utilitarian, rights-based, Kantian, Aristotelian and contractarian approaches to global justice.[10] Cosmopolitanism is, therefore, a broad church. What these approaches share is an insistence that distributive justice is global in scope and that individuals are primary. The literature in the 1990s–2000s was concerned with justifying the basic premises of cosmopolitanism and then considering their implications for morality and global governance.[11]

The counter-position is nationalism or statism. Nationalists argue that the scope of justice is restricted to the nation state because of the solidary relations that exist between co-nationals.[12] Statists reject this appeal to nationality as a shared identity that gives rise to specific moral obligations, but they insist that certain features of the state render it the appropriate site of distributive justice. For example, because the state generates conditions of reciprocity by providing access to fundamental public goods,[13] or because the state coerces citizens, it therefore has corresponding obligations of distributive justice,[14] or because

---

[9]Simon Caney, *Justice beyond Borders: A Global Political Theory* (Oxford: Oxford University Press, 2005), 3–4.

[10]See Gillian Brock, *Global Justice: A Cosmopolitan Account* (Oxford: Oxford University Press, 2009), 13–14. Singer, 'Famine, Affluence and Morality'; Henry Shue, *Basic Rights: Subsistence, Affluence, and US Foreign Policy* (Princeton, NJ: Princeton University Press, 1980); Onora O'Neill, *Toward Justice and Virtue: A Constructive Account of Practical Reasoning* (Cambridge: Cambridge University Press, 2002); Martha C. Nussbaum, *Frontiers of Justice: Disability, Nationality, Species Membership* (Cambridge, MA: Belknap Press, 2006); Beitz, *Political Theory and International Relations*.

[11]There is also 'cultural cosmopolitanism'; see Jeremy Waldron, 'What Is Cosmopolitanism?', *Journal of Political Philosophy* 8, no. 2 (2000): 227–43.

[12]David Miller, *National Responsibility and Global Justice* (Oxford: Oxford University Press, 2007); David Miller, *On Nationality* (Oxford: Oxford University Press, 1995).

[13]Andrea Sangiovanni, 'Global Justice, Reciprocity, and the State', *Philosophy & Public Affairs* 35, no. 1 (2007): 3–39.

[14]Michael Blake, 'Distributive Justice, State Coercion, and Autonomy', *Philosophy & Public Affairs* 30, no. 3 (2001): 257–96.

citizens are in some sense the co-authors of the state's laws.[15] Rawls himself argued for a statist position in his influential *The Law of Peoples* (1999).[16]

The global justice debate's discussion of the *scope* of *distributive* justice, with the implications for *individuals* in *ideal* theory, makes it an inadequate framework for thinking about global *in*justice. First, this argument over the *scope* of distributive justice has long been known to be a red herring from the perspective of the Global South. Frantz Fanon wrote back in 1961: 'The wealth of imperial countries is our wealth too.'[17] Since the wealth of the North was created by the colonization and exploitation of Southern resources and bodies, the idea that the scope of justice should be restricted to within (Northern) nation states is a Northern construct and delusion, distracting from the sources of that wealth. While cosmopolitans argue for the global redistribution of resources, it is not on the grounds of historical injustice or reciprocity with those who generated the wealth in the first place, *pace* Fanon, but rather on the basis of shared common humanity, equal entitlement to the earth's resources or contemporary relations of interdependence or coercion. In erasing history in this way, cosmopolitanism sanitizes contemporary distributions of wealth. Nationalists and statists in mainstream political philosophy tend not to consider Third World states' claims that in order to develop an effective redistributive state apparatus, what they need is a respect for their sovereignty, a principle of non-intervention in their affairs, both in terms of the economy and security, and territorial integrity.[18] Instead, they assume that a functioning redistributive apparatus exists.

The global justice debate's focus on *distributive* justice has led to the exclusion of the other dominant strand of contemporary justice theory – recognition. But as Fanon argued, if the other isn't recognized as fully human, then they will not fall within the scope of an ethical or distributive justice scheme.[19] It is not necessary to agree with Fanon that recognition precedes ethics to recognize that recognition raises profound questions for these theoretical frameworks.[20] While cosmopolitanism accepts that distributive justice should not be restricted

---

[15]Thomas Nagel, 'The Problem of Global Justice', *Philosophy & Public Affairs* 33, no. 2 (2005): 113–47.

[16]John Rawls, *The Law of Peoples* (Cambridge, MA: Harvard University Press, 1999).

[17]Frantz Fanon, *The Wretched of the Earth* (London: Penguin Classics, 2001), 81.

[18]See Rao's discussion of these factors motivating Third World countries' commitments to pluralism as opposed to global solidarism. Rahul Rao, *Third World Protest: Between Home and the World* (Oxford: Oxford University Press, 2010), 74.

[19]Lewis R. Gordon, 'Iris Marion Young on Political Responsibility: A Reading through Jaspers and Fanon', *Symposia on Gender, Race and Philosophy* 3, no. 1 (2007): 1–7.

[20]An important exception is Nancy Fraser's *Scales of Justice* where she argues that there are three spheres of justice, redistribution, recognition and representation (Nancy Fraser, *Scales of Justice: Reimagining Political Space in a Globalizing World* (Cambridge: Polity Press, 2010)). Here I'm trying to capture the 'mainstream' Western analytic philosophy approach to global justice prior to and at the time when Young was writing, as this is the framework Young's theory emerged from. Also, Fraser's book was published after Young's death.

to the nation state, it expects individuals to recognize all other human beings as equal members of a distributive justice scheme, overriding centuries of not only nationalism but also racism, xenophobia, sectarianism, lack of recognition of the 'Other', as well as sexism, homophobia and ableism. Even if this ought to be a moral requirement, without some account of recognition, it begs questions for the relevance or efficacy of cosmopolitanism as a political project.[21] Nationalists and statists restrict the scope of distributive justice to the nation state, but they fail to acknowledge that certain groups within the nation or state often do not receive the benefits of distributive justice due to failures of recognition. For instance, as a Northern Irish Catholic, I was born into a group that was historically denied civil rights through employment and housing discrimination, a limited franchise and electoral gerrymandering for much of the twentieth century, which entrenched the already unequal distribution of land and wealth between the Protestant and Catholic communities.[22] Sidelining recognition means failing to engage with permanent internal minority groups and may further entrench their disadvantage.

Another implication of focusing on distributive justice is that justice is reduced to the relationship between redistributive political institutions (the state) and *individuals*. Insofar as the question of what the scope of distributive justice is, it asks to what extent and how far states should redistribute resources to individuals (whether this is a domestic state or a world state, or some iteration of a global redistributive political institution). As Samuel Moyn puts it, 'The birth of global justice involved a remarkable philosophical consensus about the individualization of the basis of social justice. Whether as a matter of their interests or rights, all the founders argued in terms of the prerogatives of individual persons as the sole foundation of any transnational justice.'[23] This directly conflicts with the NIEO's emphasis on the collective self-determination of newly decolonized states, with the aim of reconstituting power relations *between states*. Moyn argues that this philosophical individualization of justice was a Western reaction to, and served to undermine, the NIEO's more transformative political ambitions. Rahul Rao argues that cosmopolitanism's emphasis on the individual has served as the underlying philosophical justification for US hegemony, legitimizing humanitarian intervention and economic conditionality on the grounds that these will improve

---

[21]See Rorty on the implications of these divisions for human rights. Richard Rorty, 'Human Rights, Rationality and Sentimentality', in *On Human Rights*, ed. Stephen Shute and Susan Hurley (New York: Basic Books, 1993), 111–35. But human rights are a minimalist project, whereas cosmopolitan distributive justice makes serious demands on citizens across the world.

[22]'Catholic' and 'Protestant' in the Northern Irish context are ethno-political designations and do not necessarily imply religious belief or practice. See, for example, Ed Cairns and G. W. Mercer, 'Social Identity in Northern Ireland', *Human Relations* 37, no. 12 (1984): 1005–1107. For more on the civil rights movement, see Lorenzo Bosi, 'The Dynamics of Social Movement Development: Northern Ireland's Civil Rights Movement in the 1960s,' *Mobilization: An International Journal* 11, no. 1 (2006): 81–100.

[23]Samuel Moyn, *Not Enough: Human Rights in an Unequal World* (Cambridge, MA: Belknap Press, 2018), 171.

conditions for individuals, regardless of the implications for international power relations or respect for state sovereignty.[24]

Moreover, this overweening focus on states and individuals does violence to our social reality which is made up of a constellation of actors. There are multiple other agents that contribute to global injustice. In contrast to nationalists and statists, cosmopolitans do address other actors, placing the emphasis on global governance. They recognize the impact of international institutions, such as the World Trade Organization (WTO), which determines the rules of international trade, the International Monetary Fund (IMF), which governs international finance, and the World Bank, which provides loans and collects debts. Cosmopolitans rightly observe that the impact of international trade rules and global financial regulations and regimes cannot be ignored in the twenty-first-century capitalist economy. These institutions were created with a limited remit after the Second World War, but their goals and reach have expanded significantly to the point of making 'forceful, far-reaching structural reforms' in the domestic economies of poor states.[25] The globalization of trade and finance challenges the idea that only the nation state provides the public goods needed to live a good life or that only the nation state coerces individuals.[26] But there are other actors on the global stage that are relevant to global injustice that have received much less attention from cosmopolitans. Some multinational corporations (MNCs) are worth more than many nation-states, have the power to coerce political decision-makers, and have the capacity to create and take away jobs across the globe. Also relevant are civil society actors, who sound the alarm about global, transnational or domestic injustices, campaign on issues or provide humanitarian aid and assistance, sometimes effectively and sometimes not.[27] Moreover, even if cosmopolitans do engage with other actors in the global sphere, ultimately these actors only matter insofar as they promote just distributions for individuals; their impact on power relations between collective entities is rendered secondary.

Finally, the emphasis of the debate on *ideal* theory obscures considerations that are relevant to tackling global injustice. Cosmopolitanism occludes difference, focusing on what is universal and generalizable about all human beings. It is, of

---

[24]Rao, *Third World Protest*, chap. 3. Cosmopolitanism has also been accused of cultural imperialism, by emphasizing 'tradition independent norms' developed by elites in the Global North that seek to replace the moral frameworks of other cultures, Pratap Bhanu Mehta, 'Cosmopolitanism and the Circle of Reason', *Political Theory* 28, no. 5 (2000): 619–39.

[25]IMF, *The IMF's Response to the Asian Crisis* (Washington, DC: IMF, 1998) quoted in Ngaire Woods, 'Making the IMF and World Bank More Accountable', *International Affairs* 77, no. 1 (2001): 86.

[26]Joshua Cohen and Charles Sabel, 'Extra Rempublicam Nulla Justitia?', *Philosophy & Public Affairs* 34, no. 2 (2006): 147–75; Laura Valentini, 'Coercion and (Global) Justice', *American Political Science Review* 105, no. 1 (2011): 205–20.

[27]Onora O'Neill problematized this in Onora O'Neill, 'Global Justice: Whose Obligations?', in *The Ethics of Assistance: Morality and the Distant Needy*, ed. Deen K. Chatterjee (Cambridge: Cambridge University Press, 2004), 242–60.

course, intuitively appealing to recognize the common humanity and equality of all people, but such a position can also end up doing the most disadvantaged a disservice; by ignoring differences between social groups – gender, race, ethnicity, nationality, ability, etc. – it does not tell us about the specific kinds of oppression or domination specific groups experience, and therefore, it says nothing about how to overcome these injustices.[28] As feminist, anti-racist, anti-colonial, anti-ableist groups have argued, 'claims about how the route to a just understanding of a set of unjust social circumstances must involve, not a new supposedly neutral stance, but a stance shaped by an appreciation of the suffering of the marginalised'.[29]

In idealizing the nation or state as the ideal arbiter of distributive justice, nationalism and statism obscure existing forms of injustice against individuals and social groups within the state. Far from being bastions of solidarity and comradely fellow-feeling, nations and states can be sites of oppression of minority groups, particularly in settler-colonial states where the interests of the First Nations peoples are ignored or subsumed in the interests of the dominant nation; the same can be said for multi-nation states where one nation is dominant. These minority groups actively seek international coalitions of solidarity to counter the oppression of their nation states and to reveal that their plight is transnational; think of the international activism against apartheid in South Africa or connections between colonized peoples across international borders. Also, nation- and state-building has historically been a violent process involving the elimination or suppression of social and cultural groups that defy the dominant national culture.[30] Feminists have pointed out the ways in which national culture and identity is used to subordinate women as vehicles of reproduction of the national group and culture, and feminists have sought international networks of solidarity as a result.[31]

Even though individuals are the ultimate unit of moral concern for cosmopolitans, for the most part, in cosmopolitan discourse individuals are passive recipients of redistributive schemes. This is unsatisfactory from the perspective of people who want to know what they personally can and should do in relation to global injustices, whether these be individuals in affluent states or disadvantaged individuals. When cosmopolitans do discuss the responsibility of individuals, they focus on the affluent and accord far too much weight to the individual, burdening the individual with moral responsibility for all the world's ills or burdening them with moral responsibility for all of their state's actions,

---

[28]Hye-Ryoung Kang, 'Transnational Women's Collectivities and Global Justice', in *Gender and Global Justice*, ed. Alison M. Jaggar (Cambridge: Polity Press, 2014), 40–62.

[29]Alice Crary, 'Against "Effective Altruism"', *Radical Philosophy* 2, no. 10 (2021): 39.

[30]Rao, *Third World Protest*, 94–7.

[31]Nira Yuval-Davis, *Gender and Nation* (London: Sage, 1997). Chandra Talpade Mohanty, *Feminism without Borders: Decolonizing Theory, Practicing Solidarity* (Durham, NC: Duke University Press, 2003).

as if somehow ordinary individuals have control over the global economy or what their governments do. Nationalists and statists reduce affluent individuals' role to supporting their state's 'duty of assistance' to meet basic humanitarian needs in poor countries. This does not provide affluent individuals with any guidance, and the role of disadvantaged individuals is rarely discussed in this literature, if at all.

In sum, addressing global *in*justice means considering how contemporary distributions of wealth came about. It means considering forms of injustice other than distributive injustice. It means considering injustices experienced by corporate groups (such as states) and collectives (social groups), not exclusively individuals. It means considering the complexities of these injustices in practice, rather than abstracting to an ideal world far removed from our current one.

Most fundamentally, these mainstream political philosophy frameworks fail to address power relations. They do not consider the domination and oppression of *social groups* – power relations that defy borders and that interact with nationality or citizenship in complex ways. They do not consider power relations *within states* that affect the distribution of responsibility for global injustice. They do not consider *interstate* power relations and how powerful states dominate poor states. Nor do they consider how these international and domestic power relations *came into being*. They, therefore, sidestep some of the most crucial questions for an analysis of global injustice including: Which agents are powerful on the global stage and how does this affect distributions of resources, recognition and relations of domination or oppression? How does power operate at different levels of analysis – the global, international, domestic and local? What can this tell us about global injustice and responsibility for it?

The structural injustice challenge

Meanwhile in the real world, global justice social movements had very different concerns. The Third World movement of the 1970s had dissipated and in the corridors of power a global neoliberal consensus had emerged that coalesced around the goals of the 'Washington Consensus'.[32] This neoliberal doctrine was based on the principles of rolling back the state and privatizing all public goods, as well as trade liberalization through the deregulation of domestic economies. Dissent had already begun in the 1980s with the 'IMF Riots' from 1983 to 1985 and 1989, in the Global South countries that were forced to adopt neoliberal 'Structural Adjustment Programmes' (SAPs) that undermined their burgeoning

---

[32]John Williamson, 'Democracy and the Washington Consensus', *World Development* 21, no. 8 (1993): 1329–36; John Williamson, 'A Short History of the Washington Consensus', *Law and Business Review of the Americas* 15, no. 1 (2009): 7–26.

economies.[33] The 1990s saw immense grassroots pushback on the global economic and political status quo. There were protest movements against the Bretton Woods Institutions – the IMF and World Bank – as well as the WTO, culminating in the 1998 'Battle of Seattle'. The alter-globalization movement (also tellingly sometimes called the 'global justice movement'), among other movements, highlighted that these institutions' decision-making structures, procedures and decisions were largely opaque, non-democratic and beholden to the dictates of powerful states.[34] Other social movements, such as Jubilee 2000, campaigned for debt relief. Indigenous movements were advocating for the right to retain ancestral lands, for reparations for historical injustices and for self-determination.[35] The slavery reparations movement was gaining traction.[36] Trade unions and global labour social movements were fighting for labour rights for exploited workers in global supply chains. In light of these movements, the philosophical debate was sterile and irrelevant.[37]

Iris Marion Young sought to bridge the gap between what was happening on the ground and what was going on in the Ivory Tower. In the realm of philosophy, she identified problems with both cosmopolitanism and nationalism/statism.

---

[33]Jason Hickel, *The Divide: A Brief Guide to Global Inequality and Its Solutions* (London: Windmill Books, 2017), 162.

[34]For discussions of the Battle of Seattle and the anti/alter-globalization (or global justice) movement, see Naomi Klein, *Fences and Windows: Dispatches from the Front Lines of the Globalization Debate* (London: Flamingo, 2002); David Graeber, 'On the Phenomenology of Giant Puppets: Broken Windows, Imaginary Jars of Urine, and the Cosmological Role of the Police in American Culture', in *Possibilities: Essays on Hierarchy, Rebellion, and Desire*, edited by David Graeber, Edinburgh: AK Press, 2007, 375–418.

[35]Salvador Martí i Puig, 'The Emergence of Indigenous Movements in Latin America and Their Impact on the Latin American Political Scene: Interpretive Tools at the Local and Global Levels', *Latin American Perspectives* 37, no. 6 (2010): 74–92.

[36]In the early 1990s there were two international conferences: the First World Conference on Reparations in Lagos, 1990, and the first Pan-African Conference for Reparations for African Enslavement, Colonisation and Neo-Colonisation in Abuja, Nigeria, in 1993. The topic was discussed in the UN World Conference against Racism, Racial Discrimination, Xenophobia and Related Intolerance in Durban, South Africa, in 2001.

[37]One aspect of the philosophical literature that has gained significant real-world traction is Singer's consequentialism in the form of 'effective altruism' (EA). But this is a disturbing trend because, as Alice Crary points out, it enables extremely rich individuals to believe they are doing good while maintaining the unjust system in which they operate. EA is, therefore, 'morally corrupt' (Crary, 'Against "Effective Altruism"', 40). EA also puts power into the hands of unaccountable philanthropists to determine what projects are worth financing and which people or animals are worth saving (Emma Saunders-Hastings, 'Plutocratic Philanthropy', *Journal of Politics* 80, no. 1 (2018): 149–61). Moreover, EA is in fundamental opposition to the structural injustice approach because it focuses on the rightness of proximate outcomes, failing to recognize that the combination of the outcomes of millions of disparate agents' actions can overall result in structural injustice. Indeed, billionaire philanthropy favours health and education, and 'ignores the structural inequities underlying widening wealth gaps' (Schmitz and McCollim, 'Billionaires in Global Philanthropy: A Decade of the Giving Pledge', 128). Also influential in practice have been Amartya Sen's and Martha Nussbaum's capabilities approach, which formed the basis of the UN Sustainable Development Goals, and Henry Shue's basic needs approach.

For Young, cosmopolitanism does not sufficiently explain why individuals have obligations of justice to one another: as she puts it, 'It is not enough to say the others are human.'[38] Nationalism or statism makes the mistake of prioritizing political institutions instead of recognizing that these institutions arise as a response to social connections among people; 'obligations of justice [are] generated by social connection' and the institutions are instruments for discharging those obligations.[39] At the level of political action, Young suggested that the kinds of issues social movements were raising were related to 'structural injustice', meaning *injustices that are the combined outcome of lots of diverse agents acting within the existing rules and structures, creating the conditions for the oppression and domination of disadvantaged social groups*. Some of these structural injustices are domestic, such as homelessness, but some are global, like sweatshop labour. Structural injustices do not stop at borders because they are the combined outcome of processes of production and consumption, and the institutional frameworks in which these take place, as well as social positioning in material structures and norms that construct needs and desires – processes and frameworks which are globalized.

Always with one eye on what philosophical insights mean in practice, Young argued that we need a new theory of responsibility in order to tackle structural injustices. She claimed that traditional philosophical theories of moral and legal responsibility, which were tied to individual action and identifiable causal outcomes, could not account for responding to structural injustices in the world today, since these were the outcome of millions of agents acting independently, and the cumulative outcomes of these actions were unknowable. Young argued that a new theory of responsibility should recognize that everyone connected to structural injustice should take responsibility together for overcoming it. The focus should be forward-looking, on how to improve the situation, instead of backward-looking, on identifying guilty parties, since there is no *one* guilty party. The fact that ameliorating structural injustice entails working together to overcome it meant that this responsibility is *political* – it entails collective action – rather than a moral responsibility that ushers in personalized guilt and blame.

Up until this point, the global justice debate largely took place within the tradition of Anglo-American political philosophy which continued to operate under the shadow of Rawlsian justice theory. But Young was influenced by a different philosophical tradition – critical theory. Critical theory starts with social movements, which highlight chinks in the armour of existing economic, political and social systems. It uses insights born out of political practice to think about achieving emancipation in the long term or a shift towards justice in the present.

---

[38]Iris Marion Young, 'Responsibility and Global Justice: A Social Connection Model', *Social Philosophy and Policy* 23, no. 1 (2006): 105.
[39]Young, 'Responsibility and Global Justice', 105.

The systems that concern critical theorists are not abstract 'ideal' systems that do not actually exist. They are concerned with what does exist. The kinds of systems that interest them are not only limited to political institutions but also include the capitalist economy and social norms. This alternative intellectual framework gave Young a different perspective on the global justice debate. Her focus was on political, economic and social global *injustice* in the world as it is and what could actually be done about it.

Young's theory was a huge leap forward in political theory. It opened up new avenues in global justice theory, including the role of global supply chains and capitalism, exploitation, oppression and the role of economic, political and social structures. It was one of the catalysts for the cosmopolitanism literature to focus more on 'non-ideal theory' and to take a 'policy turn'.[40] It has inspired much intellectual debate. But Young did not complete her work on this topic. She died at the age of fifty-six in 2006, without completing *Responsibility for Justice*, which was published posthumously in 2011. There are gaps and omissions in her theory. There are controversies that she did not have the opportunity to address. And, as I will argue in this book, she did not pursue the critical theory aspects of her theory far enough; in particular, she did not address power relations. I have spent the last ten years working on Young's theory. In this book, I take Young as my starting point, but I develop a new theory of structural injustice and responsibility for it, placing an emphasis on the role of power. In my view, Young conceded too much to the liberal paradigm in failing to address the power relations that underlie and constitute structural injustice. A critical theory of structural injustice incorporates power. It distinguishes types of structural injustice in order to consider whether a particular injustice is reformable or requires systemic or revolutionary change. And it is a *political* theory, not a moral theory.

The advantages and disadvantages of the structural injustice approach

The advantages of the structural injustice approach are that it overcomes several of the weaknesses of earlier philosophical approaches to global justice. First, Young discusses the responsibility of *different kinds of agents* in relation to global structural injustices, including individuals, states and corporations (although her focus is mostly on individuals). Second, she tells a more plausible story about

---

[40]For example, see Brock, *Global Justice: A Cosmopolitan Account*; Darrel Moellendorf, *Global Inequality Matters* (Dordrecht: Springer, 2009). Since the 2010s, cosmopolitans have placed much more emphasis on so-called non-ideal theory and attention is paid to specific instances of global injustice, particularly trade injustice and migration. But these developments came after Young's book was published. My aim in this introduction has been to situate Young's structural injustice theory in the philosophical literature at that time, and my focus is now on structural injustice theory itself.

the relationship between domestic and global injustice. It is palpably not the case that injustice stops at state borders: migration, sweatshops (and supply chains more generally), climate change, poverty and disease are all transnational problems. We have perhaps never felt this more acutely than during the Covid-19 pandemic. It is nonsensical to restrict discussions of these issues to within nation state boundaries or to exclusively discuss them in the global context. These issues are transnational: there are domestic, international and global factors at play. A structural injustice approach, which recognizes the various material factors, social norms, legal and institutional rules, social positions within structures and unintended consequences, can accommodate this complexity much better than a cosmopolitan or nationalist/statist framework. Most importantly, Young highlighted the role of social, political, economic and legal *structures* in perpetuating injustice, whatever its scope. Structures transcend particular agents, conditioning (but not determining) their possibilities for action.

Despite its significant insights, political theorists have highlighted a number of weaknesses in Young's approach. Of course, it bears repeating that Young died at the untimely age of fifty-six and her final book, *Responsibility for Justice*, was unfinished and was published posthumously. Perhaps she would have responded to some of these issues if she had the opportunity. But the debate has moved on in Young's absence, and these are the concerns that have been raised with the approach. Most of the debate is concerned with Young's theory of responsibility. Critics argue that Young is mistaken not to attribute moral responsibility to any agents for structural injustice.[41] When it comes to Young's political responsibility, what use is it really if there is no accountability mechanism? If agents fail to act on their political responsibility, there will be no repercussions; 'people get a free pass indefinitely', as Martha Nussbaum puts it.[42] Critics also claim that Young's theory of responsibility is too vague. It doesn't tell individuals exactly what they should do in order to combat structural injustice.[43] It doesn't specify 'who has to do what'.[44] Young also downplays the problem of responsibility-avoidance by failing to engage in sufficient depth with the reasons why individuals fail to acknowledge

---

[41]Christian Barry and Kate Macdonald, 'How Should We Conceive of Individual Consumer Responsibility to Address Labour Injustices?', in *Global Justice and International Labour Rights*, ed. Faina Milman-Sivan, Yossi Dahan and Hanna Lerner (Cambridge: Cambridge University Press, 2016); Henning Hahn, 'The Global Consequence of Participatory Responsibility', *Journal of Global Ethics* 5, no. 1 (2009): 43–56; Christian Neuhäuser, 'Structural Injustice and the Distribution of Forward-Looking Responsibility', *Midwest Studies in Philosophy* 38 (2014): 232–51.
[42]Martha C. Nussbaum, 'Foreword', in *Responsibility for Justice*, ed. Iris Marion Young (Oxford: Oxford University Press, 2011), xxi.
[43]Barry and Macdonald, 'How Should We Conceive of Individual Consumer Responsibility to Address Labour Injustices?'; Hahn, 'The Global Consequence of Participatory Responsibility'; Robin Zheng, 'What Is My Role in Changing the System? A New Model of Responsibility for Structural Injustice', *Ethical Theory and Moral Practice*, 2018, 869–85.
[44]Neuhäuser, 'Structural Injustice and the Distribution of Forward-Looking Responsibility', 242.

and act on their political responsibility.[45] Another source of contention is the way Young responds to historical injustice.[46]

These debates are rich and complex, and aspects of these issues will be touched on throughout, some in more depth than others.[47] But the focus of this book is slightly different. The aim of this book is to integrate power into structural injustice theory. In my view, the greatest weakness of Young's late work is its lack of an analysis of power. This is a strange omission, because in Young's earlier socialist-feminist work and critical theory, she foregrounded power.[48] In her later work on structural injustice, power was almost completely absent. I believe the late Young had a lot to learn from the early Young on this front. But there is also much to learn from other approaches to power. In this book, I will integrate an analysis of power into the concept of structural injustice itself. I will also integrate an analysis of power into an account of responsibility for structural injustice: I will defend Young's claim that ordinary individuals are not morally responsible for structural injustice, but I will argue against her that some agents are morally responsible – powerful agents, such as states and corporations, who have the capacity to ameliorate the injustice and fail to do so, or who deliberately perpetuate it for their own gain. Finally, I consider what an analysis of power relations can tell us about how to challenge structural injustice.

Plan of the book

In this book, I will concentrate on some lesser-explored problems with the structural injustice approach and seek to resolve them. I do so by integrating an analysis of power within structural injustice theory. In the first half of the book, I focus on structural injustice and in the second half I focus on responsibility for it.

In Chapter 2 I engage in the first systematic critique of Young's conception of structural injustice. Young's conception is the standard-bearer in political theory, and while it is undoubtedly useful, its lack of systematicity and lack of analysis

---

[45]Jade Schiff offers a book-length treatment of this problem through the lens of Arendt's views on thoughtlessness, Sartre's on bad faith and Bourdieu's on misrecognition. Jade Larissa Schiff, *Burdens of Political Responsibility: Narrative and the Cultivation of Responsiveness* (Cambridge: Cambridge University Press, 2016).

[46]For a sympathetic perspective, see Catherine Lu, *Justice and Reconciliation in World Politics* (Cambridge: Cambridge University Press, 2017). For more critical perspectives, see Alasia Nuti, *Injustice and the Reproduction of History: Structural Inequalities, Gender and Redress* (Cambridge: Cambridge University Press, 2019); Maeve McKeown, 'Backward-Looking Reparations and Structural Injustice', *Contemporary Political Theory* 20, no. 4 (2021): 771–94.

[47]For a more detailed survey of the various criticisms of Young's work on structural injustice, see Maeve McKeown, 'Structural Injustice', *Philosophy Compass* 16, no. 7 (2021).

[48]Iris Marion Young, *Justice and the Politics of Difference* (Princeton, NJ: Princeton University Press, 1990).

of power let it down. First, I outline the problem of the relationship between structure and agency. Then I highlight that Young adopted a confused social ontology when theorizing structural injustice. I adopt a more rigorous social ontology – Margaret Archer's critical realism – and show how it sheds light on the concept of structural injustice. I combine critical realism with Thomas Wartenburg's situated conception of power to explain how power operates within structures. Based on this theoretical backdrop, I argue that there are in fact three types of structural injustice. 'Pure' structural injustice is the kind of structural injustice that Young was interested in; the structural injustice is the cumulative outcome of multiple agents' actions and that no agent has the capacity to overcome; it requires systemic change. 'Avoidable' structural injustice is where powerful agents have the knowledge and capacity to remedy the structural injustice but they fail to do so. 'Deliberate' structural injustice is where powerful agents have the capacity to redress the injustice, but instead they deliberately perpetuate it for their own gain.

In Chapter 3, I assess how powerful agents act within the context of structural injustice. First, I outline the different dimensions and forms of power. Then I discuss the role of corporate power in the global economy. Finally, I look at a case study of power in the global garment industry. I argue that power can be used for good or for ill, to perpetuate or ameliorate structural injustice.

In Chapter 4, I apply the three types of structural injustice to the case studies of sweatshops (deliberate structural injustice), global poverty (avoidable structural injustice) and climate change (pure structural injustice). In each case this involves looking at the historical roots of these injustices, thinking about why these cases constitute structural injustice and what is unjust about them, and assessing the role of powerful agents in maintaining or changing these unjust structures.

After establishing this framework for thinking about structural injustice and power, I then turn to the question of responsibility. In Chapter 5, I assess the moral responsibility of ordinary individuals. I argue that Young was right to claim that ordinary individuals (meaning individuals with relatively little power within structures) are not morally responsible for structural injustice. This is a controversial claim, which Young did not defend in any detail. I defend this view through an analysis of R. Jay Wallace's account of reasons-responsive moral responsibility. I also assess consequentialist views, and the concept of complicity, and argue that they also fail to ground the moral responsibility of individuals for structural injustice.

In Chapter 6, I compare three versions of political responsibility: Arendt's *virtú* conception, socially conscious consumerism as a virtue conception and Young's conception as an ambiguous combination of the two. I argue for a politicized conception of political responsibility that is closer to Arendt's view. Political responsibility should be understood as a *political virtue*, specifically, as the responsibility to develop the capacity for political solidarity to challenge the agents with the power to change structural injustice. Working together in solidarity, individuals can become collectively empowered to provoke change.

In Chapter 7, I consider the relationship between historical and structural injustice. First, I address the question of how corporate agents can bear moral responsibility. I defend the view that corporate agents can bear moral responsibility on the grounds that they are self-asserting entities that exist through time and have an internal decision-making structure, by virtue of which they can reason about the world and act on the basis of those reasons. Hence, I argue that backward-looking reparations for historical injustice are compatible with the structural injustice framework; given that corporate entities persist through time, if they violate moral obligations, they continue to bear moral responsibility over time.

Finally, Young's approach has been critiqued for being vague and non-action guiding. By exposing the underlying power relations in structural injustices, my approach provides more guidance on how to combat structural injustice. In Chapter 8, I explore strategies for holding powerful actors to account through alternative and countering alignments. And I provide some guidelines for individuals to think about taking up their political responsibility based on a revised version of Young's 'parameters of reasoning': benefit, collective ability, interest and proximity.

Chapter 2
What is structural injustice?

Structural injustice, broadly speaking, is the fallout of social-structural processes that render groups of people vulnerable to domination or oppression. But in order to know how to tackle structural injustice we need to know more about what it is, who is responsible for it and how it can be changed. In this chapter, I focus on explaining what structural injustice is and I raise the implications this has for responsibility and change that will be explored in more detail in subsequent chapters.

Understanding what structural injustice is necessitates understanding the relationship between structure and agency. Engaging with this prolonged and intractable academic debate is daunting, but there is a reason why it has sustained interest for so long and generates such strong views:

> The urgency of the 'problem of structure and agency' is not one which imposes itself upon academics alone, but on every human being ... For it is part and parcel of daily experience to feel both free and enchained, capable of shaping our own future and yet confronted by towering, seemingly impersonal, constraints. Those whose reflection leads them to reject the grandiose delusion of being puppet-masters but also to resist the supine conclusion that they are mere marionettes then have the same task of reconciling this experiential bivalence, and must do so if their moral choice is not to become inert or their political action ineffectual. Consequently, in facing-up to the 'problem of structure and agency' social theorists are not just addressing crucial technical problems in the study of society, they are also confronting the most pressing social problem of the human condition.[1]

---

[1] Margaret Archer, *Realist Social Theory: The Morphogenetic Approach* (Cambridge: Cambridge University Press, 1995), 65.

If confronting the relationship between structure and agency is the most pressing problem of the human condition, as Margaret Archer argues, then confronting structural *injustice* is one of the most pressing problems in human relations, namely politics.

As discussed in Chapter 1, the problem of structural injustice was highlighted by Iris Marion Young in her late work in the early 2000s. Young drew attention to the injustice that results from domestic and transnational structural processes, as opposed to the emphasis of previous global justice literature on the scope of distributive justice. Since Young's statement of the problem, political theorists have tended to take her definition of structural injustice for granted. But in this chapter, I argue that Young's conception of structural injustice is ontologically confused and I offer an alternative conception based on Margaret Archer's critical realist ontology. This new conception creates space for an integration of power and structural change, which I discuss through Thomas Wartenberg's situated conception of power. It also leads me to argue that there are three *types* of structural injustice: pure, avoidable and deliberate. Once we have this typology, we have a better sense of *why* structural injustice is perpetuated over time, *who* is responsible for it and *what* can be done to change it.

Structure and agency

Since sociological ideas were first systematically articulated in the nineteenth century, there has been a debate between two opposing camps. On the one hand are collectivists. They argue that 'society' is something separate from the individuals that inhabit it. Society must be studied independently and cannot be reduced to the actions of individuals. On the other hand are individualists. Methodological individualists argue that society can be studied *only* by looking at the actions of individuals. Only individual actions are observable and, therefore, measurable – 'society' is unobservable, and therefore, theories about society cannot be empirically verified and are mere conjecture.

Both positions are unsatisfactory. Margaret Archer accuses them of conflationism. Collectivism is guilty of 'Downwards Conflation': the social whole is understood to 'have complete monopoly over causation', ruling out the role of agents in changing or shaping society.[2] But individualism is guilty of the opposite vice – 'Upwards Conflation'. Individualists argue that individuals have a monopoly on causal power.[3] Both positions claim that one factor explains causation, which is an inadequate way of understanding social reality.

---

[2]Archer, *Realist Social Theory*, 3.
[3]Archer, *Realist Social Theory*, 4.

This intractable debate persisted in twentieth-century social theory, albeit in different guises, but two theories from the latter part of the century tried to provide viable alternatives. One is Anthony Giddens's structuration theory. For Giddens, structures are made up of rules and resources. To use the analogy of language, rules are like grammar and syntax (the abstract rules that make the production of sentences possible);[4] or Giddens draws on Wittgenstein to understand rules like knowledge of children's games – the rules of the game 'cannot be strictly defined'.[5] Rules exist virtually in agents' minds. Resources are anything – material or immaterial – that can help a person achieve their goals in social interactions. Resources are divided into authoritative resources (command over persons) and allocative resources (command over objects).[6] When people use resources acting on the basis of rules, they are reproducing structures. Giddens describes this as the 'duality of structure' and uses a language analogy to explain it: 'When I utter a grammatical English sentence in a casual conversation, I contribute to the reproduction of the English language as a whole. This is an unintended consequence of my speaking the sentence, but one that is bound in directly to the recursiveness of the duality of structure.'[7]

Giddens gives the term 'structure' a different meaning from that given by other social theorists. Instead of employing 'structure' to refer to the material conditions of a society with a mechanical connotation, like the girders of a building or a skeleton holding up the body, Giddens uses it to refer to the combination of rules and resources.[8] Giddens's structure is momentary and virtual, not long-lasting and material.[9] For Giddens, the term 'structure' should be reserved for the moment of structuration: 'structure is both medium and outcome of the reproduction of practices. Structure enters simultaneously into

---

[4]William H. Sewell, 'A Theory of Structure: Duality, Agency, and Transformation', *American Journal of Sociology* 98, no. 1 (1992): 6. For accounts of structural injustice that draw on Sewell's theory of social structure, see Sally Haslanger, 'Agency under Structural Constraints in Social Systems,' in *What Is Structural Injustice?*, ed. Jude Browne and Maeve McKeown (Oxford: Oxford University Press, 2024); Sally Haslanger, 'What Is a (Social) Structural Explanation?' *Philosophical Studies: An International Journal for Philosophy in the Analytic Tradition* 173, no. 1 (2016): 113–30; and Mara Marin, 'Transformative Action as Structural and Publicly-Constituted', in *What Is Structural Injustice?*, ed. Jude Browne and Maeve McKeown (Oxford: Oxford University Press, 2024).
[5]Anthony Giddens, *Central Problems in Social Theory: Action, Structure and Contradiction in Social Analysis* (London: Macmillan Press, 1979), 68.
[6]Giddens, chap. 3; Sewell, 'A Theory of Structure', 9.
[7]Giddens, *Central Problems in Social Theory*, 77.
[8]See Jonathan Wolff, 'Structural Harm, Structural Injustice, Structural Repair'. In *What Is Structural Injustice?*, ed. Jude Browne and Maeve McKeown (Oxford: Oxford University Press, 2024) for the analogy of a house, and John B. Thompson, 'The Theory of Structurationism', in *Social Theory of Modern Societies: Anthony Giddens and His Critics*, ed. David Held and John B. Thompson (Cambridge: Cambridge University Press, 1989), 60 for the building and skeleton analogy.
[9]Giddens discusses this explicitly, saying that the terms 'structure' and 'system' 'should be understood in a rather different way from how they are ordinarily taken'. Giddens, *Central Problems in Social Theory*, 3.

the constitution of the agent and social practices, and "exists" in the generating moments of this constitution.'[10] Giddens repeats that structure 'is present only in its instantiation'[11] or structures are 'temporally "present" only in their instantiation, in the constituting moments of social systems'.[12] This is in contrast to social 'systems', which are longer-term sedimentations of social structures:[13] 'Social systems, by contrast to structure, exist in time-space, and are constituted by social practices.'[14] Systems are 'reproduced relations between actors and collectivities, organized as regular social practices'.[15] Institutions are 'the most deeply-layered practices constitutive of social systems'.[16]

Giddens was concerned to challenge functionalism (in sociology) and structuralism (in linguistics and anthropology), which both, according to him, focused on systems and structures (words they used interchangeably or with a lack of stability[17]), prioritized structure and de-centred the subject, which is a 'scandal'.[18] By drawing on the philosophy of action, Giddens sought to show how individuals actually know a lot about the social systems in which they operate – they have 'practical consciousness', a kind of tacit knowledge of social systems[19] – and they reproduce those systems through their actions in the moment of structuration. The reproduction of social systems is the unintended consequence of action.[20]

Despite being an improvement on earlier social theory because he recognizes the causal powers of both structure and agency, Archer argues that Giddens is still guilty of conflation. By insisting that structure and agency are co-constitutive, Giddens replaces the previous forms of conflation with 'Central Conflation' – conflating structure and agency, insisting on their inseparability. Giddens, therefore, cannot explain the interplay between structure and agency, how they impact upon each other and how they contribute to stability or change.[21]

---

[10]Giddens, *Central Problems in Social Theory*, 5.

[11]Giddens, *Central Problems in Social Theory*, 54.

[12]Giddens, *Central Problems in Social Theory*, 64.

[13]As Giddens puts it, 'the term "social structure" ordinarily has, as employed in Anglo-American sociology, is carried in my terminology by the notion of system: with the crucial proviso that social systems are patterned in time as well as space, through continuities of social reproduction. A social system is thus a "structured totality".' Giddens, *Central Problems in Social Theory*, 64. Critics have argued that Giddens's attempt to change the meanings of structure and system is confusing, rather than illuminating John B. Thompson, 'The Theory of Structurationism', in *Social Theory of Modern Societies: Anthony Giddens and His Critics*, ed. David Held and John B. Thompson (Cambridge: Cambridge University Press, 1989), 62; Douglas V. Porpora, 'Four Concepts of Social Structure', *Journal for the Theory of Social Behaviour* 19, no. 2 (1989): 209.

[14]Giddens, *Central Problems in Social Theory*, 73.

[15]Giddens, *Central Problems in Social Theory*, 66.

[16]Giddens, *Central Problems in Social Theory*, 65.

[17]Giddens, *Central Problems in Social Theory*, 61.

[18]Giddens, *Central Problems in Social Theory*, 38.

[19]Giddens, *Central Problems in Social Theory*, 56.

[20]Giddens, *Central Problems in Social Theory*, 59.

[21]Archer, *Realist Social Theory*, 13–14.

The other alternative social theory is critical realism.[22] This school of thought is in direct conflict with structurationism, because it insists that there are different strata of social reality (structure and agency), and it seeks to understand how properties and powers emerge out of the interplay of the two. Critical realism relies on 'analytical dualism', looking at the ways different strata impact on each other, whereas structurationism is concerned with 'interpenetration', which involves 'compacting strata rather than disentangling them'.[23] Critical realism does not suffer from any of the forms of conflation of the previous three schools of thought:

> Because the social world is made up, *inter alia*, of 'structures' and of 'agents' and because these belong to different strata, there is no question of reducing one to the other or of eliding the two and there is every reason for exploring the interplay between them.[24]

Crucially, critical realists insist that structure has *emergent properties*. 'Emergence' here does not refer to the temporal sense of emergence: something appearing for the first time or developing over time. Instead, the concept of emergence explains 'how an entity can have a causal impact on the world in its own right: a causal impact that is not just the sum of the impacts of its parts would have if they were not organised into this kind of whole'.[25] An example is water. The properties of water are different from the properties of hydrogen and oxygen. Try putting out a fire with hydrogen and oxygen, and it becomes apparent that water has properties that are more than the sum of its parts.[26] In other words, emergent properties have causal powers that are irreducible to the sum of their parts.

Applied to social structure, individualists deny that society has emergent properties, causal properties derived from the fact that it is more than the sum of its parts. They insist that society is reducible to individuals' actions. Collectivists do think that society has emergent properties, but that agents do not. Structurationists deny that society has emergent properties, because structure

---

[22]Archer at various points uses the terms 'morphogenesis', 'realism' and 'critical realism'. Critical realism has become the established term in the literature.

[23]Archer, *Realist Social Theory*, 15.

[24]Archer, *Realist Social Theory*, 62. Archer is not the only theorist in this space. She drew in particular on Roy Bhaskar's *The Possibility of Naturalism* (1978) in developing her realist social ontology and morphogenetic account of structural processes. She describes Bhaskar's book as 'the generous under-labouring of a philosopher who has actually dug beyond disciplinary bounds', whereas her approach 'is produced by a working sociologist, recognizing the obligation to go deeper into precision tooling to supply a social theory which is pre-eminently usable'. Archer, *Realist Social Theory*, 161. For another account of critical realism see David Elder-Vass, *The Causal Power of Social Structures: Emergence, Structure and Agency* (Cambridge: Cambridge University Press, 2010).

[25]Elder-Vass, *The Causal Power of Social Structures*, 5.

[26]Elder-Vass, *The Causal Power of Social Structures*, 5.

consists of rules in individuals' minds combined with individuals' perception and use of available resources.[27] But realists claim that it is not possible to study the interplay of structure and agency without acknowledging that structures condition the actions of individuals and that agents, in turn, modify structures.

Realists argue that it is through the interaction of structure and agency over time that structures evolve. For example, the role of landlord gives an individual powers over property and tenants (structure conditions the landlord's options for action). But the landlord can work within the role and decide whether or not they will try to increase their powers by working with landlords' associations or try to improve the situation for their tenants by working with tenants' associations. One individual will not have causal impact on the structures, but groups can: hence why the landlord works through a collective to achieve their goals (collective action can have an impact on and modify structures). However, groups' actions will intermingle with other groups' actions and the result may be an outcome that no individual or group intended. This starts a new cycle of the interplay between a reworked structure and reworked agency. This constitutes 'double morphogenesis' because both the structure and the agents are transformed through the process.

Young on social-structural processes

Iris Marion Young explains how social-structural processes work and how they result in structural injustice by way of an example – Sandy. A single mother of two, Sandy works in a mall and finds herself on the brink of homelessness, through no fault of her own or of anyone else.[28] A developer bought the building where she lives in the city centre and plans to convert it into condominiums. Sandy has to find a new home. She wants to live closer to work, because her current apartment is two buses away from the mall and she commutes three hours per day. But Sandy finds that there are few options for her. The housing closer to work is privately owned and the few rental options that do exist are far out of her price range. She has to rent on the other side of the city or in the city centre, but she worries the inner-city neighbourhoods are too dangerous for her kids. She decides to invest in a car and use some of the money she had earmarked for rent to pay for it. After a two-month search, Sandy finds an apartment which is a forty-five-minute drive from work. It's small; the kids will have to share the bedroom and she will sleep on a fold-out bed in the living room. There are no amenities in the building like a washer/dryer or any playgrounds nearby. But there are no other options, so she decides to take the apartment. But then she discovers that

---

[27]Elder-Vass, *The Causal Power of Social Structures*, 85.
[28]Iris Marion Young, *Responsibility for Justice* (Oxford: Oxford University Press, 2011), 43–4.

she needs to pay a three-month deposit upfront. All of her savings have been spent on the car, so she can't. Sandy and her kids face homelessness.

Young argues that the judgment that Sandy suffers from injustice does not refer to her unique story, but to the position she is in. Sandy occupies a social position whereby she is vulnerable to housing deprivation and homelessness. Whether or not Sandy and others like her will become homeless 'will depend partly on their own actions, partly on luck, and partly on the actions of others'.[29] But the crucial question from the perspective of justice is: 'whether it is right that *anyone* should be in a *position* of housing insecurity, especially in an affluent society'.[30]

So how does this happen? How is it that Sandy comes to be positioned in an affluent society so that she is vulnerable to homelessness? Young quotes William Sewell who argues that the term 'structure' can only ever be a metaphor,[31] and given the difficulty of defining structure, she offers a hybrid definition drawing on a range of theorists. Her purpose 'is only to give some depth to the claim that many judgments of social injustice refer to structural injustice'.[32] In other words, her aim is not to give a definitive definition of social structure. Young identifies four features of social-structural processes, as follows.

Objective constraint

Social structures are objective facts in that they constrain and enable individuals' options for action. There are two ways in which structures operate as objective facts. First, there are material structures. These are what Jean-Paul Sartre describes as the 'practico-inert'. Past human projects have left their mark on the world and are difficult to change. For instance, the housing stock that exists in the United States today is a product of past decisions in terms of investment, social policy and cultural preferences, and policies of racial segregation. The second way in which structures operate as objective facts is through institutional rules and social norms. Legal rules are determined by the state and enforced by the police and legal system. These are difficult to change. Social norms, while not inscribed in law, can also be resistant to change. In Sandy's case, she can only get certain jobs because of her gender and class, and she will be judged by others for superficial reasons such as her body type and style of dress.[33] As Young writes, 'She experiences the confluence of social rules as objective constraints because others behave as though they are.'[34] It is not only Sandy

---

[29]Young, *Responsibility for Justice*, 45.

[30]Young, *Responsibility for Justice*, 45.

[31]Young, *Responsibility for Justice*, 52–3; Sewell, 'A Theory of Structure', 125.

[32]Young, *Responsibility for Justice*, 53.

[33]I would include race here, but Young doesn't specify Sandy's race. In this case, then, gender and class are the relevant factors.

[34]Young, *Responsibility for Justice*, 55.

who is constrained by material and institutional/social structures. Even privileged agents will experience structures as constraining. For example, the landlord who sells Sandy's building may feel he has no choice because maintenance costs have become too high. As Young puts it, 'he faces a limited set of options that are objectively given'.[35]

Social positions

The material and institutional/social constraints are objective facts that shape people's options and behaviour. But, in order to understand social structure, it is also necessary to take a macro view of society and to look at the social positions in society and how they relate to one another. Young draws on two sociologists to explain this. Peter Blau argues that a social structure is a 'multi-dimensional space' where individuals are placed in different social positions, and the connections between those social positions create a social structure.[36] Pierre Bourdieu describes social structure as a 'field'. Individuals are placed in social positions closer to some and further away from others, and their closeness determines how likely they are to identify with those others.[37] Young argues that we cannot interpret individuals' actions in isolation, rather we have to look at the systemic relations in which individuals are embedded. Social relations 'position people prior to their interactions, and condition expectations and possibilities of interaction'.[38]

Structures produced only in action

The problem with the view that individuals are placed in different social positions is that it could lead to determinism – the view that individuals are destined to act in the ways that they do, and thus it negates agency. As we saw above, some theorists responded to this challenge with 'methodological individualism', arguing that everything in society can be explained by the actions of individuals. But Young draws instead on structurationism, that is, individuals reproduce structures through their actions. She draws on Giddens, interpreting his view as follows: 'On Giddens's account, when individuals act, they are doing two things at once: (1) They are trying to bring about a state of affairs that they intend, and (2) they are reproducing the structural properties, the positional relations of rules and resources, on which they draw for these actions.'[39] Young argues that

---

[35]Young, *Responsibility for Justice*, 56.
[36]Young, *Responsibility for Justice*, 56–7; Peter Blau, *Inequality and Homogeneity: A Primitive Theory of Social Structure* (London: Collier Macmillan, 1977).
[37]Young, *Responsibility for Justice*, 57.
[38]Young, *Responsibility for Justice*, 57.
[39]Young, *Responsibility for Justice*, 60.

people act within institutions in conformity with institutional and social rules and in doing so they reproduce structures. This may not be conscious. She brings in Bourdieu again to explain this. People act according to 'the habitus', which is the unconscious, internalized behaviour associated with an individual's social position.[40]

Unintended consequences

The outcomes of agents participating in social structures are unintended and can contradict the intentions of the participants. This is Sartre's idea of 'counter-finality'. An example is the 'tragedy of the commons' whereby each individual takes what they need from the commons without putting anything back, so eventually there is nothing left.[41] In the housing case, Young writes: 'Too many people must pay half their income for cramped and poorly maintained housing, and too many people lack private housing altogether. Presumably, in none of these cities is this situation the intended outcome of the actions of any persons or policies of any institutions.'[42]

Thus, Young argues that social-structural processes have four features:

1. Objective constraint
2. Social positions
3. Structures produced only in action
4. Unintended outcomes

Here Young combines insights from critical realism (that structure and agency are distinct, and that structures have emergent properties – 1, 2 and 4) and structurationism (3). But critical realism and structurationism are two conflicting social ontologies. They conflict in two ways. First, the former insists on the separability of structure and agency, the latter on their elision. As Archer puts it, 'The separability/inseparability issue represents the ontological parting of the ways.'[43] On Archer's morphogenetic approach to social structure, structures are already given (objective constraint), there is interaction between the structures and agents (who inhabit different social positions), the interaction between structure and agency can result in either stability or change, and because of the unpredictability of human action and of how it will affect structures, there are unintended outcomes. Structurationism takes a different perspective – structures are not already given; they only exist insofar as individual agents internalize and

---

[40]Young, *Responsibility for Justice*, 61.
[41]Young, *Responsibility for Justice*, 63.
[42]Young, *Responsibility for Justice*, 63–4.
[43]Archer, *Realist Social Theory*, 63.

act upon rules, thereby reproducing the structures (which are virtual). The second difference surrounds emergence. Critical realists believe that social structures have emergent properties, while structurationists deny this. While Giddens has a further level of analysis above structure – systems[44] – these are still patterns of routinized practices that become sedimented over time. Thus, systems do not have emergent properties; rather, they are routinized practices generated by agents reproducing structures in social practices.[45]

Young's account of social-structural processes was a sketch. But even if it was not intended to be an in-depth account, there is still an issue in that Young was trying to combine insights from different social-theoretical frameworks which conflict in important ways.[46] Therefore, there is a flaw at the core of Young's interpretation of structural injustice. There are also problems with Young's analysis, which will be elaborated in what follows. On the one hand, Young did not analyse the critical realist aspects of social structures in sufficient depth. If she had, she would have discussed the *vested interests* that come with various social positions and how this affects agents' behaviour in those positions, and how it generates *power* for particular agents. On the other hand, the inclusion of structurationism and the habitus as the explanations as to why structures persist inherits the main problems with both of these theories – they cannot account for *structural change*. Most of the literature that has followed in Young's wake has taken her definition of structural injustice for granted, but given that the approach has these problems, I am going to propose an alternative.

In what follows, I argue that critical realism is a better foundation for conceptualizing structural injustice than structurationism and that we should dispense with structurationism as part of the analysis of structural injustice. As Archer argues, the social ontology of realism leads to using the methodology of 'analytical dualism', which enables the study of the interplay between structure and agency, how they impact upon each other and how they contribute to stability or change. This separation, Archer argues, is necessary for the purposes of practical social theorizing. Crucially from my perspective, the separation of structure and agency enables an integration of power into our conception of structural injustice. In the next section, I show why structurationism provides a poor interpretation of Sandy's situation and then I apply Archer's critical realist

---

[44]Rob Stones, *Structuration Theory* (Basingstoke: Palgrave Macmillan, 2005), 54.

[45]Archer, *Realist Social Theory*, 96.

[46]There are attempts in the literature to combine the two approaches. For example, see Stones, *Structuration Theory*. But this is a minority position and Archer insists it is incoherent. Some theorists argue there is less distance between the two than Archer thinks, e.g. Anthony King, 'The Odd Couple: Margaret Archer, Anthony Giddens and British Social Theory', *British Journal of Sociology* 61 (2010): 253–60. But I would contend that the conflicts over separability/inseparability and emergence are irreconcilable.

approach to structure to highlight how this approach provides new insight into structural injustice.[47]

Sandy through the lens of structurationism

Young employs structurationism to make the point that structures are reproduced through action and exist 'only' in action.[48] Structuration theory makes the important point that structures are reproduced through action, and that is not contested neither here nor by critical realism more generally. Indeed, critical realism also insists that human agency either reproduces or transforms social structures.[49] However, the claim that structures exist *only* through action is contested. This latter point elides structure and agency, and denies the emergent properties of social structures. This can be illuminated by assessing Sandy's predicament through the lens of structuration theory.

First, we have seen that structuration theory posits that social structure only exists in its moment of instantiation. While Giddens argues that social systems are routinized and sedimented social practices, he 'denies that the relationships of a social system have any causal properties independent of the rule-following activity of human actors'.[50] But the causal properties of social relationships are self-evident. Consider the boss/employee relationship.[51] For Giddens, these social positions are an abstraction that arise from the rule-following behaviour of the agents who occupy them. However, this obscures the fact that the boss/subordinate relationship has been established by an organization and is constituted by formal rules. This institutional framework places the boss in a position of power over the employee; the boss has the power to fire or hire the subordinate and to affect their well-being in various ways. The boss has the power to dominate the employee by virtue of a pre-given social relationship

---

[47]There are other writers in the realist/critical realist tradition, but Margaret Archer is 'the dean of the critical realist movement' and so is a good place to start (Frédéric Vandenberghe, 'The Archers: A Tale of Folk (Final Episode?)', *European Journal of Social Theory* 8, no. 2 (2005): 227). Archer drew on David Lockwood's Marxist functionalism and Roy Bhaskar's critical realism to develop her morphogenetic approach across multiple books. Hers is a stand-alone approach but also a systematic rebuttal of Giddens's structurationism. Here I draw on her 1995 book, *Realist Social Theory*, which is focused on the ontological relationship between structure and agency. Her other books in the morphogenesis series focus on culture and agency, and her later work focuses on reflexivity.

[48]Young, *Responsibility for Justice*, 53, 60.

[49]Archer, *Realist Social Theory*, 217. I made the point in an earlier article that on Young's social connection model of responsibility, the kind of connection to structural injustice that generates political responsibility for it is reproduction of structures through action. For example, when I buy a T-shirt in a high-street shop, I have not caused sweatshop labour, but I am reproducing it. This point still stands within a critical realist social ontology. Maeve McKeown, 'Iris Marion Young's "Social Connection Model" of Responsibility: Clarifying the Meaning of Connection', *Journal of Social Philosophy* 49, no. 3 (2018): 497.

[50]Porpora, 'Four Concepts of Social Structure', 205.

[51]Porpora, 'Four Concepts of Social Structure', 207–8.

within an institutional hierarchy. Their social positions, and associated powers, are analytically prior to the rule-like, routinized relationship the agents go on to establish; and furthermore, this rule-like behaviour is conditioned by the causal powers of the boss. The employee acts in such a way as to anticipate the boss's powers. It is not the employee's and boss's rule-following that constitute their social positions; the social positions are already given and condition the behaviour.

To return to the example of Sandy, the landlord and Sandy reproduce social structures in their interaction when the landlord decides to sell the building and Sandy must find somewhere else to live. But there is something more fundamental underlying this process. The landlord is in a social position whereby he owns property, a power that is backed up by the state through an intricate legal framework. He is in a position of power over Sandy, which can be exercised by selling the building, rendering Sandy vulnerable to homelessness. The landlord/tenant relationship is analytically prior to any rule-following behaviour that Sandy and the landlord might engage in, either in a direct or an indirect encounter. Structurationism focuses on 'social practices' rather than the material and cultural structures that condition the landlord's and Sandy's options for action, including the institutions involved, such as the state, property ownership, property law and financial systems. Structurationism 'disallows the pre-existence of structures (roles, positions, relations) which are thus made both *co-existent* and also *co-terminous* with agency'.[52]

Second, structurationism cannot explain *why* Sandy and the landlord act in the ways that they do. Part of the answer must be to do with interests: interests that are built into social positions. As Porpora puts it, 'Among the causal powers that are deposited in social positions are interests. Interests are built into a social position by the relationship of that position to other positions in the system.'[53] For example, capitalists have an interest in maximizing profits.[54] This interest is built into the social position of capitalist by virtue of its relationship to other social positions (other capitalists, workers), and it is experienced as an external force: a law that the capitalist must obey. These interests explain the capitalists' motives, which are translated into action. In our case, the landlord has an interest in making money from his property. Sandy's position is more complicated. As a subordinate in the power relationship, she has an objective interest in overcoming this power structure, for instance, by agitating for changes to the private property regime, or at least better terms for tenants. However, Sandy has a 'real interest' at this moment in time in being an attractive tenant, a need that disincentivizes

---

[52] Archer, *Realist Social Theory*, 99.
[53] Porpora, 'Four Concepts of Social Structure', 208.
[54] Porpora, 'Four Concepts of Social Structure', 208.

acting on her objective interests.[55] (Also, Sandy likely doesn't have time for activism, right now she just needs somewhere to live.) But structurationism does not explain these interests, nor does it explain the expressed preferences or desires of agents, and therefore doesn't explain the behaviour of agents. As Archer puts it, 'Central conflationism is mute on desires: they can have no external locus, that is finding their promptings in structured positions, in vested interests or induced wants and they can have no internal locus in psychological proclivities.'[56] By contrast, recognizing that different social positions come with different vested interests explains why some agents are incentivized to reproduce structures (morphostasis), and others to push for the transformation of structures (morphogenesis).[57]

Third, structurationism 'sinks' structure into agency, rendering it incapable of explaining stability or change in structures over time. Indeed, the whole point of structuration theory is to overcome the structure/agency dichotomy and to conceive of structure as 'dual'. On the one hand, the idea of the recursiveness of structure (that it is only and constantly reproduced through individuals' action) implies 'a spurious methodological permanence', when in fact structures can and do (and always) change; even if structures are long-lasting, like feudalism, they do eventually change, and some structures are inherently short-lived, like interest rates.[58] The second implication is that structural change is possible at any moment in the ways that individual agents mobilize rules and resources. But this contradicts the idea of the recursiveness of structure – that structure is chronic. Therefore, Giddens 'has produced a pendular swing between contradictory images – of chronic recursiveness and total transformation'.[59] Giddens 'has to stress the quintessential polyvalence of each "moment", both replicatory and transformatory (reproduction always carries its two connotations)'.[60]

On either side of this coin, the analysis is wanting. On the one hand, the housing market is not immutable. It is constantly evolving due to changes in multiple structures, including legal rules and regulations, financial markets and social norms about desirable housing (witness, for example, the preference for country-housing rather than city-housing during the Covid-19 pandemic). Housing markets are also liable to sudden change, such as financial crashes or

---

[55]See Isaac for the difference between objective and real interests: 'Interests are real because they are causally effective in practice in a sense in which objective interests are not.' Jeffrey C. Isaac, 'Beyond the Three Faces of Power: A Realist Critique', in *Rethinking Power*, ed. Thomas E. Wartenberg (Albany: State University of New York Press, 1992), 50.

[56]Archer, *Realist Social Theory*, 131.

[57]Archer, *Realist Social Theory*, 221.

[58]Archer, *Realist Social Theory*, 87.

[59]Archer, *Realist Social Theory*, 88.

[60]Archer, *Realist Social Theory*, 89.

state intervention. On the other hand, any one action by an individual agent in the housing market will make no difference to the structure at any given time. Structures can outlast changes in individuals' behaviour. Giddens's inability to adequately account for structural stability or change is due to his resistance to separating structure and agency. But analytical and temporal separation of structure and agency is necessary to explain structural change.

It is undeniable that institutions like the state, property law and financial systems predate any of the landlord's or Sandy's actions and causally impact upon their options for action. Sandy or the landlord does not have to instantiate the structures in any given moment for those structures to exist. For instance, property law exists prior to their actions and either agent does not have to know the details of the laws for these laws to have an effect. As Archer puts it, laws have autonomy, are anterior and have causal influence.[61] The same can be said of the material resources of the housing market. Properties have autonomy – they are identifiable regardless of the rules and meanings attached to them by agents; they are anterior – they pre-exist any social meaning given to them by Sandy or the landlord; and they have causal influence – Sandy is locked out of the housing market, rendering her vulnerable to homelessness. There are both 'emergent cultural properties' and 'emergent material properties' that escape the claim that structure = rules and resources, and these emergent properties will continue to exist as remainders on the structuration analysis.[62] Moreover, the fact that there is a housing crisis is not only about social practices, but rather that there is an inadequate stock of housing and too many people needing housing. Sometimes sheer numbers of people create problems for policymakers regardless of their actions; this is 'the dumb pressure of numbers' and constitutes another remainder excluded from Giddens' approach.[63]

In sum, structurationism denies the emergent properties of social positions, cannot account for vested interests nor structural change. All of this suggests that the structurationism approach is not a viable way of analysing a social structure like the housing market. To return to Young briefly, Young identified four elements of social-structural processes, the other three being that structures are objectively constraining, they generate social positions and they produce unintended outcomes, so she did not insist that structurationism had all the answers when considering social-structural processes. However, she does insist that structures 'exist only in action'. This is the point I am rejecting and that I want to dispense with when conceptualizing structural injustice. Because by

---

[61] Archer, *Realist Social Theory*, 108.
[62] Archer, *Realist Social Theory*, 114.
[63] Archer, *Realist Social Theory*, 119.

inserting this structurationist ontology into the definition of structural injustice and by focusing on the ways that individuals reproduce structures, it (a) does not provide a useful diagnosis for understanding the role of social positions and vested interests in causing and maintaining structural injustice, and (b) does not explain how to change it.

Sandy through the lens of critical realism

Critical realism solves both problems. Briefly, Archer's morphogenetic approach is based on 'two simple propositions: that structure necessarily predates the actions which transform it; and that structural elaboration necessarily post-dates those actions'.[64] The morphogenetic cycle consists of three stages (see Figure 1). At T^1 there is the structure that conditions agents' actions, between T^2 and T^3 there is interaction between the structure and agency, and at T^4 there is structural elaboration, triggering a new morphogenetic cycle. The emphasis on how structure and agency impact on one another over time represents the uniqueness of the morphogenetic approach.

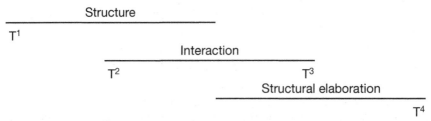

Figure 1 'The morphogenetic sequence'. From Margaret Archer, *Realist Social Theory: The Morphogenetic Approach* (Cambridge: Cambridge University Press, 1995), 76. Reproduced with permission from the Licensor through PLSclear.

Structural conditioning means that agents exist in a world not of their own making. The actions of previous generations casually affect agents in the present by having created the structural conditions in which they can act at T^1: 'They do so by shaping the situations in which later "generations" of actors find themselves and by endowing various agents with different vested interests according to the positions they occupy in the structures they "inherit" (in the class structure, in the social distribution of resources, or in the educational system, for example).'[65] We could add to this race and gender relations, as well as relations between other oppressed social groups. This analysis is a realist one, because it accepts that the results of past actions and structural elaboration have emergent properties

---

[64]Archer, *Realist Social Theory*, 90.
[65]Archer, *Realist Social Theory*, 90.

which serve as constraints or enablers of present agents' actions (something which structurationism denies).

These social positions and objective vested interests produce regular behaviour and patterns of interaction over time: 'Groups experiencing exigencies seek to eradicate them (thus pursuing structural change) and those experiencing rewards try to retain them (thus defending structural stability).'[66] So in contrast to Giddens who argues that structures only exist through the reproduction of structures through individuals' actions, critical realists assert that structures pre-exist individuals' actions, and that even though agents reproduce structures through their actions, they can also act in ways that aim to modify the structures. For example, it is in the interest of landlords to maintain the structure because they derive benefits from it. But it is in the interest of tenants to change the structure so they always have access to affordable and decent housing. Given the objective interests of agents in different social positions, some will work to change the structures and others to maintain them. Therefore, *structural interaction* recognizes that agents, as well as structures, possess emergent properties (agents can act in ways within structures that will ultimately causally impact on those structures).

At time T^2, there is interaction between the structure and the agents. The structure is already in place: knowledge of the structures, attitudes towards it and vested interests in changing or maintaining it are already distributed at T^1. It is essential to know what these are because 'without analysing these we cannot account for *when the "longue durée"* is broken, *who* is primarily responsible for changing it, or *how* it is accomplished (by collective policy, social conflict, incremental change etc.)'.[67] The influence of the structure will persist throughout T^2: 'It is essential to know whether this is because they (temporally and temporarily) resist collective pressures to change, remain because they represent the vested interests of the powerful, or are in fact 'psychologically supported' by the population.'[68]

The interaction between structures and collective agents between T^2 and T^3 results in structural elaboration at T^4, which is not merely the elimination of the prior structure but also 'the structural elaboration of a host of new possibilities'.[69] A new structure is in place, marking a return to T^1 but this time with a new structural framework and a new set of possibilities. This new structure is unlikely to resemble the intended outcome of any particular group:

> The *structural elaboration* which then ensues is interpreted as being a largely unintended consequence. The modification of previous structural properties

[66]Archer, *Realist Social Theory*, 90.
[67]Archer, *Realist Social Theory*, 78.
[68]Archer, *Realist Social Theory*, 78.
[69]Archer, *Realist Social Theory*, 79.

and the introduction of new ones is the combined product of the different outcomes pursued simultaneously by various social groups. The unintended element largely results from group conflict and concession which together mean that the consequential elaboration is often what no-one sought or wanted.[70]

Applied to Sandy's case, Sandy and her landlord have inherited a structure of the housing market at T^1. They occupy different social positions within the structure – property-owner and tenant. The state of the housing market and the positions Sandy and the landlord find themselves in are conditioned by the actions of past generations of people in their structural context. They interact with that structure in different ways between T^2 and T^3, and their actions combine with the actions of other agents, resulting in an unintended structural elaboration at T^4. Importantly, structural conditioning is not deterministic. Structures do not *force* individuals or groups to act in such a way as to further their objective interests; rather, they incentivize this behaviour by creating different opportunity costs. For example, if landlords do not act to maintain their position in the housing market, they will suffer material costs. However, conversely for agents in subordinate positions, acting to advance their vested interests can be detrimental. For instance, if Sandy acts to try to change the structures advancing her interests, she could acquire a reputation as a difficult tenant, thus getting poor references from previous landlords. Agents can, therefore, act against their self-interest. For subordinate agents, this could be because the costs of promoting their interests are too high, maybe they are unaware of their objective interests due to the dominant ideology, or a lack of critical reflection, or simple human fallibility. For privileged agents, this could be because they feel morally or politically motivated to pursue change. Archer's approach 'accommodates the possibility of reflective self-sacrifice of inherited vested interests on the part of individuals or groups'.[71] So it is possible that Sandy will act in ways that do not challenge the housing market and equally the landlord could try to challenge it, say by working with tenants' associations or within landlords' associations to promote tenants' interests. Thus, Sandy and the landlord's actions are not determined by the structure, but do come with opportunity costs. They may act in ways that seek to change the housing market for the better, but ultimately the impact of other agents' actions will also factor in and might undo or modify the effects of their actions. And, as Mara Marin points out, how their actions will be received publicly is out of their control.[72]

---

[70]Archer, *Realist Social Theory*, 91.

[71]Archer, *Realist Social Theory*, 91.

[72]Mara Marin, 'Transformative Action as Structural and Publicly-Constituted.'

Archer was writing a theory about social structure, its reproduction and modification, *in general*. She wasn't writing a theory specifically about *unjust* structures. On this point, I do not have a problem with following Young. She argues that structural injustice 'exists when social processes put large groups of people under systematic threat of domination or deprivation of the means to develop and exercise their capacities, at the same time that these processes enable others to dominate or to have a wide range of opportunities for developing and exercising capacities available to them'.[73] Filling this in with Young's earlier work on domination and oppression, domination is the structural 'constraint on self-determination' and oppression is the structural 'constraint on self-development'.[74] Domination prevents individuals from determining how they will live their lives. Oppression prevents individuals from developing their unique capacities and fulfilling their personal potential.

Critical realism is a better foundation for understanding structural injustice than structurationism. Critical realist social ontology allows us to disentangle various social strata, to understand how they impact upon each other and to explain how new powers or properties emerge from these interactions. Insisting on the separation of structure and agency for analytical purposes provides insight into how power operates within social structures. This will produce a more refined assessment of what structural injustice is and who bears responsibility for it.

Situating power

Now that we have a more developed and consistent theory of how social structures work, we can better understand how structural injustice is reproduced or changed over time. We have seen that even though agents' actions are conditioned by structures, they are not determined by structures; in the process of *structural interaction*, agents have agency to decide how they will act within structures and contest them. It is my contention that powerful agents are in a different position here to ordinary individuals. Powerful agents have more 'elbow room' to decide how they will act because they have greater resources at their disposal.[75] Furthermore, powerful agents have greater capacity to act in ways that will change the structures in the direction either of promoting justice or of

---

[73]Young, *Responsibility for Justice*, 52.

[74]This terminology comes from Iris Marion Young, *Justice and the Politics of Difference* (Princeton, NJ: Princeton University Press, 1990), 37. In *Justice and the Politics of Difference*, Young discussed domination and oppression as 'institutional' constraints. I am modifying this to structural because institutional can have connotations of intention on the part of institutional actors, which does not capture all of the ways in which structures can dominate or oppress.

[75]The term 'elbow room' is borrowed from Daniel Dennett – Daniel C. Dennett, *Elbow Room: The Varieties of Free Will Worth Wanting* (Oxford: Oxford University Press, 1984).

entrenching injustice. Therefore, this is where the action is, both in terms of understanding structural stability of change and in attributing responsibility for structural injustice. In this section, I explain how power operates within structures and what this means for conceptualizing structural injustice.

Archer's critical realist social ontology, I have argued, has provided insight into the relationship between structure and agency. But Archer does not incorporate an analysis of power.[76] My concern in this book is to theorize the role of power in structural injustice, so to that end I'm going to supplement Archer's critical realist ontology with Thomas Wartenberg's situated conception of power, which can explain how social structures generate power relationships, how those power relationships condition action and how they can be changed.

A 'situated' conception of power helps explain how power operates within structures. The social positions agents occupy within structures generate power relationships for differently placed agents. Wartenberg gives the simple example of the teacher-student relationship and the act of grading. Students' behaviour in the classroom is partly conditioned by the fact that the teacher will grade them. The teacher does not need to do anything special to get the students to behave in a certain way; the students do this in the knowledge that the teacher's grade will affect them. The power that the teacher has over the student is not interventionist, it is structural. The power relationship is not reached by agreement, where both parties have a more-or-less equal ability to affect each other; the student has no choice but to be in this situated power relationship with the teacher: 'The subordinate agent faces a situated power relationship as a given over which he can have little effect but which will have a significant effect upon him.'[77]

A bad grade can lead to parents punishing the student, or to the student not getting into college or not getting an internship or job. This reveals that the teacher's power over the student in terms of grading depends not only on the position of the teacher and student in relation to each other but also on peripheral social agents. If the parents, universities and employers did not cooperate with the grading system, then the teacher would cease to have power over the student. The coordinated practices of a range of other social agents constitute

---

[76]After developing critical realism, Archer then wrote three further books on reflexivity. In this work, she targets Bourdieu's 'habitus' as an explanation of individuals' behaviour within structures, arguing that agents can reflectively think about their social position and options for action and act on the basis of reasons and desires, as opposed to the Bourdieusian idea that habitus is unconscious. However, I am more interested here in the critical realist social ontology and the relationship between structure and agency outlined in Archer's earlier works than the habitus-reflexivity debate that came later. For a discussion of power in the context of that debate see Gisli Vogler, 'Power between Habitus and Reflexivity – Introducing Margaret Archer to the Power Debate', *Journal of Political Power* 9, no. 1 (2016): 65–82.

[77]Thomas E. Wartenberg, *The Forms of Power: From Domination to Transformation* (Philadelphia, PA: Temple University Press, 1990), 147.

the 'social alignment' that backs up and justifies the power of the teacher over the student.[78]

But the teacher is also acting within situated power relationships. The teacher 'is constrained by the alignment, just as she is empowered by it'.[79] Parents paying for education demand that their children are properly prepared for careers and receive good grades. Universities must agree that the grading system is a reliable way to assess students' capabilities, so the grades must have social meaning. The school scrutinizes teachers' grading practices to ensure that they live up to parents' expectations and the demands of universities and employers. Therefore, to say that an agent is powerful and another agent powerless in a particular social context is not to argue that these agents are powerful and powerless in all contexts. Some agents have certain forms of power in certain situations and in relation to others, but not in other situations and in relation to different others. The powerless/powerful distinction is not absolute, it is contextual and relational.[80]

In Sandy's case, her situated power relationship with her landlord affects her behaviour. Sandy knows that if she is evicted by the landlord this will make it harder to find apartments in the future, as it counts as a black mark on her record. It could render her ineligible for public housing.[81] It also entails immediate costs, such as potentially losing possessions to bailiffs or paying for expensive storage units, finding the deposit for a new place to live and the costs of moving. There is time lost at work, the cost of attending court, including travel and childcare, and all the other hidden costs related to eviction and moving. Not to mention the emotional, psychological and physical toll of eviction (which can be as extreme as clinical depression or even suicide).[82] The landlord's power to evict the tenant is similar to that of the teacher's power to grade the student. If the landlord finds the tenant undesirable, it renders the tenant vulnerable to a range of costly outcomes. The landlord's power over the tenant is backed up by a system of property rights and the judicial system, which form a comprehensive social alignment. The tenant does not enter the relationship with the landlord on equal terms. The tenant needs somewhere to live and in conditions of housing scarcity is dependent on the landlord's letting them continue to rent the property.

Scaled up to the level of social groups, rather than power alignments between particular situated individuals, Wartenberg shows how domination operates.

---

[78]Wartenberg, *The Forms of Power*, 150.

[79]Wartenberg, *The Forms of Power*, 178.

[80]It is also important to recognize that there are degrees of powerlessness and powerfulness, which will affect the degree of political responsibility that an agent has in relation to that structural injustice.

[81]Matthew Desmond, *Evicted: Poverty and Profit in the American City* (London: Penguin Books, 2016), 297.

[82]Desmond, *Evicted*, 298.

Domination refers to a relationship between social groups in which 'power is exercised by the dominating social agent over the dominated social agent repeatedly, systematically, and to the detriment of the dominated agent'.[83] The subordinated agent is harmed. The dominant agent does not need to issue a threat to coerce the subordinate, rather the dominant agent's ability to harm the subordinate is a structural feature of their relationship.[84] The rationale for the persistence of relations of domination is that the dominator receives ongoing benefits from the subordinated agent.[85] The relationship of dominators to subordinates is backed up by a social alignment.

In the landlord/tenant case, landlords accrue benefits from tenants in the form of rent. Under normal circumstances, landlords do not need to issue threats to tenants to comply with the demand for rent, tenants comply in the knowledge that they could be evicted. If tenants fail to pay rent or treat the property in a way deemed inappropriate by landlords, landlords can use coercion in the form of legal threats towards the tenant. The domination of tenants by landlords is backed up by the state.

This situated conception of power explains why social positions matter and why they precede the reproduction of social structures. Social positions come with various abilities to affect others' actions and well-being, and the power of these social positions is reinforced by social alignments. The situated conception of power explains how power operates in both individual encounters and at the structural level. It also explains why agents in positions of power over others have an interest in acting in the way that they do; one reason is that they are constrained by the social alignment, but they are also enabled to maintain their position of power. At the structural level, dominating social groups derive benefits from the actions of subordinate social groups.[86]

However, Wartenberg also provides insight into how power structures can be changed. The power relations are given by social structures, but they are reproduced through the actions of agents.[87] They are reproduced not only through the actions of the dominant and subordinated agents, however, but also of the aligned social agents.[88] Therefore, if the subordinate agents want to

---

[83]Wartenberg, *The Forms of Power*, 117.

[84]Wartenberg, *The Forms of Power*, 124.

[85]Wartenberg, *The Forms of Power*, 125.

[86]Young endorsed this view of power in *Justice and the Politics of Difference*, and she used it to develop her definition of structural domination, which is the systematic inhibition of the self-determination of social groups. She uses Wartenberg's example of the judge's power over the defendant, which is backed up by the prison wardens, recordkeepers, parole officers, lawyers and so on. Young, *Justice and the Politics of Difference*, 31. I don't know why Young didn't integrate her earlier thoughts on power into her later work on structural injustice. I think she missed a trick by not doing this.

[87]This is different from the structuration view in the sense that structures *only* exist through agents' actions for Giddens.

[88]Wartenberg, *The Forms of Power*, 172.

change the situation, they should look at the social alignment that maintains the power relation: 'The subordinate agent is always in the position of being able to challenge the aligned agents' complicity in her disempowerment. The dynamic nature of power means that the dominated are always able to seek ways of challenging their domination.'[89]

As well as approaching the social alignment that props up the dominant individual or group's power, subordinated agents also have the option of creating a 'countering alignment'.[90] For example, a trade union is a countering alignment: if an employer treats an employee badly, the union can threaten to go on strike. An 'alternative alignment' exists if the subordinates can access the same things they get from the original alignment.[91] For example, a tenant may own property elsewhere, so is not threatened with homelessness by the landlord's threat of eviction. Or if the state provided adequate social housing for citizens, this would act as an alternative alignment for tenants. Thus, through challenging the aligned agents' complicity, and through creating countering or alternative alignments, subordinate agents in power structures of domination have opportunities to contest their domination.

What can be derived from Wartenberg's situated conception of power is that powerful agents act to maintain the power structures because subordinate agents in power structures produce benefits for dominating agents. These structural power relationships are backed up by social alignments that support and enable the power of dominators. But even though these power relationships are pre-given, preceding the rule-following behaviour of individuals, this does not mean they are unchangeable. Subordinate agents can challenge their position in these structural power relationships by encouraging the aligned social agents to withdraw their support, or by creating countering or alternative alignments.

Pure, avoidable and deliberate structural injustice

Given the preceding analysis, I suggest moving beyond Young's theory of structural injustice. While Young's work has been incredibly productive, her confused social ontology and lack of analysis of power have generated an inadequate understanding of what structural injustice is. I have suggested that a critical realist social ontology provides new insight into conceptualizing structural injustice and that a situated conception of power explains how power relations are given within social structures, and also how they can be changed.

---

[89]Wartenberg, *The Forms of Power*, 173.
[90]Wartenberg, *The Forms of Power*, 174.
[91]Wartenberg, *The Forms of Power*, 175.

Incorporating power into a definition of structural injustice raises a further issue – whether structural injustice really is the unintended outcome of 'benign social processes'.[92] While the realist social ontology showed that structural elaboration rarely resembles the desired outcome of any particular agent, considering the interaction between structure and agency, and the role of powerful agents in this process, creates space for an analysis of the behaviour of powerful actors in the maintenance of structural injustice. This provides insight into different *types* of structural injustice and corresponding attributions of responsibility.

Pure versus avoidable structural injustice

Young describes the structural injustice of housing deprivation as follows:

> The all-too-common social position of being housing-deprived arises from the combination of actions and interactions of a large number of public and private individual and institutional actors, with different amounts of control over their circumstances and with varying ranges of options available to them. Most of these actors have their own perceived interests in view. While some do things that are individually wrong, such as break the law or deceive, or behave in ruthless ways towards others, many others try to be law-abiding and decent even as they try to pursue their own interests. The process nevertheless should be described as producing structural injustice, because in it some people's options are unfairly constrained and they are threatened with deprivation, while others derive significant benefits.[93]

What Young describes here I will call 'pure structural injustice'. In cases of pure structural injustice, all of the actors are constrained to the point where it is very difficult for them not to participate in reproducing the injustice, and the consequences of their actions are unintended. However, I question whether housing deprivation meets these criteria.

I argued above that agents in different social positions have different amounts of power in relation to each other and to the structural injustice in question. As suggested above, landlords want to maintain their structural position of dominance because they receive benefits from tenants by way of rent. Landlords do not benefit from homelessness, but they benefit from high rents, which price poor people out of the rental market. It is in the interest of landlords for rents to remain high. Even if a charitable view is taken on the actions of landlords charging high rents as a systemic problem and these actions interact with other factors

---

beyond landlords' control (such as social norms determining which locales are desirable), therefore rendering the outcomes of the housing market unintended, it is nevertheless also true that the outcomes are foreseeable. And, crucially, they are avoidable with state intervention.

In his Pulitzer Prize winning study of eviction in Milwaukee, Matthew Desmond offers a range of solutions to the housing crisis from small policy proposals to larger structural change. A small-scale solution is to increase legal aid. In housing courts in the United States, 90 per cent of landlords are represented by attorneys and 90 per cent of tenants are not. Legal aid would decrease evictions, prevent homelessness and give poor people a chance to retain a home. Such a programme ran in the South Bronx between 2005 and 2008, providing legal aid to families, and it prevented eviction in 86 per cent of the cases.[94] Desmond's larger-scale suggestion is for the government to provide housing vouchers to all low-income families to cover 70 per cent of their rent.[95] Fundamentally, the role of the state in perpetuating this crisis must be addressed.

> It is the government that legitimizes and defends landlords' right to charge as much as they want; that subsidizes the construction of high-end apartments, bidding up rents and leaving the poor with even fewer options; that pays landlords when a family cannot, through onetime or ongoing housing assistance; that forcibly removes a family at landlords' request by dispatching armed law enforcement officers; and that records and publicizes evictions, as a service to landlords and debt collection agencies.[96]

Desmond argues that America has prioritized the freedom of the rich to profit as much as possible from the poor, over the right to decent, affordable housing.[97] It can restore some balance with a voucher programme. The money is there, what's lacking is the political will.

I would add that ideology is also at play. Desmond describes a situation at the trailer park where he was living. The tenants found out that their landlord's annual income was close to $1 million, while they were living in poverty and under constant threat of eviction. But the tenants didn't care. He writes, 'For the most part, tenants had a high tolerance for inequality. They spent little time questioning the wide gulf separating their poverty from Tobin's [the landlord's] wealth or asking why rent for a worn-out aluminium-wrapped trailer took such a large chunk of their income. Their focus was on smaller, more tangible problems.'[98] This echoes

---

[94]Desmond, *Evicted*, 303–4.
[95]Desmond, *Evicted*, 308.
[96]Desmond, *Evicted*, 307.
[97]Desmond, *Evicted*, 305.
[98]Desmond, *Evicted*, 182.

what Susan Silbey says about ideology, which is that the poor come to believe that inequality and poverty is not only inevitable but just; at least, it is the only justice that is possible.[99]

Activist groups like tenants' rights associations are engaged in ideology critique; their very existence challenges the idea that the landlord/tenant relation is inevitable and unchangeable. But ideology critique merely opens space for thinking about social change. What Desmond's work highlights is that powerful agents in these structures could do something to change housing deprivation. Landlords do not need to rinse every available penny out of their tenants; they could ask for less rent. They could also stop evicting tenants at such a high rate. As Archer argued, structures do not determine behaviour; they *incentivise* behaviour. It is possible for agents to act in ways that further their interests while minimizing harm to others or to even act against their own interests. Furthermore, as Desmond has shown, the power of landlords is backed up by a social alignment including the government, the courts and the police. Changes in government policy and legal aid could significantly improve the relational position of tenants in this power structure. Housing policies in other parts of the world have dramatically reduced homelessness; examples are Vienna where 60 per cent of the population live in subsidized accommodation and Finland's 'Housing First' policy adopted in 2008.[100]

Therefore, I understand housing deprivation not as a 'pure' structural injustice, but as an 'avoidable structural injustice'. The category of 'avoidable structural injustice' challenges the idea that all agents are constrained by structural injustice so as to be unable to change it. It posits that not all agents are objectively constrained by the structures to the extent that they cannot change them. There are agents in positions of power that could act to change the unjust structures and fail to do so. In the case of housing deprivation, these agents are landlords and the government. Changes in the social alignment – property law, the police and so on – could also have an impact on the position of tenants in the structures. The category of 'avoidable structural injustice' also calls into question the idea that structural injustice is an unintended consequence of social-structural processes. In cases of avoidable structural injustice, the outcomes may be unintended, but they are foreseeable and avoidable. The case of housing deprivation is well-documented and thoroughly researched, and there are available solutions, what is lacking is political will.

---

[99]Susan S. Silbey, 'Ideology, Power, and Justice', in *Justice and Power in Sociolegal Studies*, ed. Bryant G. Garth and Austin Sarat (Illinois: Northwestern University Press, 1998), 293.

[100]Aitor Hernández-Morales, 'How Vienna Took the Stigma Out of Social Housing', *Politico*, June 2022; Kathrin Glösel, 'Finland Ends Homelessness and Provides Shelter for All in Need', *Scoop.Me*, 10 November 2020, https://scoop.me/housing-first-finland-homelessness/.

Deliberate structural injustice

There is a further category of structural injustice – 'deliberate structural injustice'. Powerful agents recognize that there are groups that are disadvantaged by social structures, take advantage of that situation, deliberately reproduce the injustice and reap benefits by exploiting the disadvantaged. In cases of deliberate structural injustice, all agents are constrained, but powerful agents have enough room to manoeuvre to be able to change the situation. What distinguishes avoidable from deliberate structural injustice, however, is that not only do powerful agents have the capacity to change the situation, they actively maintain it. So the consequences are not unintentional, they are intentional. Powerful agents want to maintain the vulnerability of the disadvantaged in order to continue to exploit them.

An example of deliberate structural injustice is sweatshop labour. As will be discussed in more detail in Chapter 3, multinational corporations (MNCs) in the global garment industry want to keep the costs of labour as low as possible because this is how they maintain their social position and increase profits year-on-year. They deliberately perpetuate sweatshop labour by exercising power within structures through lobbying, through setting industry standards themselves, through lax codes of corporate social responsibility and through manipulation of consumers. The power of garment MNCs is backed up by a social alignment including states (both the states where MNCs' headquarters are based and the states where sweatshops proliferate, including their legal systems and police forces), international organizations, international business lobbies, a network of global financial institutions and consumers. All of these agents form a social alignment that maintains the power of MNCs over sweatshop workers. There are measures that any one of these groups could take to improve workers' rights but, for the most part, they don't.

Of course, on the critical realist ontology, agents may act to maintain structures as they are or to change them to increase their benefits, but they do not always get what they want because their actions interact with the outcomes of the actions of other agents. Therefore, it could be objected that the maintenance of structural injustice is not intentional, it is accidental, and the idea that structural injustice is 'deliberate' is a misnomer. However, this conclusion is too quick. The fact that agents are acting to deliberately maintain structural injustice is worthy of attention. Sometimes their actions will be successful. Sometimes their actions will misfire or will be cancelled out or modified by other agents' actions. But even in the latter cases, such behaviour aimed at perpetuating injustice is still potentially blameworthy.

In most cases of structural injustice, there will be either (a) agents who could change the situation but fail to do so (avoidable structural injustice), or (b) agents who could change the situation but fail to do so and deliberately perpetuate the situation because they benefit from it (deliberate structural injustice). It is questionable whether there are, in fact, any cases of pure structural injustice. Climate change is a contender. There is clearly a lot more that powerful agents (MNCs and states) can do to mitigate climate change and insofar as they fail to do that, or have deliberately perpetuated fossil fuel extraction and consumption for their own gain, they might be blameworthy.[101] But arguably tackling climate change means abolishing capitalism, which depends upon perpetual economic growth. The growth model is incompatible with environmental preservation, as Marx and Engels pointed out during the early stages of capitalism and 'degrowth' theorists argue today.[102] Tackling climate change means not only inconveniencing powerful agents (they might have to give up some of their advantages), rather they would have to self-destruct. It may be too strong to blame agents for not wanting to self-destruct. Moreover, systemic change will require everyone working together to create a new system – one that is premised on a different economic model and different social structures – and creating different institutional actors to the ones we have now.

Young's definition of structural injustice remains vital. But I contend that it requires significant amendment. I offer the following definition:

> Within social structures agents are situated in different social positions with varying degrees of power and access to resources. The social structures are unjust when they result in the oppression or domination of certain social groups. Structural injustice is 'pure' when the injustice is unintended, unforeseeable and there are no agents with the capacity to remedy the injustice; it requires wholesale social-structural change. Structural injustice is 'avoidable' when the unjust outcomes of structural processes are foreseeable and there are agents with the capacity to remedy the injustice but they fail to do so. Structural injustice is 'deliberate' when the unjust outcomes are intended because powerful agents benefit from it so they deliberately perpetuate it, and these agents have the capacity to remedy it but they fail to do so.

Conclusion

This chapter has aimed to refine the concept of structural injustice by basing it on a critical realist social ontology, incorporating a situated conception of power

---

[101] I will discuss blame in relation to structural injustice in Chapters 5 to 8.
[102] Karl Marx and Frederick Engels, *The Communist Manifesto* (New York: Pathfinder, 1890); Jason Hickel, *Less Is More: How Degrowth Will Save the World* (London: William Heinemann, 2020).

and then identifying three different types of structural injustice. I conclude by suggesting three reasons why this typology is useful.

First, it clarifies the role of powerful agents in perpetuating structural injustice. In Chapter 4, I will discuss in more detail the ways in which sweatshops, poverty and climate change can be classified as deliberate, avoidable and pure structural injustices respectively. There will doubtless be objections to these classifications; for instance, you might think that they are all deliberate structural injustices, or all pure, or disagree with specific cases. But that, I think, is useful. The point of this typology is to generate a debate about the role of powerful agents – how their actions or omissions perpetuate structural injustice. My aim is also to problematize and destabilize the idea that there is one form of structural injustice (that it is always unintentional). I do not see the role of the political theorist as nailing down this classification, but rather opening space for creative and productive political debate based on empirical and normative research, as well as the lived experience of the agents and activists involved.

Second, understanding the role of powerful agents then helps us understand how structural change can occur. We need to know which agents are acting or failing to act, and how this maintains structural injustice, in order to know what to do about it. In cases of deliberate structural injustice, where agents are deliberately perpetuating the injustice for their own gain, those agents need to be regulated, sanctioned or even dismantled. In cases of avoidable structural injustice, there are known and feasible measures that could be taken to alleviate the injustice. In cases of pure structural injustice, systemic change and collective action are the only solutions.

Finally, Young argued that all agents connected to structural injustice share a non-blameworthy political responsibility for it. On my account, agents that deliberately perpetuate structural injustice or that have the capacity to alleviate it and fail to do so bear moral responsibility. This doesn't mean no-one can bear moral responsibility within pure structural injustice: Young always meant her liability model and social connection model to be used simultaneously. For example, in the climate case, the fossil fuel corporations and other agents that deliberately obfuscated action on climate change bear moral responsibility. But the point I will press in subsequent chapters is that in cases of deliberate and avoidable structural injustice, some agents bear moral responsibility for the structural injustice itself and not merely for particular instances of harm (a position Young would reject).

Understanding how powerful agents act to perpetuate structural injustice or fail to alleviate it, how structural change can occur and how different kinds of responsibility can be attributed represents a step forward on the previous definition of structural injustice. This analysis will form the basis for discussing these problems in the rest of the book.

Chapter 3

Power and structural injustice

Social structures are constraining. But even if structures are constraining, different agents have different degrees of power within structures and some agents have more room to manoeuvre within structures than others. In this chapter, I demonstrate this by discussing corporate power in the global economy and analysing power relations in the global garment industry. An analysis of power within this industry reveals that not all agents are constrained by structures to the point where they cannot make meaningful decisions in relation to structural injustice, and not all agents contribute to the maintenance of structural injustice unintentionally.

Building on the framework established in the previous chapter, we saw that agents act within pre-given social structures, but it is through the process of agential interaction within those structures that new structures are elaborated. The question we look at here is what powerful agents do within the period of structural interaction in order to maintain or enhance their structural advantages. Whether or not the eventual structural elaboration is within the power of any particular powerful agents is not the issue; the aim is to look at the ways in which these agents exercise power to try to maintain the injustice as it is so that they can continue to reap benefits from it.

First, I deepen the analysis of power that was briefly summarized in the previous chapter and constituted only one aspect of a multifaceted concept. The power debate is vast and highly contested. I follow Mark Haugaard in arguing that power is a family resemblance concept. I outline the five dimensions and three forms of power. Then I look at how multinational corporations (MNCs) have or exercise power in the global political economy in general. Then I focus on MNCs in the global garment industry to understand how power operates in the context of maintaining structural injustice. This descriptive analysis of power lays the groundwork for the normative argument about responsibility for structural injustice in the second half of the book.

The dimensions and forms of power

Power is a notoriously tricky-to-define concept. Debates around power have a long history. Broadly speaking, in the modern literature, there are five dimensions of power.[1] The first was identified by Robert Dahl. According to Dahl, 'A has power over B to the extent that he can get B to do something that B would not otherwise do.'[2] This is the 'most obvious and overt' way in which power operates in decision-making processes.[3] The second dimension of power was identified by Bachrach and Baratz in response to Dahl. They argued that power can also be exercised in the form of 'nondecision-making'.[4] This is where A can keep things off the agenda that are in B's interests to discuss.

The first two dimensions of power involve deliberate exercises of power which are observable. Steven Lukes developed the third dimension of power, which is where A keeps B ignorant of B's true interests.[5] A does not have to exercise power to do this; rather, the system is organized so that B is unaware of their true interests. Lukes's theory derives from earlier Marxist ideas of 'false consciousness' or Gramscian 'hegemony'. The fourth dimension of power is associated with Michel Foucault, who argued that power is productive.[6] Power constitutes the subjectivity of A and B. Power is everywhere, it is relational and it creates the subject's wants, needs, desires, personality, thought processes, habits, view and so on.

The first four dimensions of power are mostly associated with the concept of principal agents, A, having 'power over' subordinate agents, B. Often 'power over' is equated with domination. The fifth dimension of power represents a different tradition of 'power to' (Hannah Arendt) or 'power with' (Amy Allen).[7] In this tradition, power is a capacity. For Hobbes, power is the individual's capacity to obtain some future apparent good.[8] For Arendt and Allen, agents acting collectively have the power to achieve desired goals. The fifth dimension of power is associated with capacity, empowerment and emancipation.

---

[1] I borrow the term 'dimension' from Steven Lukes, who argued that Dahl's view of power was one-dimensional, Bachrach and Baratz's two-dimensional and his three-dimensional. Steven Lukes, *Power: A Radical View*, 2nd edn (London: Palgrave Macmillan, 2005). These are sometimes also referred to as 'faces' of power.

[2] Robert A. Dahl, 'The Concept of Power', *Behavioural Science* 2, no. 3 (1957): 202–3.

[3] John Scott, *Power* (Cambridge: Polity Press, 2001), 8.

[4] Peter Bachrach and Morton S. Baratz, 'Two Faces of Power', *American Political Science Review* 56, no. 4 (1962): 947–52.

[5] Lukes, *Power: A Radical View*.

[6] Michel Foucault, *Power: Essential Works of Foucault 1954–1984 Volume 3*, ed. James D. Faubion (London: Penguin, 2000).

[7] Hannah Arendt, *On Violence* (London: Harcourt, 1970); Amy Allen, *The Power of Feminist Theory: Domination, Resistance, Solidarity* (New York: Routledge, 1999).

[8] Thomas Hobbes, *Leviathan*, 2018th edn (Open Road Integrated Media, 1651), 57.

Historically in the power debate, theorists have sought to identify the core essence of power. Because this is so difficult, it has led some theorists, like Lukes, to claim that power is an 'essentially contested' concept.[9] But Mark Haugaard argues that this is a mistake. A term (like power, democracy or art) can denote a set of practices but it becomes contested when it becomes a term of commendation or condemnation, for example, that something is truly democratic or truly art is a normative evaluation rather than descriptive. There are different issues at stake when different kinds of theorists discuss power.[10] Sociologists are interested in identifying how power relations work in practice; they need an analytical tool for analysing and identifying how power operates in different areas of human activity. Political theorists, by contrast, care about how power relations *should* be. Haugaard argues that some theorists combine both descriptive and normative analyses in their definitions of power; for instance, Lukes and Foucault sometimes equate power with domination or opposed to freedom respectively, which is evaluative.[11]

Haugaard suggests that 'we treat power as a *family resemblance* concept, whereby meaning varies depending upon *language game*'.[12] The benefit of conceiving of power as a family resemblance concept is that it denotes 'concepts that overlap in usage while there is no single essence that unites all these usages',[13] which enables 'a plural view of power'.[14] It also generates clarity over descriptive and normative usages of power. In this book, I am interested in both the sociological language game (how MNCs have and exercise power in the global political economy) and the normative language game (what's wrong with this situation and why MNCs bear moral responsibility for structural injustice). I aim to be clear about when I am using power in either the descriptive sense or the normative sense. If power is considered as a family resemblance concept, then there is no need to support one dimension of power as *the* definition of power, thereby dispensing with the other four. Instead, it is possible to analyse power along the five dimensions both descriptively and normatively.

Haugaard argues further that there are three members of the power family, what I will call 'forms' of power, referring to the different ways in which power exists:

Episodic power refers to the exercise of power that is linked to agency. *Dispositional* power signifies the inherent capacities of an agent that the agent

---

[9]Lukes, *Power: A Radical View*; Mark Haugaard, 'Power: A "Family Resemblance" Concept', *European Journal of Cultural Studies* 13, no. 4 (2010): 419.

[10]Haugaard, 'Power: A "Family Resemblance" Concept', 432.

[11]Haugaard, 'Power: A "Family Resemblance" Concept', 427–9.

[12]Haugaard, 'Power: A "Family Resemblance" Concept', 424.

[13]Haugaard, 'Power: A "Family Resemblance" Concept', 424.

[14]Haugaard, 'Power: A "Family Resemblance" Concept', 419–20.

may have, irrespective of whether or not they exercise this capacity. *Systemic* power refers to the ways in which given social systems confer differentials or dispositional power on agents, thus structuring possibilities for action.[15]

Episodic power is central to the first and second dimensions of power. *A* exercises power when *A* gets *B* to do something B otherwise would not do. And *A* exercises power over *B* when *A* prevents items pertaining to *B*'s interests from reaching the decision-making agenda. In these cases, *A* exercises power in a particular moment. Episodic power is the exercise of power by a particular agent on a particular occasion.

Dispositional power – power as a capacity – refers to the second, third and fifth dimensions of power. In terms of the second dimension, *A* has the capacity to prevent issues that matter to *B* from reaching the agenda, whether or not *A* exercises this capacity. *A* may not have to actively do anything for the agenda to be set in *A*'s interests and for *B*'s to be overlooked. On the third dimension, *A* has the capacity to disseminate disinformation, or build up a sense of inevitability in its power over *B*. Again, *A* may not have to deliberately act for the sense of inevitability of *A*'s power to be part of the collective subconscious. On the fifth dimension, individuals acting alone or in concert have the capacity to initiate change. Dispositional power is a capacity that exists over time, but can also change with time and context.

Systemic power aligns with the third and fourth dimensions of power. Society is structured so that certain actors have power over others by virtue of their social position and this power does not need to be exercised or enforced; it is built into the social structure and is perceived as normal. Haugaard's concept of systemic power aligns with the 'situated' conception of power discussed in the previous chapter. There we saw how social positions within structures enable and empower some agents while constraining and disempowering other agents, although these power relations are always relational, for instance the teacher is empowered in relation to the student, but not in relation to management. Social structures produce subjects who internalize and reproduce power relations themselves without any awareness that they are doing so. Systemic power underlies social and economic structures; it confers dispositional power upon certain agents and makes it easier for certain agents to exercise episodic power over other agents.

To give an example of the five dimensions of power, consider a patient (*B*) visiting a doctor (*A*). (1) The doctor exercises power over *B* by telling *B* that they must take a certain medicine or take certain measures such as exercising more or eating differently – they get *B* to do something *B* would not otherwise

---

[15]Haugaard, 'Power: A "Family Resemblance" Concept', 425.

do. (2) The doctor constructs the conversation by deciding what is and is not relevant to the consultation; for example, B says that they are chronically fatigued, but the doctor puts this down to being a parent. (3) The modern system of medical training instils the belief in B that the doctor knows best and can solve their problem, and the doctor's belief in themselves that they are the person to solve the problem. (4) Power was productive of the doctor's subjectivity as a doctor and B's as a patient in need of medical attention. (5) If the patient feels they have been treated unfairly or negligently by the doctor they can organize with other patients into a protest or campaign group, or an association with collective bargaining power. Many such organizations exist for people who suffer from frequently misdiagnosed chronic conditions, such as endometriosis, CFS, autism and others, or groups campaigning for changes to legislation, including the legalization of medical marijuana.

In this example, we see the three forms of power at play. The doctor exercises *episodic power* over the patient in telling them what medicine to take, deciding what is in their best interests and deciding what counts as a symptom. The doctor has *dispositional power* to prescribe medications to B, and to advise B on what is in their interests, whether the doctor exercises this power or not. The doctor has this dispositional power because of a *system* of education that trains them in Western medicine, and a set of institutions – medical schools, hospitals, universities, laws – that confers these powers upon them and is defended by numerous professional associations, as well as the shared social belief that doctors have the requisite skills and knowledge to legitimately hold this power. The doctor is situated in a social alignment so as to have power over the patient.

The fifth dimension of power can also be episodic or dispositional. The patients' association has the capacity to act for change by virtue of its collective organization, whether or not it exercises this capacity. If the association does exercise this capacity, for example, by campaigning against a particular hospital or to legalize a certain drug, this is an exercise of episodic power. These associations lack systemic power; they are not positioned by the system to have dispositional power. Rather, they gain power, despite their systemic powerlessness, through collective organization.

One final aspect of power that I want to highlight before we proceed is that power is 'Janus-faced'.[16] Power can be used for good and for ill. Haugaard gives the example of a democratic election. A wins the election and in doing so exercises episodic power over B, who loses. But in exercising power over B by using the democratic electoral system, A has reproduced a system that enables B's dispositional power to participate in future elections.[17] The Janus-faced

---

[16]Amy Allen, Rainer Forst and Mark Haugaard, 'Power and Reason, Justice and Domination: A Conversation', *Journal of Political Power* 7, no. 1 (2014): 9.
[17]Mark Haugaard, 'Rethinking the Four Dimensions of Power: Domination and Empowerment', *Journal of Political Power* 5, no. 1 (2012): 36.

nature of power is important when considering the power of MNCs in the global economy, because MNCs are simultaneously in a position to increase the dispositional capacity of subordinate agents and to reduce it.

For now I set aside the fifth dimension of power, as this will be discussed in more detail in Chapter 6 on political responsibility. I turn instead to the ways in which MNCs have or exercise the three forms of power in the global political economy.

Corporate power

The role of MNCs is usually neglected in discussions of global injustice. But it doesn't make sense to discuss structural injustice without economic actors; sometimes MNCs have more power to affect structures than states. I'm going to work backwards. First, I look at the systemic power of MNCs – the way in which the global political economy is structured so as to confer dispositional power upon MNCs. Then I look at the dispositional power that MNCs have within structures. Finally, I look at the ways in which MNCs exercise power over other actors within structures. I discuss the power of MNCs in general terms, before looking at our specific case of the global garment industry. To reiterate, for the purposes of this chapter, I focus on a descriptive analysis of power, rather than normative.

Systemic power

In 1970, there were 7,000 global corporations; by 2011, there were 100,000.[18] But by the end of the twentieth century, five corporations dominated the world's major industries.[19] Power is concentrated into the hands of a few corporations.

Frequently, MNCs sales are compared with the Gross Domestic Product (GDP) of nation states to provide a rhetorical take on the size and power of corporations. But as John Mikler argues, it is more accurate to compare the sales of MNCs with states' national expenditure – a state's budget – as corporate

---

[18]John Mikler, *The Political Power of Global Corporations* (Cambridge: Polity Press, 2018), 5.
[19]Mikler, *The Political Power of Global Corporations*, 7. Mikler bases this claim on Nolan et al.'s findings that the top two aerospace companies accounted for 100 per cent of commercial aircraft sales (Boeing and Airbus), three engine makers accounted for 100 per cent of the engines that power the planes (Rolls-Royce, GE, Pratt & Whitney), six firms accounted for 68 per cent of automotive sales (Ford/Maxda/Volvo, GM, Daimler-Chrysler, VW, Toyota, Renault/Nissan), two firms for over half of brakes systems (Lucas, ITT) and three firms for half of tyre sales (Bridgestone, Michelin, Goodyear), one carbonated soft drinks firm accounted for half of world sales (Coca-Cola), two suppliers of aluminium accounted for two-fifths of global supplies (Acola/Reynolds, Alcan/Pechiney/Alusuisse) and one firm for over half of plastic bottle machinery (Sidel). Peter Nolan, Dylan Sutherland and Jin Zhang, 'The Challenge of the Global Business Revolution', *Contributions to Political Economy* 21 (2002): 101.

sales are indicative of its organizational budget.[20] From this perspective, the sales of the world's top twenty MNCs in 2013 were greater than the combined budget of the bottom 166 states. The top twenty MNCs' sales totalled $4.6 trillion, in comparison to the UK budget of $5.1 billion, or the WTO's $210 million. The size of MNCs means that 'they are in a strong position before they bargain for what they want, given their control over their sectors and the economic fortunes of even the most powerful states'.[21]

Larger structures have built up around big business, most importantly financial institutions. Top financial institutions hold blocks of shares in corporations, so that 'businesses of all kinds come to be tied together through interweaving institutional shareholdings into a network of capital relations'.[22] The directors of financial institutions take seats on company boards, establishing networks that connect MNCs.[23] In fact, some argue that there is now such a thing as a transnational capitalist class (TCC) of elite business people (mostly men), who have a shared purpose in fostering global deregulation.[24] The TCC has established itself through interlocking networks not only in financial institutions but also on company boards, think tanks and civil society organizations.[25] It comes together and develops its shared perspective and strategies in policy organizations, like the World Economic Forum, the Trilateral Commission and the World Business Council for Sustainable Development.[26]

However, the extent to which there is in fact a TCC, or whether nation state membership still matters, is up for debate. When it comes to MNCs, Dicken describes the global corporation as a 'myth'.[27] In 2004, four-fifths of the 500 top MNCs had 80 per cent of their sales and assets in their home region.[28] Just ten states account for the headquarters of 84 per cent of the FT Global 500 corporations: they are concentrated in the United States, EU and East Asia.[29] The United States accounts for almost 50 per cent.[30] Even with the rise of the BRICS countries, the majority of their largest corporations, 40 per cent,

---

[20]Mikler, *The Political Power of Global Corporations*, 11.

[21]Mikler, *The Political Power of Global Corporations*, 44–5.

[22]Scott, *Power*, 77.

[23]Scott, *Power*, 77–8.

[24]William I. Robinson and Jeb Sprague, 'The Transnational Capitalist Class', in *The Oxford Handbook of Global Studies*, ed. Mark Juergensmeyer, Saskia Sassen, Manfred B. Steger, Victor Faessel (Oxford: Oxford University Press, 2018), 309–28.

[25]Joshua Murray, 'Interlock Globally, Act Domestically: Corporate Political Unity in the 21st Century', *American Journal of Sociology* 122, no. 6 (2017): 1617–63, https://doi.org/10.1086/691603.

[26]William K. Carroll and Colin Carson, 'The Network of Global Corporations and Elite Policy Groups: A Structure for Transnational Capitalist Class Formation?', *Global Networks* 3, no. 1 (2003): 29–57.

[27]Peter Dicken, *Global Shift: Mapping the Changing Contours of the World Economy*, 7th edn (London: Sage, 2014), 115.

[28]Dicken, *Global Shift*, 168.

[29]Mikler, *The Political Power of Global Corporations*, 17.

[30]Mikler, *The Political Power of Global Corporations*, 55.

are based in China.[31] As Mikler argues, 'The data suggest the structural power possessed by global corporations is related to, and it seems reasonable to say is a reflection of, their geographical concentration in economically powerful states.'[32] In addition, the financial institutions that form an interlocking framework with the largest MNCs are 'fundamentally Anglo-American' – 'all financial roads lead to either Wall Street or the City of London'.[33] Moreover, it is worth bearing in mind, as David Ciepley argues, that corporations exist at the discretion of states. It is states that invest corporations with 'personhood' which allows them to own property and make contracts, and it is states that invest the corporation with the power to establish and enforce rules within its jurisdiction.[34]

The largest MNCs' control of markets and their geographical concentration in the most powerful states account for their systemic power.[35] Added to this is the sense that MNCs have legitimate authority to be in this position. Many factors converge to bolster the authority of MNCs. First, the emphasis over the last thirty years on economic growth, efficiency and competition has positioned business as '*the* politico-economic expert, the primary actor considered able to provide and guarantee the provision of the desired goods'.[36] Changes in technology and the economic environment and the perception that flexible responses are required mean that business is perceived as a better regulator than slow and inflexible governments.[37] There has also been a decline in trust in governments, with public regulation seen as the cause of social and economic problems.[38]

Even though business is embedded from the start in an institutional, social, economic and political context, both materially and nonmaterially, Doris Fuchs argues that business also 'plays an active role in the (re)structuring of that setting. This bi-directional dynamic is reflected in the influence of globalization on the political capacities of business and competing actors and their influence on the occurrence and shape of globalization.'[39]

Dispositional power

The way in which the global economic and political system confers systemic power upon MNCs means that they have the dispositional power – the

---

[31] Mikler, *The Political Power of Global Corporations*, 60. The BRICS countries are Brazil, Russia, India, China and South Africa.
[32] Mikler, *The Political Power of Global Corporations*, 56.
[33] Mikler, *The Political Power of Global Corporations*, 59.
[34] David Ciepley, 'Beyond Public and Private: Toward a Political Theory of the Corporation', *American Political Science Review* 107, no. 1 (2013): 143.
[35] Mikler, *The Political Power of Global Corporations*, 102.
[36] Doris Fuchs, *Business Power in Global Governance* (London: Lynne Rienner, 2007), 144.
[37] Fuchs, *Business Power in Global Governance*, 144.
[38] Fuchs, *Business Power in Global Governance*, 144.
[39] Fuchs, *Business Power in Global Governance*, 6.

capacity – to be able to make changes in structures. First, the economic power of MNCs means that they are in a position to constrain the options of other actors, whether or not they exercise this power. Drawing on Max Weber, John Scott describes economic constraint as follows:

> A person who monopolises resources that are in demand has the potential to act as a principal in a power relationship (Weber 1914: 943). The monopolist is able to influence the conduct of others by setting the conditions under which they can gain access to the desired resources and by restricting the range of options that others consider to be relevant to their intended actions. This form of domination, then, rests on mechanisms of coercion and inducement that *constrain* action alternatives. In a relation of constraint, a principal can control the actions of subalterns without the need for any explicit direction or any expression of his or her wishes. Subalterns can respond to an anticipated reaction.[40]

Countries, particularly poor countries that depend on the investment of MNCs, often act in anticipation of what MNCs want. Fuchs writes, 'This power is shown by corporations that do not even need to voice their preferences; governments will comply with them in *vorauseilen-dem gehorsam* – that is, on the basis of the anticipated reaction of MNCs, due to governments' structural dependence on economic growth, employment, and investment.'[41] Fuchs describes this as 'a passive influence on governmental agenda-setting and policy choices'.[42] As Mikler puts it, MNCs' 'global economic dominance puts them in a "privileged position" by comparison to other non-state actors like non-government organizations (NGOs) to get what they want before they need to ask for it'.[43]

NGOs, frustrated in their attempts to lobby international institutions for international treaties on social and environmental justice issues, often cooperate with MNCs. They do this because international institutions are failing to tackle these issues under the pressure of MNCs, so cooperation is 'a viable, though clearly second-best, alternative to pressuring for changes in public policy'.[44] Moreover, because of the scale and reach of MNCs, the impact of changing their procurement policies and practices could have enormous impact, more even than achieving national regulation.[45] In other words, MNCs have the capacity to be able to make changes that have significant environmental and social impact.

---

[40]Scott, *Power*, 71–2.

[41]Fuchs, *Business Power in Global Governance*, 105.

[42]Fuchs, *Business Power in Global Governance*, 105.

[43]Mikler, *The Political Power of Global Corporations*, 41.

[44]David Vogel, 'Taming Globalization? Civil Regulation and Corporate Capitalism', in *The Oxford Handbook of Business and Government* (Oxford: Oxford Scholarship Online, 2010), 477.

[45]Vogel, 'Taming Globalization?', 477.

The second aspect of MNCs' dispositional power is their relationship to states. Corporate headquarters are the 'strategic centre' of MNCs.[46] This is where decisions are made about investment and disinvestment, where the legal, financial and regulatory functions of the firm are based, and where information is relayed to the rest of the corporation.[47] As already pointed out, the majority of the top MNCs' headquarters are based in a few countries, notably the United States, EU, China and Japan. Corporate headquarters tend not to move; in fact, only one Fortune Global 500 firm moved its headquarters between 1994 and 2002.[48]

There are several effects of this. One is that the power of the largest MNCs is enhanced by being backed up by the power of the states in which they are based. Advancing MNCs' interests also advances the home state's interests, so corporations and states work together to achieve deals and advantages abroad. An example is the TRIPS agreement, which was signed by states, but increased patent payments to US corporations by $19 billion per year.[49] Both the United States and its corporations benefitted. Second, the political and legal culture of a corporation is based on that of the home state. As such, when the corporation acts abroad, other actors adapt to their home state's political and legal cultures.[50] This increases the 'soft power' of these states. Third, when these MNCs are in trouble, such as following the 2008 financial crash, their rich and powerful home states can bail them out: 'The combined stimulus expenditure of the G20 countries for 2009 was $692 billion, the equivalent of 1.4 per cent of their GDP. The USA accounted for almost 40 per cent of this.'[51]

A third way in which the systemic power of MNCs grants them dispositional power is that governments often invite MNCs to discuss policy. Politicians and bureaucrats increasingly depend on the input of business actors, due to the complexity of regulation.[52] Politicians are also involved in businesses. One study found that in 2012, of the top fifty corporations in the UK, forty-six had a member of parliament as a director or shareholder.[53] MNCs are also present in international decision-making. The complexity and cost of participating in supranational institutions, such as the EU and the Bretton Woods institutions, mean that MNCs are in a position to do this, whereas smaller businesses and civil society organizations struggle.[54] MNCs have a seat at the policy-making table, both at the domestic and international levels.

---

[46]Dicken, *Global Shift*, 142.

[47]Dicken, *Global Shift*, 142–3.

[48]Dicken, *Global Shift*, 144.

[49]Mikler, *The Political Power of Global Corporations*, 39. TRIPS refers to the Agreement on Trade-Related Aspects of Intellectual Property Rights.

[50]Mikler, *The Political Power of Global Corporations*, 89.

[51]Dicken, *Global Shift*, 188.

[52]Fuchs, *Business Power in Global Governance*, 78.

[53]Mikler, *The Political Power of Global Corporations*, 35.

[54]Fuchs, *Business Power in Global Governance*, 86–91.

In sum, by virtue of their structural position, MNCs have the capacity to get other actors to do what they would not otherwise do even if they do not act: the first dimension of power. They are also able to affect agenda-setting without actively getting involved: the second dimension of power. They shape the interests and needs of other actors in such a way that this is perceived as normal and inevitable: the third dimension of power. MNCs produce and discipline other actors within the global political economy: the fourth dimension of power.

Episodic power

MNCs are not merely in a position to make structural changes by constraining the options of other actors, by utilizing the power of their home states or by their presence in policy-making decisions; they actively exercise episodic power in order to make changes that benefit them.

Lobbying

The most obvious and direct way in which corporations affect political decision-making is by lobbying. Lobbying has grown exponentially over the last one hundred years. In 1920, one corporation had a permanent office in Washington DC; by the late 1990s, there were six hundred.[55] Lobbying intensified around the 1970s in response to the rise of civil society: the Business Roundtable was established to represent the interests of the top two hundred US corporations who account for 50 per cent of US Gross National Product (GNP); trade associations and individual firms established offices in Washington; and business political action committees (PACs) were set up.[56] Lobbying went from low to high status, with the new corporate mantra being 'get into politics or get out of business'.[57] The lobbying strength of business has increased due to the interlocking networks already mentioned among business actors formed in associations or by individual memberships on directorates and boards, as well as by the decline in the influence of NGOs and trade unions.[58]

In the United States, lobbying is often combined with campaign finance. In the 2013–14 US election, Wall Street banks and other financial institutions contributed around $1.4 billion, making them the largest source of campaign contributions.[59] Fuchs describes the EU as 'probably the world's largest playground for interest groups'.[60] In 1992, there were an estimated three thousand interest groups

---

[55]Fuchs, *Business Power in Global Governance*, 74.
[56]Fuchs, *Business Power in Global Governance*, 75.
[57]Fuchs, *Business Power in Global Governance*, 75.
[58]Fuchs, *Business Power in Global Governance*, 76–7.
[59]Mikler, *The Political Power of Global Corporations*, 36.
[60]Fuchs, *Business Power in Global Governance*, 85.

and ten thousand lobbyists in Brussels.[61] The EU business lobby consists of corporate representatives, sectoral and transsectoral, national and international associations. About 75 per cent of associations active in the EU headquarters are business associations, whereas less than 5 per cent are trade unions.[62] Some argue that the imbalance is much greater at the EU level than at the national level.[63]

At the supranational level, businesses lobby the Bretton Woods institutions. Supranational lobbying activities are often combined with national lobbying, and channelled through national governmental actors, particularly when preventing supranational regulations on social and environmental justice issues.[64] Large corporations are more present than other business interests at the supra- and international level. This has been fostered by corporations themselves, by undermining traditional associations through individual lobbying and using alternative methods of organizing, such as small informal clubs and round-tables.[65] They adopt 'single issue maximising' strategies by forming alliances on specific policy proposals on a temporary basis.[66] Corporations are also advantaged because it is too costly and difficult for trade associations, NGOs and unions to organize at this level, due to lack of funding and language and organizational barriers to coordination.[67] Corporations also benefit from the fact that supranational decision-making tends to be hidden from public view, and there is a lack of criteria for ensuring a level playing field for interest group representation.[68]

None of this is to say that businesses are always effective at getting what they want through lobbying. Sometimes, despite their best efforts, they do not get the policy they fought for. However, the fact that lobbying occurs demonstrates that MNCs attempt to exercise power to try to get what they want. The fact that lobbying is a huge business in itself suggests that it is worth investing in and is, therefore, often successful; if it was never successful, businesses would not invest in it.

Rule-setting

I pointed out above that businesses set the agenda even without acting. But they can also actively set the agenda and, more importantly, the rules. The passive

---

[61] Fuchs, *Business Power in Global Governance*, 85.
[62] Fuchs, *Business Power in Global Governance*, 85–6.
[63] Fuchs, *Business Power in Global Governance*, 86.
[64] Fuchs, *Business Power in Global Governance*, 87.
[65] Fuchs, *Business Power in Global Governance*, 88–9.
[66] Fuchs, *Business Power in Global Governance*, 89.
[67] Fuchs, *Business Power in Global Governance*, 90–1.
[68] Fuchs, *Business Power in Global Governance*, 91.

agenda-setting power of business is difficult to measure because it might not 'leave a trace'.[69] Corporations do not need to voice threats to move jobs in response to policy decisions; states act in anticipation of these threats. As such, gathering evidence on this phenomenon is difficult, making it a source of controversy among scholars.[70] The active form of agenda-setting power, however, comes in the forms of self-regulation and public-private and private-private partnerships (PPPs). As Fuchs argues,

> such arrangements provide opportunities to business actors to set rules directly. They determine issues, define problems, and design, adopt, implement, and enforce 'solutions' themselves ... Moreover, to a substantial extent this activity takes place without public influence or control. Developments in the agenda-setting power of business may thus fade into the background, when compared to the rise in its rule-setting power.[71]

Quasi-regulation is carried out by rating agencies. The Big Three rating agencies – Standard and Poor's, Moody's, and Fitch ICBA – influence 80 per cent of global financial flows.[72] They rate countries by their policies and politics, which determines whether or not MNCs will invest in those countries. Their ratings have become more important to developing countries' capital inflows than the IMF or the World Bank.[73] Coordination service firms – banks, institutional investors, hedge funds and private equity firms, multinational law and accountancy firms, and management consultants – 'exercise transnational rule-setting power by determining and enforcing standards for the behavior of business companies'.[74] Rating agencies and coordination service firms exercise episodic power in the global economy by deciding which countries are worth investing in and by determining the conduct of other economic actors.

Public-private partnerships are not new, but they have become much more significant in recent decades, especially at the global level.[75] The aim is to use private resources to achieve public policy objectives.[76] One example is the UN Global Compact (2000), which sought to improve corporate conduct. It used corporate resources to do this, but it gave corporations legitimacy and prestige without checking whether they were improving their environmental and social practices.[77]

---

[69]Fuchs, *Business Power in Global Governance*, 59.
[70]Fuchs, *Business Power in Global Governance*, 64.
[71]Fuchs, *Business Power in Global Governance*, 104.
[72]Fuchs, *Business Power in Global Governance*, 110.
[73]Fuchs, *Business Power in Global Governance*, 110.
[74]Fuchs, *Business Power in Global Governance*, 111.
[75]Fuchs, *Business Power in Global Governance*, 112.
[76]Fuchs, *Business Power in Global Governance*, 112.
[77]Fuchs, *Business Power in Global Governance*, 112–13.

An example of a private-private partnership is the Forest Stewardship Council (FSC), which sets standards for responsible forest management. This PPP filled a governance vacuum and set stringent standards, but some businesses found the standards to be too stringent and set up their own competing, weaker standards.[78] Consumers generally don't know the difference between the different labelling schemes, serving to undermine the high standards of the FSC and marginalizing it.[79]

Public-private partnerships at the national level allow businesses to be involved in agenda- and rule-setting, but they are constrained to some extent by public actors who decide which businesses get a seat at the table.[80] At the global level, however, 'PPPs can provide large business actors with considerable leeway in agenda- and rule-setting due to resource scarcity among public actors as well as civil society and a frequent lack of transparency in decisionmaking processes'.[81]

The self-regulation of business dates back to the Guilds in the Medieval era. But there has been a 'dramatic increase' in these practices.[82] Self-regulation often occurs without any government input, especially at the global level. Businesses are setting standards on environmental issues, human rights and international finance. Sector-wide regulations include the Responsible Care Program of the Chemical Industry, which was adopted following the industrial disaster at Bhopal, India, in 1984. A global example is the SA 8000 standards for environmental management and social accountability. The advantages of these practices are that business brings its organizational, technical and financial resources, as well as decentralized, flexible and efficient systems to bear on global problems.[83] However, business is able to set rules without public oversight, there is a lack of transparency and accountability, some members are advantaged in these arrangements and some actors excluded, there is no possibility for the government to step in in the global arena and there is an inherent tension between public and private interests.[84]

Corporate social responsibility

One area in which corporations set the rules themselves is corporate social responsibility (CSR). Businesses began to develop ideas of 'stakeholder relations' in the 1960s when US corporations needed to justify their activities overseas in the context of decolonization; for example, US companies like IBM and Xerox

---

[78]Fuchs, *Business Power in Global Governance*, 114.
[79]Fuchs, *Business Power in Global Governance*, 114.
[80]Fuchs, *Business Power in Global Governance*, 114.
[81]Fuchs, *Business Power in Global Governance*, 114–15.
[82]Fuchs, *Business Power in Global Governance*, 115–16.
[83]Fuchs, *Business Power in Global Governance*, 117.
[84]Fuchs, *Business Power in Global Governance*, 117.

developed the concept of 'stakeholder relations' in response to postcolonial nationalism and hostility towards US corporations and also as a response to the civil rights movements at home, which raised the problem of economic injustice.[85] Today, in general, CSR emerges in response to five pulls: top-down government regulations; market forces (consumers, employees or capital market signals); 'reputation pull'; ethics; and crisis.[86] Of these five, crisis is the most salient. Indeed, some refer to CSR as 'Crisis Scandal Response'.[87] Examples of crisis scandal response include the chemical industry's response to Bhopal, Shell's response to the Brent Spar scandal and numerous examples in the garment industry, including the Bangladesh Fire and Building Safety Accord (more in the next chapter).

The garment industry is at the forefront of codes of conduct: the first corporate code of conduct was implemented by the jeans company Levi Strauss in 1992 in response to an exposé which found that it was employing Chinese prison labour on the island of Saipan.[88] The advantages of the proliferation of codes of conduct are that businesses are learning best practices from each other and some of these practices have become routinized.[89] CSR also fills in gaps in global and state governance.[90] And, as has been mentioned, MNCs making changes can have significant impact on environmental and social policy objectives, and so is actively encouraged by many civil society actors.[91]

However, even if CSR can be seen as MNCs exercising power for good, it can also be interpreted as MNCs exercising power for ill. First, businesses decide which NGOs to engage with, and the power relationship is not equal. The FSC is an example of this, where the stringent standards set by civil society organizations have been undercut by weaker, business-created standards.[92] Second, there is no public oversight of CSR, nor involvement in its design by public actors or even all the relevant stakeholders in the companies.[93] This is a serious weakness in the garment industry's many codes of conduct, which we will come back to.[94] Third, leaving it to business means that more effective and stringent rule-setting by government can be avoided or undermined.[95]

---

[85]Robert Davies, 'Social Responsibility and Corporate Values', in *Making Globalization Good: The Moral Challenges of Global Capitalism*, ed. John Dunning (Oxford: Oxford Scholarship Online, 2003), 305.

[86]Davies, 'Social Responsibility and Corporate Values', 307.

[87]Vogel, 'Taming Globalization?', 478.

[88]Angela Hale, 'Organising and Networking in Support of Garment Workers: Why We Researched Subcontracting Chains', in *Threads of Labour: Garment Industry Supply Chains from the Workers' Perspective*, Angela Hale and Jane Wills (Oxford: Blackwell, 2005), 59.

[89]Fuchs, *Business Power in Global Governance*, 124.

[90]Fuchs, *Business Power in Global Governance*, 124.

[91]Fuchs, *Business Power in Global Governance*, 125; Vogel, 'Taming Globalization?', 475.

[92]Fuchs, *Business Power in Global Governance*, 129–30.

[93]Fuchs, *Business Power in Global Governance*, 130.

[94]Hale, 'Organising and Networking in Support of Garment Workers', 61.

[95]Fuchs, *Business Power in Global Governance*, 132.

Moreover, business's engagement in CSR builds up a perception of business actors as not merely possessing legitimate or practical authority but also moral authority.[96] Businesses are establishing the belief that they can be trusted on environmental and social issues.[97] Such a belief undermines support for public regulation of business.[98] Business power in these areas becomes normalized and legitimized.[99]

The moral and practical authority of business has also been carefully cultivated through over a century of public relations (PR) initiatives. American corporations in the early twentieth century grew at a significant rate, dwarfing the familiar world of family, church and local community; in order to establish their social and moral legitimacy, corporations had to demonstrate that they had a 'soul'.[100] By the mid-twentieth century, corporations had to develop new tactics because there was public support for more New Deal-style government intervention in the economy and a strong trade unions movement. Corporations responded by investing in local communities, making large philanthropic donations and using rhetoric/publicity.[101] They used a sophisticated range of PR techniques to avoid further advances for government and trade unions, and instead 'to redirect change in a way that minimizes the elite's loss of structural power'.[102] Nowadays the range of techniques has expanded: it still includes rhetoric, community relations and philanthropy, but also funding think tanks and political groups, interlocking networks, and corporate intelligence and spying.[103]

But the aura of businesses as responsible actors is waning, because the evidence does not back up the hype. Despite the reams of codes of conduct in the garment industry, 'there are no examples of sustained improvement in all labor standards in the global apparel supply chain, which likely accounts for the growing consensus that the private regulation model has failed to deliver, especially in the apparel industry where it began'.[104] Thus, times are changing in the world of CSR to involve more regulation at the regional and global levels. The Rana Plaza factory collapse was a catalyst for acceleration and a number of jurisdictions

---

[96]Fuchs, *Business Power in Global Governance*, 144–6.

[97]Mikler, *The Political Power of Global Corporations*, 47.

[98]Mikler, *The Political Power of Global Corporations*, 48.

[99]Mikler, *The Political Power of Global Corporations*, 48.

[100]Roland Marchand, *Creating the Corporate Soul: The Rise of Public Relations and Corporate Imagery in American Big Business* (Berkeley: University of California Press, 1998).

[101]Rami Kaplan, 'Who Has Been Regulating Whom, Business or Society? The Mid-20th-Century Institutionalization of "Corporate Responsibility" in the USA', *Socio-Economic Review* 13, no. 1 (2015): 125–55, https://doi.org/10.1093/ser/mwu031.

[102]Kaplan, 'Who Has Been Regulating Whom, Business or Society?', 129.

[103]David Miller, *A Century of Spin: How Public Relations Became the Cutting Edge of Corporate Power* (London: Pluto Press, 2007).

[104]Sarosh Kuruvilla, *Private Regulation of Labor Standards in Global Supply Chains* (Ithaca, NY: Cornell University Press, 2021), 11.

have implemented mandatory reporting on supply chains, including California's Transparency in Supply Chains Act (2015), the UK's Modern Slavery Act (2015) and France's *Loi de Vigilance* (2017).[105] The EU Non-Financial Reporting Directive 2014/95/EU required companies with more than five hundred employees to disclose their policies on 'environmental, social and employee matters, respect for human rights, anti-corruption and bribery matters'.[106] This has recently been updated with the Corporate Sustainability Reporting Directive 2022 (CSRD), so that all large EU-based companies have to disclose more detailed information on sustainability and in an accessible way, as well as MNCs with a turnover of more than 150 million euros in the EU.[107] However, a group of 220 civil society organizations signed an open statement to the EU on a draft of the directive, arguing that it does not apply to the whole supply chain, that litigation against corporations remains inaccessible and that it remains based on codes of conduct and audits which have been proven to be ineffective.[108] The UN is considering updating its UN Guiding Principles on Business and Human Rights (UNGPs) to a legally binding mechanism to hold businesses accountable for human rights abuses along supply chains, but whether or not this will be adopted and ratified by member states remains to be seen.[109] Up until now, corporations have resisted public regulation, setting the norms and rules themselves in order to present themselves in the best possible light while doing the bare minimum.

Manipulation

The final way in which MNCs exercise episodic power that I want to highlight is manipulation. Just as with the other forms of power, the debates about manipulation seek to answer two questions: the definitional question – what is manipulation? – and the normative question – when is it morally wrong?[110] The definitional question is answered in numerous ways: manipulation could mean

---

[105]Arianna Rossi, Christian Viegelahn and David Williams, 'The Post-COVID-19 Garment Industry in Asia' (Geneva, 2021), 13.

[106]Blanaid Clarke and Linn Anker-Sørensen, 'The EU as a Potential Norm Creator for Sustainable Corporate Groups', in *Cambridge Handbook of Corporate Law, Corporate Governance and Sustainability*, ed. Beate Sjåfjell and Christopher M. Bruner (Cambridge: Cambridge University Press, 2019), 199.

[107]Council of the EU, 'New Rules on Corporate Sustainability Reporting: Provisional Agreement between the Council and the European Parliament', 21 June 2022, https://www.consilium.europa.eu/en/press/press-releases/2022/06/21/new-rules-on-sustainability-disclosure-provisional-agreement-between-council-and-european-parliament/.

[108]Civil society Statement, 'Civil Society Statement on the Proposed EU Corporate Sustainability Due Diligence Directive', 2022.

[109]Anne Trebilcock, 'The Rana Plaza Disaster Seven Years on: Transnational Experiments and Perhaps a New Treaty?', *International Labour Review* 159, no. 4 (2020): 545–68.

[110]Robert Noggle, 'The Ethics of Manipulation', *Stanford Encyclopedia of Philosophy*, 2022, https://plato.stanford.edu/entries/ethics-manipulation/.

the bypassing of rationality (e.g. hypnosis), tricking someone into having the mental state (belief, desire or emotion) the principal desires, pressure to do what the principal wants (peer pressure or blackmail) or some combination of these.[111]

Corporations are typically thought to manipulate consumers through advertising. The advertising industry is premised upon finding ever novel and effective ways to manipulate consumers into buying products that they perhaps don't want or need. The current trend is away from TV and print advertising towards online advertising, as smartphones and tablets are more widely available, and people spend more time on the internet and social media.[112] While most agree that advertising is manipulative, not everyone agrees that it constitutes wrongful manipulation.[113] This debate hinges on how autonomy is understood. Depending on a philosopher's conception of autonomy, they will either find advertising to undermine individuals' autonomy or will distinguish between cases in which individual autonomy is undermined by advertising and when it is not.[114] Empirical evidence suggests that advertising does not have as much of an impact on consumers as its critics think, and there is a lively current debate among economists about the effectiveness of television and digital advertising in persuading consumers to buy specific products or visit particular websites.[115]

However, I find these debates over the effectiveness of advertising and whether or not advertising wrongfully manipulates individuals less interesting than the debate about how advertising shapes the cultural landscape more broadly. As Richard L. Lippke points out, so-called 'persuasive advertising', as opposed to 'informational advertising', occurs en masse and 'induces uncritical acceptance of the consumer lifestyle as a whole', so discussions about whether or not adverts manipulate people into buying specific products misses the point.[116] As Roland Marchand has argued in his study of American advertising in the 1920s–1930s, advertisers have an in-built status quo bias because they, and the corporations they sell products for, benefit from the status quo; they present a selective, idealized version of the contemporary society and reflect

---

[111]Noggle, 'The Ethics of Manipulation'.

[112]Trefis Team and Great Speculations, 'Trends in Global Advertising Industry: Winners and Losers Part 1', Forbes, 2015, https://www.forbes.com/sites/greatspeculations/2015/09/28/trends-in-global-advertising-industry-winners-and-losers-part-1/#6334934250ac.

[113]Timothy Aylsworth, 'Autonomy and Manipulation: Refining the Argument against Persuasive Advertising', Journal of Business Ethics 175, no. 4 (2022): 689–99.

[114]Robert L. Arrington, 'Advertising and Behavior Control', Journal of Business Ethics 1, no. 1 (1982): 3–12; Aylsworth, 'Autonomy and Manipulation'.

[115]Bradley Shapiro, Hitsch Günter and Anna Tuchman, 'TV Advertising Effectiveness and Profitability: Generalizable Results from 288 Brands', Econometrica 89, no. 4 (2021): 1855–79; Ray Fisman, 'Did EBay Just Prove That Paid Search Ads Don't Work?', Harvard Business Review, March 2013, https://hbr.org/2013/03/did-ebay-just-prove-that-paid.

[116]Richard L Lippke, 'Advertising and the Social Conditions of Autonomy', Business & Professional Ethics 8, no. 4 (1989): 39.

it back to consumers.[117] Advertising creates the impression that the consumer lifestyle and culture is inevitable and unchangeable – it is a crucial communicative component in the formation of 'capitalist realism'.[118] Thus, whether or not individuals can make autonomous choices about particular purchases belies the social conditions in which those choices are being made. As Lippke puts it, 'If individuals lack appealing and coherent alternatives to what ads tell them about how to live, they cannot make critical, rational choices about such matters' and they will judge political institutions according to their ability to deliver a consumer lifestyle rather than countervailing criteria.[119] He adds that this is particularly true of children, who do not have the capacity to see through the manipulative techniques of advertisers, and who are instilled from childhood with consumer habits that they '*carry forward* into their adult lives'.

Naomi Klein argues in *No Logo* that there was a shift in the mid-1980s from corporations as purveyors of products to purveyors of brands or 'meaning brokers', creating lifestyle philosophies and emotional connections with companies.[120] MNCs, like Nike and Gap, started spending the majority of their budget on branding. For instance, Nike's advertising expenditure rose from less than $50 million per year in 1987 to over $500 million per year in 1997.[121] The 1998 UN Human Development Report stated that global spending on advertising 'now outpaces the growth of the world economy by one-third'.[122] But *No Logo* merely signalled the advent of an exponential trend. Since the late 1990s, branding has become utterly ubiquitous. In 2019, global advertising spending reached $630 billion and is projected to reach $781 billion in 2022.[123] Every available space is used to push brands into our collective subconscious. There are adverts everywhere; most obviously on TV and in print media but also on the street, on public transport, in universities, schools, packaging, product placement in films and TV programmes, cultural and sporting events. The dawn of the internet, social media and big tech has served as fuel to the fire. With the rise of the internet, advertising seems inescapable. As Klein recently put it, 'Logos hover everywhere we look, like spots in our peripheral vision.'[124]

Therefore, whether advertising manipulates, or effectively manipulates, consumers into buying specific things and whether this is morally wrong or not is

---

[117]Roland Marchand, *Advertising the American Dream: Making Way for Modernity, 1920-1940* (Berkeley: University of California Press, 1985).

[118]Marchand, *Advertising the American Dream*; Mark Fisher, *Capitalist Realism: Is There No Alternative?* (Winchester: Zer0, 2009).

[119]Lippke, 'Advertising and the Social Conditions of Autonomy', 44, 48.

[120]Naomi Klein, *No Logo*, ed. Fourth Estate, 10th anniversary edn (London, 2010), 20–1.

[121]Klein, *No Logo*, 19.

[122]Klein, *No Logo*, 9.

[123]Statista, 'Advertising Spending Worldwide from 2000 to 2024', Statista, 2022. https://www.statista.com/statistics/1174981/advertising-expenditure-worldwide/

[124]Dan Hancox, 'No Logo at 20: Have We Lost the Battle against the Total Branding of Our Lives?', *The Guardian*, 19 August 2019.

less important than the question of how advertising is contributing to consumer culture more generally, manipulating people into believing that consumerism is the optimum lifestyle and that the capitalist economy is inevitable. Moreover, the rise of mass marketing cannot be understood in isolation. It has occurred at the same time as the diminishment of public space. In privately owned commercial spaces, political protest is suppressed. Citizens in many parts of the United States no longer encounter political debate and critique in public places, because the public town square has been replaced by the privately owned shopping mall where leafleting, petitioning and protesting are not allowed.[125] Many more live in Business Improvement Districts (BIDs) where corporations take over local government roles like security, sanitation and social services and create 'brand zones'.[126] Furthermore, many aspects of governance, from education to legal arbitration, military combat, welfare, healthcare and the provision of basic utilities, are now contracted out to private companies across liberal democracies.[127] So the sense of there being no alternative is pushed on multiple fronts, in the realm of ideas, material reality and governance.

Thus, I suggest that while advertising attempts to exercise power over individuals in terms of the first dimension – getting consumers to purchase products they would not otherwise purchase – that advertising contributes perhaps more to the third dimension – mass advertising instils general belief in society that consumerism is the optimum lifestyle, that capitalism is inevitable and the power of corporations is normal. Further, it has the Foucauldian function (the fourth dimension of power) of shaping individuals as consumers and it does this from infanthood. But corporations not only manipulate individuals into practising consumerism, they also manipulate the public sphere more broadly by creating an image of themselves as pillars of the community and experts in the economy, as we have already seen above when discussing CSR and PR.

Moreover, all of this looks like child's play in the dawn of the age of 'surveillance capitalism'. In this new era, human behaviour is intentionally manipulated and modified by big tech companies in order to generate the outcomes they desire. They do this by gathering data on individuals through social media accounts, wearable tracking devices, home smart equipment like digital thermostats, online gaming and so on. The information is used to predict and then manipulate behaviour, and has generated lucrative new markets in behavioural futures. Shoshanna Zuboff argues that this is such a paradigm shift that we cannot accurately comprehend these activities through existing conceptions of power. She argues that surveillance capitalism relies on a new form of power,

---

[125]Margaret Kohn, *Brave New Neighborhoods: The Privatization of Public Space* (London: Routledge, 2004), 189.
[126]Kohn, *Brave New Neighborhoods*, 81–4.
[127]Chiara Cordelli, *The Privatized State* (Princeton, NJ: Princeton University Press, 2020).

'instrumentarianism', which is '*the instrumentation and instrumentalization of behavior for the purposes modification, prediction, monetization, and control*' (original emphasis).[128] It is beyond the scope of this project to assess how this new era coalesces with structural injustice, but what it highlights is that corporate power has found new horizons for the twenty-first century: new sources of extraction and accumulation, ways of avoiding government regulation and self-regulating, and ways to normalize their behaviour so that we accept it as inevitable. We underestimate corporate power at our peril.

Thus, the power of MNCs is exercised along the four dimensions. MNCs exercise power in the first dimension: through lobbying and manipulation they get *B* to do what *B* would not otherwise do. They exercise power along the second dimension by active agenda- and rule-setting, through the activities of rating and coordination service agencies and through PPPs. In terms of the third dimension, the power of MNCs is given legitimate authority through CSR, which normalizes their position as legitimate moral-political actors. CSR also allows business to step into the breach of rule- and agenda-setting at the global level, thereby establishing business's authority to continue doing this. Advertising contributes to the normalization of corporate power and the sense that there is no alternative. Finally, in terms of the fourth dimension, MNCs produce actors, such as the actors that have sprung up in response to their activities in the global economy, like rating agencies and coordination services. They also produce the subjectivity of the corporate worker, who conforms to certain norms and practices in order to be able to participate in business, they shape the subjectivity and behaviour of actors who want to work with business, such as developing states, smaller businesses and civil society, and the subjectivity of consumer through marketing and advertising, instilling disciplined practices of consumption in individuals. We may even be entering a new era where corporations not only shape individuals' behaviour but instrumentalize it to suit their ends, and the ways in which surveillance capitalism will impact upon the public sphere are only beginning to be understood.

Power in the global garment industry

Global value chains

The global garment industry has increased 128-fold from the 1970s to the early 2000s.[129] In 2017, it was worth $2.4 trillion, making it the world's seventh largest

---

[128]Shoshana Zuboff, *The Age of Surveillance Capitalism* (London: Profile Books, 2019), 352.
[129]Jennifer Hurley and Doug Miller, 'The Changing Face of the Global Garment Industry', in *Threads of Labour: Garment Industry Supply Chains from the Workers' Perspective*, ed. Angela Hale and Jane Wills (Oxford: Blackwell, 2005), 17.

economy.[130] Until recently, garment consumption occurred mostly in the Global North; in 2008, the EU, United States and Japan together accounted for 75 per cent of garment imports.[131] But garment production mostly takes place in the Global South; in the 1970s, manufacturing moved from the United States, EU and Japan to Third World countries due to the 'new international division of labour' created by the proliferation of countries newly liberated from colonialism.[132]

The garment industry is characterized by *buyer-driven* commodity chains. In contrast to *producer-driven* chains, where large companies control the production process (e.g. cars, aircrafts), in buyer-driven chains brand-named retailers set up decentralized production networks in exporting countries.[133] They do not own the production facilities; rather, they outsource production to contractors. The role of retailers is to design, brand and advertise the goods, oversee the production process and distribute goods. Their profits derive from 'unique combinations of high-value research, design, sales, marketing, and financial services'.[134] Their profits also derive from keeping production costs as low as possible, which has been enabled by the new international division of labour.

The garment industry has been described as a monopsony, with few wholesale buyers and a multitude of suppliers.[135] It is difficult for newer or smaller businesses to break into the retail sector because of the high investment costs in product development, advertising and retailing.[136] But there are low entry costs to manufacturing garments, which requires only basic equipment, and in countries where labour protections are weak, wages are low and health and safety standards bypassed. Moreover, the 'big buyers' in the Global North experienced 'spectacular growth strategies' in the 1980s–1990s, using mergers and acquisitions to increase their size and reduce competition.[137] Thus, there has been a consolidation of buying power in the top retailers and an explosion of manufacturers.[138]

---

[130]Imran Amed, Achim Berg, Leonie Brantberg, Saskia Hedrich, Johnattan Leon and Robb Young, 'The State of Fashion 2017', 2016, https://www.mckinsey.com/industries/retail/our-insights/the-state-of-fashion.

[131]Gary Gereffi and Stacey Frederick, 'The Global Apparel Value Chain, Trade and the Crisis: Challenges and Opportunities for Developing Countries' (London, 2010), 3.

[132]Folker Fröbel, Jürgen Heinrichs and Otto Kreye, *The New International Division of Labour* (Cambridge: Cambridge University Press, 1980), 14.

[133]Gary Gereffi, 'The Organization of Buyer-Driven Global Commodity Chains: How U.S. Retailers Shape Overseas Production Networks', in *Commodity Chains and Global Capitalism*, ed. Gary Gereffi and Miguel Korzeniewicz (London: Praeger, 1994), 95–122.

[134]Gereffi, 'The Organization of Buyer-Driven Global Commodity Chains', 99.

[135]Ashok Kumar, *Monopsopy Capitalism: Power and Production in the Twilight of the Sweatshop Age* (Cambridge: Cambridge University Press, 2020).

[136]Gereffi, 'The Organization of Buyer-Driven Global Commodity Chains', 103.

[137]Gereffi, 'The Organization of Buyer-Driven Global Commodity Chains', 115.

[138]Gereffi, 'The Organization of Buyer-Driven Global Commodity Chains', 115–16.

The monopsony era has had significant consequences for workers. Gereffi explains,

This combination of concentrated buying power in the retail/wholesale sector and excess capacity in overseas factories has permitted the big buyers in GCCs [Global Commodity Chains] to simultaneously lower the prices they are paying for goods and dictate more stringent performance standards for their vendors (e.g., more buying seasons, faster delivery times, and better quality) in order to increase their profits.[139]

Role of the state

The meteoric rise of the global garment industry is not only the result of changes in global production processes; it has also been facilitated by states, both at the retail and manufacturing end of the supply chain. At the manufacturing end, since the 1970s, resource-poor countries have pursued export-oriented industrialization (EOI).[140] In EOI, governments create the conditions for export manufacturing, such as building infrastructure and providing subsidies for raw materials.[141] The garment industry relies on export processing zones (EPZs). Officially, EPZs are sites where imported materials can be worked on and re-exported without incurring taxes.[142] But EPZs are well-known for poor working conditions and the repression of trade unionism. In 1970, only ten countries had EPZs; by the mid-1990s, half of the world's countries had them.[143] Textile, clothing and footwear is dominant in EPZs because it is labour-intensive, is not place-bound, workers can be trained on the job and distance from market is not important because the goods are easy to transport.[144]

The retail end of the garment supply chain is fundamental when considering the role of the state in shaping and maintaining the injustice of sweatshop labour. Ever since John F. Kennedy's international trade agreement on US cotton in 1961, 'apparel production has been among the most protected manufacturing activities in the global economy'.[145] In 1974, the Multi-Fibre Agreement (MFA) established a quota system for textile and clothing exports. The effects of the MFA

---

[139]Gereffi, 'The Organization of Buyer-Driven Global Commodity Chains', 116.

[140]In contrast to larger, resource-rich economies such as Latin American and Eastern European countries, that have pursued import-substituting industrialization (ISI), that is, producing for the domestic market. Gereffi, 'The Organization of Buyer-Driven Global Commodity Chains', 100.

[141]Gereffi, 'The Organization of Buyer-Driven Global Commodity Chains', 100.

[142]Hurley and Miller, 'The Changing Face of the Global Garment Industry', 35.

[143]Hurley and Miller, 'The Changing Face of the Global Garment Industry', 36.

[144]Hurley and Miller, 'The Changing Face of the Global Garment Industry', 35.

[145]Jennifer Bair, 'Surveying the Post-MFA Landscape: What Prospects for the Global South Post-Quota?', *Competition & Change* 12, no. 1 (2008): 3.

were multifaceted. On the one hand, many countries were able to manufacture garments for export, because retailers had to source from multiple countries to bypass the quota system.[146] On the other hand, the MFA concentrated power into the hands of United States, EU and Japanese retailers, because these countries determined how much countries could export on a case-by-case basis with a view to protecting their domestic industries and MNCs. The MFA shaped the global garment industry at a time of exponential growth, in such a way as to protect the interests of the Global North.

With increasing trade liberalization under the WTO, the MFA was replaced by the Agreement on Textiles and Clothing in 1995, which aimed to phase out quotas by 2005. This process was supposed to benefit Global South countries; however, it was managed by industrialized countries.[147] The United States and EU lobbied hard to include articles that would hinder the end of quotas. The United States decided to 'end-load' the process so that only non-significant products were liberalized at first, such as parachutes and seatbelts, with 80 per cent of the products remaining under quotas by 2003.[148] The EU found itself embroiled in the 'bra wars' dispute in 2005, when it blocked imports of Chinese-made lingerie after complaints by EU manufacturers about the sudden influx of garments when the MFA did finally end; the garments were piled up in customs and checkpoints until they were eventually admitted after complex negotiations.[149] Post-MFA, the diversity of garment-exporting countries was undermined as manufacturing concentrated in low-cost countries.[150] Indeed, China was the main beneficiary, more than doubling its share of apparel exports between 1995 and 2008.[151] A new division of labour emerged with the most labour-intensive aspects of production (cut, make and trim – CMT) occurring in poorer countries, such as Cambodia, Vietnam, Bangladesh and Indonesia, and the capital-intensive production – producing man-made fibres, machinery manufacturing – in richer countries like China, India and Turkey.[152]

---

[146]Gereffi, 'The Organization of Buyer-Driven Global Commodity Chains', 101.

[147]Angela Hale and Maggie Burns, 'The Phase-Out of the Multi-Fibre Arrangement from the Perspective of Workers', in *Threads of Labour: Garment Industry Supply Chains from the Workers' Perspective*, ed. Angela Hale and Jane Wills (Oxford: Blackwell, 2005), 211.

[148]Hale and Burns, 'The Phase-Out of the Multi-Fibre Arrangement from the Perspective of Workers', 211.

[149]Andrew Brooks, *Clothing Poverty: The Hidden World of Fast Fashion and Second-Hand Clothes* (London: Zed Books, 2015), 41–2.

[150]Gereffi and Frederick, 'The Global Apparel Value Chain, Trade and the Crisis', 13.

[151]Gereffi and Frederick, 'The Global Apparel Value Chain, Trade and the Crisis', 7. However, there currently seems to be a move away from China – it accounted for 33 per cent of global apparel and footwear exports in 2019 – but China remains dominant in textile production, see Rossi, Viegelahn and Williams, 'The Post-COVID-19 Garment Industry in Asia', 4.

[152]Gereffi and Frederick, 'The Global Apparel Value Chain, Trade and the Crisis', 13–14.

A further crisis for garment-exporting countries was the 2008 financial crash. Lower demand from the United States, EU and Japan meant that smaller, more vulnerable manufacturers went out of business.[153] It also meant that retailers were demanding lower-cost production.[154] Thus, the phase-out of quotas and the financial crisis benefitted big Northern retailers and large Southern manufacturers, but not smaller firms who lacked the resources and knowledge to adapt to the changes, or garment workers.[155]

It may seem that the post-quota, newly liberalized global garment industry is powered by market forces, but this appearance is misleading. Since 2005, the United States and EU sought other strategies for preserving their advantages, mostly through bilateral and regional trade agreements.[156] The failure of the WTO's Cancun round in 2003 enabled this, after which the United States declared it would be creating its own free trade agreements.[157] Through the North Atlantic Free Trade Agreement (NAFTA), the United States has secured favourable terms for apparel production in Mexico, Central America and the Caribbean Basin. Through the Europe Agreements adopted in the 1990s with Eastern and Central European states seeking to join the EU, as well as the Mediterranean Basin, the EU has secured preferential deals.[158] As Hale and Burns put it, 'Bilateral and regional trade agreements are being used by the US and EU to bypass the WTO and establish their own rules which institutionalise their control of the industry. Although many of these agreements give preferential market access for poorer countries, even this is being used to ensure protection of US and EU business interests.'[159]

Subcontracting

Manufacturers in the Global South rely on complex supply chains that are hidden from view. As Hurley and Miller argue, 'The structure is best characterized not as a pyramid but an iceberg ... The dense and complex webs at the bottom end of the chain are invisible not just to outsiders such as government monitors, but also to the retailers that issued the order and sometimes even to the manufacturers

---

[153]Gereffi and Frederick, 'The Global Apparel Value Chain, Trade and the Crisis', 19–20.

[154]Gereffi and Frederick, 'The Global Apparel Value Chain, Trade and the Crisis', 21.

[155]Hale and Burns, 'The Phase-Out of the Multi-Fibre Arrangement from the Perspective of Workers', 216.

[156]Hale and Burns, 'The Phase-Out of the Multi-Fibre Arrangement from the Perspective of Workers', 217.

[157]Hale and Burns, 'The Phase-Out of the Multi-Fibre Arrangement from the Perspective of Workers', 217.

[158]The European Agreements have been phased out but they established a structure of production that remains. Bob Begg, John Pickles and Adrian Smith, 'Cutting It: European Integration, Trade Regimes, and the Reconfiguration of East – Central European Apparel Production', *Environment and Planning* 35 (2003): 2191–2207.

[159]Hale and Burns, 'The Phase-Out of the Multi-Fibre Arrangement from the Perspective of Workers', 217.

that subcontracted the order.'[160] Each step down the iceberg represents a step down in workers' rights and safety, and diminishing dispositional power.[161]

At the top of the iceberg are Tier 1 manufacturers. They are closest to the retailers and are large MNCs themselves, backed by foreign direct investment (FDI). They provide a range of services including 'full package' production. These manufacturers are systemically powerful and exercise power to maintain and advance their interests. They are members of employers' associations in their home countries and form strong lobbies to influence national governments on labour policies.[162] The conditions in these factories tend to be good, because they are used as showcases for inspectors and buyers. Jobs are more secure and union organizing easier, if it is allowed. Tier 1 manufacturers are more prevalent in emerging markets, who can also tap into a growing domestic demand for garments – China, India and Turkey.[163] Countries that rely on garment exports as a large percentage of their economy focus on CMT.[164]

Tier 2 manufacturers are also large, but lack the connections and international reach of Tier 1. They either receive direct orders from international or domestic buyers, or are subsidiaries of Tier 1. They focus on CMT services. The size of these companies varies depending on country. In China they have 400–1,000 workers, but in Sri Lanka only 40–80 workers. Workers have poorer terms and conditions and are less likely to be unionized. Tiers 3 and 4 are a mixture of small factories, workshops and groups of people working out of someone's house. In China, these are groups of several hundred workers, but in Sri Lanka around twenty, and the Philippines ten. These units are funded by local capital. Hurley writes, 'None were found to have very much power in the garment industry, and their circumstances were almost completely determined by the flow of orders coming from higher up the industrial chain.'[165] Workers' rights, health and safety are seriously compromised at this level.

Tier 5 refers to homeworkers, who were found in each of the nine countries in Hurley and Miller's study. These are individuals working from home, as opposed to groups of individuals working from someone's home (these are Tier 4 workers). Homeworking could either be supplementary work for the individual or constitutes their core income. It tends to be seasonal. In the supply chain, homeworkers provide 'stop-gap production' when manufacturers are under time

---

[160]Hurley and Miller, 'The Changing Face of the Global Garment Industry', 23.

[161]The following description of the different tiers is a summary of Jennifer Hurley, 'Unravelling the Web: Supply Chains and Workers' Lives in the Garment Industry', in *Threads of Labour: Garment Industry Supply Chains from the Workers' Perspective*, ed. Angela Hale and Jane Wills (Oxford: Blackwell, 2005), 97–104. The data comes from a study of the garment industry in nine countries.

[162]Hurley, 'Unravelling the Web', 97.

[163]Gereffi and Frederick, 'The Global Apparel Value Chain, Trade and the Crisis', 8.

[164]Gereffi and Frederick, 'The Global Apparel Value Chain, Trade and the Crisis', 8.

[165]Hurley, 'Unravelling the Web', 102.

pressure to finish orders. Their connection is with Tiers 4 and 3, not higher up the chain. They have to meet their own equipment and overhead costs. They are powerless in the supply chain and organizing is extremely difficult.

Subcontracting increases the power of the retailers at the top of the chain because it creates competition for their business. It benefits them by keeping costs low and turnaround times quick. It distances retailers from the poor working conditions that they can blame on companies further down the supply chain. And it creates division among workers who are already divided: 'the lower end of garment chains tend to be women, many of them (im)migrants, of low caste or class'.[166] Despite current trends in the industry towards more streamlined production with Tier 1 manufacturers gaining more power, the iceberg structure remains and is exacerbated by the increasing power of Tier 1 producers, as more workers are squeezed into the bottom rungs of the supply chain.[167]

Codes of conduct

Criticism of sub-contracting in garment supply chains peaked in the 1990s. Campaign groups sprung up in Western countries demanding brands take responsibility for the exploitative and unsafe working conditions in the Global South. Brands responded by stepping up their efforts in CSR. This started with Levi-Strauss, but soon codes of conduct became the norm in the industry. While codes of conduct have led to improvements in some cases, it is questionable whether these improvements filter down the supply chain, or only reach Tier 1 and, at best, Tier 2 manufacturers. Codes of conduct are written by the retailers themselves with no input from the workers.[168]

In 1998, the activist organization Women Working Worldwide started a four-year education programme on codes of conduct in Bangladesh, India, Pakistan, Sri Lanka, the Philippines, Indonesia and Thailand.[169] These workshops were held in the workers' few hours of leisure time and were held in secret to avoid intimidation. None of the workers had heard of the codes. Educators asked the women workers what they would put in the codes and their priorities were very different from the retailers. They wanted rights for pregnant women and mothers, freedom from sexual and physical abuse, regular working hours and stability. These issues were not part of the retailers' codes.

There are a range of private-private partnerships in the industry, such as the Ethical Trading Initiative (ETI), and public-private partnerships, such as the Fair

---

[166]Hurley, 'Unravelling the Web', 96.
[167]Rossi, Viegelahn and Williams, 'The Post-COVID-19 Garment Industry in Asia'.
[168]Hale, 'Organising and Networking in Support of Garment Workers', 62.
[169]Hale, 'Organising and Networking in Support of Garment Workers', 62. What follows is a summary of the findings.

Labour Association (FLA).[170] But these initiatives are toothless. As the Clean Clothes Campaign put it, 'by not pursuing mandatory transparency requirements or binding commitments to remediation, these MSIs [multi-stakeholder initiatives] protect brand reputation without changing actual business models, thereby doing little to effectively improve working conditions or combat violations'.[171] As mentioned above, there are more and more legal initiatives tackling the social and environmental responsibilities of big business that focus on transparency in supply chains, but critics argue that these initiatives are not going far enough.[172]

Changes in the industry

There are three main kinds of retailer in the garment industry. Those selling basic garments (e.g. underwear, T-shirts), fashion-basic garments (fast fashion – garments that are on trend but cheap) and fashion garments (branded and designer wear).[173] Basic clothing accounts for half of all clothing sold.[174] Conventional wisdom assumes that demand for clothes does not increase at the same rate as growth in incomes; clothing retailers, therefore, have to come up with new ways to encourage consumption through constant changes in fashion.[175] The current trend is a shift from fashion-basic retailers, who are beginning to struggle, and the rise of fashion. Christian Dior was the largest retailer in the world in 2019.[176] The fashion sector is more optimistic about its future earning potential than the fashion-basic sector, which is generally pessimistic.[177] The rising middle classes in India and China are the new target of the fashion sector.[178]

Of course, the Covid-19 pandemic was a huge shock to the global garment industry, which experienced some of the largest jobs and working hour losses in the manufacturing sectors.[179] Garment exports dropped by as much as 70 per

---

[170]The ETI is a consortium of corporations, NGOs and trade unions that works to improve labour standards in global supply chains. Members sign up to a labour code of practice, committing them to improving wages and working conditions across their supply chain and it focuses on the implementation of the companies' own codes of conduct. The ETI is not legally binding. The standards are not particularly stringent, enforcement is weak and membership is voluntary. The Fair Labour Association (FLA) was set up by the US government in 1999 in response to the anti-sweatshop movement and includes corporations, but not workers, in designing industry standards.
[171]Clean Clothes Campaign, 'Position Paper on Transparency' (Amsterdam, 2020), 7.
[172]Campaign, 'Position Paper on Transparency'.
[173]Dicken, *Global Shift*, 455.
[174]Hurley and Miller, 'The Changing Face of the Global Garment Industry', 29.
[175]Dicken, *Global Shift*, 455.
[176]Lauren Debter, 'The World's Largest Apparel Companies 2019: Dior Remains on Top, Lululemon and Foot Locker Gain Ground', *Forbes*, 5 May 2019, https://www.forbes.com/sites/laurendeb ter/2019/05/15/worlds-largest-apparel-companies-2019/#24e6188390a2.
[177]Business of Fashion and McKinsey & Company, 'The State of Fashion 2019' (New York, 2018), 11.
[178]Business of Fashion and McKinsey & Company, 24; Imran Amed et al., 'The State of Fashion 2022' (New York, 2022).
[179]Rossi, Viegelahn and Williams, 'The Post-COVID-19 Garment Industry in Asia', 2.

cent.[180] Many small retailers, or larger retailers who were unable to adapt to the shift online, went out of business. But the industry bounced back surprisingly quickly, especially in China, with consumers unleashing pent-up demand with so-called 'revenge buying'.[181] The trend remains as before the pandemic, with fashion on the rise in India and China.

Despite the shifting sands of the garment industry, wealth and power continue to concentrate in the hands of a few top players. As the Business of Fashion and McKinsey report 'The State of Fashion 2019' states,

> Polarization continues to be a stark reality in fashion: fully 97 percent of economic profits for the whole industry are earned by just 20 companies, most of them in the luxury segment. Notably, the top 20 group of companies has remained stable over time. Twelve of the top 20 have been a member of the group for the last decade. Long-term leaders include, among others, Inditex, LVMH, and Nike, which have more than doubled their economic profit over the past ten years … According to our estimates, each racked up more than $2 billion in economic profit in 2017.[182]

A total of 97 per cent of profits seems surprising given that there is a lot of competition on the high street and in high fashion. But the largest MNCs give the illusion of competition and choice; they own multiple brands.[183] The Covid-19 pandemic further consolidated the power of the top retailers; in 2021, only 27 per cent of retailers were value-creators (generating returns for shareholders) and they were 'the typical suspects: very strong brands with a strong balance sheet that were already in a better position when the crisis hit'.[184] The super-winners from 2019 remained largely in place by the tail end of the pandemic and through the recovery period.[185]

---

[180]Rossi, Viegelahn and Williams, 'The Post-COVID-19 Garment Industry in Asia', 3.

[181]Amed et al., 'The State of Fashion 2022', 10.

[182]Imran Amed, Johanna Andersson, Anita Balchandani, Marco Beltrami, Achim Berg, Saskia Hedrich Dale Kim, Felix Rölkens, and Robb Young, 'The State of Fashion 2019: A Year of Awakening' (New York, 2018), https://www.mckinsey.com/industries/retail/our-insights/the-state-of-fashion-2019-a-year-of-awakening.

[183]For example, VF Corporation, which has stayed in the top twenty global retailers since 2008, owns Dickies, Horace Small, Jansport, Kipling, Lee, Riders of Lee, Napapijri, Red Kap, The North Face, Timberland, Vans and Wrangler.

[184]Anita Balchandani and Achim Berg, 'The Postpandemic State of Fashion', McKinsey & Company, 2021.

[185]Imran Amed, Achim Berg, Anita Balchandani, Saskia Hedrich, Jakob Ekeløf Jensen, Michael Straub, Felix Rölkens Robb Young, Pamela Brown, Leila Le Merle, Hannah Crump, and Amanda Dargan. 'The State of Fashion 2022'. New York, 2022. https://www.mckinsey.com/~/media/mckinsey/industries/retail/our%20insights/state%20of%20fashion/2022/the-state-of-fashion-2022.pdf. Accessed 29 August 2023.

Analysis of power

Systemic power in the global garment industry lies with these top retailers. They are in a position to get what they want without asking for it. Exporting states act in the interests of these retailers, because retailers have the *dispositional power* to move jobs to cheaper countries; this is a threat they do not need to voice. The dominance of top retailers puts pressure down the whole supply chain, suppressing wages, working conditions and collective bargaining. They also *exercise episodic power* to maintain or better their positions. They merge and acquire smaller retailers, concentrating their wealth and power. They lobby national governments and international organizations: garment corporations are members of powerful business associations, such as the US Business Roundtable (Wal-Mart, Target, Caterpillar Inc.) and the European Roundtable of Industrialists (Inditex, Adidas Group), as well as a host of industry-specific associations. They set industry standards in Private-Private Partnerships, such as the ETI, bypassing more stringent governmental standards. The proliferation of CSR initiatives in the garment industry promotes the image of retailers as ethical and responsible, yet retailers have not engaged with the workers in writing these codes and the codes do not apply further down the supply chain. Retailers use ever-new marketing strategies to entice consumers to buy their goods. For instance, McKinsey notes the trend for 'woke' advertising; the use of the word 'feminist' in apparel advertising increased sixfold between 2016 and 2018.[186] Now the trend is for sustainability, which is seen as one of the top areas for growth in the industry.[187]

Other actors in the industry have systemic power. Tier 1 manufacturers tend to dominate in their home countries. They exercise power by lobbying domestic governments and forming associations to advance their own interests. Rich states exercised power by shaping the industry around a quota system that protected their own interests, manipulating the phase-out of the MFA and using bilateral trade deals to their advantage. Exporting states in the Global South established EPZs and are lax about implementing health and safety standards, and better wages, in order to encourage foreign investment. These states are undoubtedly constrained by MNCs and market forces, but this does not excuse corruption and collusion with the garment industry, which can be pernicious.

Thus, structural interaction in the garment industry since the 1970s has consisted of powerful agents (MNCs and their home states) consolidating power and pressuring less powerful actors in order to reduce the costs of production and increase their own profits. Ashok Kumar argues that this has been an era

---

[186]Business of Fashion and McKinsey & Company, 'The State of Fashion 2019', 16.
[187]Amed et al., 'The State of Fashion 2022'.

of the monopsony power of the global garment corporations, but this era is ending.[188] The combination of the phase-out of the MFA and the global financial crash of 2008 has led to increasing consolidation of producers, with small-scale suppliers going bust and the rise of 'mega-producers' (full-package Tier 1 producers). These mega-producers are investing in labour-saving technology, thereby blocking the re-entry of smaller actors; the effect is 'an increasingly calcified *symbiosis* – locking-in global buyers with global suppliers'.[189] This shift means that large-scale producers in the Global South are becoming more powerful: a shift which has the potential to increase the bargaining power of workers, who can threaten to withdraw their labour from increasingly oligopolistic producers.[190] However, the short-term impact is likely to be bad for workers; Northern brands are targeted by anti-sweatshop activists and NGOs, whereas there is less scrutiny of increasingly large Southern mega-producers.[191] The ILO agrees that workers' power could increase, but also cautions that because fewer workers will be employed in the Tier 1 factories there will be an increasing pool of workers further down the supply chain, pushing down wages and working conditions outside of Tier 1 factories.[192]

While the garment industry has recovered surprisingly quickly from the pandemic, the recovery is uneven.[193] There is still an opportunity for the garment industry to make changes in post-pandemic recovery phase, to push for structural elaboration that benefits workers and the environment. The ILO notes three ways in which the industry could proceed: repeat – go back to the status quo before the pandemic; regain – accelerate pre-pandemic trends for increasing bifurcation in the industry, which could have both positive and negative impacts for workers and the environment; or renegotiate – make fundamental changes to the industry, putting social and environmental sustainability at the core. Current evidence suggests that either repeat or regain is the most likely scenario. As McKinsey's State of Fashion 2022 report states, fashion executives are 'turning their attention to driving growth in an altered market landscape',[194] in other words, business as usual. This analysis suggests, once again, that the overall outcome of structural interaction involving multiple actors, processes and conditions will result in a form of structural elaboration that is designed by no-one and will create new structural possibilities. It remains to be seen whether this current iteration of the global garment industry will result in improvements for

---

[188]Kumar, *Monopsopy Capitalism*.

[189]Kumar, *Monopsopy Capitalism*, 11.

[190]Kumar, *Monopsopy Capitalism*, 11.

[191]Ashok Kumar, 'A Race from the Bottom? Lessons from a Workers' Struggle at a Bangalore Warehouse', *Competition & Change*, 23, no. 4 (2019): 25.

[192]Rossi, Viegelahn and Williams, 'The Post-COVID-19 Garment Industry in Asia', 10.

[193]Amed et al., 'The State of Fashion 2022'.

[194]Amed et al., 'The State of Fashion 2022', 12.

workers and the environment. What is likely, however, is that MNCs will find new and innovative ways to resist increasing pressure from workers; they will leverage what power they have within this new structural framework to continue to extract benefits and maintain the structural injustice that suits them.

Conclusion

An analysis of power of MNCs in the global economy in general, and the garment industry in particular, reveals that structural injustice is complicated by power relations. While it remains true that structural outcomes are the confluence of a wide and unknowable range of agents' actions combining and generating unintended outcomes, it is also true that powerful agents act in ways that maintain the structures for their own gain or work to change the structures to be even more advantageous for them. They are enabled to do this by structures that confer both systemic and dispositional power on powerful actors, and these actors exercise power from these positions through various means, such as lobbying, rule-setting, CSR and manipulation. We have seen that the global garment industry, while a constantly evolving structure which is the outcome of multiple processes, is also to some extent a creation of the most powerful garment MNCs operating out of, and backed up by, powerful states. While the garment industry is undergoing a new phase of structural elaboration, the powerful players will continue to do whatever they can to maintain their pre-existing structural advantages.

Chapter 4

Structural injustice in practice

What can structural injustice theory teach us about injustice in practice? In Chapter 2, I outlined a new typology of structural injustice: pure, avoidable and deliberate structural injustice. In Chapter 3, I deepened our understanding of the different dimensions and forms of power, and I provided a descriptive analysis of how power operates in the global political economy, specifically in the context of the global garment industry. Now I connect the normative and empirical through three case studies: sweatshop labour as deliberate structural injustice, global poverty as avoidable and climate change as pure. The guiding questions are: first, why is the problem a structural injustice and not a mere unfortunate structural outcome? Second, what is the role of power in the creation and maintenance of this structural injustice?

To answer the first question as to why these problems are structural injustices, I use and revise Young's definition of injustice. She argues that injustice comes in two forms: domination and oppression.[1] Domination is the systematic inhibition of self-determination. Oppression is the systematic inhibition of self-development. Young famously identified 'five faces of oppression' in the United States and other welfare-capitalist societies in the early 1990s: exploitation, marginalization, powerlessness, cultural imperialism and violence.[2] She specified that theorizing global injustices might require 'serious revision of some of these criteria, or even their wholesale replacement'.[3] In this spirit, I draw on and adapt Young's five faces. I argue that sweatshop labour is a form of structural exploitation. Global poverty involves four forms of oppression – marginalization from the global economy, powerlessness, structural violence and a form that Young did not separate out for analysis, *material deprivation*. Climate change resembles a form of structural domination because the weather arbitrability interferes with human

---

[1] Iris Marion Young, *Justice and the Politics of Difference* (Princeton, NJ: Princeton University Press, 1990), 33–8.
[2] Young, *Justice and the Politics of Difference*, chap. 2.
[3] Young, *Justice and the Politics of Difference*, 258.

activity, and it is a form of oppression as *insecurity* (another addition to Young's five faces).

To answer the second question about the role of power, this involves looking at the history of the injustice to understand how the structure emerged through the interplay of structure and agency over time. It is analysing the actions of powerful agents within these structures that leads me to categorize the structural injustices as deliberate (sweatshops), avoidable (poverty) and pure (climate change).

I conclude with some reflections on why this typology of structural injustice is useful, recalling the themes identified in previous chapters: clarifying the role of power in structural injustices, structural change and attributing responsibility. These themes occupy the second half of the book.

Deliberate structural injustice: sweatshops

Sweatshops as structural injustice

The term 'sweatshop' was first used in 1849 in the United States to refer to labour outsourced to small shops or workers' homes where they were 'sweated' by a jobber (a large buyer).[4] Sweatshops hit international attention after a fire in the Triangle Shirtwaist Factory, New York, in which 146 people (mostly women) died. Although 'sweatshop' has no fixed definition, sweatshops today are associated with poverty wages, poor working conditions, arbitrary discipline and restrictions on collective organizing.

Sweatshops today are mostly located in the Global South.[5] This is due to a profound shift in the capitalist economy in the 1960s–1970s, the period of decolonization and intensifying globalization. During the colonial period, colonies provided cheap raw materials and industrial manufacturing almost exclusively took place in Western Europe, the United States and Japan until the 1970s. At this point, production relocated to 'Third World' countries for

---

[4]Ashok Kumar, *Monopsopy Capitalism: Power and Production in the Twilight of the Sweatshop Age* (Cambridge: Cambridge University Press, 2020), 4.

[5]Sweatshops are not exclusively located in the Global South. Sweatshops persist in rich countries and in middle-income countries. They still mostly employ poor and racialized women. See for example, Miriam Ching Yoon Louie, *Sweatshop Warriors: Immigrant Women Workers Take on the Global Factory* (Cambridge, MA: South End Press, 2001); Camille Warren, 'Coming Undone: The Implications of Garment Industry Subcontracting for UK Workers', in *Threads of Labour: Garment Industry Supply Chains from the Workers' Perspective*, ed. Angela Hale and Jane Wills (Oxford: Blackwell, 2005), 133–61; Bob Begg, John Pickles and Adrian Smith, 'Cutting It: European Integration, Trade Regimes, and the Reconfiguration of East – Central European Apparel Production', *Environment and Planning* 35 (2003): 2191–2207.

at least four reasons.[6] The first is with the dissolution of European empires, a huge reservoir of labour, under-educated, unskilled, poor and willing to work for very low wages in wretched conditions, emerged. Second, the processes of production fragmented to such an extent that the most basic jobs require little skill and can be learned very quickly. Third, the development of transport and communications facilitated globalized production processes, including subcontracting. Fourth, there was a greater intensity of work among Third World workers because of few labour protections. Third World women, in particular, entered the labour market as a cheap, flexible and, for the most part, un-unionized labour force. By 2006 there were export processing zones (EPZs) in 130 countries, employing 66 million people, 70–80 per cent of whom were women.[7] Some of the reasons why women are employed in sweatshops is because they learn sewing skills at home, so they do not need to be trained;[8] women are deemed to require lower wages because they are not breadwinners;[9] and because women are seen as more docile and disciplined employees.[10]

Sweatshops are also widely associated with human rights violations and child labour. Almost everyone can agree that human rights violations (such as physical and sexual abuse) and child labour are wrong, but not everyone agrees that sweatshops minus these egregious harms are wrong. Libertarians argue that sweatshops provide jobs to people who would otherwise not have them. Corporations providing sweatshops merely add an option to the list of options available to poor people looking for work, and the work is often better paid than

---

[6]Folker Fröbel, Jürgen Heinrichs and Otto Kreye, *The New International Division of Labour* (Cambridge: Cambridge University Press, 1980), 12–13. I use the term 'Third World' here because during the 1970s, that was the term that referred to newly decolonized countries, in contrast to the First World (the West) and the Second World (the USSR). Some decolonial scholars continue to use the term 'Third World' because it designates a political bloc of countries with a decolonial agenda, as opposed to terms like 'developing' vs. 'developed' countries, which implies that all countries are aiming, and should be aiming, towards a Western, capitalist state and economy. For instance, see Rahul Rao, *Third World Protest: Between Home and the World* (Oxford: Oxford University Press, 2010), 24–30; Chandra Talpade Mohanty, *Feminism without Borders: Decolonizing Theory, Practicing Solidarity* (Durham, NC: Duke University Press, 2003).

[7]Hye-Ryoung Kang, 'Transnational Women's Collectivities and Global Justice', in *Gender and Global Justice*, ed. Alison M. Jaggar (Cambridge: Polity Press, 2014), 43.

[8]Diane Elson and Ruth Pearson, ' "Nimble Fingers Make Cheap Workers": An Analysis of Women's Employment in Third World Export Manufacturing', *Feminist Review* 7, no. 1 (1981): 87–107; Maria Fernandez-Kelly, 'Maquiladoras: The View from the Inside', in *The Women, Gender and Development Reader*, ed. Nalini Visvanathan et al. (London: Zed Books, 2011), 225–37.

[9]Elson and Pearson, 'Nimble Fingers', 96.

[10]Lourdes Benería and Martha Roldan, *The Crossroads of Class and Gender: Industrial Homework, Subcontracting, and Household Dynamics in Mexico City* (Chicago: University of Chicago Press, 1987); Deepita Chakravarty, 'Docile Oriental Women's and Organised Labour: A Case Study of the Indian Garment Manufacturing Industry', *Indian Journal of Gender Studies* 14, no. 3 (2007): 439–60.

the alternatives.[11] On this view, sweatshop labour might be exploitative – because the surplus created from the labour of sweatshop workers is unfairly divided between corporations and the workers – but it is not *wrongfully* exploitative. The exploitation is mutually beneficial; it only becomes morally wrong when human rights violations are involved. For instance, Matt Zwolinski argues, 'How ... can it be permissible to *neglect* workers in the developing world, but impermissible to *exploit* them, when exploitation is better for both parties?'[12]

As I have argued elsewhere, such a view fails to account for the background structural conditions that force certain social groups into these jobs, namely poor, racialized women.[13] It is not the case that a particular factory owner says to a particular worker, you must work here or face the alternatives of subsistence farming, domestic labour, scavenging, sex work or starvation.[14] Rather, the worker is in a social position whereby these are the available options. The individual worker's decision to work in a sweatshop appears to be a free choice, but taken as a group or class we see that they are forced either to sell their labour-power to factory owners in order to earn money to survive or to take up an even less attractive occupation. They are forced to choose these jobs because the array of alternatives available is extremely limited and often worse.

I have also argued that what is *wrong* with sweatshop labour is that it is a form of *structural exploitation*. Workers are forced to transfer their 'productive powers'. This refers to both an individual's labour power and developmental power.[15] Labour power is the ability to create use values, which can occur through traditional productive labour (the production of commodities in a factory for example) or domestic labour (cleaning, preparing meals, etc.). Developmental power is the ability to pursue one's own projects in the pursuit of developing oneself as an autonomous agent. This distinction comes from C. B. MacPherson who argues that exploited workers are giving up more than their labour power when labouring for capitalists, because the amount of time and energy spent on their labour reduces the available time and energy for pursuing their own

---

[11]Matt Zwolinski, 'Sweatshops, Choice and Exploitation', *Business Ethics Quarterly* 17, no. 4 (2007): 689–727; Nicholas Kristof, 'Where Sweatshops Are a Dream', *New York Times* (New York, January 2009), https://www.nytimes.com/2009/01/15/opinion/15kristof.html.

[12]Matt Zwolinski, 'Structural Exploitation', *Social Philosophy and Policy* 29, no. 1 (2012): 162.

[13]Maeve McKeown, 'Sweatshop Labor as Global Structural Exploitation', in *Exploitation: From Practice to Theory*, ed. Monique Deveaux and Vida Panitch (London: Rowman and Littlefield, 2017); Maeve McKeown, 'Global Structural Exploitation: Towards an Intersectional Definition', *Global Justice: Theory Practice Rhetoric* 9, no. 2 (2016): 155–77.

[14]These are some of the alternatives available to sweatshop workers in Bangladesh and Mexico, see Jeremy Seabrook, *The Song of the Shirt: The High Price of Cheap Garments, From Blackburn to Bangladesh* (London: C Hurst, 2015); Fernandez-Kelly, 'Maquiladoras'.

[15]Even though he uses these concepts slightly differently, I borrow this term from C. B. Macpherson, 'The Problems of a Non-Market Theory of Democracy', in *Democratic Theory: Essays in Retrieval*, ed. C B Macpherson (Oxford: Clarendon Press, 1973), 39–70.

projects.[16] Sweatshop labourers transfer their productive powers through the long hours of tedious, intensive labour, which allows capitalists to extract the surplus value they produce, and also diminishes the workers' capacities for self-development. It is not only the long and intensive labour that drains the developmental power of sweatshop workers, sweatshop labour is also damaging to health; sweatshop workers report problems such as back pain, allergies, fatigue, headaches and kidney problems.[17] Moreover, it is a specific social group – Third World and racialized women workers – who are positioned in the contemporary global economy through a history of colonial subjugation, more recent neoliberal restructuring of financial and trade regimes with the concomitant informalization of jobs and undermining of the state, and racist and gendered stereotyping, to be forced to work in this sector. Sweatshop labour is a form of global structural exploitation because it involves the forced transfer of the productive powers of disadvantaged social groups (in this case Third World women) to advantaged social groups (better-off consumers, capitalists). In the case of sweatshop labour, the forced transfer of the productive powers of Third World women systematically prevents their self-development.

Structural exploitation in sweatshops also enables MNCs to dominate workers by inhibiting collective organizing. The workers are structurally positioned to have very few options for alternative employment and so are restricted in their ability to resist the dictates of MNCs. Therefore, the possibilities of finding alternative or countering alignments are rarely available for sweatshop workers.[18] The structural inhibition of self-development and self-determination renders sweatshop labour a form of global structural injustice.

One of the features of social structures is that they enable and constrain all actors. It could be objected that in competitive global markets, corporations are forced to play by the rules of the game and exploit workers to stay competitive and to continue competing for business. If corporations refuse to do this, they will go bust, which is bad both for them and for the workers. Arguably, corporations in the global garment industry face 'the structural imperative of "exploit of fail"'.[19] Corporations are constrained by the rules of the capitalist game. However, we saw in the previous chapter that large garment corporations and the states that host them (the United States, EU, Japan and China) have acted in various ways to enhance their positions and power within these structures. And, as I will now argue, a recent crisis in the global garment industry suggests that powerful

---

[16]Macpherson, 'The Problems of a Non-Market Theory of Democracy', 67.

[17]Louie, *Sweatshop Warriors*, 36; Diane Elson and Ruth Pearson, 'The Subordination of Women and the Internationalization of Factory Production', in *The Women, Gender and Development Reader*, ed. Nalini Visvanathan, Lynn Duggan and Laurie Nisonoff, 2nd edn (London: Zed Books, 2011), 221.

[18]See Chapter 2.

[19]Robert Mayer, 'Sweatshops, Exploitation and Moral Responsibility', *Journal of Social Philosophy* 38, no. 4 (2007): 611.

corporations do have significant room to manoeuvre to change the industry for the better.

Using power for good and for ill: The Bangladesh Accord

In April 2013, 1,134 people died and many more were injured when the Rana Plaza factory collapsed in Dhaka, the capital of Bangladesh. It was the worst industrial disaster in the history of the garment industry. Rana Plaza gained the attention of the world, through prominent media reporting and NGO mobilization. The incident forced the global garment industry to face up to the appalling working conditions for garment workers in Bangladesh where factory fires are common, and health and safety standards are relentlessly flouted. Just five months before Rana Plaza, the Tazreen factory fire killed 112 people.[20] The garment industry employs over 4 million people in Bangladesh and is responsible for 80 per cent of the country's exports.[21]

Following Rana Plaza, 190 corporations from twenty countries signed up to the Bangladesh Accord on Fire and Building Safety.[22] This was a legally binding agreement over five years, which required signatories to agree to independent inspections of factories, to remedy any faults and to provide fire and building safety training to staff.[23] The Accord included Bangladeshi and international trade unions, and was overseen by an independent representative from the ILO. Signatories to the Accord had to accept the following terms: disclosure of their Bangladeshi suppliers and submitting them to safety inspections; public disclosure of the findings; requiring suppliers to remediate problems; paying the suppliers sufficiently to make the repairs or giving them loans; allowing worker training in health and safety; guaranteeing the right to refuse work in unsafe conditions and maintaining wages during renovations; stopping business with non-compliant suppliers.[24] The Accord's report from October 2018 states that

---

[20]Rebecca Prentice and Geert De Neve, 'Five Years after Deadly Factory Fire, Bangladesh's Garment Workers Are Still Vulnerable', *The Conversation* (London, November 2017), https://theconversation.com/five-years-after-deadly-factory-fire-bangladeshs-garment-workers-are-still-vulnerable-88027.

[21]Björn Skorpen Claeson, 'Our Voices: Bangladeshi Garment Workers Speak' (Washington, DC, 2015), 11.

[22]Bangladesh Accord Foundation, 'Accord on Fire and Building Safety in Bangladesh', http://www.bangladeshaccord.org/. They also set up an Arrangement and a Trust Fund. The Arrangement established lifelong payments to workers injured in the disaster of 60 per cent of the wage payable in October 2013, and lump sum payments to dependants of deceased workers. To finance this, the ILO set up a Trust Fund for brands to pay into, see Anne Trebilcock, 'The Rana Plaza Disaster Seven Years on: Transnational Experiments and Perhaps a New Treaty?', *International Labour Review* 159, no. 4 (2020): 545–68.

[23]'Accord on Fire and Building Safety in Bangladesh' (2013).

[24]Jaakko Salminen, 'The Accord on Fire and Building Safety in Bangladesh: A New Paradigm for Limiting Buyers' Liability in Global Supply Chains?', *American Journal of Comparative Law* 66, no. 2 (2018): 417.

since implementation, 2,104 factories were inspected and 90 per cent of the factories remedied fire and building safety issues. A total of 1.5 million workers had fire safety training; 330 health and safety complaints had been resolved. Fifty factories had been temporarily evacuated because they were unsafe and ninety-six factories were expelled from the Accord for failing to implement renovations.[25]

Improving fire safety costs very little. The Accord's guidelines specified that factories should install a fire detection and alarm system, exit lighting, fire-safe separation of hazardous areas, useable fire exits and storage facilities that do not block exits.[26] Electrical safety requirements are similarly low cost, such as proper protection and earthing of cables, and ensuring that cables are free from dust.[27] Structural changes to buildings are more financially onerous, although often the problem is overloading the factory with storage and water tanks, or using multipurpose buildings instead of industrial-standard factory buildings. This is what happened in the Rana Plaza case, where the owners added three extra floors to the multipurpose building and filled it with too many people and goods. For garment retailers who often make profits of $2 billion per year, these costs are negligible. In fact, they do not even have to meet the costs themselves; the suppliers bear the costs with support from retailers.[28] So the costs to brands were indeed minimal.

The most significant achievement of the Accord was that it was legally binding. In 2016, two global unions – IndustriALL and UNI GlobalUnion – filed cases against two Accord signatories at the Permanent Court of Arbitration at The Hague, stating that the brands had failed to ensure their supplier factories were making the required changes and they had not made it financially feasible for them to do so.[29] The claims were upheld by the court. The unions reached a settlement with the first brand to support remediation in its two hundred supplier factories, and a settlement with the second brand for US$2.3 million.[30]

While significant progress was made in improving fire and building safety in Bangladesh during the period of the Accord, other issues remained unaddressed or worsened. Wages in Bangladesh continued to be the lowest out of all garment exporting countries. The minimum wage in 2018 was US$63.60 per month, a 6.47 per cent decline since 2013.[31] The average working week was 48 hours, making the average hourly wage 31 cents per hour, which can only cover 14

---

[25]Mark Anner, 'Binding Power: The Sourcing Squeeze, Workers' Rights, and Building Safety in Bangladesh Since Rana Plaza', 2018, 10.
[26]Bangladesh Accord Sectretariat, 'Quarterly Aggregate Report – on Remediation Progress at RGM Factories Covered by the Accord and Status of Workplace Programs' (Dhaka, Amsterdam, 2018), 12.
[27]Bangladesh Accord Sectretariat, 24.
[28]Bangladesh Accord Sectretariat, 14.
[29]Anner, 'Binding Power', 13.
[30]Anner, 14. Dominic Rushe, 'Unions Reach $2.3m Settlement on Bangladesh Textile Factory Safety', *The Guardian*, 22 January 2018.
[31]Anner, 'Binding Power', 7.

per cent of living expenses.[32] Child labour remained 'rampant'.[33] There were labour law reforms after Rana Plaza due to the Sustainability Compact between Bangladesh, the EU, United States and ILO. However, there is a high threshold – 30 per cent – for union formation, and EPZs continue to be exempt.[34] Only a hundred more unions have been registered since Rana Plaza, which can be attributed to the government denying union registration and employers engaging in anti-union activities.[35] For instance, in December 2016, 1,600 garment workers were fired and thirty-four trade unionists arrested after demonstrations in Dhaka.[36] Violations of workers' collective bargaining and associative rights increased by 11.86 per cent between 2012 and 2015.[37] Intimidation and violence towards trade unionists remained commonplace.[38] Corruption is a serious problem: 10 per cent of parliamentarians in Bangladesh are factory owners or are related to factory owners.[39] Factory owners often have ties with the police, who ignore the intimidation and beatings of workers, and factory owners pay local politicians and thugs to keep unions out of their factories.[40]

Furthermore, the successes of the Accord were limited. Not all retailers active in Bangladesh signed the Accord. Notably Wal-Mart and Gap refused. They set up their own, independent initiative – The Alliance for Bangladesh Worker Safety. The Alliance lacked the groundbreaking features of the Accord: it did not require retailers to contribute to remediation costs; it lacked enforcement provisions; and it did not include worker participation in its design or implementation.[41] Crucially, 'the Alliance specifically tries not to establish a legally relevant connection between buyers and their suppliers' employees'.[42]

The Bangladesh Accord can be viewed cynically as an exercise in 'Crisis Scandal Response'. However, the Accord made tangible changes in the Bangladeshi garment industry. The Accord demonstrates the Janus-faced nature of power. On the one hand, it made significant changes to the lives of millions of workers in Bangladesh. Specifically, it effected *structural change* by improving fire and building safety across the industry, improving workers' safety. On the

---

[32] Anner, 'Binding Power', 7.

[33] Michael Safi, 'Child Labour "Rampant" in Bangladesh Factories, Study Reveals', *The Guardian*, 7 December 2016, https://www.theguardian.com/global-development/2016/dec/07/child-labour-ban gladesh-factories-rampant-overseas-development-institute-study.

[34] Anner, 'Binding Power', 8.

[35] Anner, 'Binding Power', 8.

[36] Anner, 'Binding Power', 7.

[37] Anner, 'Binding Power', 2.

[38] Simon Murphy, 'Factory That Supplied Tesco Compensated Abused Worker', *The Guardian*, 22 January 2019, https://www.theguardian.com/world/2019/jan/22/bangladeshi-factory-that-suppl ied-tesco-and-marks-and-spencer-compensates-abused-worker.

[39] Skorpen Claeson, 'Our Voices', 21.

[40] Skorpen Claeson, 'Our Voices', 21.

[41] Salminen, 'The Accord on Fire and Building Safety in Bangladesh', 420.

[42] Salminen, 'The Accord on Fire and Building Safety in Bangladesh', 421.

other hand, it allowed retailers to appear to be doing good, when they continued to exercise episodic power for ill. During the period of the Accord, they paid less to Bangladeshi suppliers than before the Accord and expected faster lead times. The Accord only addressed fire and building safety, not wages, working hours or workers' rights to unionize. Retailers continued to exert pressure on Bangladesh, while maintaining the façade that they are responsible and ethical actors. Certain retailers, like Wal-Mart and Gap, even sought to undermine the stringent fire and building safety standards of the Accord, by setting up a much weaker agreement, the Alliance. Consumers may not know the difference between the Accord and the Alliance, so signatories to the Alliance are even more culpable of 'window-dressing'.

Moreover, the Bangladesh Accord only applied in Bangladesh. Fire and building safety have not been addressed systematically in any other garment-exporting country. Wages, working hours and rights to unionize are also not being addressed in other countries. Thus, while the Accord was a force for good, it also enabled brands to continue to do harm and potentially to do more harm. In some ways, it was a smokescreen promoting an image to ill-informed consumers that brands are doing more and doing better, when they continued to act so as to perpetuate structural injustice and to use it for their own gain. The Accord expired in 2021, after a three-year extension from the initial agreement.[43] However, the Accord has a new iteration – The International Accord for Health and Safety in the Textile and Garment Industry – which 187 brands have signed up to. Currently only a twenty-six-month agreement, it seeks to maintain the successes of the Bangladesh Accord, including legal enforceability and independent factory inspections, and is currently engaging in feasibility studies in various garment-exporting countries.[44]

Deliberate structural injustice

The large-scale forces that have created the conditions for sweatshop labour today are not the fault of any one agent. Sweatshop labour is not some masterplan. Instead, it has emerged from the confluence of a history of colonialism, global

---

[43]The Bangladeshi government is seeking to expel the Accord office from Dhaka and to take over factory inspections itself via the Bangladesh Garment Manufacturers and Exporters Association, whose board consists of labour groups, brand representatives and factory owners. This new council has no legal authority. Campaign groups are livid because the government does not have the capacity of the Accord for factory inspections and such a move threatens the progress the Accord has made so far. They are calling for the retailers, as well as Northern governments, to pressure the Bangladeshi government to allow the Accord to continue its work. But brands are pushing for this new, weaker form of regulation, to effectively return to a system of self-monitoring. Elizabeth Paton, 'Fears for Bangladesh Accord', New York Times, 28 May 2021, https://www.nytimes.com/2021/05/28/business/bangladesh-worker-safety-accord.html.

[44]International Accord, 'About Us', 2022, https://internationalaccord.org/about-us.

economic restructuring in the postcolonial and globalized neoliberal eras, endemic poverty, gender stereotyping and rampant consumer culture in the Global North, as well as countless other factors. As Iris Young argues,

> Structural injustice is a kind of moral wrong distinct from the wrongful action of an individual agent or the repressive policies of a state. Structural injustice occurs as a consequence of many individuals and institutions acting to pursue their particular goals and interests, for the most part acting within the limits of accepted rules and norms.[45]

However, what the Bangladesh Accord highlights is that MNCs have the dispositional power to effect structural change. These agents have the power to change the rules of the game. MNCs have the capacity to alleviate the worst aspects of sweatshop labour – the race to the bottom that sacrifices workers' safety for the sake of increased profits. The largest MNCs had the capacity to implement these sorts of changes for decades, but until 2013 when they were forced by the worst industrial disaster in the history of the apparel industry, and the subsequent media attention and consumer pressure, they failed to do so. They are continuing to fail to implement these basic structural changes in all countries apart from Bangladesh. There are global corporations operating in Bangladesh who failed to sign the Accord.[46] And now that the Accord has run out, it remains to be seen whether signatories will continue to implement these limited changes. Omitting to make basic changes in the global garment industry, such as improving fire and building safety in all garment-exporting countries, is an exercise of episodic power; corporations with the capacity to be able to effect structural change are *choosing* not to do so. In fact, now the heat is off as time has passed since Rana Plaza, MNCs are actively working to undermine the restoration of a legally binding accountability mechanism in order to return to the good old days when they could openly flout safety regulations, and they have used the Covid-19 pandemic to push down prices and force suppliers to bear the costs of pandemic safety measures.[47]

The 'deliberate' aspect of this structural injustice is, therefore, not the creation of the injustice in the first place, but rather the deliberate *maintenance* of the injustice in order to continue extracting benefits. Where actors are acting deliberately to maintain structural injustice, I believe this raises questions about responsibility that were not adequately addressed by Young's original theory

---

[45]Iris Marion Young, *Responsibility for Justice* (Oxford: Oxford University Press, 2011), 52.

[46]Jasmin Malik Chua, '15 Major Retailers That Haven't Signed the Bangladesh Safety Agreement', Ecouterre, http://www.ecouterre.com/15-major-retailers-that-havent-signed-the-bangladesh-safety-agreement/.

[47]Paton, 'Fears for Bangladesh Accord'.

of responsibility for structural injustice. It is not sufficient to claim that these agents bear mere political responsibility – the same responsibility as ordinary individuals – for the injustice; rather, because they exercise power in order to maintain the injustice, they deserve to be blamed.

Avoidable structural injustice: Global poverty

Global poverty as structural injustice

In 1990, 1.85 billion people (36 per cent of the world's population) lived below the international poverty line of US$1 per day. By 2015, this declined to 702 million people (9.6 per cent of the world's population) living below the updated poverty line of US$ 1.90 a day.[48] The World Bank hailed this as a success; the Bank president at the time, Jim Yong Kim said that 'This is the best story in the world today – these projections show us that we are the first generation in human history that can end extreme poverty.'[49] But five years on the Bank is less optimistic. According to its own calculations, the Covid-19 pandemic threatens to plunge between 88 and 115 million people back into extreme poverty.[50] Climate change and armed conflict are also threatening to plunge hundreds of millions more people into poverty.

Defining poverty has generated much debate among political theorists, philosophers, development economists and practitioners. The World Bank poverty line is widely thought to be an inadequate way to measure poverty because it is too narrow and context-insensitive. A range of alternatives have been proposed including the basic needs approach, the capabilities approach and the rights-based approach.[51] The UN has evolved its approach from the poverty line to multidimensional indicators; first the Human Development Index (HDI) and then the Multidimensional Poverty Index (MPI). From a critical perspective, theorists and anti-poverty advocates emphasize that poverty is a relational problem that encompasses social exclusion, subordination and powerlessness.[52] As such,

---

[48]The World Bank, 'World Bank Forecasts Global Poverty to Fall Below 10% for First Time; Major Hurdles Remain in Goal to End Poverty by 2030', 2015, https://www.worldbank.org/en/news/press-release/2015/10/04/world-bank-forecasts-global-poverty-to-fall-below-10-for-first-time-major-hurd les-remain-in-goal-to-end-poverty-by-2030. This updated poverty line is adjusted for purchasing power parity (PPP).
[49]Bank, 'World Bank Forecasts Global Poverty to Fall Below 10% for First Time; Major Hurdles Remain in Goal to End Poverty by 2030'.
[50]The World Bank, 'Reversals of Fortune' (Washington, DC, 2020), V.
[51]Christian Barry and Scott Wisor, 'Global Poverty', *International Encyclopedia of Ethics*, 2013: 2162–74.
[52]Monique Deveaux, 'Beyond the Redistributive Paradigm: What Philosophers Can Learn from Poor-Led Politics', in *Ethical Issues in Poverty Alleviation*, ed. Helmut P. Gaisbauer, Goffried Schweiger, Clemens Sedmak. Dordrecht (Springer Netherlands, 2016), 230.

redistributing resources only captures one aspect of the problem. Alison Jaggar argues that all of these approaches have been developed by officials and experts who do not experience poverty, which calls into question their credibility both epistemically and morally.[53] Jaggar was part of a large, multidisciplinary team of researchers who developed a new multidimensional indicator of poverty through qualitative interviews with poor communities in a range of countries, the Individual Deprivation Measure (IDM). The IDM has fifteen indicators and is fundamentally gender- and context-sensitive.[54]

I think that the IDM is a huge improvement in the arena of public policy for measuring and tackling poverty. But here I want to delve a bit further into what the structural injustice approach can add to thinking about poverty as a form of injustice, drawing on Young's five faces of oppression. Young's theory was written in the context of the United States in the 1990s and she stated in the epilogue to *Justice and the Politics of Difference* that different forms of oppression might be more relevant in the international and global spheres.[55] We have just seen that sweatshop labour is a form of exploitation, which is one of Young's five faces. I suggest that poverty can be understood as encompassing three of Young's other faces with some revisions – marginalization, powerlessness and violence – and I will add *material deprivation*.

Young defines marginalization as follows: 'Marginals are people the system of labor cannot or will not use. Not only in Third World capitalist countries, but also in most Western capitalist societies, there is a growing underclass of people permanently confined to lives of social marginality, most of whom are racially marked.'[56] Marginalization is always multifaceted, but Young was looking at the context of Western welfare-capitalist societies. In that context, Young argues that marginalization is a combination of material deprivation, deprivation of rights and freedoms (such as the right not to be arbitrarily interfered with by state bureaucracy), and a sense of 'uselessness, boredom, and lack of self-respect'.[57]

---

[53]Alison M. Jaggar, 'Measuring Gendered Poverty: Morality and Methodology', in *British Philosophical Postgraduate Association*, 2018, 7, 1–22.

[54]The fifteen indicators are food, water, shelter, health, education, energy/fuel, sanitation, relationships, clothing, violence, family planning, environment, voice, time-use and work.

[55]She writes,

> The context-bound character of the theorizing in this book begins to emerge when we inquire about oppression in contexts other than Western societies. The five criteria of oppression that I have developed may be useful starting points for asking what oppression means in Asia, Latin America, or Africa, but serious revision of some of these criteria, or even their wholesale replacement, may be required. The categories of exploitation and cultural imperialism may stand more or less as I have defined them. But marginalization, powerlessness, and violence must be rethought, and perhaps recombined. There may be need for additional categories to describe oppression in these contexts. (Young, *Justice and the Politics of Difference*, 258)

[56]Young, *Justice and the Politics of Difference*, 53.

[57]Young, *Justice and the Politics of Difference*, 55.

Young argues that extreme material deprivation is to some extent alleviated by the welfare state, so the other two issues are more pressing.[58] In the global context, however, material deprivation is pressing, because for many citizens of poor countries there is no welfare state to fall back on. While poor states might have the responsibility to address material deprivation, they often lack the capacity. In fact, I suggest it is more useful *to separate material deprivation into its own category of oppression in the global context*, precisely because there is no global safety net and no local safety nets for large segments of the world's population.

Moreover, the other two aspects of marginalization Young identified in the United States need to be rethought in the global context. The boredom, uselessness and lack of self-respect experienced by marginals living 'a comfortable material life' in rich countries, such as the elderly, seem less applicable to the global poor, who are engaged in subsistence survival and work in the informal economy to meet their needs; the world's poor can be extremely busy and lack leisure time.[59] This is especially the case for women who might be engaged in informal labour and also face the relentless tasks of childcare and domestic labour: the famous 'double burden'. But the problem of arbitrary interference is highly relevant, because aid agencies and other international civil society actors or international institutions often decide what the poor need without input from the poor themselves. Marginalization in the context of the global poor, then, might best be defined as exclusion from the global economy, which generates vulnerability to arbitrary interference from state and non-state actors, including NGOs, civil society and MNCs.

In advanced capitalist societies, Young ties powerlessness to the division of labour. The powerless are contrasted to professionals: 'The powerless lack the authority, status, and sense of self that professionals tend to have.'[60] In contrast to professionals, the powerless do not have the opportunity to expand their skillset and progress up the professional ranks. They do not influence the actions of other people and have little autonomy at work. And they are not afforded the more general privilege of 'respectability', which can open doors outside the workplace. In the context of the global poor, this again captures some of what powerlessness entails, but not all of it. Lack of 'respectability' and a lack of opportunity to develop a skillset and progress up the ranks are relevant. But the world's poorest people sometimes do have autonomy at work. Often the poor work in the informal economy and develop small businesses based on what skills they have, like cooking, sewing or agriculture.[61]

---

[58]Young, *Justice and the Politics of Difference*, 53–4.

[59]Daryl Collins et al., *Portfolios of the Poor: How the World's Poor Live on $2 a Day* (Princeton, NJ: Princeton University Press, 2011).

[60]Young, *Justice and the Politics of Difference*, 57.

[61]Abhijit V. Banerjee and Esther Duflo, 'The Economic Lives of the Poor', *Journal of Economic Perspectives* 21, no. 1 (2007): 141–67.

Powerlessness for the poorest in the Global South might better be captured by a lack of access to financial services, opportunities and infrastructure. Nobel Prize winning economists Abhijit Banerjee and Esther Duflo explain the behaviour of the poor by looking at the constraints that they face.[62] In terms of financial constraints, the poor don't have access to formal credit and they don't have access to health insurance or life insurance.[63] The only asset the poor tend to own is land, but they often don't have the titles to the land because of a lack of historical record-keeping, which makes it difficult to sell and so they spend time protecting it. In terms of infrastructure, availability of electricity, tap water and basic sanitation is variable across poor countries. Access to education and healthcare is improving, but the quality of education and healthcare provided for the poor tends to be low. The cumulative effect of a lack of financial services, basic infrastructure and opportunities makes it difficult for the poor to live their lives in a way that promotes self-development and renders them vulnerable to more powerful and richer individuals and groups.

Young discusses violence in the US context where members of certain social groups are vulnerable to random violent attacks or harassment and intimidation, including women, members of racialized groups and LGBT people, among others.[64] Theorists of justice rarely discuss this issue, either because they see it as an interpersonal harm or because it is not a problem that distributive justice approaches can capture.[65] But Young argues that this violence is an issue of social injustice because of 'its systemic character, its existence as a social practice'.[66] Anyone who is a member of a marked social group knows 'that they are *liable* to violation, solely on account of their group identity'. The woman who jogs at night, the African American who knocks on a stranger's door, the trans person in the bustling night-time city centre – all know they are vulnerable to at least harassment and intimidation, and at worst injury or death.

Young's discussion of violence, however, still refers to 'personal violence'. Since Johan Galtung introduced the term in 1969, theorists of poverty have argued that poverty is a form of 'structural violence'. The structures of inequality that maintain poverty 'are violent because they result in avoidable deaths, illness, and injury; and they reproduce violence by marginalizing people and communities, constraining their capabilities and agency, assaulting their dignity, and sustaining inequalities'.[67] Galtung was the founder of Peace Studies and

---

[62]Banerjee and Duflo, 'The Economic Lives of the Poor'.

[63]Collins et al. argue that the poor do 'manage' to save some money through a combination of storing money at home, with other people, with banks or savings-and-loans clubs. Collins et al., *Portfolios of the Poor*, 3.

[64]Young, *Justice and the Politics of Difference*, 61.

[65]Young, *Justice and the Politics of Difference*, 61–3.

[66]Young, *Justice and the Politics of Difference*, 62.

[67]Barbara Rylko-Bauer and Paul Farmer, 'Structural Violence, Poverty, and Social Suffering', in *The Oxford Handbook of the Social Science of Poverty*, ed. David Brady and Linda M. Burton (Oxford: Oxford University Press, 2016), 47.

he argued that peace meant not only the absence of war or personal violence but also 'the absence of structural violence'.[68] Violence, for Galtung, is defined as *the difference between the potential and the actual*;[69] 'when the potential is higher than the actual is by definition avoidable, and when it is avoidable, then violence is present'.[70] For instance, death from tuberculosis in the eighteenth century was probably unavoidable, but a person dying of tuberculosis today, when this is a preventable disease, is the victim of structural violence.[71] Similarly, when a person died at age thirty in the neolithic period, that was unavoidable, but when a person dies aged thirty today due to poverty, that is structural violence.[72] Structural violence occurs when no actor directly commits violence on the person; 'The violence is built into the structure and shows up as unequal power and consequently as unequal life chances.'[73] When it comes to poverty, 'if people are starving when this is objectively avoidable, then violence is committed, regardless of whether there is a clear subject-action-object relation'.[74]

Paul Farmer's work has highlighted that structural violence is 'hard to describe' because it is distant geographically, culturally and socially from the Global North; it is invisible because it is perceived as natural or inevitable, in contrast to dramatic forms of violence like war; and it is massive, the numbers are overwhelming and unfathomable.[75] Farmer argues for 'the primacy of poverty' in terms of structural violence, and highlights its connection to other forms of violence; for instance, poverty is often the precondition for direct violence or genocide.[76] Farmer and Rylko-Bauer surveyed the relevant literature from 1997 to 2012 and found that the concept of structural violence has become embedded in the social sciences and public health.[77] It has been operationalized in the United States' National Index of Violence and Harm, which quantifies direct violence as well as violence arising from 'the structuring of society overall'.[78] Its variables of structural harm include social negligence in addressing 'basic human needs' such as food, housing, healthcare and education; infant mortality and life expectancy; employment discrimination; poverty disparity along the lines of class, race, gender and age; and gang membership.[79] As Rylko-Bauer and Farmer put it, 'The emphasis on

---

[68]Johan Galtung, 'Violence, Peace, and Peace Research', *Journal of Peace Research* 6, no. 3 (1969): 183.

[69]Galtung, 'Violence, Peace, and Peace Research', 168.

[70]Galtung, 'Violence, Peace, and Peace Research', 169.

[71]Galtung, 'Violence, Peace, and Peace Research', 168.

[72]Galtung, 'Violence, Peace, and Peace Research', 169.

[73]Galtung, 'Violence, Peace, and Peace Research', 170–1.

[74]Galtung, 'Violence, Peace, and Peace Research', 171.

[75]Rylko-Bauer and Farmer, 'Structural Violence, Poverty, and Social Suffering', 52.

[76]Rylko-Bauer and Farmer, 'Structural Violence, Poverty, and Social Suffering', 52, 53–5.

[77]Rylko-Bauer and Farmer, 'Structural Violence, Poverty, and Social Suffering', 56.

[78]Rylko-Bauer and Farmer, 'Structural Violence, Poverty, and Social Suffering', 57–8.

[79]Rylko-Bauer and Farmer, 'Structural Violence, Poverty, and Social Suffering', 58.

avoidable harm is at the heart of structural violence and raises issues of social responsibility.'[80]

Defining poverty as a combination of forms of oppression better enables an intersectional analysis than solely economic indicators. The majority of the world's poorest people live in sub-Saharan Africa and South Asia; they are Black, Indigenous and people of colour (BIPOC). Understanding poverty involves understanding why it is people of colour who are more likely to be marginalized from the global economy, to experience material deprivation and to be powerless in relation to these circumstances. It is often cited that women make up 70 per cent of the world's poor. There is a lack of statistical evidence for this claim because, as Sylvia Chant points out, sex-disaggregated data is not available across all countries.[81] Chant argues that the idea of the 'feminization of poverty' should be changed to the 'feminization of responsibility and obligation' which accounts for the ways in which 'women seem to have progressively less choice other than to assume the burden of dealing with poverty, and that their growing responsibilities have not been matched by a notable increase in agency, power to (re-)negotiate men's inputs, or personal reward'.[82] Chant also points out that the World Bank's focus on formal income neglects the fact that women are more likely to work in the informal economy, women suffer from 'time poverty' because of their domestic and reproductive responsibilities which are not accounted for in measures of income, and 'asset poverty' because they are less likely to own land or property. However, an oppression-based perspective on poverty again provides insight. Women are more likely to be marginalized from the formal economy because of their secondary status in the labour market, their responsibilities for reproductive labour and their lack of access to credit due to lack of ownership. Women can also be marginalized within the household in terms of access to resources. Women can experience powerlessness due to a status deficit both at home and in the economy. And women are rendered more vulnerable to structural violence because of these other forms of oppression.

Therefore, thinking about the injustices faced by the global poor through the lens of oppression, they are material deprivation, marginalization, powerlessness and structural violence. These are forms of oppression because the global poor are prevented from developing the capacity for self-development, and it also invites domination by preventing the poor from self-determining; often decisions are made on behalf of the global poor rather than by or with them.

---

[80]Rylko-Bauer and Farmer, 'Structural Violence, Poverty, and Social Suffering', 63.

[81]Sylvia Chant, 'Re-Thinking the "Feminization of Poverty" in Relation to Aggregate Gender Indices', *Journal of Human Development* 7, no. 2 (2006): 201–20.

[82]Chant, 'Re-Thinking the "Feminization of Poverty" in Relation to Aggregate Gender Indices', 212.

Poverty and power

As well as the question of how to define poverty, Western philosophers have focused on the question of who bears responsibility for it.[83] Their focus has been almost exclusively on the ways in which affluent individuals are morally responsible. Peter Singer argued that affluent individuals have a duty to assist those living in poverty. Others argue that affluent individuals are morally responsible for contributing to an unjust global economic order that privileges them and harms the poor. The emphasis is on poverty as a *contemporary* problem which can be solved by *individuals* in rich countries giving more of their income to charity or voting for leaders who will do more to tackle global poverty. But this discourse distracts from the fact that poverty is a *structural* and *political* problem. The moral conscience of affluent individuals in the Global North is not where the action is theoretically, politically or even morally. Understanding global poverty as a *structural* injustice requires an analysis of the underlying structures that create and maintain global poverty. Jason Hickel argues that the presentist poverty discourse obscures the long causal history of global poverty. In the development arena, experts start from the first World Bank global poverty statistics published in 1981, or the baseline of the UN Millennium Development Goals, 1990. He provides an alternative history of how current global poverty came to be, which provides much greater insight into the *structure* of global poverty and its contingency.[84]

For much of human history, living standards were comparable between people living in different parts of the world. In 1500, China and India controlled 65 per cent of the world economy. Up until 1800, living standards in Asia were better than those in Europe, with ten years more life expectancy, superior transport, better sanitation, public health and nutrition. But everything changed with European colonialism and the slave trade. In the 'New World', when the Spanish 'discovered' Latin America, they stole over 100 million kilograms of silver between 1500 and 1800 by killing 95 per cent of the Indigenous population through genocide and the spread of disease. European countries traded silver with China and India, allowing them to catch up with the larger Asian economies. European powers set up colonies in the New World and enslaved people from Africa, forcibly transporting them to the New World to work the land. The sugar and cotton industries contributed 25–30 million 'ghost acres' of productive land to Britain, which powered the Industrial Revolution. The colonies produced the products that suited the metropoles and the metropoles exported their

---

[83]Barry and Wisor, 'Global Poverty'.
[84]The following is a summary of Jason's Hickel's The Divide, Parts 2 and 3. Unless otherwise referenced, the facts here are taken from this text and only direct quotes are cited. Jason Hickel, *The Divide: A Brief Guide to Global Inequality and Its Solutions* (London: Windmill Books, 2017).

commodities to the colonies. The colonies depended on this exchange because they were prevented from developing their own industries. In Asia, Britain began the process of colonizing India in the early 1600s with the East India Company, which worked on securing trade routes, and by the 1800s, the British government had control over the country. It secured access to Chinese markets through the aggressive Opium Wars in the mid-1800s. By this point, Europeans' share of global GDP had increased to 60 per cent.

A financial crisis hit in the late nineteenth century, which precipitated the 'scramble for Africa': a bid to colonize new countries to extract precious resources and to create new dependent markets. In 1870, only 10 per cent of Africa was controlled by European powers, by 1914, it was 90 per cent. By 1913, 'Europe owned somewhere between one-third and one-half of the domestic capital of Asia and Africa, and more than three-quarters of their industrial capital.'[85] While Latin American countries gained independence from Europe under the leadership of Simón Bolívar in the early 1800s, the United States asserted its dominion over the continent under the 1823 Monroe Doctrine, which declared that the United States would militarily intervene in any attempt by Europe to recolonize Latin America. In effect, the doctrine was used to keep Latin America open to US economic interests and justified multiple invasions and occupations.

At this stage, what I would add to Hickel's analysis are the gendered and racialized dynamics of the development of today's capitalist system. Cedric J. Robinson highlighted the racist ideology that underpinned processes of colonial enclosure, extraction, enslavement and murder. Certain groups were categorized as racially inferior (in Europe: the Irish, Jews, Slavs and Roma), globally non-white people. Capitalism differentiated groups in order to expropriate their labour and resources.[86] Maria Mies highlights the ways in which capitalism drew on the reproductive labour of women, both in terms of raising children and doing the necessary domestic and caring labour to support the labour force. She notes the twin processes of colonization and 'housewifization' that contributed to capitalist development: the colonies and women suffered from 'superexploitation' – they were not exploited in formal labour markets, rather their resources and labour were considered as natural and outside of the processes of production.[87]

All of this may seem like a long time in the past, but it instantiated the contours of today's trading systems and power relations between the so-called developed and developing world. Moreover, Europe and North America have worked hard ever since to maintain their advantages carved out by force in the colonial period. During the period of decolonization in the 1960s–1970s, many newly liberated

---

[85]Hickel, *The Divide*, 99.
[86]Cedric J. Robinson, *Black Marxism: The Making of the Black Radical Tradition*, 2020th edn (London: Penguin Classics, 1983).
[87]Maria Mies, *Patriarchy and Accumulation on a World Scale: Women in the International Division of Labour*, 3rd edn (London: Zed Books, 2014).

countries tried to emulate Europe and North America's Keynesian policies, which had lifted these regions out of the Great Depression and post-war crises. Keynes argued that the way out of economic depression was to increase government spending and encourage higher wages in order to restimulate the economy. The Argentine economist Raúl Prebisch argued that similar principles should be applied to newly independent countries with additional measures, including protectionism to build up domestic industries that were suppressed under colonialism, and to develop the state and society, and land reform, nationalizing natural resources and key industries for the benefit of citizens. Prebisch's idea of New International Economic Order (NIEO) was adopted in a UN General Assembly resolution in 1974. These policies of 'developmentalism' were successful: per capita income grew in the Global South at a rate of 3.2 per cent during the 1960s–1970s, domestic wealth gaps shrunk and human welfare improved. Third World countries worked together on this project, first as the Non-Aligned Movement and then as the G77 from 1964. As Hickel puts it, 'the fight against poverty and underdevelopment during this period was understood as a *political* battle. It sought to challenge the prevailing distribution of power and resources around the world.'[88]

The Global North was horrified by the restricted access to previously open markets and the growing bargaining power of labour in these industrializing countries. Instead of the older imperial and discredited strategy of colonization, the United States turned to the military coup. In many Global South countries, the United States either installed or supported authoritarian leaders and dictators who would guarantee preferential trading terms for the West. Other Global North countries got involved in coups and assassinations too, such as Britain in Uganda, Portugal in Angola and France installed dictators across 'Françafrique'. But this strongarm tactic was soon displaced by more stealthy and ultimately crippling forms of coercion and interference.

Third World debt started as a quick fix to a short-term problem, which started with the 1967 Six-Day War in which Israel attacked Egypt and annexed neighbouring territories, including Gaza and the Sinai Peninsula from Egypt; East Jerusalem and the West Bank from Jordan; and the Golan Heights from Syria.[89] In 1973, Arab states tried to recapture the land, but the United States stepped in supporting Israel militarily. The Organization of Petroleum Exporting Countries (OPEC) hiked up oil prices by 70 per cent in response. Despite reaching a settlement, the price hikes left the OPEC awash with money and the banks didn't know what to do with it, so they invested in loans to Third World countries. What started as a quick fix turned into a multi-trillion-dollar industry. Banks focused on dictatorships, who had no qualms about signing up their populations to decades

---

[88]Hickel, *The Divide*, 139.
[89]Hickel, *The Divide*, 149.

of debt repayments. The loans were tied to the US dollar, so when US interest rates were suddenly hiked up by 21 per cent in 1981, defaults were inevitable. Mexico was the first to default in 1982, followed by Brazil and Argentina, sparking the Third World Debt Crisis. Looking for a solution, the G7 repurposed the IMF from an organization designed to avoid another depression by lending to governments with balance of payments problems, to a Third World debt collector. It helped finance debt repayments to banks, so long as member states agreed to 'Structural Adjustment Programmes' (SAPs). This meant cutting government spending on health, education and other public services and funnelling this money to debt repayments. They were also forced to deregulate their economies to encourage foreign direct investment. This one-size-fits-all policy was applied across Global South countries who were struggling to repay debts. SAPs are widely believed to have been a catastrophe for the people of the Global South. Growth rates plummeted to 0.7 per cent in the 1980s–1990s, developmentalism was stopped in its tracks. Between 1980 and 2012, the Global South paid $13 trillion in debt repayments. The money being paid does not even cover the initial loans, instead it services compound interest on the loans.

Debt is only one of the stealth tactics, 'free trade' is another. After the Second World War, world trade was governed by a Bretton Woods institution, the General Agreement on Tariffs and Trade (GATT), which was designed to lower tariffs among industrialized countries through collective bargaining. The GATT was replaced in 1995 by an altogether more aggressive organization – the World Trade Organization (WTO). While the WTO is also based on the principle of collective bargaining, bargaining power depends on market size and so rich countries end up getting what they want. Under WTO rules, poor countries are not allowed to subsidize industries and must maintain fully 'free' trade; however, rich countries do not reciprocate. Agriculture is the most famous example: the US Farm Bill and the European Common Agricultural Policy ensure that American and European agriculture is subsidized to the tune of $374 billion per year. The excess product is dumped on the global market for less than it costs to produce, undermining the capacity of Global South countries to compete.

Extraction of resources and wealth from the Global South is ongoing. Illicit financial flows refer to any money illegally transferred from one country to another. Some of this money is transferred by corrupt regimes – around 3 per cent – but the vast majority of it (around 80 per cent) is through trade misinvoicing. This could involve sending money to offshore tax havens or lying about the costs of items on invoices ('transfer mispricing'). The Global South has lost as much as $14.3 trillion from 2008 to 2018 in illicit financial flows. The rest comes from 'hot money' – transferring capital from one country to another in order to speculate on interest rates and exchange rates. A land grab is defined as a transfer of over five hundred acres converted from smallholder production, collective use or ecosystems services to commercial production. Following the world food price crisis in 2007, rich countries started buying up land in poor countries in order to take advantage of inflated prices. Britain, the United States, China and India were the biggest offenders; 4 per cent of Africa's land mass was grabbed between 2000 and 2010.

Again, I want to add to Hickel's analysis that the racial and gender dynamics persisted throughout the de- and post-colonial period. Half of all people living in extreme poverty in 2015 lived in sub-Saharan Africa and the World Bank predicts that by 2030, nine out of ten people living in extreme poverty will be in this region. Black African bodies are seen as disposable in the contemporary global economic and political system. Also, it is historically colonized and subjugated populations in Africa, Asia and Latin America that labour in sweatshops and are vulnerable to the most egregious forms of exploitation. Furthermore, it is women who are more vulnerable to poverty and exploitation due to their secondary status in the household and labour markets. Women were disproportionately affected by SAPs, because where the state pulled out, women stepped in to fulfil caring and educational responsibilities.[90] The world's poorest are a class, but their make-up is intrinsically bound up with gender and race.

Considering this lens on global poverty, the ideas that individuals in the North should forgo treats and give that money instead to charity (as Singer argues), or that individuals in the North are somehow blameworthy for the policies of powerful states and international organizations, seem inept for understanding what should be done to tackle poverty and who bears responsibility for it. These theories are superficial and have captured the hearts and minds of political philosophers for far too long. Even theories that challenge the global distribution of resources are insufficient, because they fail to engage with the underlying power structures, rules and institutions that created poverty in the first place and sustain it over time. It is time to stop basing theories of responsibility for global poverty on white liberal guilt; instead, structural and political analysis and solutions are required.

Avoidable structural injustice

Global poverty, I suggest, is an avoidable structural injustice, rather than a deliberate structural injustice. In contrast to sweatshop labour, where corporations actively work to maintain sweatshop conditions, the global system is not actively trying to keep people from living a minimally decent life. The world's poorest people are collateral damage from a system that is designed to benefit rich countries, corporations and billionaires. However, extreme deprivation is the

---

[90]Haleh Afsar and Carolyne Dennis, *Women and Adjustment Politics in the Third World* (London: Palgrave Macmillan, 1992).

foreseeable outcome of decisions by those actors in order to benefit themselves, and there are known measures they could take to alleviate it.

It could be objected from a Marxist perspective that the global system does actively work to maintain marginalization from the economy. As Marx argued, capitalism needs a reserve army of labour. In the nineteenth and early twentieth centuries, the reserve army consisted of the unemployed in domestic, industrializing economies. But in the era of the fully globalized economy, jobs can be transferred internationally at high speed and the reserve army of labour is global. However, the unemployed do not have to live in a state of extreme material deprivation in order to be of use to the capitalist system. This has been shown in welfare-capitalist economies, which provide the unemployed with the means to meet their most basic material needs. Capitalism can have its reserve army of labour (marginalization from the economy) while avoiding extreme material deprivation. The material deprivation experienced by the world's poorest people is not deliberately intended and maintained because in itself it does not benefit the capitalist class.

It could be objected that welfare-capitalist economies are dependent on the continuing poverty and exploitation of the poorest. Systemically, that seems correct.[91] However, the lack of access to the means of subsistence for the world's poorest is avoidable; from 2010 to 2020, the world's richest 1 per cent of the population captured 54 per cent of new wealth, and this accelerated to 63 per cent in 2019–20.[92] Redistribution of wealth could alleviate extreme poverty, even if it didn't tackle the underlying power structures that maintain the South's domination by the North.

I also believe it would be inaccurate to categorize global poverty as a pure structural injustice because there are multiple solutions on the table for alleviating it within the existing system: solutions that are well-known and have been for a long time. The problem is that the actors with the capacity to implement these changes refuse to do so. One solution that has been circulated for decades is debt relief. We have seen that the problem of Third World debt is relatively recent – it began in the 1970s, only fifty years ago. Dropping debt does not have to amount to a wholesale cancellation of all debts. There are many proposals on the table from all-out cancellation to more moderate forms of debt relief.[93] Indeed, there has already been an international attempt at debt relief following sustained pressure from civil society in the late 1990s – the Highly Indebted Poor Countries initiative (HIPC). Forty of the world's poorest countries were relieved

---

[91]This is what World-Systems theorists and dependency economists argue.
[92]Oxfam International, 'Richest 1% Bag Nearly Twice as Much Wealth as the Rest of the World Put Together over the Past Two Years', *Oxfam International*, 16 January 2023, https://www.oxfam.org/en/press-releases/richest-1-bag-nearly-twice-much-wealth-rest-world-put-together-over-past-two-years#:~:text=According to Credit Suisse%2C individuals,record-smashing peak in 2021.
[93]Noreena Hertz, 'Why We Must Defuse the Debt Threat', *Contributions to Political Economy* 24 (2005): 123–33..

of some debt. However, that initiative was only moderately successful; in some cases, the debt that was relieved has been replaced by new debts.[94]

A one-off amnesty on some debt will not be effective if the global economic system continues to operate solely for the benefit of the Global North. The poorest countries remain commodity dependent and therefore prone to shocks; what they need is to build infrastructure.[95] The policies of the NIFO were effective at lifting Global South countries out of poverty. A new sustainable and gender-sensitive NIEO is another option on the table, which would need to be updated to curb illicit financial flows and land grabbing.

But, again, this will not be successful if the global political and economic system continues to work against the Global South. The IMF, World Bank and WTO are undemocratic and unaccountable. The main accountability gap in the IMF and World Bank is a lack of representation of all member states.[96] From their inception, the Board of Executive Directors in both institutions only held permanent seats for the largest members (United States, Germany, France, Japan, UK, Saudi Arabia, Russia and China). All other countries were grouped into constituencies and represented by one person: in the IMF the twenty-one Anglophone African countries had one representative and only 3.26 per cent voting share, at the World Bank it's a 4.07 per cent share.[97] In 2010, both the IMF and World Bank were finally moved to embrace some reform. Quota shares were reformed to give 6.2 per cent more voting power to developing countries in the IMF and 3 per cent in the World Bank; but due to the intricacies of the agreements, the changes were in effect 'microscopic'.[98] In 2016, the IMF amended its Articles of Agreement to have an all-elected Executive Board.[99] At the WTO most decisions are made in informal 'Green Room' meetings called at the behest of the Quad (the United States, EU, Japan and Canada).[100] Decisions are therefore made without the input of Global South countries but they are bound by the decisions because the WTO is 'single-undertaking': countries have to accept all of its decisions.

---

[94]Dino Merotto, Tihomir Stucka, and Mark Roland Thomas, 'African Debt since HIPC: How Clean Is the Slate?' (Washington, DC, 2015).

[95]Merotto, Stucka and Thomas, Tihomir Stucka, and Mark Roland Thomas, 'African Debt since HIPC: How Clean Is the Slate?'.

[96]Ngaire Woods, 'Making the IMF and World Bank More Accountable', *International Affairs* 77, no. 1 (2001): 84.

[97]Woods, 'Making the IMF and World Bank More Accountable', 85.

[98]Jakob Vestergaard and Robert H. Wade, 'Still in the Woods: Gridlock in the IMF and the World Bank Puts Multilateralism at Risk', *Global Policy* 6, no. 1 (2015): 2, 6.

[99]IMF, 'Press Release: Historic Quota and Governance Reforms Become Effective', *International Monetary Fund*, 27 January 2016, https://www.imf.org/en/News/Articles/2015/09/14/01/49/pr1625a.

[100]Ngaire Woods and Amrita Narlikar, 'Governance and the Limits of Accountability: The WTO, the IMF, and the World Bank', *International Social Science Journal* 53, no. 170 (2001): 577; 'Civil Society Lampoon Exclusive "Green Rooms" in Protest Performance at the 12th Ministerial of the WTO', *Our World Is Not for Sale*, 14 June 2022, https://ourworldisnotforsale.net/2022-06-14_R_protest.

The belief that global governance of the economy is detrimental to the Global South is not a niche left-wing preoccupation. Many liberals agree that it is unjust and that change is urgently needed. For instance, Mathias Risse and Gabriel Wollner propose a 'New Global Deal', arguing that it isn't necessary to share left-wing views of dependency or the NIEO 'to agree with their insistence on stronger inclusion of developing countries into the global economy'.[101] Even Oxfam, a traditionally benign NGO which started its mission focusing on famine relief and evolving to extreme poverty, has come round to this way of thinking. In a recent report, 'The Inequality Virus', it argues that the vast gulf between the world's richest and poorest, with half the world's population living on less than $5.50 a day, 'is the product of a flawed and exploitative economic system, which has its roots in neoliberal economics and the capture of politics by elites'.[102]

Transfers of money from the Global North to the Global South might alleviate the poverty of some individuals in the present, and that is worth doing. But poverty is a structural injustice. It is a result of the accumulation of multiple processes and actions by many disparate actors over the course of time. It has long roots in the colonial period. It is bound up with patriarchy and white supremacy. It has been exacerbated and sustained by several decades of neoliberal economic policies which expand the wealth of rich states, corporations and billionaires, while robbing poor states of their capacity to develop infrastructure and support systems for citizens. At the level of what is achievable here and now, debt relief, a new NIEO and reform of global governance are all well-established and viable options. The fact that 'structural adjustment programmes' were explicitly called structural adjustment proves that international institutions and powerful states have the capacity to change the structures that underlie global poverty for the worse *or* for the better. There is no need for hundreds of millions of people to struggle for basic survival, facing marginalization from the global economy, powerlessness, extreme material deprivation, and structural violence; this structural injustice could be mitigated.

Climate change: Pure structural injustice

Climate change as structural injustice

Climate change is occurring because a build-up of carbon dioxide in the atmosphere is causing it to absorb more heat, thus warming the planet. The main

---

[101]Mathias Risse and Gabriel Wollner, *On Trade Justice: A Philosophical Plea for a New Global Deal* (Oxford: Oxford University Press, 2019), 38.
[102]Oxfam International, 'The Inequality Virus' (Oxford, 2021), 11.

reason for the excess carbon dioxide is the burning of fossil fuels. The delicate balance of the atmosphere is being rapidly undermined, which is causing an increase in extreme weather events, with disastrous effects for human, animal and plant life, including drought, flooding, landslides, hurricanes, cyclones, forest fires and rising sea levels. Our planet could become uninhabitable. The IPCC declared in 2021 that 'It is unequivocal that human influence has warmed the atmosphere, ocean and land.'[103] The report also states that this change to the climate is unprecedented and some of the damage is irreversible. The scientific consensus on climate change is now absolute. Climate change is upon us; it has been for some time.

Climate change is an injustice because it has been caused by the carbon emissions of the rich and mostly affects the poor. It is the world's poor who are first in line to be affected by the changing climate and who are the least equipped to adapt. In that sense, climate change exacerbates the existing structural injustice of poverty, including the aspects of material deprivation, marginalization from the global economy, powerlessness, and structural violence. Climate change resembles a form of structural domination: *humans are vulnerable to the arbitrary changes in the weather*, undermining their capacity for self-determination. This arbitrary interference has been caused by the cumulative effects of past and present human behaviour (particularly of humans in the Global North). Human agency is involved, but in the form of cumulatively creating a structure which is dominating. It might not be accurate to describe climate change as a structural form of domination, because it is not agential, although it has agential causes; however, like domination, it arbitrarily interferes with humans' capacity for self-determination.

Climate change is a form of oppression because it fosters *insecurity*: insecurity of life, livelihood, access to the means of subsistence, inability to plan for the future for oneself and one's family, insecurity of place and home, and by undermining the preservation of culture. All of this affects individuals' capacities for self-development. Again, it affects the poor who are most vulnerable to changes in weather and lack the capacity to adapt as individuals or at the local or state level. It affects Indigenous groups' capacities for self-development, which are often bound to specific territories with their unique flora and fauna, and cultural or spiritual significance. It also affects Indigenous groups' capacity for self-determination, because changes to habitats can offset agreements with powerful states, which are difficult to renegotiate, or they throw Indigenous groups into emergency bureaucratic processes from which they are often excluded.[104] Indigenous scholars see climate change as an intensification of

---

[103]IPCC, 'Climate Change 2021: The Physical Science Basis', 2021, 5.
[104]Kyle Whyte, 'Indigenous Climate Change Studies: Indigenizing Futures, Decolonizing the Anthropocene', *English Language Notes* 55, nos. 1–2 (2017): 154–5.

colonialism.[105] But even if climate change affects these groups imminently and most severely, it threatens to oppress *all* of the world's people with insecurity. The only likely escapees are billionaires who can move to Mars or build cities on stilts (even then, their lives will change beyond recognition).

I am going to tentatively suggest that climate change is a pure structural injustice, meaning that it is the unintended accumulation of multiple actions and processes that cannot be pinned on any one agent or group of agents. Instead, it requires systemic overhaul. This is not to say that no agents are blameworthy with regards to specific actions in relation to climate change (e.g. fossil fuel corporations' disinformation campaign), nor is it to say that no agents have a greater share of the responsibility to address it. Instead, the point is that climate change is built-in to contemporary capitalism and as such it is a pure structural injustice. To make this argument, we must look at the history of climate change.

Climate change: A brief history

Alice Bell's *Our Biggest Experiment: A History of the Climate Crisis* documents both the scientific discoveries that led to human dependency on the burning of fossil fuels for energy, as well as the scientific community's gradual realization that the burning of fossil fuels was causing climate change. It is not a linear story.

Scientists first learnt that carbon dioxide absorbs heat in 1856, when Eunice Newton Foote filled a glass cylinder with carbon dioxide and placed it by a window. She found that it became hotter than a cylinder with some air removed and others with dry and moist air. It also took a lot longer to cool down. She concluded that 'An atmosphere of that gas would give to our Earth a high temperature.'[106] This was followed by John Tyndall's similar findings in 1861. At that point, neither knew that humans were emitting vast quantities of carbon dioxide that would ultimately alter the atmosphere's composition; it was merely of scientific curiosity. Other early scientific insights include Horace de Saussure's 'heliothermometer', a device he used in the 1780s to explore how solar radiation increased with altitude in his scientific expeditions in the Alps. He thought the atmosphere worked like a solar oven: 'an early analogy for the greenhouse effect'.[107] In 1895, Svante Arrhenius presented a paper to the Royal Swedish Academy of Sciences arguing that a doubling of the earth's carbon dioxide would raise the temperature by 5–6°C. But given Arrhenius had other rather bonkers ideas, his work was dismissed almost entirely.[108]

---

[105]Whyte, 'Indigenous Climate Change Studies: Indigenizing Futures, Decolonizing the Anthropocene', 155.

[106]Alice Bell, *Our Biggest Experiment: A History of the Climate Crisis* (London: Bloomsbury, 2021), 9.

[107]Bell, *Our Biggest Experiment*, 48.

[108]Arrhenius thought that life on earth started with seeds transported through space by the pressure of light, Bell, *Our Biggest Experiment*, 75.

Other scientific breakthroughs which paved the way for climate change science include the US government investing in meteorological observations for military purposes in 1842. International cooperation followed with the establishment of the International Meteorological Organization in 1873. Meteorologists expressed concerns in the 1890s about long periods of drought in Turkestan; it relied on runoff from melting glaciers to irrigate the land, but as the glaciers shrunk, their water supply dwindled. Viennese geographer Albrecht Penck observed glaciers melting in the Alps. In 1923 he published a paper warning that Turkestan was dying and that this was a larger environmental trend. Evidence of glacier retreat and droughts was mounting and the idea that the earth was warming was becoming established among scientists. But carbon dioxide had been ruled out as the culprit at this point. Guy Callendar picked up where Arrhenius left off in 1938. He estimated that in the intervening period, humans had emitted 150,000 million tonnes of CO_2 into the atmosphere, exceeding the capacity of natural carbon sinks to absorb it. But he didn't yet argue this was a bad thing; he thought that some global warming would benefit agriculture and he was more concerned about global cooling (another ice age). His contemporaries agreed that warming was happening, but not that carbon dioxide was the cause.

July 1957 to December 1958 was the International Year of Geophysics (IGY); thirty thousand scientists, engineers and technicians across sixty-seven countries took part. There were military and strategic reasons for the project but 'ICY launched modern climate change science'.[109] It provided the funding that climate scientists had been looking for, including Roger Revelle, the 'granddaddy of climate change science' who discovered that the oceans were only absorbing one-ninth of the carbon dioxide scientists previously thought. In his 1957 paper with Hans Seuss, he wrote 'human beings are now carrying out a large-scale geophysical experiment of a kind that could not have happened in the past nor be reproduced in the future'.[110] But Revelle did not think it was time to worry, it was still a scientific curiosity. The widespread belief was that nuclear energy would replace fossil fuels, which is one of the reasons that scientists at this time did not sound the alarm.[111] Revelle's postdoc, Dave Keeling, went on to establish once and for all through his research on a volcanic outpost in Hawaii that carbon dioxide in the atmosphere had risen and that the oceans were not absorbing it. In March 1963, the first climate change conference was held that took the topic out of military geophysics and into ecology. The conference report was the first to flag concern, arguing that 'the most alarming thing about the increase of CO2 is how little is actually known about it', and that more research was urgently needed.[112]

---

[109]Bell, *Our Biggest Experiment*, 224.
[110]Bell, *Our Biggest Experiment*, 260.
[111]Bell, *Our Biggest Experiment*, 245.
[112]Bell, *Our Biggest Experiment*, 268.

Over this hundred-year period as scientists gradually became aware of carbon dioxide's role in global warming, technology and industry made rapid advances. The invention of the steam engine in the late eighteenth century was the catalyst for the Industrial Revolution. The discovery of 'rock oil' and natural gas in the 1860s, coupled with the discovery of electricity and mass-producible light bulb, generated the possibility for electric lighting in homes, workplaces and cities, for appliances like the refrigerator and, of course, the car. In 1900, there were 4,200 cars in the United States; by 1916, Henry Ford was selling 600,000 cars per year. Cars meant road-building, which meant concrete, which is an extremely high emitter of carbon. Deforestation paved the way for roads. Plastics were developed, starting in the 1840s, with Charles Goodyear patenting a strengthening process for rubber, followed by Parkesine, Celluloid, Bakelite and eventually myriad plastics by the 1930s–1940s. All of these discoveries and inventions meant that 'By the 1960s, it was hard to find any part of the US life untouched by this new, fossil energy regime. There was faster and cheaper travel, cheaper food, air conditioning as well as heating systems, and so many fun gadgets and miracle fabrics derived from oil.'[113]

This made fossil fuel companies the centre of gravity of the global economy. There was resistance to these companies from the beginning, mostly on the grounds of pollution and concerns about conservation. As we've already seen, knowledge of climate change was slow to unfold. But fossil fuel companies pushed back against all resistance. John D. Rockefeller founded Standard Oil (SO) in 1870 and by 1879, he controlled 90 per cent of America's oil refining capacity as well as dominating oil transportation. In 1914, he enlisted the PR skills of Ivy Lee to calm tensions after the bloody suppression of a coal strike. Rockefeller's monopoly was broken up in 1904, creating Exxon, Mobil, Chevron and Sohio (later the US branch of BP). But, as Bell writes, 'if anything, these companies became more powerful'.[114] There was also competition from Royal Dutch Shell, which was drilling oil in the Dutch Indies, Texaco, which discovered oil in Texas, and Mesopotamian oil, which Armenian Calouste Gulbenkian sold to Anglo-Persian (now BP), Royal Dutch Shell and French Total. Nigerian oil was drilled by BP. Colonialism and access to oil went hand-in-hand.

In the 1970s, environmentalism started to gather pace. The year 1970 saw the first Earth Day. Friends of the Earth and Greenpeace were formed. The Club of Rome published *Limits to Growth*, which argued that capitalism was going to overshoot the earth's resources leading to social collapse in the mid-twenty-first century. The UN Environment Programme was founded in 1972. And in 1974, the CIA carried out a study warning that the world was entering a new climatic

---

[113]Bell, *Our Biggest Experiment*, 229.
[114]Bell, *Our Biggest Experiment*, 192.

era, which threatened food scarcity and political instability. At this point, the fossil fuel companies mobilized. They knew that if the US government was worried, they would be in trouble. This is when the battle over climate change science really began.

The fossil fuel industry learned from the tobacco industry's PR activities in the 1950s when a link between smoking and cancer was established. The tobacco industry decided to fight science with science, investing in credible scientific research with the aim to play up the doubts, emphasizing science's commitment to questioning everything and manipulating journalism's commitment to fair and balanced reporting: 'They were turning the Enlightenment values of knowledge, scepticism and free speech in on themselves.'[115] Fossil-fuel-funded scientists published articles in popular magazines and scientific journals casting doubt on climate science: 'We now know this was a deliberate tactic to use new scientific research to distract and sometimes actively confound negative coverage.'[116] Another factor was a cultural divide between the older scientists who came of intellectual age in the Cold War and who were suspicious of the leftist tendencies of the environmental movement, and the younger climate and environmental scientists. Older generation scientists, Bill Nierenberg, Frederick Seitz and Robert Jastrow, set up the George C. Marshall Institution in 1984, which published a report in 1990 claiming that climate variation was due to the sun and would fix itself. This was popular with the right-wing White House and influenced the George Bush Sr administration's approach to climate change. This was a blow for climate change science and activism which had made significant inroads after NASA scientist James Hansen's testimony to the Senate in 1988, when he claimed that climate change was happening now and immediate action was necessary. The impact of Hansen's testimony was so significant that Bush Sr said on the 1988 campaign trail, 'Those who think we are powerless to do anything about the greenhouse effect forget about the White House effect.'[117]

But with the scientific support of the George C. Marshall Institution and climate sceptics in the White House, the fossil fuel industry sensed its moment, and 'at the start of the 1990s decided to go big on climate change scepticism as a tactic to slow the growing momentum for action'.[118] Just like the tobacco lobby before it, the plan was to 'Emphasise the uncertainty', at least this is what Exxon's public affairs department told its employees. They wanted to maintain the 'amber-light position' of Bill Nierenberg, a wait-and-see position, rather than acting now. However, climate change science continued gathering momentum. In 1988, the Intergovernmental Panel on Climate Change (IPCC) was formed,

---

[115]Bell, *Our Biggest Experiment*, 318.
[116]Bell, *Our Biggest Experiment*, 317.
[117]Bell, *Our Biggest Experiment*, 313.
[118]Bell, *Our Biggest Experiment*, 322.

with only twenty-eight countries taking part at that point. The first IPCC report paved the way for the Earth Summit in Rio in 1992. Rio led to the establishment of the UNFCCC, which set up the annual CoP meetings (Conference of the Parties signed up to the Rio Convention). By the time of the Kyoto CoP in 1997, a *New York Times* opinion poll found that 65 per cent of Americans thought that the United States should cut emissions immediately, despite a $13 million advertising campaign claiming that climate action would destroy the economy.[119] In the early 2000s, environmental NGOs finally got serious on climate change. The 2000s–2010s saw increasing media coverage and political pressure related to climate change. Greta Thunberg's 2018 school strike mobilized a new generation of climate activists.

Pure structural injustice

We can view the history of climate change through the lens of Archer's critical realism discussed in Chapter 2. Archer argues that people are born into a set of given circumstances and structures. People act within the constraints of those structures and are also enabled by them. They are situated in different social positions within structures with different capacities to affect those structures. The combination of different agents acting within structures generates unintended outcomes, which results in morphogenesis – the generation of new structures. Throughout the past two to three hundred years, scientists have made discoveries (be it the discovery of gas, oil, electricity, plastics, etc.), which they have been enabled to do by the discoveries of previous generations of scientists. These have been capitalized on by business creating new products and services, and they have been enabled to do this by processes of colonial expansion, industrialization and ongoing advances in science, engineering and tech. The combination of these processes has resulted in the emission of huge amounts of carbon dioxide. This leaves us now in a new structural situation which is the unintended outcome of the actions of past agents. Unfortunately for us, it is a dire structure in need of immediate repair. Climate change is necessarily structural. As Bell puts it,

> I'm not going to offer you villains and heroes. This is not a simple story with evil exploitative fossil-fuel baddies on one side and the goodies of renewable energy, environmentalism and climate science on the other. It's more complex than that. What's more, although individual characters played roles that we might, more or less, count as either villainous or heroic, none of them worked alone. The climate crisis is a social project – one that's always been more about the impact of groups of people than individuals.[120]

---

[119]Bell, *Our Biggest Experiment*, 328.
[120]Bell, *Our Biggest Experiment*, 16–17.

Of course, the fossil fuel industry is to blame for actively perpetuating doubt and uncertainty in the face of overwhelming certainty among the legitimate scientific community. Like the garment corporations we looked at before, fossil fuel corporations exercised power within this structure to maintain the benefits they were deriving from the structural injustice: they lobbied, set their own industry standards, implemented weak and toothless codes of corporate social responsibility, and manipulated the public into believing that their industries were essential to economic growth, and our personal and collective well-being. Identifiable agents like the Koch Brothers, the American Petroleum Institute and Exxon-Mobil bear moral responsibility for their active campaigns of disinformation and funding of denialist pseudo-science. As Bell puts it, 'The oil industry didn't start deliberately spreading doubt about climate change until the late 1980s, but it did spread doubt. We can lay the blame at its feet for at least a chunk of lost time.'[121]

Other agents exercised power too. Sociologists Riley Dunlap and Aaron McCright argue that the Reagan administration in the United States in the early 1980s exercised episodic power to quash the environmental movement, by reducing environmental regulations and appointing anti-environmentalists to key agencies like the Environmental Protection Agency and the Department of the Interior.[122] These blatant exercises of power provoked a strong backlash, so successive conservative legislators employed other forms of power. They set the agenda to exclude environmental interests and prevented the implementation of environmental policies.

However, blame should be laid not just for delaying action on climate change but for causing the problem in the first place, and for that a large share of the blame must go to rich states. While China is now the world's largest emitter of carbon, when it comes to cumulative historical emissions, it is the states of the Global North that are the biggest culprits. Taking 1850 as the base year, and then calculating the overshoot above 350 ppm atmospheric CO_2 (the safe planetary boundary which was reached in 1990), Hickel found that the United States and EU have emitted twice as much carbon as China, and that India is only responsible for 3 per cent of historical cumulative emissions. A total of 108 of 202 countries are in climate credit, with the Global North responsible for 92 per

---

[121]Bell, *Our Biggest Experiment*, 16. As Young always argued, her 'liability model' of responsibility, which attributes blame or liability, can and should be combined with the 'social connection model' of responsibility, which attributes political responsibility to all agents connected to structural injustice. This would still apply in the case of pure structural injustice, so we can blame fossil fuel corporations and others for wrongful actions, while maintaining that climate change is a pure structural injustice.
[122]Riley E. Dunlap and Aaron M. McCright, 'Challenging Climate Change', in *Climate Change and Society: Sociological Perspectives*, ed. Riley E. Dunlap and Robert J. Brulle (Oxford: Oxford University Press, 2015), 305.

cent of climate breakdown.[123] Governments not only bear moral responsibility for failing to tackle emissions, they bear legal liability for failing to fulfil legally binding climate change targets that they agreed to in international and domestic laws.

But the overall structural injustice of climate change goes deeper. The climate crisis has emerged through two centuries of innovation in science, engineering and technology, and it took time to understand what these processes were doing to damage the climate. Bell argues that social norms in the scientific and activist communities were part of the problem in failing to recognize climate change and act sooner. Climate scientists were ridiculed by other scientists for being alarmist about climate change or showing emotion, which was considered unprofessional and unscientific. There is a bias in science towards erring 'on the side of least drama'. Anyone seen as dramatic was shouted down as an activist. Scientists also tended to acquiesce to the demands of politicians instead of challenging them. And, of course, climate science lacked the funding and resources it needed, especially when it came to developing ways to communicate effectively in the public sphere about climate change.[124] Social norms among environmentalists also led to failures to focus on climate change, which they saw as an issue for pro-nuclear campaigners with links to the military, not for them with their emphasis on conservation.[125] Most importantly of all, this is a big experiment, as Revelle put it, and scientists have been learning as they go and have lacked resources throughout. If anything, Bell suggests we are lucky that we know climate change is happening, because essentially climate science has emerged through the random experiments of scientists working on other issues. Most scientists up until Dave Keeling worked on climate change as a side issue.[126]

While these social and cultural norms go some way to explaining why it took until the 2000s for climate change to be recognized as the most pressing concern of our era, the problem goes deeper still. All of this so-called progress and innovation was enabled by capitalism. And it is capitalism that is constraining action on climate change now. Capitalism depends on perpetual growth, which requires constant accumulation of natural resources and exploitation of labour. Traditionally, Marxists thought that the contradiction in capitalism that would lead to its demise is the contradiction between the production and circulation of capital. Crises of over-production regularly occur because the production of commodities outstrips demand, and capitalism has to find technological, political

---

[123]Jason Hickel, 'Quantifying National Responsibility for Climate Breakdown: An Equality-Based Attribution Approach for Carbon Dioxide Emissions in Excess of the Planetary Boundary', *The Lancet Planetary Health* 4, no. September (2020): 322.

[124]Bell, *Our Biggest Experiment*, 339–41.

[125]Bell, *Our Biggest Experiment*, 341.

[126]Bell, *Our Biggest Experiment*, 346.

or spatial fixes.[127] Eventually it will run out of these fixes. But ecological Marxists argue that there is a second contradiction in capitalism, between capitalist production and the *conditions* for that production.[128] Rather than creating the conditions for its own reproduction, capitalism is undermining these conditions by destroying the climate and the natural world. As Nancy Fraser vividly puts it, 'Simultaneously needing and rubbishing nature, capitalism is a cannibal that devours its own vital organs, like a serpent that eats its own tail.'[129]

Therefore, the emergence of the climate crisis and our knowledge of it has been the unintended consequence of multiple processes and actions by different agents accumulating over time against the background of an economic system that has a built-in tendency to destroy the conditions for its reproduction. While some agents can be blamed for their wrongful actions in relation to climate change, overall, this is an injustice which is 'baked in'[130] to our world as it is now. As climate scientist Kevin Anderson wrote in 2013,

> Perhaps at the time of the 1992 Earth Summit ... mitigation could have been achieved through significant *evolutionary changes within the political and economic hegemony*. But climate change is a cumulative issue! Now, in 2013, we ... face a very different prospect. [We have] squandered any opportunity for the 'evolutionary change' afforded by our earlier (and larger) 2°C carbon budget. Today, after two decades of bluff and lies, the remaining 2°C budget demands *revolutionary change to the political and economic hegemony*.[131]

In cases of pure structural injustice, all actors are constrained to the point where it is very difficult for them not to participate in reproducing the injustice. The injustice is unintended and there are no identifiable agents with the capacity to change it. I would suggest that stopping the climate crisis requires the creation of a new economic system that is not reliant on fossil fuels nor constant accumulation and growth. Climate change is an all-encompassing harm that cannot be changed by changing the behaviour of any particular agent; it requires a new system. However, it could also plausibly be argued that climate change was a pure structural injustice up until the 1980s when climate science became established. At that point, it was an avoidable structural injustice because there were measures that powerful agents could take to address it and they didn't, or

---

[127]David Harvey, *The New Imperialism* (Oxford: Oxford University Press, 2005).

[128]James O'Connor, 'Capitalism, Nature, Socialism: A Theoretical Introduction', *Capitalism, Nature, Socialism* 1, no. 1 (1988): 11–38.

[129]Nancy Fraser, 'Climates of Capital: For a Trans-Environmental Eco-Socialism', *New Left Review* 127, no. January–February (2021): 101.

[130]Fraser, 'Climates of Capital: For a Trans-Environmental Eco-Socialism', 102.

[131]Kevin Anderson, 'Why Carbon Prices Can't Deliver the 2°C Target', kevinanderson.info, 2013. http://kevinanderson.info/blog/why-carbon-prices-cant-deliver-the-2c-target/

it could also be interpreted as a deliberate structural injustice because fossil fuel corporations and political leaders deliberately perpetuated it in order to continue to benefit from fossil fuel capitalism. The conceptual difficulties here highlight that it may, in fact, be very difficult to find a case of pure structural injustice, because once the surface is scratched, the role of powerful agents in failing to address or deliberately maintaining structural injustice is the norm. But given that, arguably, at this point in time climate change requires systemic overhaul, I will tentatively suggest that it is a pure case.

Conclusion: Why use this typology?

Structural injustice is already a complicated concept, so why further complicate matters with this new typology? As mentioned in Chapter 2, there are three reasons why I think this is useful: it clarifies the role of powerful agents in perpetuating structural injustice, it helps explain how structural change can occur and it leads to a more accurate assessment of responsibility.

In the case studies in this chapter, we can see that powerful agents play a role in perpetuating structural injustice. Global garment corporations deliberately perpetuate sweatshop labour. International institutions and states fail to address the global economic system and global governance system that perpetuates poverty. Climate change has been the unintended outcome of a range of innovations in science, engineering and technology, which have led to the baking in of fossil fuel capitalism. With this more detailed analysis of different structural injustices and the role of powerful agents, possibilities for structural change emerge. It provides a framework for considering what alternative or countering alignments are available to subordinate agents. Sweatshops could be ameliorated by taming the power of MNCs through regulation, including global legally binding agreements on working conditions and workers' rights. Global poverty could be alleviated through a combination of debt relief, a new NIEO and more representative, transparent and accountable global governance. We might be able to adapt to or mitigate climate change with new technologies and a transition to renewable energy, but capitalism's war with the earth is built into its internal logic; systemic transformation is required.

The second half of this book will look in more detail at the problem of responsibility. Public discourse and liberal political philosophy tend to bandy about the idea that 'we' individuals in the Global North are all morally responsible for sweatshops, poverty and climate change. Young, on the other hand, argued that all agents connected to structural injustice share political responsibility to change it, regardless of how powerful they are. The reality is somewhere in between. Understanding who has the power to deliberately perpetuate or realistically remedy structural injustice provides a more nuanced account of types and gradations of responsibility.

One objection to the approach adopted here is that we cannot disambiguate these issues in the way suggested in this chapter; rather, they are all part of one system, and that system is capitalism. It is capitalism that forces people to work for a wage and that drives down wages and working conditions to increase profits for the capitalist class. It is capitalism that causes poverty; in non-capitalist societies without private property, everyone had access to, at a minimum, the means of subsistence, and in some cases, the means of production. Furthermore, capitalism created the classes of women and racialized peoples in order to specifically exploit them for their reproductive or menial labour. And it is capitalism which has caused the climate crisis and is failing to tackle it because it requires constant growth and constant accumulation of natural resources, and it is not in the interests of the capitalist class to transition to a new economy; they have too much to lose. As Nancy Fraser puts it, all roads lead to capitalism.[132]

I don't disagree with this. But what does worry me is the utopian (in a pejorative sense) implication that we will somehow transition to a global socialist economy in which there will no longer be any structural injustice anywhere. I find it hard to believe that a new political-economic system will solve all structural injustices in one fell swoop across the globe. This would be ideal, but it is unlikely. In any new system, it will remain helpful to be able to identify which structural injustices are 'baked into' the system, which are avoidable if the agents with the capacity and/or the responsibility to rectify the injustice do so, and which are being deliberately perpetuated by powerful agents for their own gain. Transition to a post-capitalist economy will be uneven in different locations and for different groups of people. Therefore, we must remain vigilant, especially about structural injustices, which are not always as easy to diagnose or to correct as straightforward repression.

Another worry is that none of these structural injustices stand alone. Take sweatshop labour: it intersects with both of the other structural injustices discussed in this chapter. It is parasitic upon global poverty; sweatshop jobs are an attractive prospect to people who might otherwise live subsistence lives outside the formal economy. The global garment industry is a significant contributor to greenhouse gas emissions; however, well-established statistics are hard to come by.[133] One recent study notes that the amount of textiles produced per person has risen from 7.6 kg fibres/person in 1995 to 13.8 kg

---

[132]Fraser, 'Climates of Capital', 96.
[133]Alden Wicker, 'Fashion Has a Misinformation Problem. That's Bad for the Environment.', *Vox*, 2020. There are studies on specific aspects of the garment industry, such as cotton production in different regions or water use, but there is a lack of empirical evidence about the overall footprint of the industry.

in 2018, an 82 per cent increase, which is clearly unnecessary.[134] But reducing the fashion industry to promote global reductions in carbon emissions could clash with securing decent jobs for garment industry workers. Thus, addressing one structural injustice has impacts on other structural injustices. What matters most? Securing decent jobs in the Global South or reducing global carbon emissions? Lifting people out of poverty or only providing decent work and work that is environmentally sustainable? Perhaps these are not contradictory goals, but they do raise practical and theoretical issues that I have not addressed here. Such intersections ought to be taken into account when looking for solutions.

---

[134]Peters, Mengyu Li and Manfred Lenzen, 'The Need to Decelerate Fast Fashion in a Hot Climate – A Global Sustainability Perspective on the Garment Industry', *Journal of Cleaner Production* 295 (2021): 2, 8.

Chapter 5
Moral responsibility

In the first four chapters of this book, I have explained what structural injustice is. I have argued that we should distinguish between different types of structural injustice, specifically deliberate, avoidable and pure structural injustices. One of the reasons for this is that if we have a better understanding of the power relations involved in any given structural injustice, we can better attribute responsibility for it. The second half of the book theorizes responsibility for structural injustice.

Iris Marion Young famously argues that ordinary individuals are not blameworthy for structural injustice, rather they bear political responsibility for it: the main difference is that if I am morally responsible, I can be blamed; if I am politically responsible, I am not blameworthy, but I should act to try to bring about change in collaboration with other politically responsible agents. Some commentators find this intuitively plausible. For instance, as Naomi Klein puts it: 'The very idea that we, as atomized individuals, even lots of atomized individuals, could play a significant part in stabilizing the planet's climate system or changing the global economy is objectively nuts.'[1] If it is objectively nuts, then why blame individuals? But many philosophers have found Young's argument controversial, insisting that individuals are blameworthy for contributing to structural injustice.[2] Part of the problem, I believe, is that Young did not defend her argument in detail. Her comments on moral responsibility are preliminary and suggestive.

In this chapter, I focus on the question of individuals' moral responsibility for structural injustice and I defend the argument that ordinary individuals are not

---

[1]Naomi Klein, *On Fire: The Burning Case for a Green New Deal* (London: Penguin Books, 2020), 133.
[2]Christian Barry and Kate Macdonald, 'How Should We Conceive of Individual Consumer Responsibility to Address Labour Injustices?', in *Global Justice and International Labour Rights*, ed. Faina Milman-Sivan, Yossi Dahan and Hanna Lerner (Cambridge: Cambridge University Press, 2016), 92–118; Henning Hahn, 'The Global Consequence of Participatory Responsibility', *Journal of Global Ethics* 5, no. 1 (2009): 43–56; Christian Neuhäuser, 'Structural Injustice and the Distribution of Forward-Looking Responsibility', *Midwest Studies in Philosophy* 38 (2014): 232–51.

morally responsible for structural injustice.[3] To defend this claim, first, I outline a brief history of the concept of moral responsibility in Western moral philosophy, explaining how philosophers have shifted from discussions of free will and determinism to normative questions about when it is permissible to blame individuals. Second, I outline Young's 'liability model' of responsibility in this context, arguing that her account is a normative theory of moral responsibility. I suggest that Young thinks that ordinary individuals are not blameworthy for structural injustice because they do not intend to reproduce it, and that their lack of intent can be demonstrated because they contribute inadvertently or because they are constrained. Third, I flesh out the argument that moral responsibility is based on intent and that individuals can be excused on the basis of inadvertence and constraint using R. Jay Wallace's detailed and influential 'reasons-responsive' account of moral responsibility. I use the example of a recent graduate, Nadia, buying an outfit for a job interview, and I complicate this example as the chapter progresses, showing how Nadia can be excused from moral responsibility on the basis of either inadvertence or social duress. Fourth, I address objections to the deontological account of responsibility and excuses from utilitarianism and the concept of complicity.

Individuals can be excused from moral responsibility for structural injustice. But the point is not to say that individuals bear no responsibility for structural injustice whatsoever. Individuals do bear responsibility – political responsibility. As Hannah Arendt argued, there are varieties of responsibility other than moral responsibility.[4] Political responsibility is a valuable form of responsibility that can explain why and how individuals should take responsibility for structural injustice. I develop the concept of political responsibility in Chapter 6, but for now, the idea that individuals are not morally responsible is our focus. In this and the following chapter, I focus on individuals; I discuss corporate agents in Chapter 7.

---

[3] I purposely refer to 'ordinary individuals' throughout to exclude the super-rich. While ordinary individuals in the Global North might over-consume, the super-rich consume significantly more. It is difficult to define exactly who qualifies as the super-rich. The Credit Suisse Global Wealth Report 2021 reports that the world's richest 1 per cent own 47.8 per cent of global wealth, Credit Suisse, 'Global Wealth Report 2021', 2021, https://www.credit-suisse.com/about-us/en/reports-research/global-wealth-report.html. To give an indication in terms of consumption, recent research has found that the average carbon footprint of an individual in the top 1 per cent of carbon emitters is 48 tCO_2 per year, compared to 11.6 tCO_2 for the next 9 per cent, 3.5 tCO_2 for the middle 40 per cent and 0.6 tCO_2 for the bottom 50 per cent: Benedikt Bruckner et al., 'Impacts of Poverty Alleviation on National and Global Carbon Emissions', *Nature Sustainability* 5 (2022): 314. At this point, the question does emerge as to what constitutes blameworthy consumption by individuals. To assess this, something like a fair shares view might be appropriate, but that is beyond the scope of this chapter, which is interested in the ways in which ordinary, everyday behaviour by the majority of individuals in the world is blameworthy or not in the context of reproducing structural injustice.

[4] Hannah Arendt, 'Collective Responsibility', in *Responsibility and Judgment*, ed. Jerome Kohn (New York: Schocken Books, 2003), 147–58.

A brief history of moral responsibility

Aristotle is the starting point for theorizing the appropriate conditions for praise and blame in Western moral philosophy, and his reflections have endured to this day. Aristotle claimed that there were two conditions for moral responsibility: an *epistemic condition* and a *control condition*.[5] If an agent *does not know* what they are doing or is *forced* to act in a certain way, they cannot be held responsible. An agent is forced if he is 'acted upon, e.g. if he were to be carried somewhere by a wind, or by men who had him in their power'.[6]

Philosophers interested in causal determinism have challenged the control condition. If control is a necessary condition for moral responsibility and if causal determinism turned out to be true – so that causal antecedents necessarily determine all of our actions – then moral responsibility is impossible, because agents cannot exercise free will. This metaphysical debate has gripped moral philosophers for centuries and continues today.[7] On the one hand are incompatibilists, who argue that moral responsibility and causal determinism are necessarily incompatible. On the other hand are compatibilists who argue that even if causal determinism is true, moral responsibility in some form would still be possible. Historically this debate has drawn on physics, but nowadays the focus has shifted to neuroscience, with philosophers interested in whether or not agents consciously control their actions.[8]

In 1967, Peter Strawson made a significant intervention in this debate. He claimed that what is important is not the metaphysical issue as to whether or not agents can control their actions; rather, what matters is the social aspect of moral responsibility. We *hold* one another morally responsible for our actions when we display 'reactive attitudes', such as blame and praise.[9] These practices do not depend on the truth or falsity of causal determinism; it is a fact of social life. Philosophers fixated on causal determinism are 'over-intellectualizing' moral responsibility.[10] The philosophical interest lies in the ways in which we hold each other morally responsible; what are we doing this for? When do we do it? When is it justified or not?

Out of this shift of focus in the moral responsibility debate has emerged a *normative* literature about when it is or is not appropriate to blame or praise

---

[5]John Martin Fischer and Mark Ravizza, *Responsibility and Control: A Theory of Moral Responsibility* (Cambridge: Cambridge University Press, 1998), 13.
[6]Aristotle, *The Nicomachean Ethics*, Oxford World's Classics (Oxford: Oxford University Press, 2009), 38.
[7]John Martin Fischer, 'Recent Work on Moral Responsibility', *Ethics* 110, no. 1 (1999): 93–139.
[8]For example, Alfred Mele, 'Free Will and Neuroscience', *Philosophic Exchange* 43, no. 1 (2013): 1–16.
[9]Peter F. Strawson, 'Freedom and Resentment', in *Freedom and Resentment and Other Essays*, edited by Peter F. Strawson (Oxon: Routledge, 2008), 26.
[10]Strawson, 'Freedom and Resentment', 33.

someone for what they have or have not done. Theorists inspired by Strawson's approach have found innovative ways of grounding moral responsibility that do not rely on causal control. The guiding idea is that adult humans are 'reasons-responsive'; that is, they can reason about the world and base their actions on those reasons. It is on this basis that we judge individuals to be morally responsible or not.[11] Whether or not determinism turns out to be true, the epistemic options that appear to be available to individuals will remain, and we will continue to base our responsibility practices on the decisions that individuals make on the basis of their apparent options.

Young's 'liability model' of responsibility

Famously, Iris Marion Young argues that individuals do not bear moral responsibility for structural injustice, rather they bear political responsibility. She distinguishes between what she calls a 'liability model' of responsibility, which generates moral and legal responsibility, and the 'social connection model', which generates political responsibility. On Young's 'liability model' of responsibility, moral responsibility requires that individuals have *directly caused* harm, with *intent* and *knowledge* of what they are doing. She writes,

> The conditions for holding an agent morally responsible are similar to those of legal responsibility: we must be able to show that they are causally connected to the harm in question and that they acted voluntarily and with sufficient knowledge of the consequences.[12]

Young recognizes that some forms of legal liability deviate from this approach in the sense that law includes the concepts of culpable negligence (responsibility for failure to do something) and strict liability (responsibility of another's actions, e.g., an employee or an animal). But the features that are common to all conceptions of responsibility on Young's 'liability model' is that they *isolate* specific individuals for blame, punishment or redress, and they are *backward-looking*. As she puts it, 'Despite their differences, these practices share an

---

[11]The field of reasons-responsive accounts of moral responsibility is large, and I cannot cover all the approaches here. What I aim to do is simply posit this as a coherent and viable grounding for moral responsibility that accords with the ideas present in Young's work. To that extent, I assume rather a lot about the plausibility of these approaches rather than seeking to independently justify them in any real depth. For fuller and competing accounts of the approach, see R. Jay Wallace, *Responsibility and the Moral Sentiments* (London: Harvard University Press, 1994); T. M. Scanlon, *What We Owe to Each Other* (London: Belknap Press of Harvard University Press, 1998).

[12]Iris Marion Young, *Responsibility for Justice* (Oxford: Oxford University Press, 2011), 97–8.

interest in identifying particular agents as the liable ones and are generally backward-looking in their purpose.'[13]

When Young was thinking about moral responsibility, she was surely speaking to the literature on normative conceptions of moral responsibility, because determinism in the sense of metaphysical or scientific causal determinism is the antithesis of the Youngian approach. Young's work on responsibility is guided by the idea that collective human political action can fundamentally change social structures. She writes,

> To be sure, no person's situation and action are *determined* by the past. We are radically free in the sense that alternative possibilities that we invent out of nothing are always open to us.[14]

However, Young's thoughts on determinism are more ambiguous than this suggests. What does interest her is the relationship of structure to agency, and the ways in which structures constrain individual agency. Young is a determinist to some extent, not in the metaphysical sense but in the sense that she thinks that agents' behaviour and attitudes, and the choices that agents are able to make, are conditioned by the social, historical, economic and cultural circumstances in which they find themselves. This is why Young thinks that individuals are not morally responsible for structures: because individuals are born into physical and social structures, and they condition our action to a large extent. But there is *a way* in which we could change them – by engaging in collective political action.[15] If we realize the radical contingency of our circumstances, we can collectively organize to change them. The relationship between structure and agency in Young's political thought is dynamic, not static. That is why she enjoins individuals to 'take responsibility' for structures, because they can be changed. She defines social structures not as fixed entities but as 'social-structural *processes*'.[16]

Young also is at pains throughout her work on responsibility to highlight that she does not reject the idea of moral responsibility on which she bases her liability model.[17] It is 'indispensible', she insists, in order to take persons seriously, to show respect for persons, and for the purposes of maintaining a legal system.[18] What she wants to do is to limit the use of the model. Instead of claiming that moral responsibility in the liability sense is somehow universalizable, she wants

---

[13]Young, *Responsibility for Justice*, 98.

[14]Young, *Responsibility for Justice*, 172.

[15]Young, *Responsibility for Justice*, 111.

[16]Young, *Responsibility for Justice*, 52–64.

[17]Young, Iris Marion, 'Responsibility and Global Labor Justice', *Journal of Political Philosophy* 12, no. 4 (2004): 368; Young, Iris Marion, 'Responsibility and Global Justice: A Social Connection Model', *Social Philosophy and Policy* 23, no. 1 (2006): 118; Young, *Responsibility for Justice*, 100.

[18]Young, *Responsibility for Justice*, 98.

to restrict its domain.[19] Young restricts the scope of moral responsibility and guilt to what an individual actually did with intent, or at least with negligence. The appropriate conditions for praise and blame are restricted.

Young's comments on why the liability model does not apply in the context of structural injustice are limited. Her explanation is as follows:

> If we contribute by such actions to the processes that produce structural injustice, we are responsible in relation to that injustice. Usually we should not be judged either morally or legally blameworthy or at fault for it, however, for several reasons. *We do not usually take the outcome as the goal of our action*, even when we can predict it as the aggregate result. We often have reasons to think that *acting within these accepted rules and practices, furthermore, is positively virtuous or useful*; it requires a wider and longer-run reflective point of view to understand how the many people who act within these accepted rules and practices interact in complex ways to produce the outcomes that many agree are unjust. We sometimes believe with good reason, finally, that *our options to do otherwise are constrained by the very same structures* to which we contribute.[20]

There are several claims to unpack here. Young argues (1) we do not *intend* structural injustice as the outcome of our actions. We do not intend it because (2) we think that acting within structures is 'positively virtuous or useful', so our contribution is *inadvertent*, and (3) we are 'constrained' by the structures in which we act, so our contribution is *unavoidable*. Thus, I take this to mean that individuals are not morally responsible for structural injustice due to a lack of intent, which is demonstrated by two excuses: inadvertence and constraint. In the next section, I will show how inadvertence and constraint can excuse an individual from moral responsibility based on an influential deontological account of moral responsibility.

But first, to give an example, consider a recent graduate, Nadia, who purchases a new outfit for a job interview from a budget retailer like Primark or ASOS. Has Nadia done something morally wrong? Nadia thinks she is 'doing the right thing' by following accepted rules and norms; she thinks that looking presentable, according to the standards of contemporary workplaces, is the appropriate, or 'positively virtuous or useful', thing to do in the job interview.[21]

---

[19]Young, *Responsibility for Justice*, 104.

[20]Young, *Responsibility for Justice*, 107–8. My emphasis.

[21]There is another way in which clothes shopping can be perceived as 'doing the right thing'. Currently in the UK there is much concern over the 'death of the high street'; as more and more people shop online, high-street shops are closing, leading to ghost-town city centres and job losses. Individuals are encouraged to shop on the high street to buck this trend and, more generally, to contribute to the growth of the economy.

She is constrained by the social norms that determine she has to look a certain way to be employable. She probably has limited funds and cannot show up to the interview in her tatty old student clothes. Like other ordinary individuals within the capitalist economy, she needs a job to earn money to survive. Her participation in clothes shopping seems 'necessary' and 'unavoidable' for participation in our current socio-economic system.[22]

Nadia does not *intend* to exploit or to perpetuate the exploitation of workers in sweatshops. She is purchasing clothes; she is not doing something that is morally wrong. The purchase of clothes only becomes problematic when placed in the context of the accumulation of the same act by millions of people.[23] Taken as an act on its own, Nadia's purchase of clothes does not demonstrate a choice to violate an established moral obligation, because there is no moral obligation not to purchase clothes. But it could be argued that there is a moral obligation not to purchase clothes that an agent *knows* have been produced in sweatshops, because by doing so the agent is reproducing the structural injustice of sweatshop labour. But even if the purchase has this effect, the agent *does not intend* to reproduce the practice of sweatshop labour. Thus, the important questions are, can the graduate's lack of intent be demonstrated by the excuses of inadvertence or constraint, as Young alludes to? And does lack of intent matter?

Excusing individuals

Young's discussion of the moral responsibility of ordinary individuals for structural injustice is suggestive but preliminary. She claims that ordinary individuals are not morally responsible for structural injustice because there is a lack of intent and potentially some excusing conditions, such as inadvertence and constraint. This section argues that Young is justified in making this claim by fleshing out the argument in more detail. The literature on moral responsibility is enormous, so to simplify I focus on one influential, mainstream, normative account of moral responsibility which builds on Strawson and that coheres with Young's preliminary thoughts on the concept: R. Jay Wallace's *Responsibility and the Moral Sentiments*. Wallace's account of moral responsibility is backward-looking, isolating and requires intentionality. Wallace's is a comprehensive and influential contemporary theory of moral responsibility. Young's point is that such an account of moral responsibility cannot explain ordinary individuals' moral responsibility for global structural injustices. I will demonstrate this by showing that on Wallace's

---

[22]Nadia's example will become more complex as the chapter progresses.
[23]We will return to the issue of the accumulation of millions of individuals purchasing clothes when discussing consequentialism.

widely adopted account of moral responsibility ordinary individuals can be excused from moral responsibility for sweatshop labour. First, I outline Wallace's account and then I apply his excusing conditions to our graduate, Nadia.

According to Wallace, philosophers have not been able to explain what we are doing when we hold others blameworthy and he seeks to resolve that problem.[24] Following Strawson, Wallace argues that moral responsibility is necessarily tied to reactive emotions. When we hold an individual morally responsible, we display certain responses towards them, from minor reproaches such as avoidance or scolding, up to punishment, or we think that these responses would be appropriate.[25] There are three reactive emotions: guilt, which one feels towards one's own behaviour; indignation, which is felt about other people's behaviour; and resentment, which is felt about other people's behaviour towards oneself.[26] Assessments of moral responsibility are tied to reactive emotions because blame is 'a form of deep assessment', an attitude that goes beyond objective assessment of another's action.[27]

Why and when do we feel these reactive emotions? Moral obligations are supported by moral reasons that are publicly justifiable.[28] If an individual supports moral reasons, it ought to motivate their behaviour. If an individual violates a moral obligation supported by reasons, it elicits the reactive emotions. The individual's action must be intentional because if the action is unintentional, 'it will generally not express any particular choice that the agent has made, and so it will not provide grounds for thinking that a moral obligation we hold the agent to has been violated'.[29]

In order to understand moral reasons and thus be able to comply with them, a person must have the requisite psychological competencies. Wallace calls these 'the powers of reflective self-control: (1) the power to grasp and apply moral reasons, and (2) the power to control or regulate his behaviour by the light of such reasons'.[30]

It would be inappropriate, or unfair, to hold an agent morally responsible for an action if it is unintentional because it would not express a choice the agent has made to knowingly violate a moral obligation. Individuals can unintentionally violate moral obligations in two ways. Either the agent does not meet the second condition – having the power to regulate behaviour in light of moral reasons – which can occur temporarily (through hypnotism, extreme stress, drug use, etc.) or persistently (mental illness, being a young child, mind control).[31] In these

---

[24]Wallace, *Responsibility and the Moral Sentiments*, 51.
[25]Wallace, *Responsibility and the Moral Sentiments*, 54.
[26]Wallace, *Responsibility and the Moral Sentiments*, 66 fn 22.
[27]Wallace, *Responsibility and the Moral Sentiments*, 78.
[28]Wallace, *Responsibility and the Moral Sentiments*, 129.
[29]Wallace, *Responsibility and the Moral Sentiments*, 133.
[30]Wallace, *Responsibility and the Moral Sentiments*, 157.
[31]Wallace, *Responsibility and the Moral Sentiments*, 155.

cases, the agent does not have the *general capacity* to behave according to moral reasons and the agent is *exempt* from moral responsibility.

Alternatively, the agent does not meet the first condition; the agent does not have the power to grasp and apply moral reasons. In these cases, the agent does have the general capacity to behave according to moral reasons, but for some reason at the *particular* moment of action, they are unable to do so. In these cases, the agent can be *excused*. Wallace calls this 'the principle of no blameworthiness without fault', which he describes as follows:

> On my approach, excuses function by showing that an agent has not really done anything wrong. When this is the case, it will not merely be theoretically improper to hold the agent to blame (because doing so would involve a false belief); it will also be morally unfair, for it is surely the case that people do not deserve to be blamed if they have not done anything wrong in the first place. As I have shown, to hold someone blameworthy is to be subject to a reactive emotion on account of what the person has done, where such emotions naturally find expression in sanctioning behaviour – condemnation, reproach, avoidance, and the like. These emotions and sanctions are essentially reactions to a moral wrong on the part of the agent who is held to blame. Hence those who have not in fact done anything wrong do not *deserve* to be subjected to the reactive emotions and the forms of sanctioning treatment that express them.[32]

Wallace argues that there are four classes of excusing conditions. First, *inadvertence, mistake or accident*. In these cases, the agent does something of kind *x*; however, it turns out that the agent does not know they were doing *x*.[33] For example, Maya goes to the fridge to get a beer not knowing that she has stepped on someone's hand. Maya is responsible for her movements towards the fridge but stepping on a person's hand was not part of her intentional plan and she was not aware she was doing it: she was not doing something of kind *x* that is knowingly wrong. Although if it was obvious that there were lots of people sitting on the floor, Maya should have looked and treaded carefully when going to the fridge; her ignorance and negligence may have been culpable. Recklessness can be a culpable quality of will because it demonstrates a cavalier attitude to risk, and this is a choice controlled by reasons. But if Maya has not been reckless, her inadvertent stepping on the hand would be excusable. As Wallace writes, an excuse of the first kind 'defeats a presumption that I did *x* intentionally,

---

[32]Wallace, *Responsibility and the Moral Sentiments*, 135.
[33]The excuses are discussed in Wallace, *Responsibility and the Moral Sentiments*, 136–47. What follows is a summary.

by showing that I did not know that I would be doing something of kind *x* at all when I chose to do whatever it was that turned out to be of kind *x*'.[34]

The second class is *unintentional bodily movements*. In these cases, the agent does not actually *do* anything, in the sense of choosing to act. Rather their body is compelled, for example, by fainting. Alternatively, the body may move by way of reflex: being accosted by a swarm of bees. Bodily movements can occur while unconscious, such as sleepwalking into a neighbour's house. Or another agent can compel a person's body to do something, such as a crowd pushing them into another person. In these cases, the bodily movements do not result from an agent's deliberative choice.

The third class is *physical constraint*. In these cases, the agent cannot act in a morally appropriate way because of the physical constraint. As Wallace argues, an omission can demonstrate a quality of will: an agent could choose to do *x* but decides to do something else instead, or they could be negligent or reckless in failing to take proper precautions. But in cases of physical constraint 'one is physically constrained from moving one's body in the way that is necessary to fulfil the obligation'.[35] For example, I am supposed to meet my friend at the airport but I am stuck in an enormous traffic jam.

The final class is *coercion, necessity and duress*. In these cases, the agent does something ordinarily considered to be morally wrong, but they do so because their options are constrained in such a way as to force them into making this choice. The act is intentional, but it is done to avoid a threat. The classic example is the bank teller handing over money to an armed thief, or the ship's captain throwing goods overboard to avoid capsizing. As Wallace puts it, 'Excuses in the final class function by showing that agent *s*'s doing *x* actually expressed a different kind of motive: not merely a choice to do *x*, but a choice to do *x*-rather-than-*y*, or *x*-in-order-to-avoid-*y*.'[36]

Young introduced us to some reasons why ordinary individuals might not be blameworthy for a structural injustice like sweatshop labour, including lack of intent and excusing conditions like inadvertence and constraint. I have discussed R. Jay Wallace's account at length because it justifies Young's understanding of moral responsibility. He argues that moral responsibility applies to specific individuals for intentional violations of moral obligations and that there are a range of excusing conditions for moral responsibility. In our example of a recent graduate buying sweatshop-produced clothes for a job interview, I suggested that the two excuses at play are inadvertence and constraint (which tallies with Wallace's coercion/necessity/duress). Now I apply these excuses to Nadia's example in more detail.

---

[34]Wallace, *Responsibility and the Moral Sentiments*, 136–7.

[35]Wallace, *Responsibility and the Moral Sentiments*, 141.

[36]Wallace, *Responsibility and the Moral Sentiments*, 144.

Excuse 1 – Inadvertence

In cases of inadvertence, the agent does something of kind x; however, it turns out that the agent does not know they were doing x, so they did it unintentionally. When Maya stepped on someone's hand when going to the fridge to get a drink, she did not intend to step on someone's hand; she did not intentionally violate an established moral obligation and so is excused. Returning to our recent graduate, Nadia, who buys an outfit for a job interview, she did one kind of act – buying clothes – but she did not intend to participate in or contribute to sweatshop labour; she did not know she was doing something of kind x that turned out to be wrong.

One response is that she *should* know and she should *take precautions* so as not to participate in the practice, otherwise her behaviour is negligent and thus blameworthy. There are two separate claims here: one is that the graduate is culpably ignorant about sweatshop labour (she *should know*) and the second is that she should act on the basis of that knowledge (she should *take precautions to avoid harm*). My question here is whether consumers are responsible *for* sweatshop labour, not whether they are responsible for not knowing about it, so I will focus on the second aspect. I will assume that Nadia does know about sweatshop labour but does not intend to reproduce it.

Can Nadia be blamed for contributing to sweatshop labour on the basis of negligence? Even if she is doing an act of one kind – buying clothes, which is not blameworthy in itself – if she knows about sweatshop labour, is her purchase blameworthy on the basis of negligence? Negligence involves tracing: tracing back to a prior moment when the agent *could have done* something to avoid harm.[37] The classic example is drink-driving; it is possible to trace back to the moment when the driver decided to carry on drinking. Or with stepping on someone's hand when going to the fridge at a crowded party, Maya *could have* surveyed the room and then stepped carefully. Perhaps Nadia buying clothes she knows have likely been produced in sweatshops is equivalent to Maya knowing it is highly likely she will step on someone's hand and does it anyway.

However, it is questionable to what extent the graduate can take precautions against her purchase contributing to sweatshop labour, because there is an empirical question as to what extent her purchase *does* contribute to sweatshop labour. There are multiple ways in which the money from any consumer purchase is used, including paying the shopworkers in the shop where the clothes were bought; paying other workers in the corporation, such as marketers, administrators and so on; paying for the shop and corporation's overheads like rent and electricity; as well as transport, distribution, advertising, design and so on. Sweatshops are far removed from the point of purchase, at the bottom of

---

[37]Manuel Vargas, 'The Trouble with Tracing', *Midwest Studies in Philosophy* 24 (2005): 269–91.

a long and complex supply chain. The consumer has no control over how the money from any purchase is used; those decisions are made by other agents. The graduate only knows that her purchase is contributing to sweatshop labour in a nebulous way. So this case is not equivalent to Maya knowing she is likely to step on someone's hand, because the graduate's purchase will not directly harm anyone.

Moreover, in cases of negligence, the agent is supposed to take precautions against their *own* actions or omissions causing harm. With drink-driving, the driver's decision to drink leads to their later causing a crash. With stepping on someone's hand, Maya's decision not to survey the room leads to her stepping on someone's hand. With sweatshop labour, the graduate's purchase does not lead to her exploiting workers. Rather, her purchase has multiple outcomes, one of which might be someone else exploiting workers. Thus, there is no linear causal connection between the earlier act (failure to take precautions) and the subsequent purchase contributing to that consumer's exploitation of workers (because in itself this act does not necessarily contribute to the exploitation of workers, and it would not be the consumer who exploits the workers).

Another implication of the tracing approach to negligence is that the harmful outcome is avoidable. The drink-driver could have avoided the crash by not drinking. Maya could have avoided stepping on someone's hand by paying more attention. As Young points out, participating in the global garment industry is unavoidable because agents are constrained by the social structures in which they act. As I will discuss in the next section, we are judged by our clothing and clothing norms are deeply embedded in many cultures. It could be objected that there are steps consumers can take to avoid participation in sweatshop labour; for example, by only buying fair trade clothes. However, this is an expensive option, so is not available to everyone and depends on class privilege. One could argue that consumers should only buy second-hand clothes, but this is not always available and if it is, it does not always supply what is needed. What if Nadia goes to every second-hand store in town and cannot find a suitably smart outfit in her size, thus jeopardizing her chances of getting the much-needed job? One could argue that consumers should not buy clothes at all, but while shopping less is a possibility, not shopping at all is implausible. Some degree of participation is inevitable, even if the extent of the participation is variable.

In sum, a consumer can get more information about sweatshop labour, but they cannot be held morally responsible on the basis of negligence. This is because the money from their purchase will be used in a multitude of ways, they will not be the agents exploiting the workers, and at times participation in clothes shopping is unavoidable. Rather their contribution to sweatshop labour is inadvertent, and thus excused.

The argument from inadvertence seems plausible for people who only buy clothes when they need to. But most people in the Global North, or people in the middle- to upper classes globally, do not restrict clothes shopping to cases of necessity. Nadia might need a smart outfit for a job interview, but she probably has a wardrobe full of clothes at home; quite possibly many more clothes than an individual needs, including clothes she never wears that are cluttering up her life. It could be argued that the more an individual purchases, the less plausible the inadvertence excuse becomes, because the more purchases one makes, the higher the probability that the money from those purchases will be used in furthering the aims of the corporation in driving down working standards in its suppliers. At this point, the behaviour looks more like recklessness than straightforward inadvertence: a cavalier attitude to the risk that one's purchases will contribute to sweatshop labour. Isn't Nadia to blame for this over-consumption, which is contributing to sweatshop labour (and thus to the oppression of mostly Third World women), environmental degradation and climate change? If this is blameworthy behaviour, can it be excused?

Excuse 2 – Coercion/necessity/duress

On Wallace's account of the excusing conditions, in cases of coercion, necessity or duress, an agent knowingly does something wrong, but they do it because of external pressures. Young describes sweatshop labour as a structural injustice, and part of the explanation as to why it is structural is that it is embedded in our attitudes, habits, customs and norms. I will argue here that the duress argument captures this.[38]

But first, let's consider coercion and necessity. Nadia is not coerced into buying sweatshop-produced clothes – there is no *agent* forcing her to do it. But this can happen; employees can be fired because of the clothes they wear in the workplace. To take just one example, in 2016, a woman was told to leave her new job as a corporate secretary at PricewaterhouseCoopers for wearing flat

---

[38] I will focus on the negative aspects of clothing culture because I want to explore the way in which duress is a feature of our relationship to clothes in contemporary Western culture, and of course this will shift depending on context, time and location. I'm thinking about the role of social conformity and control, and how these relate to social group membership, in determining what individual can and cannot wear. But it should be noted that there are positive aspects to clothing culture. Fashion is an art form. Clothes can be a source of self-esteem and pride. People bond over clothing. People communicate through and about clothes. My aim is not to deny that human relationships to clothes are multifaceted, rather my aim is to focus on the issue at hand, which is whether or not the duress argument is sufficient to excuse individuals from buying clothes that have been made in sweatshops. For more on our positive relationship to clothes, see Emily Spivack, *Worn Stories* (New York: Princeton Architectural Press, 2014); Sheila Heti, Heidi Julavits and Leanne Shapton, *Women in Clothes* (London: Particular Books, 2014). Young, Iris Marion. 'Women Recovering Our Clothes'. In ed. Iris Marion Young, *On Female Body Experience: 'Throwing Like a Girl' and Other Essays*, 62-75. Oxford: Oxford University Press, 2005

shoes.[39] In cases of strict workplace dress codes, individuals can be coerced into buying new clothes. It is therefore no stretch of the imagination to assume that people who do not wear clothing deemed appropriate by the employer in a job interview will not be hired in the first place. It could be granted that coercion is a sufficient excuse, but denied that this excuse is available to the majority of clothing consumers. The number of people who are forced into buying particular clothes is limited. So while coercion can explain why a small minority of individuals can be excused from purchasing clothes, necessity and duress seem more likely candidates as an excuse for a greater number of people.

There are times when people do genuinely need new clothes, for example, pregnancy, weight gain/loss, moving to a different climate, clothes for growing children.[40] As with coercion, this might seem to be a sufficient excuse, but is only occasionally available to consumers. Potentially Nadia does need to buy a suitable outfit for a job interview. But what if, as I suggested above, Nadia already has a wardrobe full of clothes? There might not be anything suitable for the job interview, but it is not the case that she only buys clothes in cases of necessity. Maybe she had already decided to go shopping that weekend to buy some new trainers she had coveted for months, and when she heard she got the job interview decided she would buy a sensible interview outfit instead.[41] In this case, the necessity excuse is no longer available because she was going to buy new clothes regardless, she merely decided to buy different clothes. This is a likely scenario given that the average UK consumer buys thirty-three new items of clothing per year.[42] So the excuse from necessity looks rather flimsy when the broader context of Nadia's shopping habits are taken into account.

This suggests that the excuses of coercion and necessity are highly plausible when people are forced or genuinely need new clothes for particular occasions or stages of life. But the problem when it comes to sweatshop labour is not that people are buying clothes only when they are forced to or need them, but that they are over-consuming. Perhaps this is what is morally wrong – purchasing consumer goods (in this case clothes) in the knowledge that this is contributing to the exploitation of workers, environmental degradation and climate change, when there is no identifiable need for these purchases. This is where social

---

[39]Nadia Khomami, 'Receptionist "Sent Home from PwC for Not Wearing High Heels"', *The Guardian*, 11 May 2016, https://www.theguardian.com/uk-news/2016/may/11/receptionist-sent-home-pwc-not-wearing-high-heels-pwc-nicola-thorp.

[40]Maeve McKeown, 'Sweatshops and Shame', Beauty Demands, 2017. http://beautydemands.blogspot.com/2017/08/sweatshops-and-shame_29.html

[41]I use a Frankfurt-type case to think about necessity, but in a different way to Harry Frankfurt, who was using it to disprove the principle of alternate possibilities. See Harry Frankfurt, 'Alternate Possibilities and Moral Responsibility', *Journal of Philosophy* 66, no. 23 (1969): 829–39.

[42]China and the United States account for the most spending on clothes with the average American consumer buying fifty-three items and the average Chinese consumer thirty. CO Data, 'Volume and Consumption: How Much Does the World Buy?', 2018.

duress comes in, because it provides some explanation for this behaviour. Duress is more complex than coercion and necessity, and more pertinent when considering the problem of over-consumption.

Duress operates within society in the sense that individuals must conform to certain standards, in our case, keeping up with contemporary fashions. As we saw in Chapter 4, the quantity of textiles produced per person has risen from 7.6 kg fibres/person in 1995 to 13.8 kg in 2018, an 82 per cent increase.[43] Why? Because of the rise of fast fashion. Fast fashion did not exist forty years ago. As we saw in Chapters 3 and 4, fast fashion exists now because of changes in the processes of production since the 1970s, which have enabled products to be manufactured cheaply overseas through fragmented production processes. The fast fashion industry is also a pioneer in social duress.

Inditex, the parent company of Zara, turbo-charged fast fashion by creating a new business model, changing how fashion is produced and consumed. It has factories in Asia, but it also has factories at its headquarters in Spain and in neighbouring countries, Portugal and Turkey. Zara sends a small amount of product to its stores and then it replenishes the product depending on demand, and it can do so at a fast pace due to its local factories. This agility means it responds immediately to new trends. Zara uses a range of sophisticated forms of manipulation. It buys stores that are close to designer stores on the high street, which gives the illusion that consumers are getting high-fashion clothes at a bargain price.[44] It uses cues in stores, such as few items on a rack giving the impression of scarcity.[45] The traditional fashion sector has two seasons per year and spends time developing new designs, but Zara has '52 seasons'. Because of this, 'Inditex has completely changed consumer behaviour.'[46]

The fast fashion sector that has sprung up around Zara's success typically addresses its target market (young women aged fifteen to twenty-nine) not via traditional advertising or through retail stores but on social media, using influencers and copying the designer looks worn by celebrities.[47] Fast fashion sells the high-fashion lifestyle on a budget; it has made fashion accessible through price and ecommerce.[48] The most recent example is Shein, which in the space of a few years has become a rival to Zara and H&M. It targets teenagers

[43]Greg Peters, Mengyu Li and Manfred Lenzen, 'The Need to Decelerate Fast Fashion in a Hot Climate – A Global Sustainability Perspective on the Garment Industry', *Journal of Cleaner Production* 295 (2021): 2, 8.
[44]Suzy Hansen, 'How Zara Grew into the World's Largest Fashion Retailer', *New York Times Magazine* (New York, November 2012).
[45]Shirpa Gupta and James W. Gentry, 'Evaluating Fast Fashion: Examining Its Micro and the Macro Perspective', 2018, 8.
[46]Hansen, 'How Zara Grew into the World's Largest Fashion Retailer'.
[47]Hala Abdel-Jaber, 'The Devil Wears Zara: Why the Lanham Act Must Be Amended in the Era of Fast Fashion', *Ohio State Business Law Journal* 15 (2021): 237.
[48]Abdel-Jaber, 'The Devil Wears Zara', 241.

online with a range of 'dark patterns' including putting countdowns on deals, aggressively using cookies to anticipate what shoppers will like and producing three thousand 'hyper trendy' new styles per day sometimes copied directly from independent designers.[49] In other words, the fast fashion industry preys on contemporary social norms that favour celebrity, wealth and luxury lifestyles, saying to ordinary people (especially younger, women consumers) that they can emulate this lifestyle by purchasing their products.

Perhaps this is over-stating the point. As Daniel Dennett puts it, what is required to make moral choices is 'elbow room', room within obvious limitations generated by the external world, and Dennett claims that advertising is simply one of those influences.[50] But Dennett was writing in 1984, before the explosion of brands and their grip on public culture and public space. He was writing before the internet, social media and fast fashion. There is also a practical or material aspect, as mentioned in Chapter 3. Public space is not only dominated by advertising, but it has also been bought by corporations. The rise of neoliberal capitalism throughout the last thirty years has decimated public spaces in cities, so there are few areas to convene and pass time with others that are free from corporate influence. Shopping has become a pastime for so many because there is literally nothing else to do.

Furthermore, there is pressure, particularly on women, to 'look the part' (i.e. to be dressed in a manner deemed appropriate according to social norms) in all aspects of their lives and their many different social roles: professional and authoritative at work, sexy in the 'right' contexts, good mother and so on.[51] Women are judged especially harshly on what they wear; many are riven with anxiety about clothes. A Marks & Spencer's survey from 2016 found that women spend six months of their working lives deciding what to wear.[52] At the time of writing, a Google search on 'deciding what to wear' generated 48.2 billion hits. And there are social pressures to conform to clothing norms that vary according to social group membership. For example, if our graduate is a woman of colour, lesbian, a trans-woman or a Muslim woman who wears hijab, she will experience the pressure to conform to workplace clothing norms in different ways to a cis-, white, heterosexual woman.[53] Therefore, many people are pressured to buy

---

[49]Rob Hastings, 'Shein: Fast-Fashion Workers Paid 3p per Garment for 18-Hour Days, Undercover Filming in China Reveals', *Inews*, 15 October 2022, https://inews.co.uk/news/consumer/shein-fast-fashion-workers-paid-3p-18-hour-days-undercover-filming-china-1909073.

[50]Daniel C. Dennett, *Elbow Room: The Varieties of Free Will Worth Wanting* (Oxford: Oxford University Press, 1984), 66.

[51]McKeown, 'Sweatshops and Shame'.

[52]Jess Edwards, 'We Spend Six Months of Our Working Lives Deciding What to Wear', *Cosmopolitan* (London, June 2016), https://www.cosmopolitan.com/uk/fashion/style/news/a43849/deciding-what-to-wear-six-months/.

[53]For instance, women of African descent face pressure to dress in Western-style clothes at work, otherwise their appearance could be deemed threatening and aggressive, Akilah S. Richards, 'How Blackgirl Natural Hair Is Shamed from Infancy to Adulthood', *Everyday Feminism*, 2014. Trans-women

new clothes (indeed, a range of clothes) to fit into the dominant social norms associated with work-clothing culture in multicultural and pluralist societies.

In advanced capitalist societies, for many people the primary way to assert individual identity is through clothing. As Andrew Brooks puts it,

> Consumption has become an incredibly important force in defining identity. Increasingly people are what they buy, which in particular places enormous financial and psychological pressure on the young to participate in what one might call a 'consumption arms race'. Teenagers have to buy the latest style to take part in distinction-making so they can simultaneously subscribe to current norms of behaviour and try to narrate their own identity.[54]

Moreover, the pressure to dress to conform to gender roles is deep-seated and phenomenological (a result of lived experience and socialization), not always the outcome of rational choice. Young argues in an early essay, 'Women Recovering Our Clothes', that young girls are given dolls to play with and dress up, associating clothes with adult femininity in the crucial early years of development. The association of looking pretty, dressing up, pleasing the male gaze and using clothes to do so is taught to girls from infanthood.[55]

To return to our example, the graduate, Nadia, might not have *needed* the cool new trainers in the sense that the trainers do not satisfy a basic need. But she might have *felt* she needed the trainers to stay in line with her peer group and to be socially accepted. And this desire will partly come from that individual, but it has also been manufactured by corporations throughout this young person's life. The graduate does not remember a time before the internet, before mass marketing, before fast fashion. It has also been manufactured by social norms around gender, race, sexuality, faith, ability, and class that not only subconsciously influence how a person wants to dress but also affects how they will be perceived by dominant groups in society.[56] She lives in a context of widespread over-consumption, in which fashion changes constantly and pressure to keep up with one's peers, and even celebrities and influencers, is immense, especially since the advent of social media. It is a context in which looking 'right' (i.e. socially acceptable) depends on the context; looking right at

---

may face pressure to 'pass' as cis-women, to reduce the possibility of discrimination and stigma, Vivian, 'I'm a Trans Woman and I'm Not Interested in Being One of the "Good Ones"', *Autostraddle*, 2013. Women wearing hijab have been discriminated against because white, Western employers consider them as submissive, John Bingham, 'Hijab-Wearing Muslim Women Being Passed over for Jobs in Last Form of "acceptable" Discrimination – MPs', *The Telegraph*, 11 August 2016.

[54]Andrew Brooks, *Clothing Poverty: The Hidden World of Fast Fashion and Second-Hand Clothes* (London: Zed Books, 2015), 33.

[55]Marion Young, 'Women Recovering Our Clothes'. .

[56]Alisa Bierria, 'Missing in Action: Violence, Power, and Discerning Agency', *Hypatia* 29, no. 1 (2014): 129–45.

work is different to at university, in the club, on a date, at the gym and so on.[57] And the contexts in which Nadia finds herself will shift over time, for example, with motherhood or climbing the career ladder.

Furthermore, it is not only the underlying social norms but also the economic conditions that need to be investigated. Capitalism depends upon ever-increasing consumption. It constantly seeks new markets in order for capital to accumulate. It convinces consumers that they need new things in order to achieve status and happiness. Capital is enabled by political systems that privilege economic growth over human welfare and environmental preservation. And the political economy of clothes is essential to understanding the acceleration of fast fashion in recent years. It was the end of the Multi-Fibre Agreement (MFA) in 2005 (see Chapter 3), when the global garment industry was liberalized, that unleashed vast imports of affordable clothing in the Global North; clothing prices in the 2000s fell by 26.2 per cent in Europe and 17.1 per cent in the United States.[58] Instead of blaming individual consumers, therefore, we should focus on the social norms and the economic and political systems that are causing this injustice, and take political responsibility together to change them.

In sum, I have argued that Young's conception of moral responsibility on the liability model can be fleshed out with R. Jay Wallace's comprehensive deontological theory of moral responsibility. On this view, an agent deserves blame if they intentionally violated a moral obligation. Some ordinary individuals who buy clothes produced in sweatshops are not morally responsible because they can be excused on the basis of inadvertence; when purchasing clothes, they do not intentionally violate a moral obligation. Others are recklessly over-consuming clothes, but they can be excused on the basis of social duress.

A lot of people will find this argument unsatisfactory. They feel a strong intuition that they are morally responsible (blameworthy) for purchasing clothes they know have been made in sweatshops, especially in the context of over-consumption rather than consumption to satisfy basic needs. It could be objected that the individual's 'quality of will' does not really matter. What matters is what the agent did. In our example, Nadia purchased clothes on a regular basis knowing that there was the possibility that the money from her purchases would contribute to the perpetuation of sweatshop labour and that is enough to ground moral responsibility.

Hannah Arendt, who will we discuss in the next chapter, makes this point vividly in her assessment of Adolf Eichmann, a high-ranking Nazi administrator who organized transport to death camps. Eichmann's situation is different to a case of structural injustice in the sense that he was a perpetrator of genocide, rather than an ordinary individual merely living his life in the context of unjust

---

[57]McKeown, 'Sweatshops and Shame'.
[58]Brooks, Clothing Poverty, 68.

structures, but her point is worth engaging with because it captures this intuition that what matters is the deed, not the intention. In his trial, Eichmann claimed that he was not anti-Semitic, and he did not *want* to kill Jews. Eichmann seemed to lack the relevant 'quality of will' that is necessary to be found morally responsible on Wallace's account. Indeed, in the trial it was difficult to prove that Eichmann displayed *mens rea*, which was necessary to find him criminally responsible.[59] We want to find Eichmann morally responsible for his acts but it appears to not be possible on an intentionality-based account of moral responsibility. It is for this reason that Arendt argues we should not bother worrying about an agent's quality of will when they acted; all that matters is what they did.[60]

The 'quality of will' account of moral responsibility, however, can be rescued from Arendt's powerful objection, because for an agent to be exempt or excused from moral responsibility they must meet either an exempting or excusing condition. Consider first that Eichmann certainly does not meet the exempting conditions for moral responsibility: he was a 'normal' adult insofar as he had fully functioning mental capacities, as confirmed by several psychiatrists.[61] He was not insane or suffering from any kind of cognitive disability that would rule him out from ascriptions of moral responsibility. So Eichmann cannot be exempted from moral responsibility. Can he be excused?

Eichmann claimed that he did not *intend* to cause the suffering and deaths of millions of victims in the Holocaust. Does this claim undermine the necessary condition for blameworthiness? If Eichmann's supposed lack of intention could be backed up by one of the excusing conditions, then possibly it would. The first excusing condition is inadvertence, mistake or accident. Eichmann did not organize transportation to concentration camps inadvertently, by mistake or by accident; rather it was a methodical, highly organized process that extended over several years, so this excuse is not open to him. The second is unintentional bodily movements. Again, as his work was methodical and long term, it cannot be explained by momentary physical incapacity. The third excuse is physical constraint. Eichmann was not physically constrained in any way or physically forced into carrying out his work. The final excuse that might prove lack of intent is the class of coercion, necessity or duress. This may plausibly seem available to Eichmann. He argued that he had to do what he did. But we know this to be false. As Arendt points out, there was not a single case in which a member of the SS who refused to take part in an execution was himself executed.[62] Eichmann was able to ask for a transfer to a different job or department. There was never

[59]Hannah Arendt, *Eichmann in Jerusalem: A Report on the Banality of Evil*, 5th edn (London: Penguin Books, 2006), 17.
[60]Arendt, 'Collective Responsibility', 148.
[61]Arendt, *Eichmann in Jerusalem*, 25.
[62]Arendt, *Eichmann in Jerusalem*, 91.

a threat of death or physical harm to Eichmann. And as he could simply have transferred to another 'well-paying job' there is no excuse from necessity.[63]

Arendt's objection to the quality of will account is important. However, the quality of will account can deliver the right verdict in this case. Eichmann may have claimed to not intend what he did, but on closer inspection this claim seems utterly disingenuous. None of the excusing conditions are available to him and so we can reject his claim to be excused.[64]

The claim that intention is at the core of a plausible, deontological, reasons-responsive account of moral responsibility is a strong one. It does seem that, at least in ordinary circumstances, we are interested in whether someone meant to cause harm or not. We care about whether or not an individual can be exempted or excused for what they did. My claim is that this account of moral responsibility based on intentionality can excuse ordinary individuals from blame for sweatshop labour. Individual consumers can be excused either because they inadvertently contribute to sweatshop labour, because the money from their purchases will be spent on multiple things and because other agents are causing the harm, or they are participating due to social duress. Both arguments point to the structural nature of sweatshop labour – the multiple processes, practices and agents, whose actions together produce an unjust outcome. However, perhaps this is precisely the problem – buying clothes is wrong because cumulatively it is wrong – one act makes an imperceptible difference in terms of a global injustice, but it is a difference nevertheless.

Consequentialism

Arguably clothing consumers are negligent because they know that their action has a harmful outcome when combined with the actions of millions of others. Thus, the negligence argument could be interpreted as a consequentialist argument based on imperceptible causal contributions to harm. Perhaps, then, consequentialism will find consumers morally responsible for sweatshop labour.

Derek Parfit argues that even though our individual acts have imperceptible effects on others, some of our acts are wrong because *together* they make large numbers of people worse off.[65] This can explain why *we think* our actions

---

[63] Arendt, *Eichmann in Jerusalem*, 92.

[64] Scholarship after Arendt has challenged her view, demonstrating that Eichmann was deeply anti-Semitic and proud of his role in the genocide. I'm not trying to make any claims about whether Arendt was right or wrong, instead the point is to consider whether intentions and excuses matter, or whether only deeds matter. Arendt's assessment of this point, I claim, is wrong. For the most developed recent assessment of Eichmann see Stangneth, Bettina. *Eichmann before Jerusalem: The Unexamined Life of a Mass Murderer*. (New York: Vintage, 2014).

[65] Derek Parfit, 'Five Mistakes in Moral Mathematics', in *Reasons and Persons*, ed. Derek Parfit (Oxford: Clarendon Press, 1987), 83. This discussion appears in my article Maeve McKeown, 'Iris

in the global economy are not causally and morally significant (because the effects are trivial or imperceptible) but this is mistaken.[66] Parfit uses the example of the Harmless Torturers: a thousand torturers flick a switch that inflicts an imperceptible amount of pain on a thousand victims. At the start of each day the victims are suffering mild pain, but by the end of the day, when each torturer has flicked the switch, they are suffering severe pain.[67] He writes,

> It is not enough to ask, 'Will my act harm other people?' Even if the answer is No, my act may still be wrong because of its effects. The effects that it will have when it is considered on its own may not be its only relevant effects. I should ask, 'Will my act be one of a set of acts that will *together* harm other people?' The answer may be Yes. And the harm to others may be great. If this is so, I may be acting *very* wrongly, like the Harmless Torturers.[68]

This argument, however, cannot generalize to global structural injustices like sweatshop labour, for at least two reasons. First, in the Harmless Torturers case, even though the harm caused by each torturer is imperceptible, the harm is direct. There is a direct linear connection between the torturer's act and the pain suffered by the victim. In structural injustice there is no such linear causal connection. Global supply chains are extremely complex; the harm is brought about by the interactions and behaviour of multiple agents of different kinds, doing different things and with different degrees of power. Young herself points out this difference as a reason for needing the social connection model of responsibility: 'I have developed a social connection model of responsibility as distinct from responsibility as liability precisely because there are good reasons to distinguish such direct connections from more mediated connections.'[69]

Second, the acts of consumers do not add up to an aggregate harm because the acts of *intermediary agents* change the nature of the harm and could alleviate it. On a micro level, many individuals within supply chains make decisions about the costs of garments, how budgets will be allocated, what workers will be paid and so on. The consumer is unaware of these processes. And on a

Marion Young's "Social Connection Model" of Responsibility: Clarifying the Meaning of Connection', *Journal of Social Philosophy* 49, no. 3 (2018): 484–502. Andrea Sangiovanni argues that the Harmless Torturers example can be applied to structural injustice on the grounds that 'What matters is whether their [individuals] causal contribution makes an *expected* marginal moral difference given what others can be expected to do.' Andrea Sangiovanni, 'Structural Injustice and Individual Responsibility', *Journal of Social Philosophy* 49, no. 3 (2018): 478. But I disagree for the reasons I will now argue for.
[66]Derek Parfit, 'Five Mistakes in Moral Mathematics', in *Reasons and Persons*, ed. Derek Parfit (Oxford: Clarendon Press, 1987), 75.
[67]Parfit, 'Five Mistakes in Moral Mathematics', 80.
[68]Parfit, 'Five Mistakes in Moral Mathematics', 86.
[69]Young, *Responsibility for Justice*, 158.

macro scale, the world's major clothing companies could collectively decide to pay garment workers a global minimum wage and to implement legally binding safety agreements.[70] In the Harmless Torturers case, the individuals themselves must stop flicking the switch. In the case of sweatshop labour, if consumers collectively boycott then corporations could move their production or output elsewhere and the practice would continue. The problems do not have the same structure because of the role of intermediary agents.

Thus, Parfit's argument from imperceptible difference, where refraining from doing the act in question will make a difference either over time or in conjunction with others, is not applicable in relation to structural injustice. This is because there is no direct connection between the consumer's act and sweatshop labour, and there are intermediary agents who could make a difference to the processes.

Shelley Kagan argues that there are no collective action cases where an individual's act makes *no* difference to the outcome; rather there are only 'triggering' cases, and consequentialism can easily accommodate triggering cases.[71] He gives the chicken example. If the butcher orders chickens in batches of twenty-five, if Ayesha buys the twenty-fifth chicken, then the butcher orders another batch.[72] Ayesha's act triggered the buying of more chickens. However, everyone who bought a chicken bears moral responsibility because there was a *possibility* that their act would be the one that triggers the new order. The expectation of generating overall negative utility renders each individual blameworthy.

Clothes buying has the same structure. Ayesha's purchase of a pair of jeans could be the purchase that triggers the order of a hundred more pairs of jeans. Every person who buys a pair of jeans is morally responsible, because their purchase had the potential to trigger a new order. Kagan admits that his example is 'artificially simple'; the butcher will call their supplier, who will order more chickens from the farm when a suitable number of butchers have placed a new order, and the chicken farm only increases its number of chickens when they have sold enough.[73]

In the clothes case, setting aside the point that it is more complex than the artificial example and that there are intermediary agents who are making decisions about how and where to produce the clothes, there is an important difference to the chicken case. Torturing and killing chickens obviously generate negative utility (if animals are included in the calculus). But giving people jobs

[70]See the example of the Bangladesh Fire and Building Safety Accord, which is a legally binding agreement over five years (extended for a further three), which 190 brands signed up to, discussed in Chapter 4.

[71]Shelly Kagan, 'Do I Make a Difference?', *Philosophy & Public Affairs* 39, no. 2 (2011): 140.

[72]Kagan, 'Do I Make a Difference?', 122.

[73]Kagan, 'Do I Make a Difference?', 122.

making clothes does not. We saw in Chapter 4 that there is debate about whether or not sweatshop labour is wrongfully exploitative. Libertarians argue that sweatshops provide jobs to people who would otherwise be worse off, and they generate economic growth for poor countries. I argued, however, that sweatshop labour is still a form of injustice because it systematically uses the productive powers of mostly Third World women for the benefit of consumers and capitalists.

Nevertheless, in both the Harmless Torturers example and the chicken example, there is a clear-cut implication for what the individual participant should do. The torturers should not flick the switch and if they do, they are doing something wrong. The chicken buyer should not buy the chicken. But there is not an analogous act for clothing consumers. As Young points out, consumer boycotts can lead to job losses, which is not necessarily what sweatshop workers want.[74] What they want is better pay and working conditions. So the appropriate response will be something like encouraging other consumers to complain to, or publicly shame, the company into paying the garment workers better wages and providing better and safer working conditions. This is less of a 'do or don't situation', and more of an 'act in a certain way' situation – act in a politically savvy way that involves gathering knowledge about the victims' needs and encouraging others to act on it. This implies using one's discretion, ongoing commitment and looking for forward-looking solutions.[75]

Changes in consumer habits can change what gets produced, but no particular abstention from purchasing clothes will make this change. Moreover, boycotts might generate *more* negative utility overall because they lead to job losses. An appropriate response to sweatshop labour, therefore, requires collective action and organization over time to change the processes of production in a way that is responsive to the needs of the workers. From the consequentialist perspective, it would make more sense to argue that consumers are morally responsible for failing to collectively organize to demand changes in the garment industry, rather than blaming them for particular purchases of clothes. Focusing on individual consumption practices offers false solutions for how to respond to structural injustice.

Furthermore, the consequentialist focus on individual imperceptible causal contributions to harm or triggering cases is a red herring, because it focuses our attention on the wrong issues – on the individual culpability of consumers – rather than on the structures and the agents with power to change those structures. Focusing on the point of consumption obscures the processes of production.

---

[74]Young, *Responsibility for Justice*, 134.
[75]McKeown, 'Iris Marion Young's "Social Connection Model" of Responsibility', 499.

Complicity

I've argued that an intentionality-based deontological reasons-responsive account of moral responsibility will excuse ordinary individuals from moral responsibility for sweatshop labour. I've also argued that a consequentialist theory does not provide an adequate analysis of moral responsibility for sweatshop labour, because it assumes a linear connection between an individual's action and the harm caused, it ignores the role of intermediary agents and it suggests clear-cut solutions; even if consequentialist arguments do allow for more causal complexity, they place too much emphasis on the capacity for the actions of individual consumers to change structural processes and they ignore the role of producers. For these reasons, I believe that traditional deontological and consequentialist accounts do not ground individuals' moral responsibility for structural injustices like sweatshop labour. But this is too narrow a focus. Our moral repertoire is larger than this. One concept that could explain why individual consumers are morally responsible for sweatshop labour is complicity.[76]

In an influential account of complicity, Christopher Kutz argues that individuals who participate in a collective action are liable for the harm done by virtue of the fact that they intended to participate in the group.[77] Individual liability for the outcome of the group's act is grounded in 'participatory intent'. Kutz's primary example is the bombing of Dresden in the Second World War, in which the city and its inhabitants were annihilated, an act that many historians and other observers consider disproportionate. The harm was overdetermined: about eight thousand crewmen participated in the bombing, so the harm cannot be traced to the action of any one bomber and no one individual's act made a difference to the overall outcome. This means that the normal conditions for moral responsibility do not hold. Kutz calls these (1) the 'individual difference principle': I am accountable for harm if my act made the difference to the resulting state of affairs; (2) the 'control principle': I am accountable if I could control the harm's occurrence.[78] Because these conditions do not obtain, Kutz argues for a new principle:

The Complicity Principle: (Basis) I am accountable for what others do when I intentionally participate in the wrong they do or harm they cause.

---

[76]Our moral repertoire extends beyond the concept of complicity. There are many theories of moral responsibility in the Continental philosophy tradition, feminist philosophy and philosophies from other cultures that are relevant. I have restricted the scope of this chapter to the Anglo-American philosophical tradition because this is the terrain the debate has taken place on. However, Young incorporated Continental philosophy into her conception of political responsibility, and I discuss these theories more in the next chapter.

[77]Christopher Kutz, *Complicity: Ethics and Law for a Collective Age* (Cambridge: Cambridge University Press, 2000), 122.

[78]Kutz, *Complicity*, 116.

(Object) I am accountable for the harm or wrong we do together, independently of the actual difference I make.[79]

Kutz goes on to discuss complex cases relevant to our discussion in which it is harder to apply the complicity principle: including cases where an individual facilitates another's autonomous act (a gun-seller selling a gun to someone who uses it to commit a crime) and individuals making imperceptible contributions to a public bad or 'unstructured collective harm' (drivers using CFC cooling systems in their cars, which damage the ozone layer). He groups these cases together because in both cases the individual's act makes no difference to the outcome, and so there is little in Western mainstream ethical thought that would encourage these individuals to not carry on as they are.[80]

In the gun-seller case, the seller intended to participate in the financial transaction of selling the gun but did not intend to contribute to the commission of a crime and cannot be held responsible for the autonomous act of the person who did commit the crime.[81] This relates to my critique of consequentialist approaches to the moral responsibility of clothing consumers. Consumers may purchase clothes, which funds the operations of global garment corporations, but it is the producers who make the decisions about how and where to produce the clothes. The consumers cannot be held responsible for these autonomous decisions.

In the climate case, drivers could purchase cooling systems for their cars that do not use CFCs, but these are much more expensive and less effective.[82] Drivers do not intend to harm the ozone layer, and they are not engaged in any kind of joint enterprise with other drivers, so the complicity principle does not apply.[83] Again, this relates to consumers purchasing clothes produced in sweatshops: they do not intend to harm workers and they are not engaged in a joint project with other consumers.

Kutz offers a 'piecemeal solution' to grounding individual accountability in these harder cases.[84] First, he argues that individuals can develop a sense of 'quasi-participatory accountability'. To do this, they should emphasize 'the moral significance of pre-existing networks of collaboration'.[85] Gun-sellers should consider how their trade as a whole contributes to a culture of violence and drivers can realize that their way of life contributes to environmental damage.[86]

---

[79]Kutz, *Complicity*, 122.
[80]Kutz, *Complicity*, 176.
[81]Kutz, *Complicity*, 169.
[82]Kutz, *Complicity*, 171.
[83]Kutz, *Complicity*, 172.
[84]Kutz, *Complicity*, 191.
[85]Kutz, *Complicity*, 188–9.
[86]Kutz, *Complicity*, 189.

Second, individuals can take a 'character-based' or 'symbolic' approach to accountability.[87] Drivers can make the decision to buy the environmentally friendly cooling system, and gun-sellers can refuse to sell to people with known mental instability, as a symbolic gesture, which can potentially affect others' decision-making. Both motives are individualistic: 'Reflection on who we are can thus supply accountability for what we together do.'[88]

Kutz's piecemeal solution is not entirely convincing for our case. While the gun-seller case shares similarities with the clothing case – it enables others to cause harm – a gun is a lethal weapon. Buying clothes is not equivalent. It is only when clothes are produced and purchased in the vast quantities they are today that it results in labour and environmental harms. The gun-seller has a prima facie reason for being concerned about the products they sell. Clothing consumers do not have a prima facie reason for moral reflection on buying clothes. In fact, consumers can claim they are contributing to job creation in Global South countries and economic growth. Kutz could respond that together consumers create and perpetuate a culture that endorses fast fashion, constantly sets new trends and views clothing as a disposable item. However, even if consumers do together perpetuate this culture, is this enough to ground liability? As I argued above, consumers perpetuate this culture, but this is at least facilitated by producers who channel huge amounts of money into various forms of manipulation. Also, consumers are constrained to some extent by social norms.

The driver case also shares features of our case: the drivers do not intend to contribute to environmental damage, are not engaged in a joint project and only collectively cause harm. But Kutz does not consider the role of the corporations who make the cars. Why do the corporations not see themselves as having quasi-participatory accountability and why don't they make the symbolic gesture of replacing the cooling systems with environmentally better alternatives as standard? Better yet, why don't governments legislate to ensure that car manufacturers install the non-ozone-depleting cooling systems? Kutz could respond that together producers and consumers create the environment where car use is normalized, high-spec cooling systems are demanded and the environmental impact is not a priority. The consumers and producers could all see themselves as having 'quasi-participatory accountability' and it is within the power of both individual consumers and producers to take up 'symbolic' accountability; thus, they are all complicit.

However, each consumer who purchases a car or cooling system makes a marginal or imperceptible difference to the harm. But if the producers stopped producing the cooling systems, then consumers would not be able to buy them, and the harm would stop. It is within the power of the producers to stop the

---

[87]Kutz, *Complicity*, 190.
[88]Kutz, *Complicity*, 191.

harm. Why then is the consumer's and the producer's responsibility equivalent? Seeking to attribute complicit accountability to all participants, no matter how minimal their participation, deflects attention from the agents who are properly accountable on the standard definitions of moral responsibility. Similarly in the clothing case, each individual consumer's purchase of a garment makes no difference. But a producer could implement better working practices across their supply chain. The significant difference in the size of the contribution to harm and the potential impact the agents could have on the harm mean that the agents do not all share the same kind of responsibility for the harm.

Young finds Kutz's account of the Dresden bombing persuasive: she finds it 'an excellent account of complicity in an endeavor where many people participate and coordinate their actions to bring about determinate results'.[89] I, however, am less persuaded. The complicity principle is plausible in cases where individuals have more-or-less equal power to decide to participate or not in a joint enterprise. But in cases where individuals have little or no choice, for example, they are conscripted, or they face economic or social ostracization if they refuse to participate, then it is less convincing. There is a lack of analysis of power in Kutz's analysis, and indeed in Young's, as I have already argued.

When it comes to unstructured collective harms, however, Young is not persuaded. She argues that 'In the absence of an *intent* to produce the outcome, surely those who participate should not be found *guilty* in the same way that those who participate in a war crime are.'[90] The lack of intent means that agents should not be held accountable for the harms. Young argues that 'What we should seek is not a variation on a weaker form of liability, but rather a different conception of responsibility altogether.'[91] On this point, I agree with Young. Why do we need to seek the *accountability* of each individual who participates in everyday practices that have unintended harmful outcomes?

Alison Jaggar and Corwin Aragon agree that Kutz's theory of complicity does not apply to structural injustice. However, they do not agree with Young that this renders the concept of complicity altogether unhelpful. Instead, they argue that a different conception of complicity could do the work. They argue that *interpersonal* complicity refers to the actions, attitudes or intentions of specific individuals in connection with intentional wrongdoing. *Institutional* complicity refers to the complicity of all agents who are members of a collective that commits wrongdoing. Both of these forms of complicity are 'liability lite'.[92] But *structural* complicity is different; it doesn't require *mens rea*. Instead, it refers

---

[89]Young, *Responsibility for Justice*, 102.
[90]Young, *Responsibility for Justice*, 103.
[91]Young, *Responsibility for Justice*, 104.
[92]Corwin Aragon and Alison M. Jaggar, 'Agency, Complicity, and the Responsibility to Resist Structural Injustice', *Journal of Social Philosophy* 49, no. 3 (2018): 449.

to the complicity of individuals in unintentionally perpetuating unjust social structures. They write,

> When social structures are unjust, they orient individuals to re-enact injustice and when people act on habituated dispositions to think, feel, and act in conformity with unjust structures, they are complicit in the injustice of those structures.[93]

Jaggar and Aragon recognize that individuals might be 'forced' into participating in structural injustice and do not intend to cause harm. However, they argue that

> 'Going along' with unjust processes is not morally neutral, regardless of our intention; instead it reinforces and normalizes those processes. Without complicity, injustice could not happen. To be complicit is to be morally compromised; our characters and conduct are morally tainted by being involved in wrongness and acting out the orientation to reproduce injustice.[94]

This structural complicity grounds moral responsibility to remedy the injustice. This moral responsibility involves reflecting on our complicity, working to change ourselves and the unjust social structures.[95]

However, both Kutz's theory and Aragon and Jaggar's approach fail to include an analysis of power. Consider Kutz's car example and our clothes case. In these cases, the producers could stop the harm. If producers did not create CFC cooling systems, then consumers couldn't buy them. If garment producers didn't produce fast fashion, consumers couldn't purchase it. In these cases, it is not only the lack of intent that is worrying in terms of attributing complicity to ordinary individuals, it is the difference in power. Why is the consumer's responsibility equivalent to producers when they do not have the same power to change the structures? The concept of structural complicity also elides power relations and obscures what is structural about structural injustice. It is too strong to argue that individuals bear complicity for the economic, social, political and ideological structures into which they are born. Aragon and Jaggar argue that their account is an improvement on Young's because structural complicity is 'a normative concept with a negative moral valence which provides a moral rationale for our responsibility'.[96] But that is precisely what Young was trying to avoid, and for good reason. Attaching negative moral responsibility to ordinary individuals merely for trying to live their lives in the context of unjust structures

---

[93]Aragon and Jaggar, 'Agency, Complicity, and the Responsibility to Resist Structural Injustice', 450.
[94]Aragon and Jaggar, 'Agency, Complicity, and the Responsibility to Resist Structural Injustice', 451.
[95]Aragon and Jaggar, 'Agency, Complicity, and the Responsibility to Resist Structural Injustice', 452.
[96]Aragon and Jaggar, 'Agency, Complicity, and the Responsibility to Resist Structural Injustice', 447.

is too strong and unfair. Political responsibility is a more helpful concept when considering responsibility for structural injustice.

Conclusion

I have argued that ordinary individual consumers are not morally responsible for sweatshop labour. This conclusion is potentially disturbing. *We know* that sweatshop labour exists, so how can consumers not be blameworthy? On the 'liability model' at least, consumers are not blameworthy because they do not demonstrate a faulty 'quality of will' when purchasing clothes. When purchasing clothes, individual consumers do not intentionally violate a moral obligation; rather their behaviour can be excused because the contribution to harm is inadvertent or the result of social duress. The lack of direct causal connection and lack of intent mean that holding individuals blameworthy for sweatshop labour is unfair.

Despite appearances, this does not let consumers off-the-hook. What I have shown in this chapter is that a well-established deontological conception of moral responsibility is not equipped to deal with sweatshop labour. I have also argued that consequentialist and complicity-based arguments struggle in the case of sweatshop labour. However, there is another tradition of moral responsibility in Western philosophy that I have not yet discussed – virtue ethics. In the next chapter, I argue that Youngian political responsibility looks suspiciously like a virtue: it is a forward-looking responsibility for justice, it is based on role responsibility, it is discretionary, it requires practical wisdom to implement it and it involves criticism without blame.

But I will not argue in support of the virtue ethical perspective of political responsibility that I attribute to Young. Instead, I will argue that we should focus on a *political* conception of political responsibility. Moral responsibility is only one type of responsibility; it is one part of a bigger picture. Young's key insight is that it is essential to create a supplementary framework that can deal with structural injustice. That is what Young sought to achieve with her 'social connection model' of responsibility and the political responsibility that it generates: we cannot *blame* individuals for structural injustice, but we can *hold them responsible*. In Chapter 6 I develop a different interpretation of political responsibility: that it is a responsibility to develop the capacity for political solidarity. In the final chapter, I look at what this entails in practice.

Chapter 6
Political responsibility

Many philosophers have lamented philosophy's inability to account for responsibility under the conditions of globalized, advanced capitalism. Hans Jonas pointed out back in 1984 that traditional theories of ethics and moral responsibility were becoming anachronistic.[1]

> Modern technology has introduced actions of such novel scale, objects, and consequences that the framework of former ethics can no longer contain them … To be sure, the old prescriptions of the 'neighbor' ethics – of justice, charity, honesty, and so on – still hold in their intimate immediacy for the nearest, day-by-day sphere of human interaction. But this sphere is overshadowed by a growing realm of collective action where doer, deed, and effect are no longer the same as they were in the proximate sphere, and which by the enormity of its powers forces upon ethics a new dimension of responsibility never dreamed of before.[2]

Other philosophers also believed that traditional conceptions of responsibility were fundamentally challenged by the new circumstances of the late twentieth century. John Ladd responded to the Bhopal explosion of 1984 – at that point, the biggest industrial disaster in history – that 'the adherence by most philosophers to a narrow, legalistic notion of responsibility … has rendered meaningful discourse about moral responsibility in contexts like the Bhopal disaster impossible, if not incoherent'.[3] Samuel Scheffler argued that 'restrictive' theories

---

[1]Young opens her 2004 paper with a quote from Jonas: Iris Marion Young, 'Responsibility and Global Labor Justice', *Journal of Political Philosophy* 12, no. 4 (2004): 365. She also cites him on the idea that 'Political responsibility seeks not to reckon debts, but aims rather to bring about results'. Young, 'Responsibility and Global Labor Justice', 379.

[2]Hans Jonas, *The Imperative of Responsibility: In Search of an Ethics for the Technological Age* (London: University of Chicago Press, 1985), 6.

[3]John Ladd, 'Bhopal: An Essay on Moral Responsibility and Civic Virtue', *Journal of Social Philosophy* 22, no. 1 (1991): 73.

of moral responsibility, which focus on small-scale, interpersonal interactions, are deeply entrenched in our psyche and practices but are invalid in the context of modern science, technology, communication, travel and economic and political interdependence. While consequentialists have a response – holding individuals responsible for all the possible outcomes of their actions across the whole world – this is not internalizable by most people. He concludes, 'the net effects of these developments may be, not to encourage the substitution of a non-restrictive conception of responsibility for more restrictive ideas, but rather to leave our thinking about responsibility in some disarray'.[4] Young thought that Scheffler had 'identified a key problem in contemporary moral theory and practice',[5] but she disagreed that our ethics are left in disarray. Instead, she argued that 'we need a plausible way of conceiving responsibility that connects individual agency to structural processes'.[6] She aimed to work towards this with her conception of political responsibility.[7]

In the previous chapter, I argued that a person can be held morally blameworthy when they intentionally violate a moral obligation. When it comes to structural injustice, the lack of intent and the lack of direct causal connection means that holding each other blameworthy for structural injustice is inappropriate; individuals' contributions to structural injustice are inadvertent or the product of social duress and therefore excused. This does not deny the fact that there is injustice that needs to be acknowledged and remedied; rather, it shows that the traditional frameworks of moral responsibility are not equipped to deal with responsibility for structural injustice. These traditional frameworks, however, are only one part of a much bigger picture. In this bigger picture, we contribute to the harming of social groups, or masses of distant people, or to the background structural injustice that disadvantages certain groups and privileges others; but we contribute unintentionally and in a causally indirect or negligible way. Nonetheless, we are somehow connected to and involved in this harm. As Young writes,

> If social philosophy assumes that intended and deliberate action is the primary focus of moral judgment, it risks ignoring or even excusing some of the most important sources of oppression.[8]

---

[4]Samuel Scheffler, 'Individual Responsibility in a Global Age', in *Boundaries and Allegiances: Problems of Justice and Responsibility in Liberal Thought* (Oxford: Oxford University Press, 2001), 46.

[5]Young, 'Responsibility and Global Labor Justice', 374.

[6]Iris Marion Young, 'Political Responsibility and Structural Injustice', *The Lindley Lecture* (University of Kansas, 2003), 8.

[7]Young, 'Responsibility and Global Labor Justice', 8.

[8]Iris Marion Young, *Justice and the Politics of Difference* (Princeton, NJ: Princeton University Press, 1990), 150.

Young thought it essential to create a supplementary framework of responsibility that can account for responsibility for structural injustice. This is what she aimed to do with her 'social connection model' of responsibility.[9] On the social connection model, individuals share *political* responsibility for structural injustice they are connected to. This political responsibility is nonblameworthy – individuals can be criticized but not blamed for structural injustice or for failing to act on political responsibility or doing so in an inappropriate way.[10] The responsibility is shared among everyone connected to structural injustice, instead of isolating individuals or groups for blame or recrimination. Political responsibility is forward-looking – it aims to overcome structural injustice, not to attach blame for one-off actions or to reckon debts. And it can only be discharged through collective action.

This new conception of responsibility has generated a lot of philosophical attention and critique. Critics argue it is too vague: what does political responsibility actually entail?[11] They also claim that it is non-motivating: why would anyone act on this responsibility if they are not blamed for structural injustice, nor blamed for failing to act on political responsibility?[12] Some philosophers and political theorists have sought to expand traditional conceptions of moral responsibility,[13] or to find new, innovative approaches to moral responsibility or complicity, to explain ordinary individuals' moral responsibility for structural injustice or to correct for Young's perceived mistakes.[14] But I think that Young, and the other theorists mentioned above, are right. It is legitimate to continue using the traditional models of moral and legal responsibility for their intended purposes. But our world has changed, and instead of trying to reshape or modify existing models of responsibility, it makes sense to rethink it anew. As Young puts it,

---

[9]Iris Marion Young, *Responsibility for Justice* (Oxford: Oxford University Press, 2011), 104–13.

[10]Young, *Responsibility for Justice*, 113–22, 144.

[11]Christian Barry and Kate Macdonald, 'How Should We Conceive of Individual Consumer Responsibility to Address Labour Injustices?', in *Global Justice and International Labour Rights*, ed. Faina Milman-Sivan, Yossi Dahan and Hanna Lerner (Cambridge: Cambridge University Press, 2016), 92–118; Robin Zheng, 'What Is My Role in Changing the System? A New Model of Responsibility for Structural Injustice', *Ethical Theory and Moral Practice* 21 (2018): 869–85; Christian Neuhäuser, 'Structural Injustice and the Distribution of Forward-Looking Responsibility', *Midwest Studies in Philosophy* 38 (2014): 232–51; Henning Hahn, 'The Global Consequence of Participatory Responsibility', *Journal of Global Ethics* 5, no. 1 (2009): 43–56.

[12]Martha C. Nussbaum, 'Foreword', in *Responsibility for Justice*, ed. Iris Marion Young (Oxford: Oxford University Press, 2011), ix–xxv; Zheng, 'What Is My Role in Changing the System? A New Model of Responsibility for Structural Injustice'.

[13]Barry and Macdonald, 'How Should We Conceive of Individual Consumer Responsibility to Address Labour Injustices?'

[14]Charlotte Knowles, 'Responsibility in Cases of Structural and Personal Complicity: A Phenomenological Analysis', *The Monist* 104 (2021): 224–37; Corwin Aragon and Alison M. Jaggar, 'Agency, Complicity, and the Responsibility to Resist Structural Injustice', *Journal of Social Philosophy* 49, no. 3 (2018): 439–60; Zheng, 'What Is My Role in Changing the System? A New Model of Responsibility for Structural Injustice'; Mara Marin, *Connected by Commitment: Oppression and Our Responsibility to Undermine It* (Oxford: Oxford University Press, 2017).

'What we should seek is not a variation on a weaker form of liability, but rather a different conception of responsibility altogether.'[15] This makes even more sense when the arguments of this book are taken into account. I have suggested, using a critical realist social ontology, that structural elaboration is the unintended outcome of the actions of all the agents in a given time; the resulting structures are unpredictable and unintended. In other words, agents do not control what the structural framework will look like in the future. Moreover, to the extent that any agents do have any control over this, or perhaps more plausibly 'influence' over this, they are powerful corporate agents like multinational corporations or states, not ordinary individuals acting alone. Powerful agents have more of a chance of getting what they want, either maintaining structures as they are or creating new structures that benefit them. In light of this, seeking to blame ordinary individuals *for the structures* is nonsensical.

In this chapter, I want to defend the concept of political responsibility as a new way of thinking about responsibility for structural injustice, but I take a different perspective on it to Young. First, I outline three different ways of conceiving of political responsibility: Arendt's conception, which I argue is a *virtú* conception; *virtue* conceptions, including socially conscious consumerism and the role-ideal model of responsibility; and Young's conception, which is an ambiguous combination of the *virtú* and virtue approaches.[16] In the second part of the chapter, I outline a new conception of political responsibility borrowing Arendt's concept of a 'political virtue'. I argue that political responsibility entails the responsibility to develop the capacity for political solidarity, because it is only through acting in solidarity with others that structural injustice can be overcome.

Political responsibility as *virtú*

Arendt made the distinction between legal, moral and political responsibility in response to Joel Feinberg's essay 'Collective Responsibility'. Feinberg argued

---

[15]Young, *Responsibility for Justice*, 104.

[16]The reader might recognize the virtue/*virtú* distinction from Bonnie Honig, *Political Theory and the Displacement of Politics* (New York: Cornell University Press, 1993). But Honig uses terms differently to me. Honig identifies Kant, Rawls and Sandel as virtue theories, because their theories 'displace conflict, identify politics with administration and treat juridical settlement as the task of politics and political theory'. Whereas Nietzsche and Arendt's *virtù* theories characterize 'politics as a disruptive practice that resists the consolidations and closures of administrative and juridical settlement for the sake of the perpetuity of political contest'. Honig argues that virtue theories of politics, in their quest to settle politics in forms of legal administration, have anti-democratic tendencies. Ultimately, politics will always involve both settlement and contestation. While I have been inspired by Honig's set-up of the virtue-*virtù* distinction, I am using it in a more literal sense to question whether the specific concept of political responsibility is a virtue, something that is morally praiseworthy and related to character, or a *virtù*, something that is political, responds to changing circumstance and does not have moral goodness at its centre.

that 'Guilt consists in the intentional transgression of a prohibition.'[17] Thus, *'there can be no such thing as vicarious guilt'*.[18] Only the individual who intentionally transgressed a prohibition (be it legal or moral) can be said to be 'guilty' and should 'pay for his sins'.[19] Arendt agrees with Feinberg that legal and moral standards 'always relate to the person and what the person has done'.[20] But this posed a problem. Arendt wanted to understand what kind of responsibility 'ordinary Germans' bore for the Holocaust. Because legal and moral responsibility depend on personal responsibility, Arendt believed individuals were not legally nor morally responsible, unless they themselves committed a crime. So in what way can these others be said to have been responsible?

According to Arendt, Feinberg assumes that all issues can be subjected to moral or legal judgments, rendering political issues no more than a 'special case' that can be judged according to these same standards. She argues that the rise of Christianity has imposed a hierarchy of values: the strictest standards are moral, and then legal standards are next, with 'customs and manners' coming in last.[21] Arendt aims to rehabilitate the concept of 'political responsibility' as an equally important and distinct kind of responsibility; it is a collective responsibility shared by citizens.

There are important practical reasons for clarifying the roles of legal, moral and political responsibility. For Arendt, the aim of legal responsibility is clear; it exists to protect the political community. When assigning legal responsibility, she thinks that 'it is irrelevant who is better off, the wrongdoer or the wrong-sufferer. As citizens we must prevent wrongdoing since the world we all share, wrongdoer, wrong-sufferer, and spectator, is at stake; the City has been wronged.'[22] The idea that legal responsibility should protect the political community is not particularly controversial. H. L. A. Hart has a similar understanding of the function of the law: we punish 'to protect society from the harm that crime does and not to pay back the harm that they have done'.[23] Arendt's conception of moral responsibility, by contrast, is highly idiosyncratic.

Arendt considers moral responsibility to be self-regarding. She claims that the most influential moral principles are self-referential – 'love thy neighbour as *thyself*', 'Don't do unto others what you don't want to be done to *yourself*' and Kant's maxim, 'Act in such a way that the maxim of your action can become a

---

[17]Joel Feinberg, 'Collective Responsibility', *Journal of Philosophy* 65, no. 21 (1968): 676.
[18]Feinberg, 'Collective Responsibility', 676.
[19]Feinberg, 'Collective Responsibility', 676.
[20]Hannah Arendt, 'Collective Responsibility', in *Responsibility and Judgment*, ed. Jerome Kohn (New York: Schocken Books, 2003), 148.
[21]Hannah Arendt, 'Thinking and Moral Considerations', in *Responsibility and Judgment*, ed. Jerome Kohn (New York: Schocken Books, 2003), 182.
[22]Arendt, 'Thinking and Moral Considerations', 182.
[23]H. L. A. Hart, *Punishment and Responsibility: Essays in the Philosophy of Law*, 2nd edn (Oxford: Oxford University Press, 2008), 201.

general law for all intelligible beings.'[24] All of these rules, she writes, 'take as their standard the Self and hence the intercourse of man with himself'.[25] Retaining moral integrity involves living according to Socrates' advice: 'It is better to suffer wrong than to do wrong.'[26] It is worse to do wrong because a person is in constant dialogue with oneself; they are 'two-in-one'.[27] She interprets Socrates as implying that 'If I disagree with other people, I can walk away; but I cannot walk away from myself, and therefore I better first try to be in agreement with myself before I take all others into consideration.'[28] The ability to think for oneself and judge oneself is a non-technical, pre-philosophic ability, which all people possess, and is practised in solitude.[29] The moral person is the person who learns to think for themselves.

We tend to think that morality imposes a set of obligations, as does the law; but Arendt claims that 'the problem of making moral propositions obligatory has plagued moral philosophy since its beginning with Socrates'.[30] This is because, unlike with legal responsibility, moral responsibility imposes no real-world sanctions, and the threat of 'future rewards and punishments' in the afterlife is no longer a plausible philosophical foundation, nor a motivation for moral action for many individuals.[31] Arendt also rejects thinking about morality in terms of obligations because she claims that one set of obligations can easily be exchanged for another. This is how she interprets the collapse of morality in Nazi Germany, where morality 'stood revealed in the original meaning of the word, as a set of *mores*, of customs and manners, which could be exchanged for another set with no more trouble than it would take to change the table manners of a whole people'.[32] Persons who hold fast to moral principles are not to be trusted, because they accept rules that are given to them; it is 'the doubters and skeptics' who will constantly ask themselves whether they can live with what they are doing.[33]

Arendt's account of moral responsibility poses many problems. Peter Steinberger considers it nihilistic, creating 'a certain kind of intellectual anarchy' by undermining our existing categories.[34] Whatever the validity of Arendt's

---

[24]Hannah Arendt, 'Some Questions of Moral Philosophy', in *Responsibility and Judgment*, ed. Jerome Kohn (New York: Schocken Books, 2003), 76. Her emphasis.

[25]Arendt, 'Some Questions of Moral Philosophy', 76.

[26]Arendt, 'Some Questions of Moral Philosophy', 90; Arendt, 'Collective Responsibility', 151.

[27]Arendt, 'Some Questions of Moral Philosophy', 92.

[28]Arendt, 'Some Questions of Moral Philosophy', 90.

[29]Arendt, 'Some Questions of Moral Philosophy', 93.

[30]Arendt, 'Some Questions of Moral Philosophy', 72.

[31]Arendt, 'Collective Responsibility', 153.

[32]Hannah Arendt, 'Personal Responsibility under Dictatorship', in *Responsibility and Judgment*, ed. Jerome Kohn (New York: Schocken Books, 2003), 43.

[33]Arendt, 'Personal Responsibility Under Dictatorship', 45.

[34]Peter J. Steinberger, 'Hannah Arendt on Judgment', *American Journal of Political Science* 34, no. 3 (1990): 819.

position on moral responsibility, we need to understand it to consider Arendtian political responsibility. For Arendt, 'In the center of moral considerations of human conduct stands the self; in the centre of political considerations of conduct stands the world.'[35] The 'world' means something specific to Arendt; the world is the public sphere which enables individuals to voice their plural perspectives on common affairs (plurality) and provides a space for enacting new beginnings (natality). Arendt likens the world to a table – it separates individuals from each other yet allows them to communicate about common themes and to consider common concerns from each other's point of view.[36] The world precedes our birth and outlasts our death.[37] It must be maintained in order that a space in which individuals can communicate continues to exist: 'If the world is to contain a public space, it cannot be erected for one generation and planned for the living only; it must transcend the life-span of mortal men.'[38]

What Arendt hoped to encourage by identifying the concept of political responsibility was that all individuals would take up their responsibility for the maintenance of the world. The end of the world is when the common world is seen from one perspective, which presents itself as the *only* perspective.[39] Many people in Nazi Germany abdicated their political responsibility, allowing the evil of totalitarianism to take its place: dictators put their faith in absolutist ideologies that preached the inevitable outcomes of human history, people like Eichmann reduced themselves to 'cogs in the machine' who existed to obey orders, and more controversially, 'unpolitical Jews' failed to rise up and fight the destruction of the world which would have allowed their viewpoints to be heard.[40]

Political responsibility is distinct from legal responsibility because legal responsibility entails obeying the law, regardless of whether the law is justified. By contrast, political responsibility insists that individuals remain vigilant as to the political system under which they live and ensure that the public/political/plural human world is maintained or reconstituted. Therefore, civil disobedience, breaking the law or revolution may be the *politically responsible* thing to do when the human world is threatened. Political responsibility is also sharply distinguished from moral responsibility in Arendtian thought. The morally responsible person will not do wrong, but the politically responsible person might have to. Arendt often quotes Machiavelli who instructed the Florentine Prince to learn 'how not to be

---

[35]Arendt, 'Collective Responsibility', 153.
[36]Hannah Arendt, *The Human Condition*, 2nd edn (London: University of Chicago Press, 1998), 52.
[37]Arendt, *The Human Condition*, 55; Lawrence J. Biskowski, 'Practical Foundations for Political Judgment: Arendt on Action and World', *Journal of Politics* 55, no. 4 (1993): 879.
[38]Arendt, *The Human Condition*, 55.
[39]Arendt, *The Human Condition*, 58.
[40]Margaret Canovan, *Hannah Arendt: A Reinterpretation of Her Political Thought* (Cambridge: Cambridge University Press, 1994), 52.

good' – to place the city's needs above his own clean conscience.[41] She writes, 'The political answer to the Socratic proposition would be "What is important in the world is that there be no wrong; suffering wrong and doing wrong are equally bad". Never mind who suffers it; your duty is to prevent it.'[42] Another difference is that legal and moral responsibility attribute 'guilt' to individuals for particular events and are judged according to the law or the self, respectively, but political 'responsibility' is collective and is judged in relation to the world.

The aim of conceptualizing political responsibility is to find a form of responsibility that does not imply guilt but does imply some sort of responsibility for the world. The aim is not to let ordinary individuals off the hook, but instead to more accurately determine the kind of responsibility they have. Their responsibility is not legal or moral, but it is political. In fact, Arendt argues that claiming that all German citizens of the time were morally responsible for the Nazis' crimes was *harmful* because it obscured where guilt truly lies – with the people who actually committed immoral and illegal acts.

> Morally speaking, it is as wrong to feel guilty without having done anything specific as it is to feel free of all guilt if one actually is guilty of something. I have always regarded it as the quintessence of moral confusion that during the postwar period in Germany those who personally were completely innocent assured each other and the world at large how guilty they felt, while very few of the criminals were prepared to admit even the slightest remorse. The result of this spontaneous admission of collective guilt was of course a very effective, though unintended, white-wash of those who *had* done something: as we have already seen, where all are guilty, no one is.[43]

Arendt was not the only post-war philosopher who thought that attributing guilt to the German people was unwise. Karl Jaspers also made the distinction between 'criminal guilt', which applied to the perpetrators of actual crimes related to the genocide, and 'political liability', which extended to German citizens – a responsibility to pay for the crimes of the regime under which they were governed.[44] According to Jaspers 'there can be no collective guilt of a people or a group within a people – except for political liability. To pronounce a

---

[41]For example, Arendt, 'Collective Responsibility', 154; Arendt, 'Some Questions of Moral Philosophy', 80.

[42]Arendt, 'Collective Responsibility', 153.

[43]Arendt, 'Personal Responsibility under Dictatorship', 28.

[44]Jaspers unhelpfully uses the terms 'political guilt' and 'political liability' interchangeably. But he makes it clear that when liability is 'political' it is different in kind to moral or criminal guilt. He writes: 'Guilt … is necessarily collective as the political liability of nationals, but not in the same sense as moral and metaphysical, and never as criminal guilt.' Karl Jaspers, *The Question of German Guilt* (New York: Dial Press, 2000), 55–6.

group criminally, morally or metaphysically guilty is an error akin to the laziness and arrogance of average, uncritical thinking.'[45] There are similar dynamics at play when individuals express their guilt for structural injustices which are far beyond their control, like poverty, sweatshops and climate change. These individual effusions of guilt distract us from where guilt truly lies – with the agents who have it within their power to do something about it.

Young versus Arendt

Indeed, Young's theory of political responsibility was inspired by Arendt's. But Arendt sought to theorize responsibility for the past crimes of the Holocaust, whereas Young's question is different: 'How shall moral agents think about our responsibility in relation to structural social injustice?'[46] She writes of Arendt's distinction:

> I think that Arendt's effort to distinguish guilt from political responsibility is important and, with several refinements, can contribute to an answer to my starting question. I find highly unsatisfying, however, the meaning she gives to political responsibility.[47]

Young identifies two problems with Arendt's conception of political responsibility. The first is that Arendt ties the conception to membership of a political community. Young writes, 'It is a mystification to say that people bear responsibility simply because they are members of a political community, and not because of anything at all that they have done or not done.'[48] And Young argues that Arendt is inconsistent on this point. In contrast to the essay 'Collective Responsibility', in the book *Eichmann in Jerusalem*, Arendt discusses the failure to take up political responsibility not only of Germans but also of other nation states and foreign nationals who failed to resist deportations.[49] Arendt also finds the Danes, who stood up to Hitler and refused to deport Jews, a prime example of taking up political responsibility.[50] Thus, Young thinks that political responsibility 'derives from something more specific and active than mere membership'.[51] She writes that 'On this interpretation, political responsibility entails *doing* things (and perhaps not doing things), but doing things that indirectly contribute to the enactment of crimes or wrongs.'[52]

---

[45]Jaspers, *The Question of German Guilt*, 36.
[46]Young, *Responsibility for Justice*, 75.
[47]Young, *Responsibility for Justice*, 79.
[48]Young, *Responsibility for Justice*, 79.
[49]Young, *Responsibility for Justice*, 87.
[50]Young, *Responsibility for Justice*, 90–1.
[51]Young, *Responsibility for Justice*, 86.
[52]Young, *Responsibility for Justice*, 80.

Arendt may have been inconsistent in her use of the concept of political responsibility; nevertheless, there are good reasons within Arendt's overall framework for tying political responsibility to membership of a political community. As discussed above, Arendtian political responsibility is a responsibility to maintain the 'world', which is something that *citizens* share in common. An individual can avoid legal and moral responsibility, but political responsibility is unavoidable. The only way to avoid political responsibility is to leave a political community.[53] But for Arendt, leaving a political community means no longer being able to participate in a public sphere, thus engaging in political action and realizing oneself as an individual. Refugees and stateless people are the only persons who can avoid political responsibility, but this 'innocence' is completely undesirable: 'It is precisely this absolute innocence that condemns them to a position outside, as it were, of mankind as a whole.'[54] Therefore, tying political responsibility to membership is consistent with Arendt's conception of political action in the world.

The second issue Young raises with Arendt's conception of political responsibility is that it is 'backward-looking'. She writes, 'In Arendt's discussion, political responsibility seems to be a concept just as backward-looking as guilt. Her primary case is the Nazi Holocaust, whose events are in the past.'[55] Young wants to conceptualize political responsibility as 'forward-looking', in contrast to legal and moral responsibility, which are backward-looking. She writes, 'One *has* the responsibility always *now*, in relation to current events and in relation to their future consequences.'[56] Arendt was asking what responsibility ordinary Germans bore for the Holocaust, so she was necessarily considering responsibility for the past. However, as I have argued, Arendt's political responsibility is an ongoing responsibility for the world and entails the constitution of a new world should the current world be under threat or corrupted. Thus, even though Arendt is discussing a past event, she is still interested in the responsibility that German citizens had when the event was occurring. In other words, like Young, Arendt is arguing for a 'present and ongoing' responsibility. Her point is that Germans abdicated this responsibility in the past.

The real difference between Young and Arendt, as I see it, is the following. Arendt has a clear explanation of the distinction between moral and political responsibility: the latter is necessarily tied to political community – the world – and is amoral; the former is self-regarding and tied to conscience. Young has a different understanding of moral responsibility compared to Arendt's. Young explicitly cautions against a self-regarding interpretation of morality, claiming that

---

[53]Arendt, 'Collective Responsibility', 150.
[54]Arendt, 'Collective Responsibility', 150.
[55]Young, *Responsibility for Justice*, 92.
[56]Young, *Responsibility for Justice*, 92.

individuals who feel blameworthy for their role in perpetuating injustice are self-centred.[57] Morality, for Young, concerns others. She writes,

> A responsible person tries to deliberate about options before acting, makes choices that seem to be the best for all affected, and worries about how the consequences of his or her action may adversely affect others.[58]

And Young's starting question is different to Arendt's: she asks how we as 'moral agents' should conceptualize our responsibilities for justice, not how we as political agents (or citizens) ought to relate to the world. Thus, Arendt can make a sharp distinction between moral and political responsibility, but Young cannot. Both moral and political responsibility are other-regarding in Young's thought. She needs an explanation, then, as to why political responsibility is not simply a form of moral responsibility. Young hinges this distinction on the backward-lookingness of moral responsibility compared to the forward-lookingness of political responsibility. This way of framing the distinction, however, is questionable; there can be forward-looking varieties of moral responsibility – virtue.

Political responsibility as a virtue

In the previous chapter, I considered and rejected deontological and consequentialist models of moral responsibility for thinking about responsibility for structural injustice; but another way of thinking about it is through the lens of virtue ethics. Many modern versions of virtue ethics take their cues from Aristotle. Most of the Aristotelian virtues are self-regarding. Indeed, Rosalind Hursthouse and Glen Pettigrove argue that modern virtue ethical theories mainly employ three concepts from ancient Greece, which are all self-regarding: 'These are *arête* (excellence or virtue), *phronesis* (practical or moral wisdom) and *eudaimonia* (usually translated as happiness or flourishing).'[59] However, for Aristotle, there is a fundamental relationship between virtue and politics. The *Nicomachean Ethics* opens by stating that 'The science of human good is politics.'[60] Individual virtue is other-regarding in the sense that the more virtuous citizens there are, the better the society and political order will be.[61] It is important to cultivate virtue not only for one's sense of integrity and happiness but also to create a just society

---

[57]Young, *Responsibility for Justice*, 118.
[58]Young, *Responsibility for Justice*, 25.
[59]Rosalind Hursthouse and Glen Pettigrove, 'Virtue Ethics', *Stanford Encyclopedia of Philosophy*, 2016.
[60]Aristotle, *The Nicomachean Ethics*, *Oxford World's Classics* (Oxford: Oxford University Press, 2009), 3.
[61]Gisela Striker, 'Aristotle's Ethics as Political Science', in *The Virtuous Life in Greek Ethics*, ed. Burkhard Reis (Cambridge: Cambridge University Press, 2006), 140.

for all. This way of connecting morality and structural injustice can be seen in the current trend of socially conscious consumerism and Robin Zheng's 'role-ideal model' of responsibility.

Socially conscious consumerism

Socially conscious consumerism is a growing trend and a way that many individuals try to act on their political responsibility for global structural injustice. According to Kate Soper, socially conscious consumers ride bikes, buy organic food and fair trade, and opt for environmental goods and services, promoting a new way of thinking about the 'politics of consumption' and rejecting the negative by-products of our industrialized, polluting and materialistic way of life.[62] While citizen-consumers are in a minority, Soper views them as practicing an 'avant-garde consumer ethic', which, if it were implemented by more and more people, could lead to sustainable development and altruistically motivated consumption in the Global North and South.[63] Soper argues that the 'citizen-consumer' is not necessarily an activist but someone who feels that their potential for living the good life has been compromised by the environmental degradation and fast consumption practices of contemporary life.[64] In other words, their capacity for happiness or flourishing – *eudaimonia* – has been compromised by globalized neoliberal capitalism.

Michele Micheletti argues that this brand of virtue ethics has emerged because of the collapse of traditional categories of public and private, economy and government. In the advanced capitalist, globalized economy, government is slow to respond to global problems created by mass consumption, and corporations are often more powerful than governments. These conditions have generated a new virtue ethics, which emphasizes modern versions of traditional Aristotelian virtues, especially empathy, social justice and solidarity, and also patience (i.e. acknowledging that change will be slow and incremental); knowledge (a kind of enlightened self-interest about consumption); and a meta-virtue of wisdom, which is needed to decide how and when to act, and in what way, within the politicized global economy. She argues that 'Democratic political consumerism is a virtue-practicing activity. As such, it is an example of *phronesis*: virtues in action in everyday settings.'[65]

Through empirical research, Micheletti has found that socially conscious consumerism is having an impact. It is too early to assess how much of an impact,

---

[62]Kate Soper, 'Rethinking the "Good Life": The Consumer as Citizen', *Capitalism, Nature, Socialism* 15, no. 3 (2004): 115.

[63]Soper, 'Rethinking the "Good Life"', 114.

[64]Soper, 'Rethinking the "Good Life"', 112–13.

[65]Michele Micheletti, *Political Virtue and Shopping* (New York: Palgrave Macmillan, 2003), 150.

but it does have a range of benefits.[66] It gives, what she calls, 'simple folks' a tool for challenging corporations. It makes up for the weakness of traditional political institutions in dealing with globalized economic injustice. It is used in underdeveloped democracies – for example, boycotting Shell in Nigeria. It has revitalized established political bodies like NGOs and trade unions and increased their negotiating strength. And it is often used as a complement to other forms of civic engagement, not as an end in itself. Furthermore, socially conscious consumerism builds bridges between diverse organizations that come together to work on single-issue topics. For example, the Forest Stewardship Certification (FSC) labelling scheme brought together Indigenous groups, environmental groups, forest owners and furniture makers, who all had different public or private motives for preserving forests, but who were able to work together to create a successful campaign.[67]

Lucy Atkinson interviewed socially conscious consumers and found that they were generally motivated by an implicit conception of virtue ethics. They were concerned with 'being a good person', living a good life or a sense of personal integrity or authenticity:[68] in other words, capturing *arête* (virtue) and *eudaimonia* (flourishing). Rather than being purely selfish, however, Atkinson notes how they were practising a new kind of citizenship – one that merged private attitudes and behaviour with public goods. She writes, 'Among socially conscious consumers, marketplace behaviors offer a viable and meaningful way to connect their private concerns with concerns for their community, both near and distant. It is by attending to their private, individual concerns that consumers address moral and ethical issues at the collective level.'[69]

Socially conscious consumerism is an understandable response to the moral quandaries imposed upon individuals by globalized advanced capitalism. The literature stresses the intricacy of this response and the necessary integration of private and public concerns and rationales. As Micheletti points out, political consumerism is *one* strategy for challenging consumption and production practices.[70] There are other strategies, which usually combine with socially conscious consumption. It is also not generally lauded as a panacea for global structural injustice. As Soper puts it, to practice socially conscious consumerism 'is to acknowledge how minimal one's power is as an individual consumer – and then to use it nonetheless'.[71]

---

[66]Micheletti, *Political Virtue and Shopping*, 161–4.

[67]Micheletti, *Political Virtue and Shopping*, 154.

[68]Lucy Atkinson, 'Buying in to Social Change: How Private Consumption Choices Engender Concern for the Collective', *Annals of the American Academy of Political and Social Science* 644, no. 1 (2012): 196–203.

[69]Atkinson, 'Buying in to Social Change', 192.

[70]Micheletti, *Political Virtue and Shopping*, 166.

[71]Soper, 'Rethinking the "Good Life"', 115.

Despite having some attractive features, understanding political responsibility as a private consumerist virtue is not the right approach. If political responsibility is private virtue, it implies that good people cultivate and practice this virtue; thus, presumably, bad people don't. As Hursthouse and Pettigrove argue, 'The concept of a virtue is the concept of something that makes its possessor good: a virtuous person is a morally good, excellent or admirable person who acts and feels as she should.'[72] The literature on socially conscious consumerism shows that these consumers tend to be middle-class, well-educated and white, and often women.[73] They have the time and resources to be able to think about their consumption practices, spend more time shopping and spend more money on products, whereas other social groups are not in the same position. There is something troubling about positioning this group as the 'avant garde of contemporary ethics', as 'good' people in contrast to the 'bad' or 'less good' people who don't engage in these practices. There is a danger of reproducing 'class and gender stereotypes about which sorts of people are susceptible to a relative lack of proper virtue'.[74]

Furthermore, socially conscious consumerism individualizes the political and could even undermine collective action. As W. Lance Bennett argues, it is 'less like conventional social movements with leaders, organizations, and collective identity frames than ... *individualized collective action* where large numbers of people join in loosely coordinated activities centered on more personal emotional identifications and rationales'.[75] The problem is that 'the individualized orientation of the citizen-consumer further undermines the appeal of adopting collective identifications with party, ideology, or conventional movements'.[76] Socially conscious consumption could also undermine the generation of more radical proposals aimed at fundamentally challenging the global capitalist economy. It is an easy way out, providing a momentary salve for liberal guilt without threatening the privilege of consumers in the Global North. As Andrew Brooks puts it, 'Liberal-minded citizens in the global North can indulge in their consumption habits without calling for large-scale structural changes that could threaten their own privileged status in global society.'[77] Finally, empirical research suggests that despite having good intentions, ethical consumers 'rarely' purchase ethical

---

[72]Hursthouse and Pettigrove, 'Virtue Ethics'.

[73]Atkinson, 'Buying in to Social Change', 195; Micheletti, *Political Virtue and Shopping*, 157.

[74]Clive Barnett, Philip Cafaro and Terry Newholm, 'Philosophy and Ethical Consumption', in *The Ethical Consumer*, ed. Rob Harrison, Terry Newholm and Deirdre Shaw (London: Sage, 2005), 8.

[75]W. Lance Bennett, 'The Personalization of Politics: Political Identity, Social Media, and Changing Patterns of Participation', *Annals of the American Academy of Political and Social Science* 644, no. 1 (2012): 26.

[76]Bennett, 'The Personalization of Politics', 26.

[77]Andrew Brooks, *Clothing Poverty: The Hidden World of Fast Fashion and Second-Hand Clothes* (London: Zed Books, 2015), 216.

products; there is an 'intentions-behaviour gap' created by environmental factors, such as time pressure, competing ethical demands and the accessibility of cheaper alternatives.[78]

The role-ideal model of responsibility

Robin Zheng does not draw on Aristotelian virtues, but instead highlights the moral responsibility individuals bear to perform their social roles well. Zheng argues that responsibility for structural injustice is grounded in our existing social roles because *'roles are the site where structure meets agency'*.[79] All agents fulfil various social roles, such as parent or professional of some sort. In performing their social roles, they reproduce social structures. So instead of arguing that individuals bear responsibility for structural injustice by virtue of their connection to it, as Young argues, Zheng argues they bear responsibility because they reproduce it through performance of social roles. Drawing on the sociological theory of structural-functionalism, she argues that society is a *'boundary-maintaining system'* – if people deviate too far from their social roles, the system will restore order.[80]

However, social roles are necessarily open to interpretation. This is an insight from another sociological theory, symbolic interactionism, which highlights that social structures are built from interpersonal interactions that are constantly re-negotiated by individuals rethinking what their social roles entail. What makes a good parent or a good teacher depends on each individual's values, abilities and experiences. Thus, individuals can define their own 'role-ideal'.[81] And they can define their role-ideal for all the various social roles in their lives. The role-ideal model of responsibility posits that 'structural transformation is made possible when all individuals through-out the entire system *push the boundaries of their social roles'*.[82] The pressure of individuals pushing the boundaries of their social roles can create incremental change or eventually result in 'ruptural changes'.[83] Individuals must continually push their social roles 'so as to bring about the conditions of possibility for transformative change'.[84] Zheng argues that individuals are already committed to this because they are committed

---

[78]Michal J. Carrington, Benjamin A. Neville and Gregory J Whitwell, 'Why Ethical Consumers Don't Walk Their Talk: Towards a Framework for Understanding the Gap between the Ethical Purchase Intentions and Actual Buying Behaviour of Ethically Minded Consumers', *Journal of Business Ethics* 97 (2010): 139–58.
[79]Zheng, 'What Is My Role in Changing the System?', 870.
[80]Zheng, 'What Is My Role in Changing the System?', 874.
[81]Zheng, 'What Is My Role in Changing the System?', 875.
[82]Zheng, 'What Is My Role in Changing the System?', 877.
[83]Zheng, 'What Is My Role in Changing the System?', 877.
[84]Zheng, 'What Is My Role in Changing the System?', 878.

to living up to the role-ideals of their social roles, and good role-ideals aim at structural transformation. Zheng argues that this model of responsibility is more actionable than Young's, because individuals are already expected to perform their social roles well and will face sanctions if they don't. She gives the example of a teacher asked to diversify a curriculum.[85] If the teacher fails to do it, she will be sanctioned; not only is she expected to improve as a teacher, but she is also expected to push her social role in such a way that contributes to structural transformation.

Zheng tries to push the approach in a more political direction than socially conscious consumerism by emphasizing that individuals should push their social roles to enable transformative structural change. But she underestimates the fact that the kinds of activities she notes as pushing for justice – diversifying curricula, using gender-neutral language and so on – have been borne out of social movements, not out of individuals acting alone. It is a history of collective action that has paved the way for individuals to incorporate these sorts of activities into their daily social roles. Furthermore, she assumes that individuals designing their role-ideals will adopt an intersectional feminist theory of justice and that this will be supported by the institutions they work or participate in. However, subscriptions to this way of thinking about justice are not mainstream. Many people will design their role-ideal in a different way to what Zheng would envision as a good role-ideal. For example, take a cis-white, heterosexual man who works in a global garment corporation.[86] He is a libertarian, so he thinks that sweatshops provide jobs to workers who want and need them. He thinks that being a good employee involves maximizing profits and being accountable to shareholders. He thinks that he is performing his role well. Zheng wants to disagree because he's failing to challenge the intersectional exploitation of sweatshop labour. But he can simply disagree. Even after debating with others, he can hold fast to his capitalist-libertarian theory of justice. He can continue to promote his theory of justice, which will have very different outcomes to the ones Zheng wants. Moreover, the company he works for fully endorses his way of thinking about justice, not an intersectional-leftist-feminist perspective. This company, therefore, is not going to punish him for not pushing his social role in the direction of transformative structural change. In fact, the vast majority of people in the workforce, who are working for private companies, are not going to be encouraged to push their social roles (at least in the workplace) in the direction of transformative structural change because this is not in the interests of private businesses; they might actually be punished for doing so. This can also

---

[85]Zheng, 'What Is My Role in Changing the System?', 882.

[86]I use this example in Maeve McKeown, 'ETMP Discussion of Robin Zheng's "What Is My Role in Changing the System? A New Model of Responsibility for Structural Injustice"', Pea Soup, 2018.

be the case in public sector institutions, who ostensibly have an agenda more aligned with social justice.[87]

Ultimately, my main worry about virtue-ethical approaches to responsibility for structural injustice is that they are individualized and privatized and, therefore, play into pre-existing neoliberal ideals about responsibility. In his essay 'Good for Nothing', Mark Fisher argues that 'responsibilisation' is the greatest ideological success of neoliberal capitalism. He writes, 'Each individual member of the subordinate class is encouraged into feeling that their poverty, lack of opportunities, or unemployment, is their fault and their fault alone. Individuals will blame themselves rather than social structures, which in any case they have been induced into believing do not really exist (they are just excuses, called upon by the weak).'[88] A virtue understanding of political responsibility plays into this narrative. It implies that there is an ethical imperative upon the individual to work on one's character or social roles to be able to overcome structural injustices. It places an unreasonable ethical burden on the individual to counteract forces that are beyond their control and suggests that they are a bad person if they fail to do so.

Chandra Talpade Mohanty locates feminist practice at three levels: daily life, collective action in groups, and theory and pedagogy.[89] Zheng and socially conscious consumers are engaging in the third level (theory and pedagogy) and give us an account of the first level (action in our daily lives), but they don't tell us much about the second level – collective action. That is missing from their accounts, when in fact it is the precondition for their approaches. Collective action is something Young wanted to focus on, which brings us to Young's theory of political responsibility.

Youngian political responsibility

Young started out by asking what responsibility moral agents bear for structural injustice. Given the limitations of the liability model of responsibility in regard to structural injustice, she argues that agents are not morally responsible for it, but they are politically responsible. Youngian political responsibility, I suggest, is an ambiguous combination of Arendtian political responsibility, or *virtú*, and moral virtue.

---

[87]For a discussion of complaints being suppressed in the university sector, see Sara Ahmed, *Complaint!* (Durham, NC: Duke University Press, 2021).

[88]Mark Fisher, 'Good for Nothing', in *K-Punk: The Collected and Unpublished Writings of Mark Fisher*, ed. Darren Ambrose (London: Repeater Books, 2018), 749.

[89]Chandra Talpade Mohanty, *Feminism without Borders: Decolonizing Theory, Practicing Solidarity* (Durham, NC: Duke University Press, 2003), 5.

Young grounds political responsibility in 'connection' to structural injustice. While the meaning of connection is unclear – sometimes she refers to causal connection (contribution, participation), sometimes dependence on structural injustice and sometimes existence within unjust structures – I believe connection refers to reproduction of unjust structures through action.[90] Young understands political responsibility as having five features: it is not isolating, it judges background conditions, it is more forward-looking than backward-looking, it is a shared responsibility and it is discharged only through collective action.[91] It is the element of collective action that gives this responsibility its political flavour. She writes,

> Thus we can come around to Arendt's idea that this is a specifically *political* responsibility, as distinct from privately moral or juridical. Taking responsibility for structural injustice under this model involves joining with others to organize collective action to reform the structures. Most fundamentally, what I mean by 'politics' here is public communicative engagement with others for the sake of organizing our relationships and coordinating our actions most justly.[92]

Youngian political responsibility, therefore, wants to keep some aspects of Arendtian *virtú* – the emphasis on collective responsibility, the need for political action and willingness to endorse radical change. But she also wants to incorporate aspects of the moral approaches. She is considering how 'moral agents' should respond to structural injustice and what 'responsible' individuals should do (meaning people who consider others). In fact, there are good grounds for understanding Young's conception of political responsibility as a virtue. Political responsibility, as Young conceives of it, shares at least six features with moral virtues.

First, virtues are not acquired through having done or not done a specific act in the past. Instead, a virtue is a disposition which the moral individual has an ongoing responsibility to cultivate. The orientation of virtue is forward-looking. Second, tying political responsibility to 'justice' – a moral category – rather than the 'world' – a political and contingent circumstance – suggests that it falls into the category of virtue rather than *virtù*. Youngian political responsibility is a *forward-looking* responsibility for *justice*. Third, political responsibility involves engaging in collective action, but the first steps are acquiring knowledge of structural injustice, listening to the claims of victims and encouraging others

---

[90] I develop this argument in detail in Maeve McKeown, 'Iris Marion Young's ' "Social Connection Model" of Responsibility: Clarifying the Meaning of Connection', *Journal of Social Philosophy* 49, no. 3 (2018): 484–502.

[91] Young, *Responsibility for Justice*, 104–13.

[92] Young, *Responsibility for Justice*, 112.

to act with you;[93] in other words 'being' a conscious and engaged, politically responsible person. The sense of 'responsible' is thus different from when we talk about whether or not an agent is causally responsible for a harm that has occurred or is occurring. Young acknowledges that political responsibility draws on the idea of *role responsibility*,[94] a form of responsibility often associated with virtue ethics. It involves assuming an ongoing role as a politically responsible actor and being responsible within that role.

Fourth, Young's conception of political responsibility is criticized for being too vague, for failing to provide action-guidance.[95] But the vagueness of political responsibility is deliberate. This is because Young argues that it is *discretionary*, and it is open for individuals to decide how to act on their political responsibility depending on their social position and on how much power, privilege, interest or collective ability they have in relation to a particular structural injustice.[96] Virtue ethics is often criticized along the same lines – that it is 'unable to provide action-guidance'.[97] But virtue ethics is not in the business of telling people what to do; instead, it encourages individuals to develop the moral character required to figure out what to do.[98] So, fifth, we could argue that just as with other kinds of virtue, political responsibility requires the cultivation of *practical wisdom* (*phronesis*). Practical wisdom develops with experience. The person who has developed practical wisdom knows how to discern the relevant features of a situation and how to act in the most responsible way – that is, the best for all concerned.[99] As Julia Annas puts it, virtue ethics 'is not a theory which tells us what to do ... we neither have nor should want any such thing. Rather, it guides us by improving the practical reasoning with which we act.'[100]

Sixth, Young argues that individuals should not be blamed for failing to act on their political responsibility. But we could, as with virtues, avoid the use of the deontic terms right and wrong and discuss political responsibility in *axiological* terms – good and bad, better or worse.[101] Say a person lacks courage; it's not

---

[93]Serena Parekh, 'Getting to the Root of Gender Inequality: Structural Injustice and Political Responsibility', *Hypatia* 26, no. 4 (2011): 681.

[94]Young, *Responsibility for Justice*, 104.

[95]Kate MacDonald and Christian Barry, 'How Should We Conceive of Individual Consumer Responsibility to Address Labour Injustices?', in *Global Justice and International Labour*, ed. Faina Milman-Sivan, Yossi Dahan and Hanna Lerner (Cambridge: Cambridge University Press, 2016), 110; Henning Hahn, 'The Global Consequence of Participatory Responsibility', *Journal of Global Ethics* 5, no. 1 (2009): 49–50. Zheng, 'What Is My Role in Changing the System? A New Model of Responsibility for Structural Injustice', 879.

[96]Young, *Responsibility for Justice*, 142–7.

[97]Hursthouse and Pettigrove, 'Virtue Ethics'.

[98]G. E. M. Anscombe, 'Modern Moral Philosophy', *Philosophy* 33, no. 124 (1958): 1–19.

[99]Hursthouse and Pettigrove, 'Virtue Ethics'.

[100]Julia Annas, 'Being Virtuous and Doing the Right Thing', *Proceedings and Addresses of the American Philosophical Association* 78, no. 2 (2004): 73.

[101]Hursthouse and Pettigrove, 'Virtue Ethics'.

blameworthy that they failed to display courage in a particular situation, but they can work on and improve their moral character by recognizing this weakness and developing it for the future. Similarly, Young writes that 'we can and should be *criticized* for not taking action, not taking enough action, taking ineffective action, or taking action that is counterproductive'.[102] As with other virtues, criticism without blame can lead to a person working on that virtue.[103]

Thus, there is a compelling case to be made that political responsibility is a moral virtue. However, there are reasons for thinking that Young would not have endorsed either of the virtue conceptions of political responsibility presented here. Young's name comes up a lot in the socially conscious consumerism literature. Her theory of individualized responsibility taking is seen as an inspiration, lending theoretical credibility to the concept.[104] However, I'm not convinced that Young would endorse this approach. One of the reasons Young adopted a distinct conception of political responsibility over some version of moral responsibility is because she thinks that ordinary individuals who admit that they are to blame for their role in perpetuating injustice 'become more focused on themselves, their past actions, the state of their souls and their character, than on the structures that require change'.[105] This 'self-indulgence' is a distraction from the real task of getting involved in collective political action for change.[106] The empirical evidence shows that while thinking about the wider social benefits of their behaviour, socially conscious consumers *are* focused on the states of their soul or their character, which Young actively discredits. Even if socially conscious consumption is one strategy among many, and is other-regarding and publicly minded, it is nevertheless concerned with moral character and the good life. The *eudaimonia* aspect of this approach makes it an unsuitable candidate to fill in the blank of what Youngian political responsibility refers to.

Zheng takes Young as her starting point, but she also wants to create a new model of responsibility. Young's approach differs in at least two respects. First, Young drew on the concept of role responsibility to think about political responsibility, but Young pointed out that working within existing roles might be part of the problem. There are times when dismantling old roles and creating new ones is what's called for.[107] Second, Zheng's is an explicitly moral theory about the appropriate behaviour of individuals in social roles. But Young wants

---

[102]Young, *Responsibility for Justice*, 144.

[103]Michael Slote, *From Morality to Virtue* (Oxford: Oxford University Press, 1995), 121–4.

[104]Atkinson, 204; Clive Barnett, Philip Cafaro and Terry Newholm, 'Philosophy and Ethical Consumption', in *The Ethical Consumer*, ed. Rob Harrison Terry Newholm and Deirdre Shaw (London: Sage, 2005), 4–5; Michele Micheletti and Andreas Follesdal, 'Shopping for Human Rights. an Introduction to the Special Issue', *Journal of Consumer Policy* 30, no. 3 (2007): 168.

[105]Young, *Responsibility for Justice*, 118.

[106]Young, *Responsibility for Justice*, 118.

[107]Young, 'Responsibility and Global Labor Justice', 384–5.

to de-individualize political responsibility, making it a shared responsibility that demands collective action. Young insists that political responsibility has a political dimension; it involves collective action for change.

So, on the one hand, Youngian political responsibility does appear to be a virtue. On the other, there are strong reasons for thinking she would not endorse the more fully-fleshed-out virtue ethical conceptions of political responsibility. What, then, is Youngian political responsibility? My view is that Youngian political responsibility *is a form of moral responsibility*. As I interpret her, in Young's thought, there are two types of moral responsibility. This is an established view in moral philosophy: moral responsibility can refer to the appropriate conditions for praise and blame and what it is to be a morally responsible agent. In *Justice for Hedgehogs*, Ronald Dworkin distinguishes between moral responsibility as a virtue and moral responsibility as 'a relation between people and events'.[108] When we use the term 'moral responsibility' in the virtue sense, we are talking about whether 'someone behaved responsibly' or whether they are a responsible person.[109] When we talk about moral responsibility in a relational sense, we are interested in whether or not someone 'is or is not responsible for some event or consequence'.[110]

Mark Bovens describes the distinction as the difference between active and passive responsibility. Moral responsibility as accountability is a passive, *backward-looking* form of responsibility that asks for an account of what has happened and may involve some form of retribution – 'The central question is, "Why *did* you do it?" '[111] Moral responsibility as virtue is an active and *forward-looking* form of moral responsibility; it requires agents to think about preventing future harm – 'The central question here is: "what *is* to be done?" '[112] The relationship between the two forms of moral responsibility – accountability and virtue – is dynamic. Accountability encourages the cultivation of virtue in the future.[113]

Similarly, Young has an account of responsible agency, rather than just passive accountability. She thinks that the responsible person takes an active stance towards their responsibility and always considers others. For Young, a 'responsible person' deliberates before acting, makes choices in the interests of all who will be affected and worries about the consequences of those actions. Young thinks 'being responsible' implies thinking about others, not oneself.

---

[108]Ronald Dworkin, *Justice for Hedgehogs* (London: Belknap Press of Harvard University Press, 2011), 102.

[109]Dworkin, *Justice for Hedgehogs*, 102.

[110]Dworkin, *Justice for Hedgehogs*, 102.

[111]Mark Bovens, *The Quest for Responsibility: Accountability and Citizenship in Complex Organisations* (Cambridge: Cambridge University Press, 1998), 27.

[112]Bovens, *The Quest for Responsibility*, 27.

[113]Bovens, *The Quest for Responsibility*, 38–9.

Young also has an account of the relationship between backward-looking and forward-looking responsibility. She argues that moral and legal responsibility are 'primarily backward-looking'[114] and acknowledges the forward-looking elements (e.g. deterrence and reform).[115] The forward-looking/backward-looking distinction is not a sharp normative dichotomy but a description of how these practices function and interact with each other. This claim makes sense once we understand the two forms of moral responsibility as accountability (primarily backward-looking) impacting on moral responsibility as virtue (forward-looking).

Thus, as I read Young, the theory that there are two models of moral responsibility is implicit in her account. Young thinks there are two forms of moral responsibility in the other-regarding sense.[116] First, interactional – do not directly harm others. Directly harming others activates the 'liability model' of responsibility; the agent will be held to account. Second, structural – think about whether and how our actions contribute to structural injustice. It is the second form that constitutes 'political responsibility'. This is an active, or virtue, sense of responsibility. She writes, 'Just as it is appropriate to distinguish moral judgment about individual interaction from moral judgment about social-structural processes and their effects, it is necessary to distinguish a conception of individual responsibility in relation to each.'[117] Therefore, my suggestion is that Youngian 'political' responsibility is distinguished from 'moral' responsibility as follows: political responsibility is a moral responsibility individuals have towards structures and requires the cultivation of virtue; moral responsibility is a responsibility in relation to direct interactions with others, and it entails ascriptions of praise and blame.

While this seems like a neat solution, Young's position is more ambiguous than this suggests, for three reasons. First, moral responsibility as virtue can accommodate forward-lookingness and responsible agency, but it is self-regarding – which Young wants to avoid – and struggles to account for collective action – which Young wants to emphasize.

Second, as Zheng points out, Youngian political responsibility is more about 'the *unjust outcomes* that are produced by structural processes, and not the moral quality of individual agents'.[118] Thus, Zheng claims that Youngian political responsibility is closer to Dworkin's relational responsibility, or Bovens's passive responsibility, or the liability model than a virtue theory of responsibility. Young points this out herself when discussing the relationship between her conception of political responsibility and role responsibility. She says that political responsibility

---

[114]Young, 'Responsibility and Global Labor Justice', 368.

[115]Young, 'Responsibility and Global Labor Justice', 378.

[116]Young, *Responsibility for Justice*, 73.

[117]Young, *Responsibility for Justice*, 73–4.

[118]Robin Zheng, 'What Kind of Responsibility Do We Have for Fighting Injustice? A Moral-Theoretic Perspective on the Social Connections Model', *Critical Horizons* 20, no. 2 (2019): 112.

draws more on the idea of role responsibility than the liability usage, but it shares with the liability model 'a reference to the causes of wrongs – here in the form of structural processes that produce injustice'.[119]

Third, Young was influenced by a range of Continental theories of responsibility – not only Arendt but also the thought of Hans Jonas (as mentioned at the beginning), Jacques Derrida, Emmanuel Levinas and Larry May.[120] All these thinkers were grappling with something other than the traditional Western theories of moral responsibility with their emphasis on appropriate ascriptions of praise/ blame or responsible agency and more with what it means to be existentially responsible for the unjust circumstances into which one is born. While Young ultimately wants to locate the source of political responsibility in action (the reproduction of unjust structures), there is a lingering remainder of responsibility that arises through no fault of one's own, from simply existing in the circumstances of injustice.

Ultimately, therefore, I think that Young's conception of political responsibility is somewhat ambiguous. It does not have the clarity of Arendt's conception, nor the coherence of the virtue-ethical conception. She is grappling with a range of different conceptions of responsibility but leaves the tensions somewhat unresolved. In the next section, therefore, I will offer a potential solution for thinking about political responsibility.[121]

Political virtue

In trying to make sense of political responsibility for structural injustice, I suggest we return to Arendt. I have suggested that political responsibility is amoral for Arendt; Arendtian political responsibility is permissive in terms of what individuals are allowed to do in order to preserve the public sphere from the threat of tyranny. But there are limits to this amorality. Because the aim is to preserve the world, Arendt admits two 'moral precepts' into politics. These are forgiving and promising.[122] Forgiving is essential, because action in the world

---

[119]Iris Marion Young, 'Responsibility and Global Justice: A Social Connection Model', *Social Philosophy and Policy* 23, no. 1 (2006): 119.

[120]On Derrida and Levinas see Young, *Responsibility for Justice*, 118–22. On Larry May see Young, *Responsibility for Justice*, 110–11; Young, 'Responsibility and Global Justice', 122; Young, 'Responsibility and Global Labor Justice', 380.

[121]Zheng offers an alternative reading: she argues that Youngian political responsibility is grounded in causal contribution to structural injustice, which generates a prospective kind of responsibility as accountability (a kind of remedial responsibility for structural injustice). Such a responsibility does not licence blame, but rather the burden to collectively organize with others. Zheng, 'What Kind of Responsibility Do We Have for Fighting Injustice?'.

[122]Suzanne Duvall Jacobitti, 'The Public, the Private, the Moral: Hannah Arendt and Political Morality', *International Political Science Review* 12, no. 4 (1991): 287; Honig, *Political Theory and the Displacement of Politics*, 84; Arendt, *The Human Condition*, chapters 33–4.

has unknowable consequences. If people are going to be able to continue acting in the world, they need to be able to forgive each other when things go wrong. Promising is essential for similar reasons; we don't know what's going to happen next, so promises are the only way to maintain some guarantees and some stability.

These two moral precepts are not the same as private virtues. They are specifically political virtues because they depend upon the presence of others.[123] Promising happens in the form of contracts or treaties between agents. Forgiving releases actors from their past mistakes, when they trespassed against others, so that new beginnings are again possible. Arendt argues that these moral precepts do not derive 'from some supposedly higher faculty or from experiences outside action's own reach. They arise, on the contrary, directly out of the will to live together with others in the mode of acting and speaking, and thus they are like control mechanisms built into the very faculty to start new and unending processes.'[124]

Young doesn't discuss this, but Arendt's political virtues are relevant to her. Young argues that political responsibility is non-blameworthy: we shouldn't argue about what went on in the past, we shouldn't blame each other for not acting on political responsibility, and we shouldn't blame each other when things go wrong. This sounds a lot like Arendt's moral precept of forgiveness in politics. If we are to work together in collective action, we need to be able to forgive.[125] Also relevant is promising. For Arendt, 'the force of mutual promise or contract' keeps collectives together to enact new beginnings.[126] Indeed, Young recognizes the importance of promising to political responsibility in the form of solidarity. She writes,

> The sort of solidarity I am invoking is a relationship among many people who recognize and take up a shared responsibility in relation to the social institutions and practices they enact and support, to make them just. This solidarity is an ideal, *a promise*, and an engagement.[127]

Here, I think, is the crux of the matter. My suggestion is that we should understand political responsibility as a *political virtue* and specifically as *political solidarity*. Solidarity is a specifically political virtue because, like promising and forgiving, it depends on the presence of others; there can be no solidarity without people to be in solidarity with. Political solidarity is necessary if individuals are going to engage in the kinds of collective action that could disrupt and overcome

---

[123]Arendt, *The Human Condition*, 238.
[124]Arendt, *The Human Condition*, 246.
[125]Arendt, *The Human Condition*, 240.
[126]Arendt, *The Human Condition*, 245.
[127]Young, *Responsibility for Justice*, 121. My emphasis.

structural injustice. Political virtue is the point where politics and morality meet, but it is not the same as private virtue. The virtue conception implied that there is an ethical imperative to work on one's character to counteract structural injustice and had the potential to suggest that an individual is a bad person if they fail to do this. On the political virtue approach, the individual does not have a bad character and is not a bad person if they are not challenging structural injustice through socially conscious consumerism or virtuously fulfilling an existing social role with a view to ameliorating injustice; rather to be a moral person in the context of structural injustice, an agent ought to develop their capacity for political solidarity and then act on it.[128] Thus, individuals do not have to develop the *right character* to live the good, virtuous life but the *right capacities* to participate in collective action.[129] In the remainder of this chapter, I explain how political responsibility relates to empowerment, the work individuals must do in order to be politically responsible individuals, and why political responsibility does not involve blame.

Individual and collective empowerment

Philosophers in the Western traditions tend to focus on the responsibility of the privileged in relation to 'distant others'.[130] But one of the most striking aspects of Young's theory of political responsibility was her attempt to counteract this tendency by including everyone connected to structural injustice in shared responsibility for it. Of course, this was not Young's innovation; the responsibility to stand up and resist comes up time and again in the literature from, what Angela Davis calls, The Black Freedom Movement, which encompasses everything

---

[128]Other theorists have emphasized the necessity of a theory of solidarity to accompany Young's social connection model of responsibility. Ann Ferguson calls this 'transformational solidarity' and Carol Gould 'transnational solidarity.' Ann Ferguson, 'Iris Young, Global Responsibility, and Solidarity', in *Dancing with Iris: The Philosophy of Iris Marion Young*, ed. Ann Ferguson and Mechthild Nagel (Oxford: Oxford University Press, 2009), 185–99; Carol C. Gould, 'Varieties of Global Responsibility: Social Connection, Human Rights, and Transnational Solidarity', in *Dancing with Iris: The Philosophy of Iris Marion Young*, ed. Ann Ferguson and Mechthild Nagel (Oxford: Oxford University Press, 2009), 199–213.

[129]It could be argued that there is a step prior to cultivating the capacity for solidarity and acting on it, and that is 'cultivating responsiveness' to structural injustice in the first place, overcoming the Arendtian thoughtlessness, Sartrean bad faith, or Bourdieusian misrecognition that enables the constant reproduction of structural injustice. I decided not to engage with this problem in this book because I think Jade Schiff has already written an excellent book-length treatment of it, to which I would direct the reader – Jade Larissa Schiff, *Burdens of Political Responsibility: Narrative and the Cultivation of Responsiveness* (Cambridge: Cambridge University Press, 2016). Also, I suspect that any reader of this book will already be responsive to structural injustice and sensitive to their responsibilities for it. My aim here is not to find a solution to how to generate that responsiveness in others, but rather to focus on the integration of power into an understanding of what structural injustice is and responsibility for it.

[130]For example, see the edited volume Deen K. Chatterjee, *The Ethics of Assistance: Morality and the Distant Needy* (Cambridge: Cambridge University Press, 2004).

from emancipation from slavery, to reconstruction, Civil Rights, struggles against colonialism and critical race theory and practice today.[131]

What constitutes a 'victim' of structural injustice? The victims are not powerful in relation to the injustice; they do not have the systemic or dispositional power to effect structural change like large corporations or states. They also don't benefit from the injustice: the opposite is true; the victims are people who are rendered vulnerable to domination or oppression from structural injustice. Victims are structurally situated so as to be powerless in relation to, and rendered vulnerable by, structural injustice – this is why they are victims. However, they are victims only in this narrow sense. Victims are not solely victims; they are also *agents*.[132]

The desire to absolve victims of political responsibility to stand up for themselves and get involved in movements for justice corresponds to a tendency identified by post-colonial feminists – the tendency to objectify victims. Mohanty argues that the group 'Third world women' are constructed in Western feminist literature, 'as a homogenous, "powerless" group'.[133] Categorizing Third World women as inherently powerless victims 'robs them of their historical and political *agency*'.[134] Victims tend to be seen as non-agents in need of rescue, rather than as agents who can and do engage in acts of resistance. As bell hooks forcefully argues, oppressed people know they are oppressed and are often already engaged in resistance.[135] She argues that women who are oppressed do not want to think of themselves as victims because they want to focus on what they *can* do. Furthermore, 'Women, even the most oppressed among us, do exercise some power.'[136]

The modes of power discussed so far in this book – episodic, dispositional and structural – and the underlying unjust power relations of domination

---

[131]Angela Y. Davis, *Freedom Is a Constant Struggle: Ferguson, Palestine, and the Foundations of a Movement* (Chicago: Haymarket Books, 2016), 64. For an early statement of this view, see Frederick Douglass, 'West India Emancipation: Speech Delivered an Canandaigua, New York', ed. University of Rochester Frederick Douglass Project, 1857, http://www.lib.rochester.edu/index.cfm?PAGE=4398. There is also a recent debate in analytic political philosophy about whether victims have a moral duty to resist their oppression, for a helpful summary, see Ashwini Vasanthakumar, 'Recent Debates on Victims' Duties to Resist Their Oppression', *Philosophy Compass* 15, no. 2 (2019): e12648.

[132]Carol Gould emphasizes this worry with Young's theory. She acknowledges that Young's view does not amount to victim-blaming since it is not based on the liability model and that victims do have 'some residual freedom of choice', but that including the victims in political responsibility does not take sufficiently seriously the fact of their exploitation and that they lack the power to change the systems. They are coerced into participating and it is 'unfair' to include them in political responsibility. Gould, 'Varieties of Global Responsibility', 203.

[133]Chandra Mohanty, 'Under Western Eyes: Feminist Scholarship and Colonial Discourses', *Feminist Review* 30, no. 1 (1988): 66.

[134]Mohanty, 'Under Western Eyes: Feminist Scholarship and Colonial Discourses', 79.

[135]bell hooks, *Feminist Theory: From Margin to Center* (Boston, MA: South End Press, 1984), 10. See also James C. Scott, *Weapons of the Weak: Everyday Forms of Peasant Resistance* (New Haven, CT: Yale University Press, 1987).

[136]hooks, *Feminist Theory*, 90.

and oppression, do not take into account the more positive sense of power as empowerment. Amy Allen criticizes Young on precisely this point: 'A fully satisfactory critical theoretical analysis of power needs to be able to highlight not only domination or oppression but also individual and collective empowerment and the complex interconnections between these different modalities of power.'[137]

Including an account of empowerment shows how why and how victims can be included in sharing political responsibility. Many transnational women's collectivities have arisen in response to global structural injustices. Hye-Ryoung Kang highlights the Central American Network of Women in Solidarity with Maquila Workers, the Asian Women's Immigrant Advocates, Feminists Against Sweatshops and the East Asia-US-Puerto Rico Women's Network Against Militarism.[138] Kang argues that by engaging with others who are also experiencing oppression, two mutually reinforcing processes occur.[139] Through discussion, consciousness is raised and victims are enabled to call their situation injustice – we can call this individual empowerment. And collectivities are more able to broadcast and vocalize justice claims than isolated individuals – collective empowerment. Individual and collective empowerment are co-constitutive: the individual might need the conceptual and normative resources generated by social movements in order to become individually empowered.[140] But, in turn, these social movements emerge because of empowered individuals coming together in large enough numbers to create these resources and to build a critical mass that is taken seriously. Brooke Ackerly assessed the strategies of 125 women's rights activist organizations and found that a core strategy across the board was to develop the self-advocacy skills of victims: 'These human rights defenders practice the normative value that even those with unsecure freedom can and should exercise their capacity to take political responsibility and should do so in ways that develops others' capacities for doing so.'[141]

Including the victims in shared responsibility for structural injustice is not tantamount to victim blaming. On the liability model of responsibility, including the victims would be victim blaming because it isolates particular individuals for blame, thereby absolving others.[142] But political responsibility is a shared and non-blameworthy responsibility to cultivate the capacity for political solidarity. An agent does not need to be privileged to develop the capacity for political

---

[137]Amy Allen, 'Power and the Politics of Difference: Oppression, Empowerment, and Transnational Justice', *Hypatia* 23, no. 3 (2008): 163.
[138]Hye-Ryoung Kang, 'Transnational Women's Collectivities and Global Justice', in *Gender and Global Justice*, ed. Alison M Jaggar (Cambridge: Polity Press, 2014), 57.
[139]Kang, 'Transnational Women's Collectivities and Global Justice', 52.
[140]Allen, 'Power and the Politics of Difference', 167.
[141]Brooke A. Ackerly, *Just Responsibility: A Human Rights Theory of Global Justice* (Oxford: Oxford University Press, 2018), 184.
[142]Young, *Responsibility for Justice*, 105–6.

solidarity; people from all walks of life participate in solidaristic actions all the time. Not including the victims would be to marginalize and objectify them.

The work of solidarity

Individual and collective empowerment depend on solidarity. The victims of structural injustice could be excluded from solidarity, however, depending on how solidarity is understood. Some theorists have expressed concerns over the concept of solidarity on the grounds that it is often exclusionary. Solidarity can be a means to cement existing social, civic or political relations rather than to create new ones. We see this to some extent in Arendt's conception of political responsibility. Taken at face value, if political responsibility is tied to the political community, it would seem to exclude those who are not members of the community. In pre-nineteenth-century conceptions of solidarity, it implied social cohesion, which was particularly pernicious in the colonial context where the imperial metropole was the epicentre of cohesion or in religious traditions in which dissent was suppressed.[143] From the nineteenth century on, the term shifted to signify group interests and political struggle, in the work of Marx and Engels and Max Weber.[144] This is what we still tend to mean by solidarity. Critics argue, however, that such a meaning continues to promote group unity and, thus, exclusion and the denial of difference, a problem that has particularly plagued feminist movements.

But Jodi Dean argues that while some versions of solidarity are problematic, we should not throw the baby out with the bathwater.[145] Some kinds of solidarity do suffer from exclusion, such as affectional solidarity (solidarity with those to whom we have personal ties) or conventional solidarity (Marxist, religious or identity-based solidarity, which imposes group unity and posits an 'us' versus 'them'). But it is possible to have a conception of solidarity that is respectful of difference. She calls this 'reflective solidarity', which depends on 'openness to difference which lets our disagreements provide the basis for connection'.[146] Reflective solidarity does not assume that a given identity or common interest is sufficient to ground solidarity; instead, 'Reflective solidarity urges that we replace ascribed identities with achieved ones and substitute an enforced commonality of oppression with communities of those who have chosen to work and fight together.'[147]

---

[143]Rubén A. Gaztambide-Fernández, 'Decolonization and the Pedagogy of Solidarity', *Decolonization: Indigeneity, Education & Society* 1, no. 1 (2021): 49.

[144]Gaztambide-Fernández, 'Decolonization and the Pedagogy of Solidarity', 48.

[145]Jodi Dean, *Solidarity of Strangers: Feminism After Identity Politics* (Berkeley: University of California Press, 1996), 17.

[146]Dean, *Solidarity of Strangers*, 18.

[147]Dean, *Solidarity of Strangers*, 180.

If difference and disagreement are integral components of creating and maintaining solidary relationships, then solidarity is no longer straightforward. As Dean puts it, reflective solidarity 'has to be achieved', and it is 'never easy and always at risk'.[148] Developing the capacity for solidarity involves *work* in order to be willing and able to engage in creating and maintaining relationships across difference. This work will look different depending on the social position of the agent involved. Starting with the *oppressed*, it may involve a process of introspection and self-recognition prior to or in tandem with engaging in collective action. For instance, Fanon discusses a patient who told him of a dream where he was in a room with white men and realized that he was white too.[149] Fanon argues that the man is suffering from an 'inferiority complex' and that he has to do two things: one is to work on himself to overcome his lack of self-recognition and the other is to struggle against the social structures that generate the complex in the first place.[150] hooks argues, similarly to Fanon, that victims need to reflect on the ways in which they are socialized so that their behaviour perpetuates the status quo.[151] But hooks also argues that self-evaluation and self-critique is something that the *privileged* must engage in.[152] This involves unlearning what privileged individuals think they know. For instance, hooks writes of the feminist movement that white women will have demonstrated their political commitment to eliminating racism 'when they work to unlearn racist socialization' before they assume leadership roles, writing theory or working with women of colour.[153] In other words, privileged individuals need to work on themselves to overcome prejudices, biases or a sense of entitlement.

hooks also argues that the oppressed must participate in emancipatory struggle because of 'the special vantage point our marginality gives us and make use of this perspective to ... envision and create a counter-hegemony'.[154] Young also draws attention to the epistemic insight of the oppressed in understanding their situation and thus being better placed to know what to do about it.[155] But again this raises a corresponding responsibility on the part of the privileged. The

---

[148]Dean, *Solidarity of Strangers*, 47. Various versions of this thought have emerged in recent literature. Solidarity has been conceived of as relational (Gaztambide-Fernández, 'Decolonization and the Pedagogy of Solidarity'), networked (Carol C. Gould, 'Transnational Solidarities', *Journal of Social Philosophy* 38, no. 1 (2007): 148–64.), 'intersectionality of struggles' (Davis, *Freedom Is a Constant Struggle*, 144), amongst others. The underlying idea throughout is that difference and disagreement are at the root of solidarity.

[149]Frantz Fanon, *Black Skin, White Masks* (London: Pluto Press, 2008), 74.

[150]Fanon, *Black Skin, White Masks*, 74.

[151]hooks, *Feminist Theory*, 43.

[152]hooks, *Feminist Theory*, 46–7. See also Christopher Lebron, 'Equality from a Human Point of View', *Critical Philosophy of Race* 2, no. 2 (2014): 125–59.

[153]hooks, *Feminist Theory*, 55.

[154]hooks, *Feminist Theory*, 15.

[155]Young, *Responsibility for Justice*, 146.

privileged cannot rely on the oppressed to educate them about injustice because this amounts to epistemic exploitation.[156] The time, effort and emotional toll it takes to repeatedly explain how oppression manifests itself for any individual or social group is an unfair extraction of labour from the oppressed. As Françoise Vergès writes, white women 'need to understand how tiring it is, always having to educate them about their own history. After all, whole libraries on this topic are available to them. What is holding them back? Why are they waiting to be educated?'[157] So while the oppressed should engage in collective action against structural injustice because of their knowledge of and insight into it, this shouldn't be abused by the privileged as license not to learn about injustice and to expect the oppressed to do all of the intellectual and epistemic labour.

So far, the forms of work I have associated with political virtue are largely introspective, focused on learning or unlearning received views about oneself or others. However, the ultimate goal is to build solidaristic relations with others in order to engage in collective action. José Medina argues that agents need to foster 'resistant imaginations': ways of imagining both at the object level and meta-level. He gives the example of Nazi Germany. Resistant imagination at the object level would be to challenge the stigmatization of Jews, homosexuals, the Roma and Sinti and so on. At the meta-level it means resisting the idea that humanity is divided into inferior and superior races.[158] Medina argues that resistant imagining isn't a solo affair. Engaging with others' resistant imaginings, which may be different to our own, generates 'epistemic friction' and can provide the grounds for radical solidarity. He writes: 'Our social imaginings have to be radically pluralized and opened up to epistemic friction in order to meliorate our social sensibilities and to create or improve relations of solidarity.'[159] With plural social imaginations, social perceptions can be changed, individuals can better perceive others' problems, interests and needs on their own terms and in relation to their own and become invested in them.[160]

Young also acknowledged this imperative of solidarity to listen to others. She writes, 'People who understand that they share responsibility in relation to injustice and justice call on one another to answer before a public. The political process consists in the constitution of a public in which members raise problems and issues and demand of one another actions to address them.'[161] But, if people are going to work together and genuinely listen to each other, a further form of work that the privileged need to do is to learn how to interact with

---

[156]Nora Berenstain, 'Epistemic Exploitation', *Ergo* 3, no. 22 (2016): 569–90.

[157]Françoise Vergès, *A Decolonial Feminism*, ed. Ashley J. Bohrer (London: Pluto Press, 2021), 26.

[158]José Medina, *The Epistemology of Resistance: Gender and Racial Oppression, Epistemic Injustice, and Resistant Imaginations* (Oxford: Oxford University Press, 2013), 256–7.

[159]Medina, *The Epistemology of Resistance*, 306.

[160]Medina, *The Epistemology of Resistance*, 306.

[161]Young, *Responsibility for Justice*, 122.

victims in a spirit of solidarity and respect. hooks highlights the phenomenon of individuals who opportunistically seek legitimacy for their actions, rather than acting with victims in a spirit of solidarity. For example, she argues that white feminists 'condescended' towards black feminists, 'that we were able to participate because they allowed it, even encouraged it; after all, we were needed to legitimate the process. They did not see us as equals. They did not treat us as equals.'[162] To engage in political solidarity means recognizing the oppressed as equal active participants in movements to undermine the injustice that affects them, rather than using them as a means to an end of legitimizing one's own activism.

And as Arendt pointed out, it also means not treating the oppressed as needy people who can be patronized and who 'good' privileged people are trying to help.[163] Arendt rejected the entrance of emotions like pity into politics, because acting in the interests of the 'good of others' is hubristic and objectifies people, rather than respecting them as equal political participants.[164] She attributes the terror after the French revolution to the entrance of pity into the public sphere, because it rendered *le peuple* as an indistinct mass, rather than recognizing them as separate persons, thereby paving the way for mass violence.[165] As Lawrence Biskowski writes, 'When our actions are inspired by pity or some other emotion, we begin to lose our bearings, precisely because such emotions take no account of, and are harmful to, the "in-between" that separates and relates human beings.'[166] Pity is patronizing and homogenizing, whereas solidarity depends upon respect.[167]

A form of work that *all* participants in collective action need to do is to acknowledge that difference and disagreement are necessary components of political organizing. Any sort of shared identity or interest (gender, race or class, for example) is not sufficient to generate solidarity, nor to dilute disagreement. hooks gives the example of a group of students she was working with. Despite some ostensible shared identities or interests, the group as a whole learnt that

---

[162]hooks, *Feminist Theory*, 11.

[163]Derrida too recognizes the importance of distance in his conception of political friendship: 'The co-implication of responsibility and respect can be felt at the heart of friendship, one of the enigmas which would stem from this distance, this concern in what concerns the other: a respectful separation seems to distinguish friendship from love.' Jacques Derrida, *The Politics of Friendship* (London: Verso, 2005), 252.

[164]Suzanne Duvall Jacobitti, 'The Public, the Private, the Moral: Hannah Arendt and Political Morality', *International Political Science Review* 12, no. 4 (1991): 287.

[165]Biskowski, 'Practical Foundations for Political Judgment', 883.

[166]Biskowski, 'Practical Foundations for Political Judgment', 883.

[167]Canovan, *Hannah Arendt*, 171. Canovan points out that 'Arendt knew from direct experience what it was to be one of "the unfortunate", a member of a persecuted and suffering minority, grateful for authentic *compassion* but infuriated by the patronage of *pity*, and craving the respect *solidarity* implies.'

'our different experiences often meant that we had different needs, that there was no one strategy or formula for the development of political consciousness. By mapping out various strategies, we affirmed our diversity while working towards solidarity.'[168] Another form of work that all participants have to grapple with is sustaining political solidarity over time. As Sally Scholz points out, sustaining praxis is difficult. Groups can disperse; once a goal has been overcome, individuals with weak commitments might leave and individuals with strong commitments might burn out or lose interest in the group.[169]

Thus, being able to engage in political solidarity requires the development of certain skills and capacities. The work involved depends on an agent's social position, which will vary depending on the structural injustice they are seeking to address. Some of the forms of work involved are the following (but this is not exhaustive): unlearning received biases and prejudices, both conscious and unconscious in relation to oneself and others; keeping distance or space between oneself and the others with whom one is working in political solidarity, to avoid patronizing or objectifying them, or using them, rather than engaging with them in terms of mutual respect; developing the capacity to listen to others, and to acknowledge and accept their different and competing concerns or points of view; fostering a resistant imagination oneself and through communication with others; reflecting on how one's own behaviour reproduces injustice; being responsive to changes in the collective or changes in the circumstances in which the collective is acting; and developing stamina for continuing to engage. These skills and capacities are learned over time, through engaging with others and through trial and error. And, as Medina puts it, 'The tasks of radical solidarity are indeed not easy tasks.'[170] My claim is that political responsibility is the responsibility an individual has to do this work.

Of course, this is not only an individual-level responsibility. Groups also do this work when struggling against structural injustice. In her empirical assessment of women's human rights groups, Ackerly identifies ten core strategic activities.[171] We have already seen that these groups develop the self-advocacy skills of individuals and, relatedly, they develop community capacities. Several strategies involve integrating inequality and epistemic lacunae: engaging in intersectional analysis – integrating an understanding of how structural injustice affects differently positioned individuals and groups; making cross-issue connections – for instance women's economic exploitation and domestic violence; analysing external threats and opportunities; assessing internal strengths and weaknesses; and organizational learning. Another group of strategies focus on

---

[168]hooks, *Feminist Theory*, 58.
[169]Sally J. Scholz, *Political Solidarity* (Pennsylvania: Penn State Press, 2008), 223.
[170]Medina, *The Epistemology of Resistance*, 281.
[171]Ackerly, *Just Responsibility*, 183–5.

solidarity: networking, developing potential partnerships, and building bridges with potential stakeholders. These strategies are politically expedient, but sometimes they don't work; however, they all reflect a normative commitment to continuous learning and cultivating solidarity across difference.

Responsibility without blame

Young argues that political responsibility does not involve blame. Many theorists have challenged this particular aspect of political responsibility. Martha Nussbaum famously calls this the 'free pass' objection – if individuals are not blamed for failing to take up political responsibility, then they get a free pass to continue as they are.[172] But distinguishing responsibility from blame is not only possible, it is essential to realizing political responsibility for structural injustice.

Hanna Pickard has developed a conception of 'Responsibility without Blame' in the context of clinical psychiatry, particularly in the treatment of service users with personality disorders. Such people often behave in ways that we ordinarily think of as blameworthy – they bully, manipulate, harm others, self-harm for effect and sometimes commit grave offenses which leads to their hospitalization.[173] The appropriate stance towards these service users is Responsibility without Blame. This stance enables clinicians to recognize both that these people are agents who have it within their power to behave differently, but also that they have been shaped by histories of adversity, including childhood trauma, abuse, neglect and circumstances like war and poverty. Blaming people for their behaviour 'risks creating feelings of rejection, anger, shame, hopelessness, and desperation ... thereby undermining the possibility that responsibility and accountability may enable learning and change'.[174] But not holding them responsible fails to enable them to make different choices in future by supporting them to learn new skills, improving their capacity for control and enabling them to better recognize their feelings and motivations.[175] This is the 'rescue-blame trap', which clinical practice aims to avoid.[176]

Westerners struggle to distinguish between blame and responsibility, Pickard argues, because Western cultures tend to thread the two together. However, they are in fact quite clearly distinct: 'responsibility is about *the other person*, while blame is about us and how *we choose to respond to that person*'.[177] A person is responsible for their actions if they meet the criteria of having done

---

[172]Nussbaum, 'Foreword', xxi.
[173]Hanna Pickard, 'Responsibility without Blame: Therapy, Philosophy, Law', *Prison Service Journal* 213 (2014): 10.
[174]Pickard, 'Responsibility without Blame', 15.
[175]Pickard, 'Responsibility without Blame', 12.
[176]Pickard, 'Responsibility without Blame', 12.
[177]Pickard, 'Responsibility without Blame', 13.

something wrong and they chose to do it. But whether or not they are blamed for that action depends on the response of the people around them. Blame involves holding and displaying negative feelings towards that person, such as anger, resentment or disgust; it involves negative judgments about the person's actions or even their character; and it could involve punitive behaviour like aggression or ostracism.[178] In a clinical context, clinicians are enabled to avoid blaming patients because they have a duty of care towards patients, there are guidelines establishing how to speak to patients, there is a norm of enabling the service user to take responsibility, and clinicians have developed their 'poker face' knowing how to mask their emotions and refrain from acting on them.[179] Most importantly, clinicians learn about and pay attention to the service user's history, enabling them to understand the behaviour in the context of that person's life story.

Pickard argues that the criminal justice system can learn from this insight. In the criminal justice context, similarly to the clinical context, blaming offenders leads to feelings of hopelessness and desperation, which runs counter to the goal of rehabilitating them and reducing crime in future.[180] Instead, we should develop 'an attitude of concern, respect, and compassion for the offender', which 'may do better to help them address their offending behaviour and enable learning and change'.[181] If such a stance is possible in contexts where people have committed crimes, why is it not possible in relation to people who are going about their daily lives and inadvertently reproducing structural injustice? Moreover, Arendt and Jaspers argued in favour of political responsibility in the context of the Holocaust – an extreme situation where extended moral responsibility might seem warranted. Structural injustice does not reach these heights. It is mundane and ingrained in the system. As Young puts it,

> Structural injustice is not as horrible as systematically perpetrated genocide; I think of it as 'ordinary' injustice. Such injustice must be of concern to us as moral and political agents, precisely because it is more everyday, and often conditions other criminal acts. I find the idea of political responsibility that I have interpreted and developed out of Arendt's texts particularly useful for giving an account of responsibility in relation to structural injustice.[182]

Blame in this context is disproportionate and unfair. But just because we shouldn't blame people does not mean we can no longer recognize them as responsible agents who can take responsibility for their reproduction of unjust structures

---

[178]Pickard, 'Responsibility without Blame', 14.
[179]Pickard, 'Responsibility without Blame', 14.
[180]Pickard, 'Responsibility without Blame', 15.
[181]Pickard, 'Responsibility without Blame', 15.
[182]Young, *Responsibility for Justice*, 93.

through their actions. We do not need to know every individual's entire life story in order to do this; we simply need to recognize that they were born into unjust social structures and have been socialized into reproducing these structures. We can also accept that changing unjust social structures is beyond the power of that individual. But we can recognize that every individual can develop the capacity for political solidarity and work with others to try to bring about change. Avoiding blame can be difficult since it is the immediate response of people socialized in Western cultures, but Pickard argues that 'As a first step, and quite generally, we can keep the distinction between responsibility and blame clearly before our minds, and undertake to challenge our own sense of righteousness and entitlement while cultivating a commitment to treating all people ... with respect, concern and compassion.'[183]

But there is an ambiguity in Young's discussion of blame. It is unclear whether agents are not blamed for their reproduction of structural injustice or whether they are not blamed for failure to take up political responsibility. It seems to be both for Young. But other theorists have separated the two. For instance, Catherine Lu does not blame agents for reproduction of structural injustice but does blame them for failure to act on political responsibility.[184] In my view, blame is still inappropriate here. Zheng provides a useful way to think about this. Drawing on an analogy with pedagogy, she distinguishes between summative and formative criticism. Summative criticism is criticism against a benchmark – for example, being graded for an exam. Formative criticism is feedback on how the student is doing, without recourse to a grade. Zheng applies this to 'moral criticism'. A person who knowingly violates a moral obligation would be a candidate for summative criticism, and hence blame. But a person who is lagging behind in their political responsibility would be a candidate for formative criticism, or 'course correction'.[185] They could be reminded that there is more they could be doing and steered in the right direction, rather than scolded and blamed.

I would add that this is especially true when we consider that challenging structural injustice entails engaging in collective action, and engaging in collective action entails developing the capacity for political solidarity, which is a process. As Barrett Emerick argues in relation to our loved ones, we should 'play the long game with someone, and to be with them through their moral development – just as we need others to be with us in ours'.[186] We also need to play the long game in individuals' political development, since we are shaped and socialized in the context of injustice and working to develop ourselves to be effective

---

[183]Pickard, 'Responsibility without Blame', 14.

[184]Catherine Lu, *Justice and Reconciliation in World Politics* (Cambridge: Cambridge University Press, 2017), 259.

[185]Robin Zheng, 'Moral Criticism and Structural Injustice', *Mind* 130, no. 518 (2021): 514.

[186]Emerick, Barrett, 'Love and Resistance: Moral Solidarity in the Face of Perceptual Failure', *Feminist Philosophical Quarterly 2*, 2016, p. 15 quoted in Zheng, 'Moral Criticism and Structural Injustice', 518.

participants in collective action for justice takes time and will be full of mistakes. Identifying agents as blameworthy or bad plays a minimal role in considerations of political solidarity. Instead, the focus is on working together to achieve the goal of overcoming structural injustice. As Scholz puts it, 'political solidarity requires a concerted effort to work with others to alleviate some oppression or injustice and, given the intransigency of both, blame laying plays a very insignificant part. Instead, members owe each other a continued commitment to the cause that also affects their relationships with each other.'[187]

Conclusion

The responsibility that individuals bear for structural injustice is political responsibility, which is a responsibility to develop the capacity for political solidarity and act on it. Political solidarity is the grounds for individual and collective empowerment and will lead to effective collective action. Understanding political responsibility as a specifically political virtue – it arises from the need to work with others, not from character-based virtue – overcomes the dichotomous thinking between morality or politics. As Mohanty puts it, 'solidarity is a political as well as ethical goal'.[188] Or to borrow from Chantal Mouffe, it is an 'ethico-political' concept.[189] The concept of political virtue better captures what is at stake when conceiving of responsibility for structural injustice than the virtue or *virtù* approaches, or Young's ambiguous combination of the two. Political responsibility is the responsibility individuals bear for unjust social-structural processes, and on my interpretation, it involves the development of the capacity for solidarity in order to be able to participate in collective action for change. Individuals should not be blamed for failing to do this, but rather the fact that we are all born into and shaped by structural injustice should be recognized. Thus, we can take a compassionate approach and steer each other in the right direction, encouraging both individual and collective empowerment.

---

[187]Scholz, *Political Solidarity*, 91.
[188]Mohanty, *Feminism without Borders*, 3.
[189]Chantal Mouffe, *The Return of the Political*, 2nd edn (London: Verso, 2005), 66.

Chapter 7

Corporate responsibility and historical injustice

In this book, I have argued that ordinary individuals are politically responsible for structural injustice, but powerful agents with the capacity to alleviate structural injustice and fail to do so, or who deliberately perpetuate it for their own gain, bear moral responsibility. This raises the question, 'How can corporate agents bear moral responsibility?' The first half of this chapter will answer that question. I will argue that corporate entities can bear moral responsibility for their wrongdoings, and their responsibility persists as long as that entity continues to exist. This leads to another controversial topic in structural injustice theory – historical injustice. Since some corporate entities exist over decades or even centuries, they continue to bear moral responsibility on the liability model for their wrongdoings through time.

I address two difficulties raised by state liability through time in comparison to the responsibility of other corporate entities like corporations: the fact that states change and that citizens have to bear the costs. Next, I compare my approach to the other approaches relating structural and historical injustice – namely, that of Young and recent book-length treatments of the subject by Catherine Lu and Alasia Nuti. On my view, the continuation of corporate responsibility through time gives greater weight to the liability model in relation to historical injustice than the other structural injustice approaches, while retaining the overarching structural injustice framework.

Corporate responsibility

Throughout this book, I have suggested that powerful corporate agents like states and corporations can be held morally responsible for structural injustice, either by omission (avoidable structural injustice) or action (deliberate structural injustice). But what does it mean to hold a corporate entity morally responsible?

Not all groups can bear responsibility. Peter French distinguishes between 'aggregate' and 'conglomerate' collectivities.[1] An aggregate collectivity could be one of two types: either a group defined by shared characteristics, such as all people with green eyes, or a group that is thrown together by spatial and temporal contiguity, such as a crowd, a mob or people at a bus stop. Such groups are merely the sum of their parts. Changes in membership will change the group. Aggregates are 'not intentional agents in and of themselves'.[2] Such groups might be causally responsible for wrongdoings – for example, a mob rioting and damaging property – but moral responsibility can only be attributed to individual group members depending on their actions and whether or not they can be excused.[3]

A conglomerate collective is different. A conglomerate collective, or what Toni Erskine calls an 'institutional moral agent', has four characteristics that distinguish it from a mere aggregate.[4] First, they are more than the sum of their parts. Take the example of Lloyds of London, a corporation that acts as 'an independent guardian' of insurance markets, who I will say more about when we come to historical injustice.[5] The corporation Lloyds of London will remain Lloyds of London whether or not specific personnel stay or go. It can change operative, administrative and executive staff, and clients, and still remain Lloyds of London. Second, conglomerate collectives have an internal decision-making structure, by virtue of which they make decisions about how to act as a group. Such a structure creates the capacity for the group to deliberate and come to a decision about how to act purposively as a group agent. In contrast to aggregate collectives who are not intentional agents, institutional moral agents are.

Third, they have an identity over time. Take Lloyds of London again. It has existed for over 350 years and has maintained its identity as a corporate agent throughout this time.[6] French highlights that this means these agents are 'project-making' entities that can access past memories and make future plans. Erskine adds a fourth dimension, which is that these entities are self-asserting. Lloyds of London acts in the world as Lloyds of London, not as a collection of individual members. It defines itself as a group, rather than being externally defined.[7]

---

[1] Peter A. French, *Collective and Corporate Responsibility*, ed. Peter A. French (New York: Columbia University Press, 1984), 5.
[2] French, *Collective and Corporate Responsibility*, 11.
[3] French, *Collective and Corporate Responsibility*, 9–10.
[4] French, *Collective and Corporate Responsibility*, 13–14; Toni Erskine, 'Assigning Responsibilities to Institutional Moral Agents: The Case of States and Quasi-States', *Ethics and International Affairs* 15, no. 2 (2001): 71.
[5] Lloyd's, 'The Lloyd's Corporation', n.d., https://www.lloyds.com/about-lloyds/the-corporation; Kevin Rawlinson, 'Lloyd's of London and Greene King to Make Slave Trade Reparations', *The Guardian*, 18 June 2020, https://www.theguardian.com/world/2020/jun/18/lloyds-of-london-and-greene-king-to-make-slave-trade-reparations.
[6] Lloyd's, 'Our History', n.d., https://www.lloyds.com/about-lloyds/history/.
[7] Erskine, 'Assigning Responsibilities to Institutional Moral Agents', 72.

Corporate agents, as I will call them, are organized so that responsibility for wrongdoing falls on the corporate entity itself, not on individual members.[8] So when Lloyds of London facilitated an insurance market for slave ships, the responsibility fell on the corporation. Whether or not individual employees, executives or clients bear some sort of responsibility (be it legal, moral or political) is a separate question to the responsibility of the corporation itself. Moral judgments about corporate agents' behaviour are claims about the group agent, not necessarily claims about the individual members' behaviour. As Virginia Held puts it, 'Corporation Z should not have done A.'[9]

But there are many sceptics who refuse to accept the idea that corporate agents can bear moral responsibility. As the Lord Chancellor of England, Edward the First Baron of Thurlow (1731–1806) evocatively put it, a corporation has 'no soul to be damned, and no body to be kicked'.[10] If bearing moral, or legal, responsibility depends on having a conscience that can be affected, which is displayed through appropriate emotions like remorse, or a body that can be punished by imprisonment or other measures, then there is no way of holding corporations responsible because they do not fulfil these criteria. Manuel Velasquez fleshes out these concerns when he argues that responsibility depends on displaying *mens rea* (intent) and carrying out the *actus reus* with one's own body.[11] He argues that 'an act is intentional only if it is the carrying out of an intention formed in the mind of the agent whose bodily movements bring about the act'.[12]

Since the conception of moral responsibility used so far in this book depends on both intent and causation, Velasquez's critique seems to fundamentally damage my claim that corporate agents can bear moral responsibility. In Chapter 5, I drew on R. Jay Wallace's reasons-responsive account of moral responsibility that claimed that an agent must have carried out the act with intent in order to be held morally responsible for it. The agent themselves must have done something that violated a moral obligation. However, despite appearances, a reasons-responsive account can in fact easily respond to both of Velasquez's criticisms.

On the point about the *actus reus*, it is not the case that the agent themselves had to use their own bodily movements to carry out the act. It is well established

---

[8]French, *Collective and Corporate Responsibility*, 15.

[9]Virginia Held, 'Can a Random Collection of Individuals Be Morally Responsible?', *Journal of Philosophy* 67, no. 14 (1970): 474.

[10]John C. Coffee Jr., ' "No Soul to Damn: No Body to Kick": An Unscandalized Inquiry into the Problem of Corporate Punishment', *Michigan Law Review* 79 (1981): 386.

[11]Manuel Velasquez, 'Why Corporations Are Not Responsible for Anything They Do', in *Collective Responsibility: Five Decades of Debate in Theoretical and Applied Ethics*, ed. Larry May and Stacey Hoffman (Oxford: Rowman and Littlefield, 1991).

[12]Manuel Velasquez, 'Why Corporations Are Not Responsible for Anything They Do', 120.

that in a principal-agent relationship, a principal can authorize an agent to carry out an act on their behalf, but that the principal would still be responsible for it. Take a hitman for instance. The person who ordered the hit is legally and morally responsible for murder, just as the hitman is legally and morally responsible for carrying out the act with their own body. When it comes to corporate agents, the corporate agent authorizes the employee or functionary to carry out an act on its behalf. The individual employee or functionary might bear moral responsibility if what they are doing is wrongful – for instance, a buyer in a garment MNC ordering clothes from a supplier that is known to violate labour laws and provide unsafe working conditions for staff. But the corporation is also responsible for ordering the act.

There is a complication here, though, which is that the corporation itself is an 'artificial person' to use Hobbes's terminology.[13] This means that the corporation comprises individual members who authorize the corporation to act on their behalf. So, in fact, the structure of a corporate agent is tripartite. The members are the principal who authorize the corporate entity as an agent. But then the corporate entity, by virtue of its internal decision-making structure, can make decisions, and it becomes the principal. It can then authorize employees/functionaries to act as agents on its behalf. Sceptics of the idea of corporate responsibility would claim that this intermediary step, of the corporate entity becoming a principal by virtue of its internal decision-making structure, is wrong. The responsibility simply devolves onto individual members of the collective.

This leads to the issue of *mens rea*. A corporate entity does not have an individual mind and a conscience in which it makes decisions based on a mix of rational reasoning and emotions. Corporate entities do not have the same capacity for moral reasoning as humans – the ability to think in solitude, to be in dialogue with oneself, two-in-one, as Arendt puts it.[14] But instead of having this internalized capacity, corporate entities have this capacity by virtue of having deliberative processes between persons. They have a *social capacity* for moral reasoning by drawing on the reasoning capacities and moral emotions of members who talk to each other about what the corporate entity ought to do. This is not the same as an individual's capacity for moral deliberation, but it is equivalent, because this decision-making structure activates the powers of reflective self-control, which Wallace argues are essential for an agent to be capable of bearing moral responsibility.[15] An internal decision-making structure

[13]See Elizabeth Wolgast, *Ethics of an Artificial Person: Lost Responsibility in Professions and Organizations* (Stanford, CA: Stanford University Press, 1992).
[14]Hannah Arendt, 'Thinking and Moral Considerations', in *Responsibility and Judgment*, ed. Jerome Kohn (New York: Schocken Books, 2003), 159–93.
[15]See Chapter 6.

gives the corporate agent the capacity to (a) reason about the world and (b) act on the basis of those reasons.

Moreover, the intention of corporate action is not reducible to the intention of the individual carrying out the action. The action of the individual employee/functionary is not only authorized by the corporate agent via its internal decision procedure, but is also a product of a corporate culture and a set of policies and rules. As French puts it, 'When the corporate act is consistent with, an instantiation or an implementation of established corporate policy, then it is proper to describe it as having been done for corporate reasons, as having been caused by a corporate desire coupled with a corporate belief and so, in other words, as corporate intentional.'[16] For example, when the buyer orders clothes from a substandard supplier, they are not doing this off their own bat. They are doing this because they are part of a corporate agent that buys clothes in bulk in order to retail them and does so at the lowest possible price point.

Of course, there are constraints on corporate agents. The structural injustice framework insists that agents face objective constraints when they make decisions about how to act or when they do act. We saw in Chapter 2 that a critical realist social ontology argues that agents find themselves in structures not of their own making at time T^1; there is a period of structural interaction in which all sorts of agents act in their own ways (often based on vested interests aligned with pre-existing social positions), and this results in structural elaboration at time T^4, which is a new structural framework that is not intended by any agents. In the same way that ordinary individuals face multiple constraints when they decide how to act, powerful corporate agents do too. Corporations are bound to secure the interests of their shareholders and by regulation (although this is often minimal and has been designed in collaboration with large corporations).[17] States are constrained by democratic processes, judicial review, the demands of shape-shifting politics, the decisions of global institutions, the demands of big business and the markets and so on. Nonetheless, these entities have the capacity to think about moral reasons and to act on them. Ordinary individuals also face multiple constraints when deciding how to act, but we still hold them responsible for their actions. And, as I've been suggesting throughout, corporate agents have *more* capacity to act on their decisions by virtue of their greater power and resources in comparison to individuals acting alone. Social structures place certain corporate agents at the top of the power hierarchy (they have systemic power), and they have the dispositional power (capacity) to act in ways that are not available to individuals.[18] Thus, corporate agents have more 'elbow

---

[16]Peter A. French, 'The Corporation as a Moral Person', in *Collective Responsibility: Five Decades of Debate in Theoretical and Applied Ethics*, edited by Larry May and Stacey Hoffman (Oxford: Rowman and Littlefield, 1991), 145.
[17]See Chapter 3.
[18]See Chapter 3.

room', as Daniel Dennett puts it, to decide how to act within structures.[19] And due to their size and systemic and dispositional power, they are more likely to get what they want in the period of structural interaction (even if they don't always achieve this).

Moreover, the origin of the reasons-responsive account of moral responsibility was Peter Strawson's claim that philosophers have been over-intellectualizing moral responsibility. The fact is that individuals *hold* one another morally responsible as a social practice. This is an important part of social relations, irrespective of philosophical questions about causal determinism. And the same applies to corporate agents. We hold corporate agents responsible when they violate moral obligations, and we do this irrespective of debates about corporate moral agency. For example, when the Rana Plaza factory collapse occurred, many people held the corporations morally responsible who were supplied by the factory. When we hold an individual morally responsible, we display reactive attitudes towards them, such as indignation, scolding or reproach. This also occurs with corporations.

In the case of corporate agents, however, they do not feel guilt, shame or remorse because they are not a human being with a conscience. Rather they are a collection of human beings, incorporated into a group by law, and the artificial person that is created is devoid of human emotion. As sceptic Elizabeth Wolgast puts it, 'It is implausible to treat a corporation as a member of the human community, a member with a personality (but not a face), intentions (but no feelings), relationships (but no family or friends), responsibility (but no conscience), and susceptibility to punishment (but no capacity for pain).'[20] But I don't think that this matters as much as sceptics suggest. Holding agents responsible serves multiple purposes. With an individual human, we want to know that they are sorry and won't do the same thing in future, and they express this through emotions and future actions. With a corporate entity, we also want to know that they are sorry and won't do the same thing in future, and they express this through a public apology, other reparatory measures like compensation and future actions. The lack of genuine emotions, if emotion depends on an individual's affective state, doesn't really matter. Corporate agents perform emotion, and this is perceived as important. For instance, Prime Minister Tony Blair's statement of remorse in 1997 for the Irish potato famine of the mid-nineteenth century was perceived as an important moment in the peace process in Northern Ireland.[21]

---

[19]Daniel C. Dennett, *Elbow Room: The Varieties of Free Will Worth Wanting* (Oxford: Oxford University Press, 1984).

[20]Wolgast, *Ethics of an Artificial Person*, 87.

[21]Jason A. Edwards and Amber Luckie, 'British Prime Minister Tony Blair's Irish Potato Famine Apology', *Journal of Conflictology* 5, no. 1 (2014): 43–51.

In fact, corporations act as though they are moral agents all the time. They make apologies for wrongdoing, write codes of conduct, get involved in social justice and philanthropic initiatives, engage in public–private partnerships and take responsibility for human rights and climate treaties, and the law holds them accountable for moral endeavours like upholding human rights.[22] Moreover, as Philip Pettit and Christian List argue, 'Why should any group of individuals be allowed to incorporate under an organizational structure that deprives the group of the ability to assess its options normatively, thereby making it unfit to be held responsible for its choices?'[23] There must be mechanisms in place for group agents to make moral decisions, otherwise there would be very strong reasons for preventing these agents from existing in the first place.

However, another form of scepticism arises when thinking specifically about capitalist corporations. It could be argued that corporations are not moved by moral considerations and conform to one motive only – the profit motive. They are not moral actors; they act only to increase capital. This is a structural imperative; they must grow or fail. Morality doesn't come into it. Capitalists would concede that corporations bear responsibilities, but those responsibilities are to their shareholders – to increase profits. While I am sympathetic to the view that there is not much point in trying to constrain corporations by moral argument, since they are impervious to moral reasoning, I still believe there is value in claiming that corporations bear moral responsibility for structural injustice that they deliberately perpetuate or fail to redress when they can, and this is for six reasons.

First, as corporate agents, they simply can bear moral responsibility for the reasons already outlined. Since they are candidates for blame, not holding them responsible would create 'a deficit of responsibility'.[24] Pettit and List give the example of the 'Herald of Free Enterprise', a ferry that capsized in the English Channel in 1987, killing nearly two hundred people. An official inquiry found out that 'From top to bottom the body corporate was infected with the disease of sloppiness', but no individual member of the corporation was seriously enough at fault to be held responsible in court.[25] Failing to hold the corporation itself to be legally liable meant that there was a responsibility deficit. Moreover, Pettit and List argue that not holding corporate agents responsible creates the perverse incentive of encouraging individuals to become a corporation in order to carry out wrongdoings and to benefit from this responsibility deficit.[26]

---

[22]See Florian Wettstein, 'Corporate Responsibility in the Collective Age: Toward a Conception of Collaborative Responsibility', *Business and Society Review* 117, no. 2 (2012): 155–84.

[23]Philip Pettit and Christian List, *Group Agency: The Possibility, Design, and Status of Corporate Agents* (Oxford: Oxford University Press, 2011), 159.

[24]Pettit and List, *Group Agency*, 165.

[25]Pettit and List, *Group Agency*, 166.

[26]Pettit and List, *Group Agency*, 166. Pettit and List also discuss how corporate responsibility is not mutually exclusive with the responsibility of individuals. I agree, but it is beyond the scope of this chapter to discuss the relationship of individual employees/functionaries and the corporate agent's

Second, some responsibilities can only be imputed to corporate agents: for example, responsibility for upholding the Paris Agreement to curb carbon emissions. As Toni Erskine puts it, 'If only individuals, and never institutions, are seen to be moral agents, the possibility of assigning responsibility for some actions is lost.'[27] An individual 'has neither the scope nor the power to coordinate and enforce systematic changes in how goods are produced, consumed, and disposed of'.[28] So not only does failure to acknowledge corporate responsibility result in responsibility deficits for past wrongdoing in which the corporate agent itself was at fault, it also results in a responsibility deficit for prospective responsibilities, if only corporate agents have the capacity to bear them.

Third, public blaming of corporations can be a spur to action. We saw in Chapter 3 that Corporate Social Responsibility is also known as 'Crisis Scandal Response'. Corporations respond in the aftermath of a crisis if there is concerted public political pressure. They fear reputational damage, they are sensitive to public opinion and image, and so blaming corporations is a way to force them to act. The PR industry exists precisely in order to improve the reputation of corporate agents in the public eye.[29] Blaming corporations for moral wrongdoing generates efforts to amend their behaviour in order to restore their public reputation, which they need to do to continue operating and making profits. Blame moves corporate agents in similar ways to individuals; they act to restore damages and make future changes. This might only last for a short period of time – as long as the crisis and scandal are prominent in the media or at the top of the agenda for international civil society – but something can be better than nothing. While not all the corporations connected to the Rana Plaza factory collapse were moved to sign up to the legally binding Bangladesh Fire and Building Safety Accord, many of them did sign, and they did implement changes in fire and building safety in Bangladesh. They also paid compensation to direct victims and their families.[30] These initiatives show that public blame and pressure gets results (even if those results are limited).

---

responsibility in any depth. It could be the subject of a whole other book to try to disentangle the degrees of responsibility within corporate entities, given the hierarchies of power. So, in this book, I make the simpler distinction between the moral responsibility of powerful corporate agents versus the political responsibility of ordinary individuals. I hope to address the internal dynamics within corporate entities in future work. To anticipate, it seems to me there is more room for a concept like straightforward blameworthiness when considering the higher-ups in these organizations, to complicity or implication when thinking about members of staff further down the hierarchy, and perhaps even mere political responsibility for those who are powerless in the corporate entity and are there out of necessity of employment. But there is much to discuss on this front.

[27] Erskine, 'Assigning Responsibilities to Institutional Moral Agents', 83.
[28] Erskine, 'Assigning Responsibilities to Institutional Moral Agents', 83.
[29] Roland Marchand, *Creating the Corporate Soul: The Rise of Public Relations and Corporate Imagery in American Big Business* (Berkeley: University of California Press, 1998).
[30] Anne Trebilcock, 'The Rana Plaza Disaster Seven Years On: Transnational Experiments and Perhaps a New Treaty?', *International Labour Review* 159, no. 4 (2020): 545–68.

Fourth, blaming corporations could lead to action that includes changes in law, which creates the possibility of holding them legally liable. Once legal liability is in place, it is more difficult for corporations to continue pursuing particular harmful courses of action. For instance, the EU's new Corporate Sustainability Reporting directive places tighter regulations on corporations' environmental practices and could serve as the basis for future legal actions.[31]

Fifth, corporations have the capacity and resources to be able to implement significant changes in their industries. As we saw in Chapter 3, NGOs often work with corporations precisely for this reason. Corporations might be better placed on some occasions to pursue specific environmental or social justice agendas because of their transnational reach, their purchasing power and their sometimes larger capacity than states.

Sixth, the kinds of changes implemented by corporations, while small and certainly nothing to touch the sides of global capitalist relations of exploitation, still have the potential to improve the lives of workers, and people affected by their activities, in the here and now. This sort of incrementalism is frowned upon by the most ardent Marxists who await the revolution and who may even seek to accelerate the degradation of the masses in order to precipitate revolution sooner. However, I believe that making people's lives better in the here and now is a goal worth striving towards. Reducing suffering is a worthwhile objective.

In sum, corporate agents can bear moral responsibility for their actions because they can exercise intentional agency. There are many reasons for wanting to hold corporate agents morally responsible, most importantly to avoid retrospective and prospective responsibility deficits.

Corporate responsibility through time

We have seen that rejecting the concept of corporate responsibility results in both retrospective and prospective responsibility deficits. But there is a further responsibility deficit created by the denial of corporate responsibility – responsibility through time. Not only do individuals lack the capacity in terms of power and resources to fulfil certain prospective responsibilities, such as treaties and certain kinds of contracts, but they also cannot bear responsibility for the potential duration of the agreement, if it lasts for several generations. If only

---

[31]Council of the EU, 'New Rules on Corporate Sustainability Reporting: Provisional Agreement between the Council and the European Parliament', 21 June 2022, https://www.consilium.eur opa.eu/en/press/press-releases/2022/06/21/new-rules-on-sustainability-disclosure-provisional-agreement-between-council-and-european-parliament/; Blanaid Clarke and Linn Anker-Sørensen, 'The EU as a Potential Norm Creator for Sustainable Corporate Groups', in *Cambridge Handbook of Corporate Law, Corporate Governance and Sustainability*, ed. Beate Sjåfjell and Christopher M. Bruner (Cambridge: Cambridge University Press, 2019), 190–203.

an individual can bear moral responsibility for what they have done, once the individual dies, the responsibility dies too. But some responsibilities transcend the lifetime of particular individuals. Treaty obligations and corporate contracts do not expire once the individual who signed them dies. People who deny the idea of corporate responsibility cannot explain responsibility through time.

Since corporate agents are more than the sum of their parts and have a self-asserting identity over time, they are able to bear responsibility over time. Consider Lloyds of London again. In 2020, it decided to apologize and pay reparations for its involvement in the Transatlantic slave trade. It released a statement saying, 'We are sorry for the role played by the Lloyd's market in the eighteenth and nineteenth century slave trade. This was an appalling and shameful period of English history, as well as our own, and we condemn the indefensible wrongdoing that occurred during this period.'[32] The firm decided to implement an affirmative action programme, provide education on slavery, and review its 'organisational artefacts to ensure that they are explicitly non-racist'.[33]

Corporations in the United States have long been the target of reparations lawsuits.[34] While there have been controversies over establishing legal liability, there is less complication when attributing moral responsibility. If corporate agents can bear moral responsibility and they continue to bear this as long as they exist, then the moral responsibility for wrongdoing continues through time. Individuals voluntarily join corporations and so knowingly sign up for the benefits and burdens, including outstanding reparative obligations. The employees and clients of Lloyds of London can be expected to bear the costs of profits diverted to reparations or jobs denied due to affirmative action policies. They opted in to this company.

But things get more complicated when considering states. There are two worries about state liability over time: the fact that states change and that citizens will bear the costs. Let's take the first problem, the fact that states change over time. The US state, for instance, had a limited franchise at the time of slavery, but now all citizens, including African Americans and women, can vote. Also, the United States covers a much larger territory with a bigger population and has a stronger federal government than at the time of slavery.[35] Such changes might be thought to render the concept of state liability over multiple generations void. The United States then is not the same as the United States now. But, as David Boonin points out, the US Constitution remains the same. He writes, 'the

---

[32] Rawlinson, 'Lloyd's of London and Greene King to Make Slave Trade Reparations'.
[33] These efforts have been criticized as inadequate. Rashaad Lambert, 'Exclusive: Lloyd's of London Responds to T.I'.s Open Letter Calling Out Its Ties to Trans-Atlantic Slave Trade', *Forbes*, August 2020.
[34] Adoja A. Aiyetoro, 'Formulating Reparations Litigation Through the Eyes of the Movement', *NYU Annual Survey of American Law* 58 (2001): 457–74.
[35] David Boonin, *Should Race Matter? Unusual Answers to the Usual Questions* (Cambridge: Cambridge University Press, 2012), 119.

question of what constitutes a distinct national government seems to have a relatively straightforward answer, at least in the case of a national government like that of the United States: what constitutes the government is, as its name suggests, the Constitution'.[36]

There is a straightforward answer, then, for some states. But not for all states. There are many states in the world today that are much newer than the United States. And some states that are seemingly old but that have changed constitutions multiple times. Take Germany as an example. Germany became a unified state in 1871 as the *Kaiser Reich*. This imperialistic regime was dismantled following the First World War and a new constitution was signed, the Weimar Constitution. The Weimar Republic was toppled by the Nazis' Enabling Act in 1933. After the Second World War, Germany was divided into the Federal Republic of Germany, or West Germany, and the German Democratic Republic, or East Germany. Germany formally reunified on 3 October 1990. So the straightforward answer of constitutional continuity does not apply in this case.

Nevertheless, West Germany took responsibility for the crimes of the Nazis despite constitutional change. It paid reparations to Israel and to individual survivors of the Shoah and returned stolen property to individuals; it also engaged in widespread education and memorialization initiatives.[37] This might seem justified on the basis that if West Germany failed to take responsibility for the preceding administration, there would have been an enormous responsibility deficit – failure of any corporate responsibility for the Shoah, which would have left an untenable gap in terms of memorializing the dead, helping living victim-survivors and repairing the harm done to international trust and cooperation.

However, Germany has not only acknowledged responsibility for the crimes of the Nazis, but is also engaged in an ongoing conversation about responsibility for the earlier crimes of the *Kaiser Reich*. The German administration in 1915–16 was aware of the Ottoman genocide of over one million Armenians but did nothing because the Turks were a strategic ally. After a public political debate on this issue, the German Parliament commemorated the genocide in June 2016.[38] Michael Schefczyk argues that this is justified on the basis that the newer German constitutional regimes bear 'second-hand responsibility' for the crimes committed by past iterations of the German state.[39]

---

[36]Boonin, *Should Race Matter?*, 122.

[37]Andrea Armstrong and Ariel Colonomos, 'German Reparations to the Jews after World War II', in *The Handbook of Reparations*, ed. Pablo de Greiff (Oxford: Oxford University Press, 2006), 390–420.

[38]Michael Schefczyk, 'Modern Germany and the Annihilation of the Ottoman Armenians: A Note on the Political Avowal of Shame and Guilt', in *Der Genozid an Den Armeniherlinnen: Beiträge Zur Wissenschaftlichen Aurfarbeitung Eines Historischen Verbrechens Gegen Die Menschlichkeit* (Wiesbaden: Springer VS, 2018), 86.

[39]Schefczyk M, 'Moral Responsibility for Historical Injustice' in *The Routledge Handbook of Philosophy of Responsibility*, ed. Maximilian Kiener (London: Routledge, 2023).

This seems plausible to me, again on the basis that failure to assume responsibility results in an untenable responsibility deficit. If states fail to assume the responsibility for the obligations of earlier versions of the state, including positive treaty commitments and negative reparatory obligations, this creates responsibility deficits that will make international cooperation difficult, if not impossible, and will leave the victims of state wrongdoing bereft of compensation. Whether second-hand responsibility is as strong as first-hand responsibility, or weakened in some sense, is up for debate. But the idea that such a responsibility exists is highly plausible, especially since states do take on this responsibility, as the German example shows.

Arendt discusses the practice of states taking on responsibility for the actions of previous iterations in 'Collective Responsibility'. She writes,

> Every government assumes responsibility for the deeds and misdeeds of its predecessors and every nation for the deeds and misdeeds of the past. This is even true for revolutionary governments which may deny liability for contractual agreements their predecessors entered into. When Napoleon Bonaparte became the ruler of France, he said: I assume responsibility for everything France has done from the time of Charlemagne to the terror of Robespierre. In other words, he said, all this was done in my name to the extent that I am a member of this nation and the representative of this body politic. In this sense, we are always held responsible for the sins of our fathers as we reap the rewards of their merits; but we are of course not guilty of their misdeeds, either morally or legally, nor can we ascribe their deeds to our merits.[40]

Arendt brings out two points here. First, not only must states take on the burdens of the past, because otherwise there will be responsibility deficits, but in the same way that later versions of the state benefit from the earlier state's accomplishments, it also must bear the burdens of its wrongdoings. Second, she separates the responsibility of the state from the citizens. Citizens now are not 'guilty' – not morally nor legally responsible – for the crimes of the past. However, if the state continues to bear responsibility, whether it is moral responsibility, second-hand responsibility or mere liability, the costs will be passed on to citizens.

This leads to the second problem with state liability. Corporations and states are different in a crucial way. Individuals voluntarily join corporations and so knowingly sign up for its benefits and burdens. But most citizens did not voluntarily join their state; they were born into it. If a state bears liability for its

---

[40]Hannah Arendt, 'Collective Responsibility', in *Responsibility and Judgment*, ed. Jerome Kohn (New York: Schocken Books, 2003), 149–50.

wrongdoings, citizens will have to bear this cost through their taxes, and why should they do that if they themselves were neither involved in the wrongdoing nor signed up for the burdens associated with this corporate agent?

This complex issue has been tackled in a number of ways by philosophers. According to 'democratic authorization' views, the state's liabilities transfer to citizens only if the state fulfils certain conditions of legitimacy. On a weak Hobbesian-inspired view, the state is a necessary background condition to live one's life.[41] On a stronger Kantian-inspired view, states have to provide enfranchisement, some redistribution and effective citizenship.[42] Other accounts focus on the depth of citizens' commitment to the state. Citizens 'intentionally participate' in the state by accepting its benefits and not demonstrating resentment by say leaving, forming autonomous communities or agitating for succession; as such, they bear complicity for the state's actions.[43]

However, I do not find these views persuasive. In terms of intentional citizens, citizens might accept the benefits of state membership, but their options to do otherwise are extremely limited. The world is organized into states; not participating in a state is not an option for the vast majority of the world's people. Even Indigenous and autonomous communities usually come under a state's jurisdiction whether they want to or not. And for the majority of the world's citizens, if they want to live their lives, they simply have to participate in one state or another. Participation, therefore, does not signal willingness to be complicit in the state's actions. As for democratic authorization views, they are retroactively trying to justify a practice that exists in order for international relations to be possible. And the means by which they justify the practice sets the bar too high. In the past, citizens did not democratically authorize states. Many states today still do not meet the requirements of democratic authorization. But that does not invalidate the state's past commitments or reparative obligations.

Treaty-making is a necessary component of international cooperation. It would not be possible for international cooperation to function without states making commitments to each other and making amends for wrongdoing. Cooperation between states has been necessary as long as states have existed, in order to prevent war, facilitate trade and maintain relationships. Reparations have been paid by aggressor states, such as Germany post–First World War, in order to restore international trust and pay for damages. Arguably, international cooperation is more important today due to increased global interdependence, including responding to transnational harms like climate change and pandemics.

---

41 John M. Parrish, 'Collective Responsibility and the State', *International Theory* 1, no. 1 (2009): 119–54.
42 Anna Stilz, 'Collective Responsibility and the State', *Journal of Political Philosophy* 19, no. 2 (2011): 190–208.
43 Avia Pasternak, 'Limiting States' Corporate Responsibility', *The Journal of Political Philosophy* 21, no. 4 (2013): 361–81.

Such cooperation necessarily entails intergenerational commitments. As Thompson puts it, 'By their nature treaties are "posterity-binding": they are meant to impose obligations on our political successors as well as ourselves. To be perpetually valid, or even valid for a reasonable period of time, a treaty has to bind citizens of the future.'[44]

What is important, I would argue, is not the justification for how liability for transgenerational obligations, both good and bad, transmits to citizens – it simply does in order for the international state system to function. What matters is that these commitments themselves meet certain standards of legitimacy. Basic legitimacy entails transparency and accountability: citizens should know what intergenerational commitments they are paying for and have mechanisms by which to hold the state accountable for that. Different generations of citizens should have the possibility of revising those commitments. Two recent examples from the UK bring out this point. One is the Brexit referendum. The UK officially joined the EU on 1 January 1973. In doing so, it signed up to a wide range of posterity-binding obligations. Through a referendum in 2016, forty-three years later, citizens voted to renounce these obligations. I, personally, disagree with this decision and the way in which the referendum was conducted was, I believe, anti-democratic.[45] Nevertheless, the point is that citizens had an opportunity to revise an intergenerational commitment. By contrast, the British government had been paying former slave owners reparations for their lost property from 1835 until 2015. The government paid £20 billion to these individuals and their descendants over nearly two hundred years.[46] The British public had no say in revising this intergenerational commitment, which surely, they would have rejected as illegitimate. As Thompson puts it, 'Above all, we should want our successors to maintain arrangements that all parties can continue to respect and regard as acceptable. They ought to interpret and apply treaties, change or re-negotiate them, in a way that will maintain respect, trust and mutually accepted terms of cooperation.'[47]

In sum, corporate agents can bear moral responsibilities over time. They do this in the form of contracts and treaties. Denial of corporate responsibility means denial of intergenerational responsibilities. While it is straightforward to suggest that the responsibility will devolve onto individual members of corporate agents

---

[44]Janna Thompson, *Taking Responsibility for the Past: Reparation and Historical Injustice* (Cambridge: Polity Press, 2002), 15.

[45]It was anti-democratic for at least four reasons: there was no plan so citizens did not know what they were voting for; there were no protections for minority groups like a supermajority, weighting towards young people who would bear the costs the most, or the inclusion of sixteen- to eighteen-year-olds; Northern Ireland should have been weighted because it threatened the stability of peace; there were criminal activities and disinformation propagated by the Leave.EU campaign.

[46]Kris Manjapra, 'When Will Britain Face Up to Its Crimes against Humanity?', *The Guardian*, 29 March 2018.

[47]Thompson, *Taking Responsibility for the Past*, 20.

where membership is voluntary, it is more difficult for states. States change over time, and liability for the state's costs, both positive and negative, fall on citizens. However, treaty-making and accepting reparative obligations for past iterations of a state is an essential component of international relations in order to maintain cooperation and trust between states and to avoid responsibility deficits. Instead of retroactively trying to justify this practice, I suggest it makes more sense to try to ensure its legitimacy by enhancing transparency and giving future citizens the option to revise intergenerational commitments.

Structural injustice and historical injustice

Some of the most sophisticated literature on structural injustice has been on the topic of the relationship between structural and historical injustice. Young discussed this in the final, unfinished chapter of *Responsibility for Justice*, and two books have addressed this topic in exemplary fashion – Catherine Lu's *Justice and Reconciliation in World Politics* (2017) and Alasia Nuti's *Injustice and the Reproduction of History* (2019). In this section, rather than giving a detailed exposition of Lu and Nuti's approaches, I will briefly explain their views and highlight where we converge and where we disagree. I will argue that these approaches neglect the topic of this chapter so far – corporate responsibility through time.

One of the most important insights of structural injustice theory is to call our attention to the background conditions in which action takes place. In cases of structural injustice, the background conditions are themselves unjust and ought to be changed. Catherine Lu laid the groundwork for integrating the structural and historical injustice literature.[48] She argues that colonialism was not merely an 'interactional' harm – a perpetrator-to-victim harm that deviates from a normal baseline – but was also the product of an unjust international order. Moreover, it preyed upon existing structural injustices, like the subordination of women, manifesting in different forms in different contexts; she gives the example of the South Korean 'comfort women', women and girls who were forced into sexual slavery by the imperial Japanese army during the Second World War. She also highlights that there were many different subject positions in relation to colonialism other than simply victims and perpetrators, including victim-perpetrators – people in colonies who collaborated with the colonizers. Lu has

---

[48]Catherine Lu, 'Colonialism as Structural Injustice: Historical Responsibility and Contemporary Redress', *Journal of Political Philosophy* 19, no. 3 (2011): 261–81; Catherine Lu, *Justice and Reconciliation in World Politics* (Cambridge: Cambridge University Press, 2017).

shown how the structural injustice approach can enrich our understanding of historical injustice.

Young and Lu agree that when discussing responsibility for contemporary structural injustice, both the liability model and the social connection models of responsibility should be used simultaneously. But when it comes to historical injustice, they argue that losses should lie where they fall. When all the direct victims and perpetrators are dead, the past cannot be repaired. Instead, the emphasis should be on forward-looking political responsibility for contemporary structural injustice. Young discussed reparations for slavery in the final chapter of *Responsibility for Justice* and rejected them in favour of forward-looking responsibility: 'The remedies for racialized structural injustice in the United States concern institutional reform and investment, rather than payment construed as compensation to some present persons for wrongs done directly to other persons before they were born.'[49]

Historical injustice is not irrelevant to either thinker. For Young, understanding historical injustice is essential to understanding contemporary structural injustice and how to address it, and there is a responsibility to reconsider historical narratives.[50] For Lu, historical injustice ought to be acknowledged, but it cannot be repaired because all of the victims and perpetrators are dead.[51] She writes, 'Past unjust acts or interactions are not rectifiable by contemporary agents and thus constitute a permanent blight on the historic agents who lived and participated in them.'[52]

However, it is my view that Young and Lu have not given sufficient weight to corporate agents. Corporate agents exist over time. If they commit wrongdoings, they continue to bear obligations to make repair. In fact, Young admits this in relation to corporations. She discusses the City of Chicago's ordinance requiring companies to disclose whether they profited from slavery and suggests, 'The liability model potentially works here; the agent being held liable is the same agent that more than one hundred years ago did business involving slavery or slave owners, and there may be records to prove it.'[53]

While Young is open to the idea that corporations can bear liability over time, she resists the idea that the US state can bear liability over time for three reasons. First, she argues that while the US state legalized slavery and failed to deliver on Reconstruction, it has also 'made explicit reforms aimed at providing some remedy', such as civil rights and voting rights bills and the Fair Housing Act.[54] However, this objection to state liability can swiftly be rejected. The US

---

[49]Iris Marion Young, *Responsibility for Justice* (Oxford: Oxford University Press, 2011), 185.
[50]Young, *Responsibility for Justice*, 182.
[51]Lu, *Justice and Reconciliation in World Politics*, 251.
[52]Lu, *Justice and Reconciliation in World Politics*, 149.
[53]Young, *Responsibility for Justice*, 176.
[54]Young, , *Responsibility for Justice*, 176.

state in taking these measures merely gave African Americans their rights.[55] In a democracy, voting and having protections against housing discrimination are basic. This does not amount to reparations.

Young's second criticism goes deeper. She argues that the state is not 'a specific agent distinct from the society it governs', so responsibility for slavery and associated harms would 'belong in some sense to the people of the United States, or at least to some of them'.[56] However, I would argue that the people who were participating in slavery and its aftermath are all dead, whereas the US state continues. The moral responsibilities of those individuals died when they died. But the moral responsibility of the US state lives on, because it lives on. Just because the individuals who made up US society at the time are dead, this does not invalidate the claim that the US state continues to bear a responsibility for repair.

Young's third argument is that it is not possible to determine how much compensation should be paid to African Americans. If the aim of compensation and damages is to restore a person to the material condition they would have been in had the harm not occurred, then this is not possible in relation to slavery. She claims that 'No one can make objective and verifiable claims about such a vague and sweeping counterfactual.'[57] On this point, Lu agrees with Young. Lu also rejects the idea of state liability over time on the basis of the counterfactual objection. She argues that an interactional approach to historical injustice would assume that the economic benefits and burdens in the present are the direct result of past wrongdoing, which 'relies on a controversial assumption of a causal connection between past and present distributions of holdings'.[58]

Lu specifically objects to Daniel Butt's argument that reparations can be calculated according to a hypothetical just baseline: the distributions of resources that would have obtained had slavery and colonialism not occurred.[59] Lu rejects this for two reasons. First, it assumes that there will be justice in holdings as long as there is justice in transfer, but unjust distributions of resources can result from just market processes, as Rawls observed.[60] Second, it denies the agency of states who make their own decisions about how to utilize resources. For instance, China was not colonized; instead, contemporary distributions can be traced to Mao's policies.[61] Counterfactual reasoning is not possible in relation to

---

[55]Maeve McKeown, 'Backward-Looking Reparations and Structural Injustice', *Contemporary Political Theory* 20, no. 4 (2021): 781.

[56]Young, , *Responsibility for Justice*, 177.

[57]Young, , *Responsibility for Justice*, 179.

[58]Lu, *Justice and Reconciliation in World Politics*, 151.

[59]Lu, *Justice and Reconciliation in World Politics*, 150; Daniel Butt, *Rectifying International Injustice: Principles of Compensation and Restitution between Nations* (Oxford: Oxford University Press, 2008).

[60]Lu, *Justice and Reconciliation in World Politics*, 151.

[61]Lu, *Justice and Reconciliation in World Politics*, 151–2.

slavery and colonialism, and so restoring people now to a situation they would have experienced if these harms had not occurred is impossible.

But Young and Lu are equating reparations with restoration on the basis of counterfactual reasoning. This is unnecessary. Reparations in political practice take multiple forms in cases of transitional justice (transitioning from conflict or mass human rights violations). It could involve individualized payments in the form of compensation, such as the payments made to Japanese Americans who were interned during the Second World War, or the restitution of property to individuals, such as property restored to individuals in former Soviet countries.[62] But these forms of reparation as restoration do not exhaust the possibilities of reparations. There have also been state- or community-building reparations, such as the payments made by West Germany to Israel between 1953 and 1965, or development programmes in post-dictatorship Latin American countries.[63] Reparations can also take the form of memorialization, such as official apologies, building memorials, removing memorials, changing street names, museums, cultural institutions and education programmes.[64]

My claim here is that corporate agents continue to bear responsibility for their wrongdoings as long as they continue to exist. States can continue to bear moral responsibility for historical wrongdoings, and the reparations they pay do not have to be in the form of compensation to individuals, but rather could be a broader programme of development or memorialization, as is already practised in transitional justice contexts. In equating reparations with restoration and rejecting reparations on the basis that it involves impossible counterfactual reasoning, Young and Lu ignore the broad range of approaches to reparations that already exist in political practice.

If reparations could involve programmes of development, however, now the worry emerges that such broader programmes will conflict with the need to address contemporary structural injustice, and since states' resources are limited, focusing on the present and future is more urgent and necessary. I have two responses to this worry. First, to repeat, reparations can take multiple forms. Some forms of reparation cost nothing – for example, an official apology. Others cost little, like changing street names or removing statues of slave holders or other

---

[62]Christopher Kutz, 'Justice in Reparations: The Cost of Memory and the Value of Talk', *Philosophy and Public Affairs* 32, no. 3 (2004): 277–312; Elazar Barkan, *The Guilt of Nations: Restitution and Negotiating Historical Injustices* (New York: W. W. Norton, 2000), chapter 2.

[63]Clemens Nathan, 'The Value of Experience: What Post World War II Settlements Teach Us about Reparations', in *Colonialism, Slavery, Reparations and Trade: Remedying the Past?*, ed. Fernne Brennan and John Packer (Oxon: Routledge, 2012), 209–20; Pamina Firchow, 'Must Our Communities Bleed to Receive Social Services? Development Projects and Collective Reparations Schemes in Colombia', *Journal of Peacebuilding and Development* 8, no. 3 (2013): 50–63.

[64]Brandon Hamber and Ingrid Palmary, 'Gender, Memorialization, and Symbolic Reparations', in *The Gender of Reparations: Unsettling Sexual Heirarchies While Redressing Human Rights Violations*, ed. Ruth Rubio-Marin (Cambridge: Cambridge University Press, 2009), 324–81.

compromised individuals. Others cost something, but not enormous amounts, like building memorials, museums or education programmes. Yet others could be a matter of diverting existing funding into those areas; for instance, instead of paying 'development aid', which implies beneficence on the part of the givers, call it reparations and frame it as payment for the harms done to former colonies in the past.[65] As Charles Mills argues, it matters whether distributions of resources are framed as a matter of charity or of paying a debt for harms done.[66] So the worry about conflicts with contemporary justice programmes are overstated. It all depends on what form reparations actually take. Detractors often fail to acknowledge the wide range of potential reparatory measures.

Second, this worry about conflicts of justice is overly focused on states; it assumes that the state is the only agent that owes reparations for historical injustice. But the state is not the only agent that could owe reparations, since, as I have argued, corporate agents that continue to exist over time continue to bear reparative obligations. This can include corporate agents like corporations, churches, universities, clubs and associations and so on. The perceived conflict of justice does not apply to these agents who do not bear responsibility for contemporary distributive and social justice.[67] They can pay reparations without raising these sorts of concerns. The Legacies of British Slavery database at UCL has documented all of the British companies and cultural institutions who have connections to slavery.[68] Thus, at least when it comes to Britain, these actors have already been identified. Some, like Lloyds of London, Greene King, the University of Glasgow and All Souls College, Oxford, have made some gestures at reparations.[69]

Failing to recognize the ongoing responsibility of corporate agents over time results in a responsibility deficit for historical wrongdoings, when this doesn't have to be the case since there are a range of liable agents and a range of forms of reparations. Merging all reparations claims into a generalized forward-looking

---

[65]Lu acknowledges this possibility when discussing German payments to Namibia for the genocide of the Hereo and Nama.

> In this case, since acknowledgment of past injustice is the purpose of acknowledgment payments, they need to be specified between Germany and those groups that were the explicit targets of genocidal policies and therefore should be distinct from any 'development assistance' that Germany pays to the postcolonial state of Namibia. The insistence of German officials on categorizing any financial transfer as 'development assistance' further obscures the proper role of such payments, which is to fulfil Germany's responsibility to acknowledge forthrightly its historic responsibility for the injustice. (Lu, *Justice and Reconciliation in World Politics*, 251)

[66]Charles W. Mills, 'Race and Global Justice', in *Domination and Global Political Justice* (New York: Routledge, 2015), 181–206.
[67]Daniel Butt, 'What Structural Injustice Theory Leaves Out', *Ethical Theory and Moral Practice* 24, no. 1 (2021): 1171.
[68]UCL, 'Legacies of British Slave-Ownership Project', 2020, https://www.ucl.ac.uk/lbs/project/project.
[69]Jonathan Guthrie, 'Lex in Depth: Examining the Slave Trade – "Britain Has a Debt to Repay,"' *Financial Times*, 28 June 2020.

approach to structural injustice ignores the persisting responsibility of corporate agents and the multiple forms of reparations they can and should pay. Backward-looking reparations can be combined with forward-looking responsibility for contemporary structural injustice when the range of reparative measures is taken into account as well as the range of agents who can pay for them.

Alasia Nuti agrees with me that 'dismissing backward-looking reparations demands would leave a significant gap in the moral framework of structural approaches'.[70] She claims that Young and Lu have 'under-theorised' history, and we ought to 'de-temporalise' justice.[71] Following historian Reinhard Koselleck, she argues that history can be understood in two ways: either as a series of 'events' or as 'long-term structures'.[72] Understanding history as structural allows us to consider how historically unjust structures are newly reproduced in the present. This is what Nuti calls 'historical-structural injustice' (HSI). For example, in the past African Americans were subordinated through legalized chattel slavery, but their subordination continued in different forms in subsequent generations, from Jim Crow to a range of manifestations today, including the 'radical' – such as the prison-industrial complex and arbitrary police killings – and the 'banal' – for example, negative stereotypes. The underlying long-term structure of the subordination of African Americans needs to be addressed, rather than particular historical events.

Nuti argues that the US state owes reparations to African Americans because it has accumulated a 'structural debt' for persistently reproducing their subordination through legislation. She writes,

> Reparation demands for injustices such as slavery point out that fully de-temporalising injustice – that is, separating the past and the present in our reflecting upon justice – entails not only forward-looking responsibilities but also a backward-looking normative analysis searching for powerful agents that, over history, have significantly enabled the structural reproduction of unjust history. It requires that such agents be held accountable for what can be called their *structural debt* – that is, a debt they have accumulated over time through their actions (and inactions) within unjust structures.[73]

Nuti's framework is complementary to mine in the following sense. Her framework of historical-structural injustice explains how powerful corporate agents that fail to address or deliberately perpetuate structural injustice continue to bear liability

---

[70]Alasia Nuti, *Injustice and the Reproduction of History: Structural Inequalities, Gender and Redress* (Cambridge: Cambridge University Press, 2019), 157.
[71]Nuti, *Injustice and the Reproduction of History*, 19.
[72]Nuti, *Injustice and the Reproduction of History*, 23.
[73]Nuti, *Injustice and the Reproduction of History*, 157.

for that over time. This is what she calls their 'structural debt'. To put this in the terms of the critical realist framework employed here, agents are born into structures, and over time, there is interaction between structure and agency, and new forms of structural elaboration emerge that are intended by no one. However, over time, certain groups continue to experience domination and oppression in new structural elaborations, now in a different form. The examples Nuti gives are African Americans and women. These groups repeatedly experience domination and oppression despite the emergence of new social structures, but the form of their domination and oppression shifts as the social structures change. Since there have been agents who had it within their power to ameliorate this structural injustice and failed to do so, or agents who deliberately perpetuated it for their own gain, these agents bear a 'structural debt' for these actions or omissions, and this structural debt persists, and even increases, over time.[74] Thus, Nuti's framework explains how the moral responsibility of powerful corporate agents for avoidable and deliberate structural injustice travels through time.

However, Nuti argues that 'Unlike backward-looking approaches, the account of HSI does not claim that the unjust past grounds obligations of justice in the present per se. Quite the contrary, it claims that we should pay normative attention to the unjust past because *it is present* in terms of unjust long-term structures.'[75] So the only historical injustices that warrant repair, on Nuti's account, are those that persist in contemporary unjust structures. And this is where we disagree. What I would add to Nuti's framework is that corporate agents that persist through time continue to bear liability for specific wrongdoings committed in the past, for the reasons outlined in this chapter. Thus, in contrast to Nuti who insists that only historical injustice that continues to be present in social structures is a candidate for reparations, my approach retains backward-looking reparations. My approach insists that if historical perpetrator agents continue to exist, they continue to bear responsibility on the liability model for their wrongdoings.

Backward-looking reparations for historical injustice are important because it means that historical wrongdoers that continue to exist are not let off the hook. Nuti cautions against backward-looking reparations for historical injustice that is no longer present because these will run into the 'impracticability objection' – the claim that there are so many historical injustices that we cannot repair all of them.[76] But my approach based on corporate liability through time does not face this objection because it only calls for repair in cases where the perpetrator agents continue to exist.[77] I argue that this responsibility exists in addition to

---

[74]Nuti, *Injustice and the Reproduction of History*, 161.
[75]Nuti, *Injustice and the Reproduction of History*, 47.
[76]Nuti, *Injustice and the Reproduction of History*, 15.
[77]Janna Thompson calls this an 'obligations-dependent approach'. Thompson, *Taking Responsibility for the Past: Reparation and Historical Injustice*, 39.

cases of structural debt for failing to ameliorate or deliberately perpetuating unjust social structures over time.

As well as avoiding responsibility deficits for historical wrongdoing, my approach also ensures that communities who are claiming backward-looking reparations are taken seriously. For instance, some reparationists not only want to address present-day forms of repression and structural injustice faced by African Americans or the wider African diaspora, but rather want acknowledgement that chattel slavery itself was a crime against humanity.[78] The uniqueness of certain historical 'events' could be forgotten in an approach that only acknowledges historical injustice that continues to persist in contemporary unjust structures. Nuti risks ignoring the uniqueness and significance of specific cases of wrongdoing that no longer persist, like chattel slavery.

Finally, Nuti argues that reparations for structural debt serves an educative dimension, but I would argue that reparations for historical events can also serve this purpose. Young makes this point when discussing the City of Chicago's ordinance, that it is 'a move to encourage public discussion of the historic injustice of slavery among Americans, not only in schools and universities, but also in commercial and industrial enterprises'.[79] Thomas McCarthy argues that America needs to engage in 'historical consciousness-raising' and that reparations lawsuits can ignite this conversation. He draws on Habermas's classic essay, 'On the Public Use of History', to discuss the importance of public education and remembrance:

> Public remembrances and commemorations of the suffering of victims – through artistic as well as historical representations, in public rituals and public places, in school curricula and mass media – play crucial roles in transforming traditions and in determining what will or will not be passed on to future generations. Whether or not past evils are kept present in public consciousness, whether or not their victims are still mourned, Habermas continues, are central elements of who 'we' (Germans) are and who 'we' want to be. For recognizing past evil as integral to German history, as issuing 'from the very midst of our collective life' – rather than as marginal or accidental to it – 'cannot but have a powerful impact on our self-understanding ... and shake any naïve trust in our own traditions'. It is, in fact, an essential ingredient in any genuine effort to re-form national identity in full awareness of the horrors that issued from its previous formations.[80]

---

[78]CARICOM, 'Ten Point Action Plan' (Institute of the Black World 21st Century, 2014), http://ibw21. org/commentary/caricom-reparations-ten-point-plan/; McKeown, 'Backward-Looking Reparations and Structural Injustice'; Hilary McD. Beckles, *Britain's Black Debt: Reparations for Caribbean Slavery and Native Genocide* (Kingston: University of West Indies Press, 2013).
[79]Young, *Responsibility for Justice*, 183; Lu, *Justice and Reconciliation in World Politics*, 162–4.
[80]Thomas McCarthy, *Race, Empire, and the Idea of Human Development* (Cambridge: Cambridge University Press, 2009), 102–3.

As mentioned above, reparations can take the form of memorialization, including public education initiatives, memorials, changing memorials and place names and so on. All this contributes to a rethinking of collective subjectivity, which is a necessary part of the process of ensuring that such catastrophes never happen again. Since such a reckoning has never occurred in relation to slavery and colonialism, in the United States and European colonizer states, claims of never again ring hollow. The contemporary and future social structures need to be addressed, but also the specific harms of the past.

One final worry that is persistent across this literature is, who are the relevant recipients of reparations programmes if all the direct victims are dead? Lu and Young both cite this as a reason for rejecting reparations for historical injustice.[81] Nuti tries to solve this problem by arguing that 'historical-structural groups' are the appropriate candidates – groups that are the 'structural descendants' of historically victimized groups, meaning they have inherited the same social position and categorization as the dead; if they had been alive at the time of the injustice, they would have experienced it too.[82]

What I want to highlight in regard to this point is, again, that it depends on the kind of reparations programmes being proposed. Reparations can take multiple forms, including development programmes and memorialization. Such forms of reparations have broad targets and do not require the identification of specific individuals, or even social groups, as beneficiaries. So, again, whether or not this problem arises will depend on the kind of reparations programme that is being discussed.

To take an example of a reparations proposal, the Caribbean Community (CARICOM) announced a 10-Point Plan for reparations in 2013, which includes a range of measures.[83] It calls for memorialization reparations: an apology, cultural institutions and an African knowledge programme. And it calls for development programmes for Indigenous peoples, addressing of public health and education deficits in the region and debt cancellation. With such an approach, the target of the reparations programmes is essentially everyone who lives in the Caribbean. While some groups will specifically be allocated funding – Indigenous peoples – for the most part, the application of the reparations measures will be broad-brush.

When reparations are conceived of in this way, the supposed philosophical sticking point of who counts as an appropriate beneficiary loses its bite. We could think of the recipients in this case as the 'structural descendants' of the

---

[81]Young, *Responsibility for Justice*, 177–8; Lu, *Justice and Reconciliation in World Politics*, 159–66.
[82]Nuti, *Injustice and the Reproduction of History*, 62.
[83]For a detailed discussion of this case see McKeown, 'Backward-Looking Reparations and Structural Injustice'; CARICOM, 'Ten Point Action Plan'; Verene A. Shepherd, 'Part Imperfect, Future Perfect? Reparations, Rehabilitation, Reconciliation', *Journal of African American History* 103, no. 1 (2018): 19–43; Beckles, *Britain's Black Debt*.

enslaved and victims of Indigenous genocide in the Caribbean, but these sorts of initiatives will be more inclusive than that. The benefits of memorialization will reach the diaspora and visitors to the region. And the benefits of development will reach recent immigrants and could even benefit those from former perpetrator communities. None of this strikes me as a reason to reject such a reparations programme: being over-inclusive is better than being under-inclusive. Moreover, the same sorts of issues of inclusion and exclusion apply to contemporary reparations programmes for transitional justice and are also not a reason for rejecting those programmes. Instead, these problems are worked through as a matter of political debate in consultation with the relevant stakeholders. Thus, just as the worry about conflicts of justice was overstated, the worry about who counts as a beneficiary of reparations for historical injustice tends to be overstated. This will often come down to questions of institutional design and political debate, rather than being an insurmountable philosophical obstacle.

Furthermore, raising the questions of political debate and institutional design also address Lu's concerns that an interactional reparations programme would only include perpetrators and victims, excluding other relevant agents. Lu herself acknowledges that, in practice, reparations programmes in contexts of contemporary transitional justice include a wide range of participants – from liable states, to external states, the society of states and global civil society.[84] The practice of reparations can combine both the structural injustice and interactional approaches when dealing with contemporary 'political catastrophes'. So positioning the structural versus the interactional approach creates a false dichotomy. I would argue that the two can be combined not only in contemporary cases but also in historical cases, and this will largely be a question of institutional design; how the two work together, relate to each other and impact on each other in practice.

Conclusion

Young argues that the present disadvantages experienced by African Americans are not the 'direct result' of slavery: 'It is in the nature of structural causation that one cannot for the most part trace a direct lineal causal relationship between particular actions or policies and the relatively disadvantaged circumstances of particular individuals or groups.'[85] I agree that the interaction between structure and agency over time is complex and unpredictable, and so claims about historical injustice should not be based on distributions of holdings over time or counterfactual reasoning. But the argument of this chapter shows that this is not

---

[84]Lu, *Justice and Reconciliation in World Politics*, 222.
[85]Young, *Responsibility for Justice*, 185.

the only, or even the best, way to think about the problem of responsibility for historical injustice. I have shown that corporate agents can bear responsibility and can do so over time. Their responsibility for wrongdoing persists, even if they committed these wrongdoings in the past. It is on that basis that they should pay reparations.

Catherine Lu might object that this interactional approach 'cannot tell the whole story about responsibility for many colonial injustices'.[86] The structural injustice approach 'identifies other contributory agents and structures in the production of colonial injustices and raises the question of the responsibilities of those other contributory agents, including *of international society, as well as of and among* colonized peoples'.[87] Again, I agree. The structural injustice framework calls attention to the background conditions, the role of multiple agents in contributing to historical injustice, and includes those with complex subjectivities. The structural injustice approach improves our understanding of historical injustice and responsibility for it. But this is not a reason for rejecting interactional reparations. Instead, it is a reason for combining an interactional approach with a structural approach. What this will look like in practice is up for political debate.

I conclude that structural injustice theory ought to take corporate responsibility more seriously and the way in which corporate responsibility persists through time. Failing to recognize corporate responsibility over time will result in responsibility deficits and while this raises difficult questions in relation to states, these are not insurmountable. The challenges that Young and Lu raised to state liability over time are not strong. Reparations can take multiple forms, some of which do not conflict with present-day concerns about justice, nor involve counterfactual reasoning, and states are not the only agents who bear outstanding historical responsibilities. Alasia Nuti's approach is a fruitful complement to mine in terms of explaining how responsibility to address or stop deliberately perpetuating contemporary structural injustice generates a structural debt. But her account can be supplemented with an account of the backward-looking responsibilities of corporate agents. By acknowledging the corporate responsibility of powerful agents over time, structural injustice theory more fully integrates the liability model of responsibility, ensuring a more accurate and actionable distribution of responsibility for structural and historical injustice.

---

[86]Lu, *Justice and Reconciliation in World Politics*, 116.
[87]Lu, *Justice and Reconciliation in World Politics*, 117.

Chapter 8
Acting on political responsibility

Every day, billions of individuals and collective agents go about their normal lives, and the result is structural injustice. From material infrastructure, economic and political systems, to law and social norms, habits, attitudes and behaviour, everything coalesces to produce and reproduce injustice. Sometimes this injustice is deliberately perpetuated by powerful agents because they benefit from it, such as when multinational clothing corporations lobby governments and international organizations for lax labour laws and spend billions on manipulation to convince consumers to keep shopping. Sometimes the injustice is not deliberately perpetuated, but could be alleviated if only powerful agents would take responsibility for it: the case of global poverty – the money is there and structural changes are on the table, what is lacking is political will. And sometimes the injustice is genuinely the fallout of cumulative processes and requires systemic overhaul, such as climate change; we must replace the capitalist system that is based on constant accumulation and growth, and fossil fuel extraction and consumption.

Because ordinary individuals are born into and trapped in these unjust systems, constraining their options for action, it is wrong to blame them for structural injustice; their contributions are either inadvertent or the result of social duress. However, ordinary individuals are not off the hook. They bear political responsibility to collectively organize to challenge structural injustice. Powerful agents bear moral responsibility – they are blameworthy – when they deliberately perpetuate structural injustice or fail to alleviate it when it is in their power to do so.

We now know what structural injustice is and who bears responsibility for it. The next question that naturally arises is, what do we do about it? In this concluding chapter, I offer some thoughts on how to address structural injustice. The underlying principle is based on the situated conception of power (see Chapter 2). The way to challenge the powerful is to create alternative alignments, so that individuals are no longer dependent on those powerful agents, or to create countering alignments. Also, powerful agents are enabled by a social alignment that legitimates and props up their power, which provides multiple avenues for contestation. Thus, in this chapter, I offer some suggestions for ordinary individuals taking up political responsibility based on this situated conception of power. First, I will discuss the moral responsibility of powerful agents for structural injustice and how they cannot be relied upon to do the right thing. Second, I make some suggestions regarding alternative alignments, countering alignments and challenging the social alignment. Third, I discuss Young's 'parameters of reasoning' about political responsibility, which are supposed to help individuals to decide which structural injustice to act on. Young suggested four parameters – power, privilege, interest and collective ability. I remove power, given its more central place in my account of structural injustice, and add proximity.

Corporate responsibility: State and economy

Throughout this book, I have emphasized the role of powerful agents in perpetuating structural injustice either through acts or omissions. I highlighted in Chapter 2 that structure and agency interact; agents have some room to decide how to act within structures. Powerful agents have more elbow room to decide how to act than relatively powerless agents. They also have greater resources, giving them a better chance of getting what they want. Their interests are given by their social position, and so they usually act to maintain or improve that position; but this is not predetermined – they could act otherwise. In Chapter 7, I argued that corporate agents can bear moral responsibility for their actions. This is because corporate entities, such as states or MNCs, have internal decision-making structures by virtue of which they reason and make decisions. They then act as a principal, authorizing other agents (employees or functionaries) to carry out actions on their behalf. Therefore, corporate agents meet the conditions for moral responsibility and can bear moral responsibility for their actions.

When global garment corporations lobby to reduce workers' rights or fossil fuel corporations propagate climate denialism, they are acting to deliberately perpetuate structural injustice for their own gain, and are blameworthy. When states ignore tax avoidance and fail to rein in global finance, they are failing to take measures that could alleviate global poverty, and are blameworthy. The question is, what follows?

Corporations *are* acting to alleviate global problems. As we saw in Chapter 3, corporations are engaged in a range of activities promoting justice. Corporations are engaged in private–private partnerships, such as the Forest Stewardship Council (FSC) or Ethical Trading Initiative, writing codes of conduct and creating frameworks for the regulation of industries.[1] Significantly, states and corporations are coming together to tackle global problems through public–private partnerships (PPPs), like The Global Compact, The Global Fund to Fight Aids, Tuberculosis and Malaria, and the Global Polio Eradication Initiative.[2] These are a new form of governance because they involve co–decision-making by states and corporations and the pooling of resources.[3] Liliana Andonova argues that 'the emergence of global public-private partnerships created as new hybrid governance to complement state-driven multilateralism and their impact on global problems cannot be underestimated'.[4] PPPs are now so established that most UN Agencies are engaged in partnerships, one of the Sustainable Development Goals (SDGs) is 'Partnership for the Goals' (SDG 17), and there is a UN Fund for International Partnerships that brokers agreements between the UN and businesses.[5] The rise of PPPs means that a 'post-Westphalian order' is emerging, where hybrid forms of governance are normalized and corporations have 'private political authority'.[6]

There are three implications of this emerging phenomenon that are relevant here for responsibility, for states and for individuals. The first is the implication for the social connection model of responsibility. Florian Wettstein sees the emergence of PPPs as a promising example of the social-connection model of responsibility in practice. He argues, similarly to me, that 'it is those with the greatest power to have a potential positive impact on the situation who bear the largest share of responsibility'.[7] For Wettstein, this means that corporations share a forward-looking 'collaborative responsibility' to fulfil human rights obligations, particularly socio-economic rights. They are currently doing this through PPPs and should do more.

But I disagree. Corporations, I believe, bear backward-looking moral responsibility on the liability model for deliberately perpetuating structural injustice or failing to remedy it when it is in their power to do so. This is not the same as saying that corporations should work with each other or with governments to take forward-looking political responsibility to fulfil socio-economic human rights

---

[1]As discussed in Chapter 3, there are a range of criticisms of private–private partnerships. They are often toothless because they are not legally binding. When these partnerships are stringent, like the FSC, some corporations opt out and create more diluted standards, confusing consumers. And they undermine the possibility for government regulation.

[2]Liliana B. Andonova, *Governance Entrepreneurs: International Organizations and the Rise of Global Public-Private Partnerships* (Cambridge: Cambridge University Press, 2019), 1.

[3]Andonova, *Governance Entrepreneurs*, 27.

[4]Andonova, *Governance Entrepreneurs*, 1.

[5]Andonova, *Governance Entrepreneurs*, 14, 18.

[6]Stephen J. Korbin, 'Private Political Authority and Public Responsibility: Transnational Politics, Transnational Firms, and Human Rights', *Business Ethics Quarterly* 19, no. 3 (2009): 349–74.

[7]Florian Wettstein, 'Corporate Responsibility in the Collective Age: Toward a Conception of Collaborative Responsibility', *Business and Society Review* 117, no. 2 (2012): 170.

more broadly or distributive justice. The arguments against such a scenario are familiar. Corporations lack accountability mechanisms. In democratic states, the rulers can be ousted at elections, but corporations are not accountable to the people whose human rights they would be fulfilling; there is no mechanism for those affected by corporations' actions to remove their CEOs or even to question their practices. Corporations are often not transparent, and their decision-making processes are not required to be transparent. They are selective in terms of what they choose to fund and support, which can depend on the whims, pet projects or vanity projects of incumbent CEOs. This creates a problem of uneven distribution of corporate/philanthropic resources over different global problems. To put it more starkly: is it a desirable world where Coca-Cola, Nike or massive philanthropic organizations like the Bill & Melinda Gates Foundation are responsible for addressing global injustice?

PPPs might seem to alleviate some of these worries because corporations are working together with the UN or states. Thus, as Andonova argues, the 'corporate takeover' worry is insufficiently nuanced; PPPs are constrained by the norms and legal rules of global governance.[8] But the problems with PPPs go further than that. My point is that corporations should be held morally responsible for the structural injustices they contribute to, either by act or omission. But the PPPs that corporations contribute to are often not related to the injustices they contribute to. The majority of PPPs focus on global health, environment, disaster response, nutrition and education.[9] To give an example, the Global Business Coalition for HIV/AIDS is touted as a success story in the global partnerships and business ethics literature.[10] Two of the partners in this venture are the oil giants Chevron and Exxon Mobil.[11] But should oil companies be trying to eradicate HIV/AIDS or focus on the structural injustice they are most implicated in – that is, burning fossil fuels and making the planet uninhabitable? It could be argued that the two are not mutually exclusive – if corporations have the funds, why shouldn't they contribute to the fight against HIV/AIDS while also getting their own house in order? But the problem is that corporations use these partnerships to give the illusion of being responsible and ethical actors while simultaneously continuing to behave in irresponsible and unethical ways in their own sectors.[12]

Another problem with PPPs is that these initiatives are unlikely to attempt to make more sweeping ideological and material changes that might be warranted when tackling structural injustices like climate change, sweatshops and poverty.

---

[8]Andonova, *Governance Entrepreneurs*, 28.

[9]Andonova, *Governance Entrepreneurs*, 14.

[10]Wettstein, 'Corporate Responsibility in the Collective Age'; Andonova, *Governance Entrepreneurs*; Korbin, 'Private Political Authority and Public Responsibility:'.

[11]GBC Health, 'Our Parnters', accessed 7 January 2023, https://www.gbchealth.org/partners.

[12]Critics argue that PPPs have the effect of 'blue-washing' corporations – giving them the cloak of UN legitimacy. Andonova, *Governance Entrepreneurs*, 28.

They are unlikely to challenge neoliberal orthodoxy, to dismantle existing institutions and create new ones that fundamentally put people and the planet at the centre of decision-making. To return to Wettstein's suggestion, therefore, my argument is not that corporations bear forward-looking collaborative responsibility for fulfilling socio-economic rights. Rather, I believe that they bear backward-looking moral responsibility for deliberately perpetuating the structural injustices that suit them and for failing to tackle the ones that they could address. This means that corporations ought to be held accountable for their particular activities within their sectors, not given more discretionary power over larger bodies of people.

The second implication of the emergence of hybrid global governance is for the role of states. States continue to have a role in creating legislation that protects workers, and people generally, from the power of corporations. A Fossil Fuel Non-Proliferation Treaty would protect people from continued expansion of the fossil fuel industry. Such a treaty proposes to leave any remaining fossil fuels in the ground. It would be modelled on the Nuclear Non-Proliferation Treaty's three pillars of non-proliferation (no more extraction of fossil fuels), disarmament (documenting the remaining resources and protecting them) and peaceful use (regulated use of current stocks).[13] In the garment industry, states could require their corporations to agree to global legally binding agreements on working conditions, like the International Accord, and increase the scope of such an agreement to include wages and rights to unionize. States could also implement joint-liability legislation. For instance, after sustained activism by the International Ladies Garment Workers Union (ILGWU), sweatshops were virtually eliminated in the United States between 1947 and 1990. This was because buyers bore legal liability to ensure minimum wages and working conditions in their factories, to allow unionization and to guarantee payments if factories went bust.[14] While this is more difficult to achieve globally than in a domestic jurisdiction, the Bangladesh Accord was essentially an exercise in joint liability and was successful while it lasted.[15] In terms of alleviating poverty, states could demand higher corporation tax, outlaw tax havens, alleviate debts and agree to reforms of global governance institutions. At the time of writing, the UN General Assembly has just adopted a resolution on a New International Economic Order, echoing the 1974 resolution. A total of 123 countries voted in favour and 50 against – essentially the West, or

---

[13]Peter Newell and Andrew Simms, 'Towards a Fossil Fuel Non-Proliferation Treaty', *Climate Policy* 20, no. 8 (2020): 1043–54.

[14]Mark Anner, Jennifer Bair and Jeremy Blasi, 'Toward Joint Liability in Global Supply Chains: Addressing the Root Causes of Labor Violations in International Subcontracting Networks', *Comparative Labour Law & Policy Journal* 35, no. 1 (2013): 1–44.

[15]Anner, Bair and Blasi, 'Toward Joint Liability in Global Supply Chains'; Maeve McKeown, 'The Law's Contribution to Deliberate Structural Injustice', in *Structural Injustice and the Law*, ed. Virginia Mantouvalou and Jonathan Wolff (London: UCL, 2024).

states that share geopolitical or economic interests with the geographical West (United States, UK, some EU states, Canada, Australia, Israel, South Korea and Japan).[16] States could take responsibility and actually implement this resolution this time.

As Iris Young wisely argues, 'Prudence calls for mistrust of state institutions, even when we affirm their importance.'[17] This is where the role of individuals arises and our political responsibility kicks in. Citizens in democracies can hold states accountable through elections, interactions with politicians, the media and civil society. It is through action in civil society that citizens can hold the state to account for its perpetuation or failure to alleviate structural injustice. But political responsibility no longer only entails vigilance about what the state is doing and maintaining an institutional framework in which plurality is possible (as Arendt argued); it also requires vigilance about what corporations are doing, since they are now also public-political actors. The political responsibility of individuals involves holding corporations to account directly (public shaming, direct action, etc.) and indirectly by pressuring governance institutions to create appropriate legal frameworks, including the suggestions above. As a basic starting point, more stringent transparency and accountability requirements should be demanded of corporations, as these values are the bare minimum required for political legitimacy. Through these methods, individuals can contribute to corporations and states fulfilling their moral responsibilities for structural injustice.

Individuals in civil society

According to Thomas Wartenberg's situated conception of power (see Chapter 2), subordinated agents have the option of creating alternative alignments (providing the goods or services denied by the powerful by other means) or countering alignments (a countervailing powerful force like a trade union or social movement). He also argues that any agent's power is enabled by a social alignment.[18] For instance, the power of landlords is backed up by the state, the courts and the police. Therefore, challenging power can be a matter of addressing the powerful agents themselves or the social alignment that backs them up.

All of this occurs already in civil society. Instead of thinking of civil society in spatial terms, Young argues that we should think of it as a set if activities for the purposes of 'free self-organising' and 'limiting power and democratizing

---

[16]Ben Norton, 'West Opposes Rest of World in UN Votes for Fairer Economic System, Equality, Sustainable Development', Multipolarista, 22 December 2022.

[17]Iris Marion Young, Inclusion and Democracy (Oxford: Oxford University Press, 2002), 194.

[18]Thomas E. Wartenberg, The Forms of Power: From Domination to Transformation (Philadelphia: Temple University Press, 1990).

its exercise'.[19] Through civil society activities, individuals can challenge the powerful agents that perpetuate or fail to tackle structural injustice. Normally, the discussion is about 'citizen' participation in civil society, but since many migrants are not afforded full citizenship rights and there are a least 10 million stateless people in the world today[20] – with the number of migrants and stateless people set to increase exponentially with the intensification of climate change – I prefer to talk about individuals. Also, there is no global state and since we are talking about global structural injustice, in the global sphere, individuals' civil society activities do not necessarily target states on the basis of citizenship.

Alternative alignments

One role of civil society organizations is to provide *goods and services* where governments fail to do so.[21] Examples abound in the women's movement, such as networks of Rape Crisis Centres, domestic abuse shelters and abortion support services like Women on Waves or the Abortion Support Network. These organizations, made up of private donations, volunteers and sometimes small workforces, provide support or services that victims of gender-based violence, or pregnant people, are unable to access from their governments.

One of the concerns of this kind of organizing is that it plugs the gap created by government, removing the government's incentive to properly address the problem.[22] The idea of 'leave it to civil society' can be a convenient way for government to avoid its responsibilities or to impose an ideological agenda of the small state. The current proliferation of food banks across the United Kingdom, where there are now more food banks than McDonalds fast-food outlets, is a case in point.[23] It is a symptom of the government failing to adequately address the spiralling 'cost-of-living crisis', where incomes fail to match rising gas prices and interest rates, especially for workers in the public sector or those on benefits. However, Jonathan Wolff cautions that we shouldn't forget about the needs of people experiencing structural injustice now, focusing attention only on long-term and difficult-to-achieve structural solutions. He writes 'although there is an urgency in trying to address structural injustice, there can be even greater

---

[19]Young, *Inclusion and Democracy*, 159.
[20]UNCHR, 'Statelessness around the World', United Nations High Commission for Refugees, accessed 6 January 2023, ttps://www.unhcr.org/ibelong/statelessness-around-the-world/.
[21]Young, *Inclusion and Democracy*, 165.
[22]Anna Coote, 'Cameron's "Big Society" Will Leave the Poor and Powerless Behind', *The Guardian*, 19 July 2010.
[23]There are an estimated 2,500 food banks compared to 1,463 McDonald's. Bethany Dawson, 'Many in the UK Face a Grim Choice This Winter between Eating and Heating as a Cost-of-Living Crisis Grips the Nation', *Business Insider*, 9 October 2022.

urgency in trying to relieve the particular difficulties faced by the victims of structural injustice'.[24]

I agree. Addressing structural injustice by only focusing on long-term structural solutions risks leaving people to a miserable fate in the short term. But we can work on both simultaneously – they are not mutually exclusive. Some of these organizations both provide goods or services and do advocacy on behalf of their service-users, pushing governments to provide access to these resources. Even if these organizations don't do advocacy, their mere existence signals that there is a problem that needs to be addressed, which subsequent, more sympathetic administrations might do.

Civil society organizations have also provided *alternative institutional frameworks* for the protection of workers. A compelling example is the Fair Food Program (FFP) in the United States. Farmworkers in Immokalee, Florida, started to organize in 1993 in response to rampant forced labour and workers' rights abuses.[25] Many of the workers came from Latin American and Caribbean countries and were used to a model of Popular Education, which emphasizes participatory dialogue and a continuous process of critical analysis and reflection. They realized that, much like the garment industry, workers' wages were being driven down by retailers, like the fast-food giant Taco Bell. In 2001, they launched a campaign with the slogan 'Taco Bell makes farmworkers poor'. They held meetings at schools, churches and community centres across the country and used social media and protests to mobilize consumer support. The result of this 'painstaking work' was the Fair Food Program (FFP) adopted by the industry in 2011. This programme has been credited with eliminating forced labour and sexual violence and harassment from Florida's agriculture industry. The FPP is built on five pillars: (1) Fair Food Agreements – contracts between corporations and farms, which place a Fair Food Premium on each pound of produce; (2) a Fair Food Code of Conduct – a worker-written code for participating farms; (3) an informed workforce – new employees are fully briefed of their rights in writing and on video, the materials are created by workers and are available in multiple languages and there is an ongoing education program; (4) a complaint mechanism – workers have a right to make complaints with no threat of reprisal and there is a 24/7 helpline, again in multiple languages, staffed by auditors who know the farms; and (5) in-depth audits – a minimum of 50 per cent of the workforce is interviewed on every farm. This is a private regulatory system, but it has been effective because of its foundation in Worker-Driven Social

---

[24]Jonathan Wolff, 'Structural Harm, Structural Injustice, Structural Repair', in *What Is Structural Injustice?*, ed. Jude Browne and Maeve McKeown (Oxford: Oxford University Press, 2024).
[25]This paragraph is a summary of the account in Greg Asbed and Steve Hitov, 'Preventing Forced Labor in Corporate Supply Chains: The Fair Food Program and Worker-Driven Social Responsibility', *Wake Forest Law Review* 52 (2017): 497–531.

Responsibility (WSR). Workers know the issues that affect them, they have come up with solutions and they are all educated in the FPP, so hold employers to account; the FPP 'effectively deputizes tens of thousands of workers as frontline defenders of their own human rights'.[26]

Alternative institutional frameworks have also been created by the anti-sweatshop movement. In response to sweatshop scandals in the late 1990s, the Clinton administration created the Fair Labour Association (FLA), an association of firms, NGOs and unions. Since the FLA's board was controlled by firms, students rejected the FLA and formed an alternative organization, United Students Against Sweatshops (USAS). USAS researches, organizes protests and does advocacy around university licencing deals – where universities work with a brand like Nike or Adidas, who get exclusive use of the university logo, and in return, the university gets 7–8 per cent of the profits.[27] USAS then formed a monitoring organization, the Workers' Rights Consortium (WRC), which does independent, unannounced factory inspections. Like the Fair Food Program, the USAS and WRC are founded on the principle of workers' empowerment. This is a normative and philosophical choice, but it is also strategic.[28] It is through direct collaboration with sweatshop workers and local unions that they get their information, develop demands and design campaigns. For instance, it is due to worker empowerment that the US anti-sweatshop movement has generally avoided boycotts, since workers were clear that they wanted to keep their jobs, and boycotts would undermine that.[29] They have had at least two successes: getting workers reinstated and a pay rise at the Kukdong factory in Mexico in 2001 and similar results for Honduran workers at Fruit of the Loom factories in 2008.[30]

Greg Asbed and Steve Hitov argue that the Fair Food Program 'models an approach that can succeed in a multitude of low-wage environments around the globe'.[31] They believe that private worker-designed and worker-implemented programmes in industries that are dominated by global MNCs, backed by consumer support, offer a promising alternative alignment to the dominance

[26]Asbed and Hitov, 'Preventing Forced Labor in Corporate Supply Chai', 520.
[27]Dreier, Peter. 'The Campus Anti-Sweatshop Movement'. *The American Prospect*, 19 December 2001. Matthew S. Williams, 'Global Solidarity, Global Worker Empowerment, and Global Strategy in the Anti-Sweatshop Movement', *Labor Studies Journal* 45, no. 4 (2020): 397.
[28]Williams, 'Global Solidarity, Global Worker Empowerment, and Global Strategy in the Anti-Sweatshop Movement', 402.
[29]They have used boycotts sparingly, for instance in cases where the companies already fired all the workers, so there were no jobs to be lost. Williams, 'Global Solidarity, Global Worker Empowerment, and Global Strategy in the Anti-Sweatshop Movement', 410.
[30]Williams, 'Global Solidarity, Global Worker Empowerment, and Global Strategy in the Anti-Sweatshop Movement'; Ashok Kumar and Jack Mahoney, 'Stitching Together: How Workers Are Hemming Down Transnational Capital in the Hyper-Global Apparel Industry', *Working USA* 17, no. 2 (2014): 187–210.
[31]Asbed and Hitov, 'Preventing Forced Labor in Corporate Supply Chains', 531.

of global capital. But the limited successes of the anti-sweatshop initiatives demonstrate that it is more difficult to organize and enforce such a framework in global supply chains, as opposed to a domestic American supply chain. For instance, one of the pillars of the FFP is the 24/7 phoneline staffed by auditors of the factories. Implementing such an initiative globally would be extremely difficult logistically. Also, workers' rights regimes are a lot less effective in many parts of the world compared to the United States, so there would not be the same background framework of state support. And where US consumers feel a sense of national solidarity with US farmworkers (perhaps, in this case, even expanding to migrant workers who are at least working on US soil), the same cannot be said about workers across the globe. Brands know that they can get away with egregiously exploiting distant workers in poor and corrupt countries without provoking the same kind of backlash from US consumers or from those states. This is why I argue in Chapter 6 that political responsibility involves cultivating the political virtue of solidarity across difference. Such global solidarity currently exists in initiatives like the USAS, but only on a small scale.

Countering alignments

Countering alignments typically take the form of trade unions or social movements. Trade unions provide a form of structural countering power by embedding workers' bargaining power into the system. This is why the right to unionize is fundamental across industries. Social movements respond to a range of injustices, not only workers' rights, and tend to be temporary in nature. In response to the structural injustices discussed in this book, there have been multiple social movements, such as the anti-sweatshop movement, anti-poverty movements like Jubilee 2000, Make Poverty History, and poor-led anti-poverty movements and environmental movements. These movements use a range of tactics, such as protests and varieties of non-violent direct action, like blockades, sit-ins, disruption, flashmobs, performance art and so on.

Typically, social movements address the powerful agents themselves. For example, in recent years Indigenous movements have been extraordinarily successful in Turtle Island (North America). Activism across twenty-one areas has resulted in stopping 1.8 billion metric tonnes of CO_2 emissions, the equivalent of 28 per cent of 2019 United States and Canadian emissions.[32] Indigenous activists engage in this resistance, often at great personal risk; in 2017, 312 Indigenous defenders in twenty-seven countries were murdered.[33] Tackling the powerful head-on can be an essential component of organizing and can achieve

---

[32]Dallas Goldtooth, Alberto Saldamando and Kyle Gracey, 'Indigenous Resistance Against Carbon' (Washington, DC, 2021), 12.
[33]Goldtooth, Saldamando and Gracey, 'Indigenous Resistance Against Carbon', 5.

important immediate-term results. However, on its own, this strategy might only offer limited results: for example, the sporadic successes of the anti-sweatshop movement or Jubilee 2000's short-term gains of a one-off debt amnesty.[34] Tackling the social alignment that shores up the powerful is an important long-term strategy, but it requires mobilization on many different fronts.

A good example is the anti–fossil fuel movement. The fossil fuel industry's resources far outstrip that of civil society. It had created a 'denial machine' made up of at least ten different kinds of actors: corporations and trade associations, opposition coalitions and front groups (e.g. Global Climate Coalition); PR firms; astroturf groups (appear to be grassroots groups but are actually funded by corporations); conservative philanthropists and foundations; conservative think tanks; contrarian scientists; conservative media; Republican politicians; and denial bloggers.[35] In the short term, these groups fight particular issues or fund electoral candidates. But the long-term strategy is to mould the cultural and intellectual infrastructure to support the status quo, including funding academic programmes and individuals, philanthropy, advertising, and getting academic ideas into policy via think tanks, advocacy and PR.[36] The fossil fuel lobby has been so successful in quashing climate science that 'Since the first IPCC report was published in 1990, more anthropogenic fossil CO_2 has been released into the atmosphere than previously throughout all of human history.'[37]

The anti–fossil fuel movement has nothing like the kinds of resources necessary to pull off this level of networking, propaganda and obfuscation. But civil society has one advantage – moral legitimacy.[38] It can leverage this advantage by tackling the social alignment that shores up the fossil fuel industry. Activists have already found myriad pressure points and creative tactics to attack them. Aaron Thierry identifies seven areas in the social alignment that activists have targeted, often with success.[39]

First, legislation. Since the legally binding Paris Agreement was adopted in 2015, every country in the world now has one law addressing climate change

---

[34]Ann Pettifor, 'The Jubilee 2000 Campaign: A Brief Overview', in *Sovereign Debt at the Crossroads: Challenges and Proposals for Resolving the Third World Debt Crisis*, ed. Chris Jochnick and Fraser A. Preston (Oxford: Oxford University Press, 2006), 297–318.

[35]Robert Brulle, 'The Structure of Obstruction: Understanding Opposition to Climate Change Action in the United States', 2021.

[36]Brulle, 'The Structure of Obstruction'.

[37]Isak Stoddard et al., 'Three Decades of Climate Mitigation: Why Haven't We Bent the Global Emissions Curve?', *Annual Review. of Environment and Resource* 46 (2021): 679.

[38]Fergus Green, 'Anti-Fossil Fuel Norms', *Climatic Change* 150 (2018): 103–16.

[39]This was in a Twitter thread dated 9 November 2022, https://twitter.com/ThierryAaron/status/1590 329428030021632. I then reached out to Dr Thierry and he shared the slides of his presentation that the Twitter thread was based on. The framework and sources in the following three paragraphs are from there, but I also read the sources and took some different ideas from them, and added a few other sources.

or transition to a low-carbon economy.[40] There are proposals for even bigger ideas, such as the Fossil Fuel Non-Proliferation Treaty mentioned above. At the time of writing, the European Parliament and WHO have signed up, as well as two states (Vanuatu and Tuvalu), and seventy-four local governments worldwide; and activists are providing tools for people to support this treaty at the level of local government.[41] There is also a movement to get the crime of Ecocide codified in law.[42] Second, litigation. Litigation is 'a costly strategy, with uncertain outcomes'.[43] But activists have employed litigation in three ways: to target high-carbon projects or policies to stop them – for example, stopping the third runway at Heathrow airport; as a stepping stone to a broader strategy – for example, divestment activists; and to name and shame governments or corporations for failure to live up to existing legislation – for example, *Milieudefensie* in The Netherlands representing 17,000 citizens against Shell.[44] Litigation can have immediate-term benefits such as stopping high-carbon projects or changing policy, but it also has 'a long tail' creating legal precedents, generating publicity and forcing companies and governments to act in anticipation of potential lawsuits.[45]

Third, divestment. What started as a student movement has led to over 1,500 institutions divesting from fossil fuels, including universities, government institutions, cultural institutions, pension funds and faith-based organizations.[46] The divestment movement has also been instrumental in creating a strong anti–fossil fuel norm.[47] Fourth, the PR industry has been fundamental to the fossil fuel industry's disinformation campaign and 'green-washing' strategies (giving the impression of engaging with sustainability while failing to make real change).[48] Clean Creatives is a civil society organization encouraging PR and advertising professionals to not work with the fossil fuel industry.[49] Activist group *Reclame*

---

[40]Kim Bouwer and Joana Setzer, 'Climate Litigation as Climate Activism: What Works?' (London, 2020), 5.

[41]Fossil Fuel Treaty Campaign Hub, 'The Fossil Fuel Free Cities Toolkit', accessed 6 January 2023, https://campaign.fossilfueltreaty.org/cities/toolkit.

[42]Stop Ecocide International, 'Activating a Law to Protect the Earth', accessed 6 January 2023, https://www.stopecocide.earth/.

[43]Bouwer and Setzer, 'Climate Litigation as Climate Activism: What Works?', 4.

[44]Bouwer and Setzer, 'Climate Litigation as Climate Activism: What Works?', 7.

[45]Bouwer and Setzer, 'Climate Litigation as Climate Activism: What Works?', 10.

[46]Global Fossil Fuel Commitments Databse, 'The Database of Fossil Fuel Divestment Commitments Made by Institutions Worldwide', accessed 6 January 2023, https://divestmentdatabase.org/.

[47]Green, 'Anti-Fossil Fuel Norms'.

[48]William F. Lamb et al., 'Discourses of Climate Delay', *Global Sustainability* 3, no. 17 (2020): 1–5; Robert Brulle and Carter Werthman, 'The Role of Public Relations Firms in Climate Change Politics', *Climatic Change* 169, no. 8 (2021).

[49]Clean Creatives, 'The Future of Creativity Is Clean', accessed 6 January 2023, https://cleancreatives.org/.

Fossielvrij (Fossil Free Advertising) successfully persuaded Amsterdam to ban fossil fuel advertising.[50]

Fifth, activist groups are campaigning to '#stopthemoneypipeline' by stopping banks investing in fossil fuel corporations and pressuring the insurance industry to stop insuring them.[51] Sixth, recruitment. Student groups are encouraging students to not enter the fossil fuel industry and pressuring universities to stop the recruitment pipeline.[52] The industry is struggling to recruit young people.[53] Seventh, sponsorship. The performance art group *Liberate Tate* first gatecrashed an event at London's Tate gallery in 2010 celebrating its twenty-year relationship with BP and spilling an oil-like substance on the floor in protest at the Deepwater Horizon Disaster.[54] They are still going today and have inspired other groups like The Reclaim the Shakespeare Company, Shell Out Sounds, BP or Not BP, and BP Out of Opera.[55] Cultural sponsorship encourages support for fossil fuel companies by increasing their cultural capital in the countries where they are most consumed, and they also grant access to political power for corporate executives through socializing with politicians at swanky events.[56] Ending sponsorship for cultural institutions, and also sporting events, cuts off a source of their legitimacy.

I would add an eighth area, which is the media. Famously, Noam Chomsky argued that the media 'manufactures consent' to the capitalist political economy. In the UK, for example, the Media Reform Coalition found that just three companies owned 90 per cent of the newspaper market in 2021.[57] And, as we saw in Chapter 4, since the 1980s, the fossil fuel industry has manipulated traditional media's supposed commitment to balance and impartiality by insisting that climate denialism is featured in conversation with climate change science. But credible investigative journalism can be an important area of resistance. For instance, around 400 International Consortium of Investigative Journalists (ICJ) worked together to report on the Panama Papers, which exposed global tax avoidance; the US government, as a result, recovered $1.2 billion in taxes and

[50]Reclame Fossielvrij, 'Historical! Amsterdam First City World Wide That Wants to Ban Fossil Fuel Advertising', 2020, https://verbiedfossielereclame.nl/amsterdam-wants-to-ban-fossil-fuel-ads/.

[51]Insure Our Future, 'Our Best Insurance Is to Keep Fossil Fuels in the Ground', accessed 6 January 2023, https://global.insure-our-future.com/.

[52]Rachael Grealish, 'NUS Calls for Unis to End Relationships with Fossil Fuel Companies', *Freshered*, 2022. /

[53]Emily Pickrell, 'Oil and Gas Industry Must Get Serious about Climate Change to Compete for Millennial and Gen Z Workforce', *Forbes*, January 2021, https://www.stopecocide.earth/.

[54]Emma Mahony, 'Opening Spaces of Resistance in the Corporatized Cultural Institution: Liberate Tate and the Art Not Oil Coalition', *Museum & Society* 15, no. 2 (2017): 126.

[55]Mahony, 'Opening Spaces of Resistance in the Corporatized Cultural Institution', 127.

[56]Mahony, 'Opening Spaces of Resistance in the Corporatized Cultural Institution', 128.

[57]Media Reform Coalition, 'Media Ownership and Control', accessed 8 January 2023, https://www.mediareform.org.uk/key-issues/media-ownership-and-control.

penalties.[58] The UN reported this year that journalists globally are increasingly facing threats to press freedom and to their lives.[59] In established democracies where press repression is more subtle, Dan Hind argues that citizens should push for media reform, including public ownership and oversight of the media.[60] The Media Reform Coalition is pushing for a Media Commons.[61] There is also the option of alternative media; platforms like OpenDemocracy are funded by grants and donations and provide investigative journalism and representation for under-represented voices in traditional media.[62] In 2020, Extinction Rebellion launched their 'Free the Press' campaign by blockading Rupert Murdoch–aligned printworks in London, Glasgow and Liverpool.[63] As the so-called 'fourth estate', the media is a crucial area of contestation when addressing structural injustice. Activists have also used social media to directly communicate with each other internationally, to signal when crises are emerging and to organize.[64]

We can see that the social alignment that shores up the fossil fuel industry is multifaceted and can be targeted on many fronts. But as Stoddard et al. point out, 'powerful vested interests can shift their positions if they come under significant pressure from investors, regulators, and the public'.[65] For instance, fossil fuel companies have recently adopted the tactic of positioning oil and gas as transition fuels and adopting net-zero strategies (that don't stand up to scrutiny). The powerful have the resources to shift their narrative and image to suit whatever demands the social alignment make of them. They employ the PR industry and propagate ever-more subtle forms of climate denialism.[66] So vigilance must be constant. As Asbed and Hitov put it when discussing the Fair Food Program,

> ridding corporate supply chains of unwanted behavior requires ongoing vigilance. It is not like painting a house, where the hard work is done up front

---

[58]Andrea Carson, 'Why Investigative Reporting in the Digital Age Is Waving, Not Drowning', *The Conversation*, August 2019, https://theconversation.com/why-investigative-reporting-in-the-digital-age-is-waving-not-drowning-121045.

[59]UN, 'UN Expert Warns of Dangerous Decline in Media Freedom', United Nations Office of the High Commissioner, 2022, https://www.ohchr.org/en/stories/2022/07/un-expert-warns-dangerous-decline-media-freedom.

[60]Dan Hind, 'To Achieve Press Freedom, We Must Rewrite Journalism', *Open Democracy*, 30 April 2021, https://www.opendemocracy.net/en/opendemocracyuk/achieve-press-freedom-we-must-rewrite-journalism/.

[61]Media Reform Coalition, 'Our History', accessed 6 January 2023, https://www.mediareform.org.uk/about/our-history.

[62]OpenDemocracy, 'About Us', accessed 6 January 2023, https://www.opendemocracy.net/en/about/.

[63]Extinction Rebellion, 'Free the Press', accessed 6 January 2023, https://extinctionrebellion.uk/act-now/campaigns/free-the-press/.

[64]Paul Mason, *Why It's Kicking Off Everywhere* (London: Verso, 2012).

[65]Stoddard et al., 'Three Decades of Climate Mitigation, 662.

[66]Brulle and Werthman, 'The Role of Public Relations Firms in Climate Change Politics'; Lamb et al., 'Discourses of Climate Delay'.

and one can then enjoy the fruits of that labor for years to come. Rather, maintaining a clean supply chain, a supply chain free of human trafficking, is more like weeding a garden. No matter how thorough a job one does up front, without constant attention the weeds will return.[67]

Stoddard et al. also point out a number of other areas in the fossil-fuel social alignment that require attention. Within the group of powerful agents, activists and critical research have targeted the fossil fuel industry itself and governance, but the military is largely underdressed, despite the fact that the military is a huge emitter of carbon; for instance, the US military is the world's largest consumer of petrol, and if it were a country, would be the 55th largest emitter.[68] Geopolitical competition over extraction in places like the Arctic and the oceans is backed by the military, and climate change has the potential to cause future wars.[69] The 'Enabler Cluster' includes mainstream economic's approaches to climate change that focus on money and trade, resulting in 'solutions' like carbon markets and green securitization as well as inadequate mitigation modelling. Perhaps most important is the realm of ideology; there is a lack of alternative 'social imaginaries'.[70] There is a tendency to believe that There Is No Alternative, as Margaret Thatcher put it.[71] Contemporary schools and universities fail to educate students beyond the status quo, have marginalized alternative knowledge traditions to industrial modernity and are themselves based on marketized practices, all of which creates an 'epistemological monoculture'.[72] I would argue that creating alternative social imaginaries is key to sustaining alternative alignments, so that people can begin to perceive that there is a viable alternative way of life to modern industrial capitalism. Without visions of an alternative present and futures, we remain dependent on fossil-fuel capitalism.

Individual action

I suspect that many people don't get involved in activism because they think they have to do everything themselves and don't know where to start. But this is wrongheaded. Many activist groups already exist. Sometimes it does take someone starting from scratch; for instance, feeling frustrated that no real action was occurring on climate change, Greta Thunberg took it upon herself to start a school strike and millions followed in her wake. But the majority of people do

---

[67]Asbed and Hitov, 'Preventing Forced Labor in Corporate Supply Chains', 528.

[68]Stoddard et al., 'Three Decades of Climate Mitigation', 663.

[69]Stoddard et al., 'Three Decades of Climate Mitigation', 663–4.

[70]Stoddard et al., 'Three Decades of Climate Mitigation', 675.

[71]Mark Fisher, *Capitalist Realism: Is There No Alternative?* (Winchester: Zer0, 2009).

[72]Stoddard et al., 'Three Decades of Climate Mitigation', 666.

not have to do this. It is possible to become a member of existing organizations or, if there are none locally, to start a chapter of an existing organization, drawing on their resources, knowledge, networks and practices. In any case, the point of acting in groups is that different people bring different attributes to the group. Anybody's existing skill set, knowledge or resources might contribute something to an already-existing group. It can still be difficult to get involved, however, due to time constraints. Not everyone can be involved in activism all the time; there will be times in an individual's life when it isn't feasible due to caring responsibilities, illness, work pressures and so on. In these times, individual politically responsible actions might be the best we can do. So what would that look like?

Brooke Ackerly has developed a theory of 'just responsibility', which means taking responsibility for structural injustice in a way that is accountable to the people who experience it.[73] She identified five normative principles for guiding politically responsible action, which I will summarize as questions:

1. Is the action intersectional, including varied experiences of marginalization and oppression?
2. Does the action make connections across people and issues?
3. Does the action develop the capacity for collective- and self-advocacy of those affected by structural injustice?
4. Does the action contribute to solidaristic network building?
5. Is there a learning process in order to improve future actions and knowledge of structural injustice?[74]

The principles can be applied to philanthropic giving and volunteering. For many people in the Global North, donating money will be their main way to contribute to struggles against structural injustice. Through giving to NGOs and charities that adhere to the principles-in-practice 'individuals can contribute to transformative political change despite not knowing the specifics of the circumstances that need to be transformed, relying instead on an intermediary to do the research'.[75] This is similar to democratic politics, where an individual might join a political party on the basis that they do not have the time to analyse every political issue for themselves, but rather choose a party with which they are broadly sympathetic, taking some of the work out of democracy. Similarly,

---

[73]Brooke A. Ackerly, *Just Responsibility: A Human Rights Theory of Global Justice* (Oxford: Oxford University Press, 2018), 250. She derived the theory from existing political practice by studying the grant applications of 125 women's rights organizations across twenty-six countries and then engaging in a dialogue with some of the organizations about the validity of the principles established from this analysis.
[74]Ackerly, *Just Responsibility*, 223.
[75]Ackerly, *Just Responsibility*, 233.

with donating one's time through volunteering, the principles-in-practice can help determine whether the organization is challenging structural injustice itself.

In Chapter 6, I critiqued the conceptions of political responsibility in socially conscious consumerism and the role-ideal model of responsibility. But Ackerly argues that these can be forms of political responsibility if they encompass the five principles-in-practice. For example, socially conscious consumerism becomes politically conscious consumerism when the consumer engages in actions to support workers' rights to unionize, such as letter writing to pressure garment corporations to sign the Accord.[76] Or the role-ideal model of responsibility could entail individuals drawing on the five principles-in-practice to the extent that they can in their professional role.[77]

Parameters of reasoning

I have made some suggestions about alternative and countering alignments, including how to address the social alignment that props up the powerful. But a further question arises: how can an individual or groups decide which structural injustice to act on? In this book I have focused on three structural injustices – sweatshops, poverty and climate change – but there are many more structural injustices in the world today. The number and scale of structural injustices is overwhelming. Young helpfully gave four 'parameters of reasoning' to help individuals decide which structural injustice to focus on: power, privilege, interest and collective ability. In this section, I briefly discuss the parameters of reasoning. I have argued throughout this book that power confers moral responsibility, not political responsibility, on powerful agents, so I set power aside. I change privilege to benefit (because that is the core of Young's claim that some people are privileged in relation to structural injustice – they benefit from it), and I add one other parameter of reasoning – proximity.

Young's position is philosophically interesting for two reasons. First, many philosophers argue that two of the remaining parameters of reasoning – benefit and collective ability – confer moral responsibility on agents. Second, many philosophers argue that a theory of responsibility for justice must be 'action-guiding' – it should specify duties that individuals have in relation to injustice.[78]

---

[76]Ackerly, *Just Responsibility*, 228.

[77]Ackerly, *Just Responsibility*, 236.

[78]Christian Barry and Kate Macdonald, 'How Should We Conceive of Individual Consumer Responsibility to Address Labour Injustices?', in *Global Justice and International Labour Rights*, ed. Faina Milman-Sivan, Yossi Dahan and Hanna Lerner (Cambridge: Cambridge University Press, 2016), 92–118; Henning Hahn, 'The Global Consequence of Participatory Responsibility', *Journal of Global Ethics* 5, no. 1 (2009): 43–56; Robin Zheng, 'What Is My Role in Changing the System? A New Model of Responsibility for Structural Injustice', *Ethical Theory and Moral Practice* 21 (2018): 869–85; Robert Jubb, 'Social Connection and Practice Dependence: Some Recent Developments in the Global Justice Literature: Iris Marion Young, Responsibility for Justice. Oxford: Oxford University Press, 2011; and Ayelet Banai,

I side with Young on both counts. In this section, I will explain why privilege and collective ability do not confer moral responsibility for structural injustice on ordinary individuals. But first, I address action-guidingness.

Action guidingness does not depend on specifying duties. A duty is the requirement to do a specific act on a specific occasion, in comparison to a responsibility, which encompasses a sphere of responsibility.[79] For example, a babysitter might have a duty to feed the baby at 5 p.m., but they also have a general sphere of responsibility for making sure the baby is well looked after, and they can employ a range of strategies to achieve this. Acting on their responsibility might even involve violating a duty specified by the parents, such as not leaving the house; if there is a fire, the babysitter should take the baby outside, in order to fulfil their broader responsibility to look after the baby.[80] Applied to individuals' political responsibility, there is no need to specify what exactly any individual should do in relation to structural injustice. Instead, political responsibility is a sphere of responsibility – an individual should cultivate the political virtue of solidarity and then act on it and can employ a range of strategies to do this.

Moreover, it is not the place of an armchair philosopher to come up with duties that apply to individuals across the world who are all differently positioned in relation to structural injustice along multiple axes, including class, profession, nationality, race, gender, age, ability, knowledge and so on. It is impossible for a philosopher to do that, and it is not remotely desirable. Once power is integrated into the analysis, this further complicates any assessment of what any particular individual ought to do. The power-based analysis of this book dictates that attention to power in context is a fundamental component of acting on political responsibility, and each individual will have to consider what that looks like for themselves.

Benefit

Young argues that privilege is distinct from power, in the sense that agents can occupy privileged positions within social structures with respect to a particular structural injustice; nevertheless, they are relatively powerless to change the structures. Their privilege consists in the fact that they *benefit* from the injustice in some sense.[81] If an agent benefits from a structural injustice, this could be the

---

Miriam Ronzoni and Christian Schemmel, Social Justice, Global Dynamics. Oxford: Routledge, 2011.' *Critical Review of International Social and Political Philosophy* 16, no. 5 (2013): 698–713.

[79]H. L. A. Hart, *Punishment and Responsibility: Essays in the Philosophy of Law*, 2nd edn (Oxford: Oxford University Press, 2008), 213; Robert E. Goodin, 'Responsibilities', *Philosophical Quarterly* 36, no. 142 (1986): 50–6.

[80]Henry S. Richardson, 'Institutionally Divided Moral Responsibility', *Social Philosophy and Policy* 16, no. 2 (1999): 218–49.

[81]Iris Marion Young, *Responsibility for Justice* (Oxford: Oxford University Press, 2011), 145.

structural injustice they focus on. For instance, middle-class clothing consumers benefit from the vast range of clothes available at affordable prices, and they are more able to change their behaviour and pay more for clothes than low-income consumers across the globe.[82]

Several philosophers, however, argue that benefit generates moral responsibility to compensate rather than political responsibility.[83] For instance, Goodin and Barry use the example of an individual who was admitted to Harvard because his father bribed an admissions officer.[84] The man discovers evidence of the bribe fifty years later when clearing out his father's estate. He tracks down the man who lost his place at Harvard, who was distraught at his rejection, became a car mechanic and has been in and out of jail ever since. The innocent beneficiary in this case cannot 'give back' thirty years of life, but he should 'make up' the loss. It is the fact of benefitting from wrongdoing that generates the obligation. Innocent beneficiaries of wrongdoing 'are wrongly enriched, and it would be wrong for them to keep those riches'.[85]

However, it is not possible to scale up from an example of a discrete, bounded wrongdoing (a one-off bribe) to cases of structural injustice. The first difference is that structural injustice is ongoing, whereas the Harvard bribe is a past, bounded event, and the wrongdoer and the bribed officer are no longer around. In the case of sweatshop labour, there are agents who could be considered wrongdoers, and therefore, they should be the first point of compensation.[86] MNCs are not only benefitting from the practice of sweatshop labour, but deliberately perpetuate it. Governments are at fault for failing to implement labour standards. By contrast, consumers are not doing anything wrong by buying clothes (see Chapter 5); they are benefitting from the unjust practices of more powerful agents, and it is these powerful agents who ought to do the compensating.

This points to a second difference, which is that there is a chain of beneficiaries in cases of structural injustice. MNCs benefit to a much greater extent from sweatshop labour than do consumers. By charging large sums of money for clothing that cost very little to produce, they amass billions of dollars in profit. High-ranking employees in the supply chain, like designers and buyers, benefit by having well-paid, professional careers. Shareholders benefit from returns on their investments. Even if consumers can be said to benefit from sweatshop labour

---

[82]Young, *Responsibility for Justice*, 145.

[83]Robert E. Goodin and Christian Barry, 'Benefiting from the Wrong-Doing of Others', *Journal of Applied Philosophy* 31, no. 4 (2014): 363–76; Daniel Butt, 'On Benefiting from Injustice', *Canadian Journal of Philosophy* 37, no. 1 (2007): 129–52; Avia Pasternak, 'Voluntary Benefits from Wrongdoing', *Journal of Applied Philosophy* 31, no. 4 (2014): 377–91.

[84]Goodin and Barry, 'Benefiting from the Wrong-Doing of Others'.

[85]Goodin and Barry, 'Benefiting from the Wrong-Doing of Others', 368.

[86]I take this to be uncontroversial – Goodin and Barry agree that if the wrongdoer is around, they should compensate the victim. Goodin and Barry, 'Benefiting from the Wrong-Doing of Others', 370.

in the sense of having a range of clothing at affordable prices, this is a marginal benefit compared to the gains of MNCs, their employees and shareholders. We can ask, then, do the agents that benefit most bear the responsibility to disgorge the benefits or do all beneficiaries have to disgorge their benefits even if they only benefit in marginal ways?

The third difference is a question of scale. In the Harvard example, there are identifiable perpetrators, victims and beneficiaries (even if we raise the number of victims or beneficiaries). Structural injustice involves a mass of disorganized beneficiaries and a mass of disorganized victims. And they benefit and are victimized to different degrees. On the beneficiary side, some consumers buy large amounts of cheap clothing even when they could afford to buy fair-trade clothing, thus taking advantage of the situation, while other consumers infrequently buy clothing but are still benefitting. How do we work out how much any individual beneficiary owes? On the victim side, there is a high turnover of staff in sweatshops – some will have worked for short periods of time, others for years. Perhaps the fact that some people cannot get long-term jobs is part of the injustice, and they should be compensated more. Or should those who have worked more be compensated more because they have suffered this particular injustice for longer? How do we work out what each victim is entitled to? How do we know who the victims are if staff records are not routinely kept or work has been subcontracted further down the supply chain?

Also, there is not a 'thing' that has been given to the consumers instead of the garment workers; I assume the garment workers do not want consumers to return the clothes to them. Goodin and Barry argue that when there is no 'thing' to give back, the beneficiary should give 'the cash equivalent of the subjective value of the thing they received'.[87] But even if we could work out what that cash equivalent is given the different degrees of benefit, we are still left with the question of to whom would it be given? If the consumers don't know who the victims are and the victims don't know who the beneficiaries are, can the claim to disgorge the benefits be enforceable? The scale of the problem means that cash transfers directly from beneficiaries to victims is not plausible. In any case, it is doubtful that what sweatshop workers want is a one-off cash transfer from consumers. What they want are decent jobs, which consumers are not in a position to give.

These differences of ongoing harm, chains of beneficiaries and scale are not just practical difficulties. These issues point to an underlying, fundamental difference – injustice is structural and requires a structural solution, whereas a discrete wrongdoing could be remedied through compensation. Goodin and Barry are adopting the liability model to deal with the responsibility of an innocent

---

[87]Goodin and Barry, 'Benefiting from the Wrong-Doing of Others', 368.

beneficiary from a discrete wrongdoing, but the problems I have highlighted in scaling this up to structural injustice bears out Young's argument that the liability model cannot successfully deal with structural injustice. Whatever the validity of paying compensation to the victim of a discrete wrongdoing from which one innocently benefits, this does not apply to structural injustices because it is not a structural solution. Burdening individuals with guilt for the benefits they receive and over which they have no control is unhelpful. It makes more sense to say that we have a forward-looking political responsibility to try to improve unjust structures than that we have moral responsibilities to compensate for all the injustices from which we benefit. When considering benefit from structural injustice, the focus should be on structural solutions rather than individualized moral atonement. But if an individual knows they benefit from a particular structural injustice, this can be a useful method for deciding which structural injustice to act on.

Collective ability

Young argues that 'the shared responsibility for undermining injustice can be discharged only through collective action'.[88] She uses 'collective ability' as a way of thinking about how to go about this. She writes,

> Some agents are in positions where they can draw on the resources of already organized entities and use them in new ways for trying to promote change. Unions, church groups, and stockholder organizations, to name just a few, sometimes can exercise significant power not because they can coerce others to do what they decide, but because they have many members who act together.[89]

In other words, individuals can discharge their political responsibility by becoming active within a group in which they are already a member. Young cites student anti-sweatshop activists who target their universities' licensing agreements with sportswear brands.[90] Another more recent example is fossil fuel divestment campaigns, where universities, church groups, cultural institutions, pension funds and so on have cut ties with fossil fuel corporations after sustained internal activism.[91] This can be an effective mechanism for change, and it is a convenient way for time- and resource-poor individuals to act on their political responsibility. However, as Young herself points out, convenience 'is not always a reason to give priority to that issue, for such ease of organization may be a sign that the

---

[88]Young, *Responsibility for Justice*, 146.
[89]Young, *Responsibility for Justice*, 147.
[90]Young, *Responsibility for Justice*, 147.
[91]Databse, 'The Database of Fossil Fuel Divestment Commitments Made by Institutions Worldwide'.

action makes little structural change'.[92] The existing institutional set-up may be the thing that needs to change.[93]

Sometimes, then, taking up political responsibility will involve creating new collectivities. In the philosophical literature, the dominant argument is that when there is a need to create a group to solve a problem, individuals have a moral responsibility to do this.[94] Larry May describes a 'putative group' as a group of people who are capable of acting in concert, but currently lack decision-making apparatus or a formal institutional structure.[95] A putative group can be found guilty of 'collective inaction': 'the failure to act of a collection of people that did not choose as a group to remain inactive but that could have acted as a group'.[96]

Virginia Held gives the example of three pedestrians walking down a street when a building collapses, trapping a man's leg. The three people know that they need to apply a tourniquet to the man's leg but they disagree over how to move the debris. They also know that any of the suggested actions would be better than no action, yet they fail to come to a decision. She argues that 'the random collection can be held morally responsible for failing to make a decision on which action to take – for failing, that is, to adopt a decision method'.[97] She claims that moral responsibility can be ascribed to this group of individuals, 'when it is obvious to the reasonable person that action rather than inaction by the collection is called for'.[98] Held extends this argument to claim that individuals are morally responsible for failing to create a group decision-making procedure for deciding how to deal with systemic political problems.[99]

Peter French thinks that, whatever the merits of the small-scale emergency examples, like the collapsed building, these are simply not analogous to global problems. How could Held's reasonable person test be applied to global problems?[100] Suppose that Upper- and Middle-Class People from the

---

[92]Iris Marion Young, 'Responsibility and Global Justice: A Social Connection Model', *Social Philosophy and Policy* 23, no. 1 (2006): 129.

[93]Iris Marion Young, 'Responsibility and Global Labor Justice', *The Journal of Political Philosophy* 12, no. 4 (2004): 384–5.

[94]Larry May, *Sharing Responsibility* (London: University of Chicago Press, 1992); Virginia Held, 'Can a Random Collection of Individuals Be Morally Responsible?', *Journal of Philosophy* 67, no. 14 (1970): 471–81; Joel Feinberg, 'Collective Responsibility', *Journal of Philosophy* 65, no. 21 (1968): 674–88; Florian Wettstein, 'Corporate Responsibility in the Collective Age: Toward a Conception of Collaborative Responsibility'.

[95]May, *Sharing Responsibility*, 109.

[96]May, *Sharing Responsibility*, 107.

[97]Held, 'Can a Random Collection of Individuals Be Morally Responsible?', 479.

[98]Held, 'Can a Random Collection of Individuals Be Morally Responsible?', 479.

[99]Held, 'Can a Random Collection of Individuals Be Morally Responsible?', 480.

[100]Peter A. French, 'The Responsibility of Inactive Fictive Groups for Great Social Problems', in *Individual and Collective Responsibility*, ed. Peter A French (Rochester, Vermont: Schenkman Books, 1998), 255.

Western Industrial Democracies (UMCPWIDs) are morally responsible for world hunger:

> To be held morally responsible for it, however, the UMCPWIDs must be in a position to override the actual causal factors and either perpetuate the hunger or relieve it. And how is so nebulous a group as the UMCPWIDs to do anything like what is required? It makes little sense to say that they can unless they are transformed radically. But transformed into what? The UMCPWIDs must be turned into a corporation-like entity (or entities) in the fullest sense of the term, with vast powers on the global scene. But is such a corporate entity actually formable? What would it look like? How would it function? As these questions become more and more intractable, the sense of the original responsibility ascription fades. In their disorganized states, fictive inaction groups certainly do not have the requisite control for moral responsibility. Inaction is all one can expect from a group gathered only in the moralist's imagination.[101]

French, and Young, are right. Putative groups do not bear moral responsibility for global structural injustice, but political responsibility, and this is precisely for the reason that French points out – even if individuals do collectively organize they do not have the dispositional power to effect the required structural change. The reality is that if UMCPWIDs did organize, they would not have dispositional power on the global scene. It is more likely that they will organize into a social movement, which is a group that is collectively empowered and has collective ability, which is a form of power, but it is not the same as dispositional power to change social structures. Perhaps if the group was sufficiently large, it could become a revolutionary group, in which case it could have the power to affect structural change. But most such groups will not grow to this size and capacity. And even if individuals did organize into a global revolutionary force, they would not bear backward-looking moral responsibility for structural injustice on the liability model, because there was nothing they could have done about it until that point.

Collective ability is distinguished from dispositional power, because dispositional power implies a structural position that confers the capacity to change the structures, whereas collective ability generates the capacity to pressure or influence the powerful. Influence can coincide with dispositional power (e.g. business lobbies), but there are many agents with collective ability but not dispositional power (e.g. trade unions, social movements). Having collective ability in relation to a structural injustice can be another way of deciding which structural injustice to work on.

---

[101] French, 'The Responsibility of Inactive Fictive Groups for Great Social Problems', 254–5.

Interest

For Young, interest applies to the victims of structural injustice, who 'have unique interests in undermining injustice, and they ought to take responsibility for doing so'.[102] The meaning of interest here is having a vested interest in a particular structural change by virtue of one's social position. We have seen in this book that corporations and states have vested interests that conflict with the victims of structural injustice. Vested interests within structures clash. Having a vested interest in ameliorating structural injustice means fighting for it.

The normative reasons for the inclusion of victims of structural injustice have been discussed in Chapter 6. Here, I want to add two further comments about the strategic importance of their inclusion. First, there is an epistemic reason. Young writes, 'It is they who know the most about the harms they suffer, and thus it is up to them to broadcast their situation and call it injustice.'[103] Inhabitants of various social positions usually know most about what their interests are. They should be consulted because 'unless the victims themselves are involved in ameliorative efforts, well-meaning outsiders may inadvertently harm them in a different way, or set reforms going in unproductive directions'.[104] Young cites some of the 'ineffective or paternalistic' interventions of the anti-sweatshop movement, such as campaigning to shut down factories or pushing for inspections of factories without guaranteeing the safety of workers who participate.

We have seen already that successful anti-sweatshop initiatives used the philosophy of worker empowerment, both for normative and strategic reasons. One of the strategic reasons is that workers have the knowledge of what their interests are and how best these can be met. It was sweatshop workers who convinced American student anti-sweatshop groups to avoid boycotts because these result in job losses. Another interesting example Asbed and Hitov cite is the use of buckets for picking tomatoes in Florida's agricultural sector. Tomato harvesters are paid per bucket. For decades they were required to 'cup' the bucket (overfill it, like an ice-cream cone) and they weren't given credit for the extra tomatoes. This was wage theft and often the flashpoint for violence. After negotiations, it was decided to include a photograph of an appropriately filled bucket in worker training leaflets, which became the industry standard.[105] These are examples of knowledge that can only be gained from being embedded in a workplace. Well-meaning outsiders will not have access to this knowledge.

Second, these examples show that successful interventions in structural injustice will be grounded in the concerns of the victims and potentially designed

---

[102]Young, *Responsibility for Justice,*, 145.
[103]Young, *Responsibility for Justice*, 146.
[104]Young, *Responsibility for Justice*, 146.
[105]Asbed and Hitov, 'Preventing Forced Labor in Corporate Supply Chains', 515.

and shaped by them also. This is why I have emphasized the importance of cultivating the capacity for political solidarity across difference. Working with the victims of structural injustice is the best way to counteract it. Often victims are already struggling against structural injustice. There are trade unions fighting for garment workers' rights across the globe, poor people organizing to empower themselves and each other and to push their governments for change, Indigenous groups fighting for climate justice and so on. The role of the privileged is to support them in an appropriate way.

But I want to highlight another meaning of interest and that is *being interested in* something, rather than *having* an interest in it. I first got involved in anti-sweatshop protesting as a teenager because I was shocked when I learnt about the working conditions of the people making my clothes. I didn't have any particular connection with the injustice other than being a person who likes and wears clothes. Since there are so many structural injustices in the world and it is impossible to be active against all of them, simply being interested in an injustice can be a reason for choosing it. Just caring about a particular injustice can be enough reason to focus on that injustice as the site of your political responsibility, although I hasten to add the caveat that this depends on going about it in a way that centres the victims and is not patronizing, disrespectful or counterproductive (see Chapter 6).

Moreover, as bell hooks points out, demonstrations of support can be fleeting, but solidarity requires sustained commitment.[106] Being interested in a particular injustice can help sustain commitment and support over time. The more you learn about something that interests you, often the more you want to know. This interest can, therefore, sustain commitment to a cause over time. For instance, my interest in sweatshops has sustained a commitment to research this structural injustice over time. An interest in how climate change is affecting the oceans or how poverty intersects with racial injustice, to take just two examples, can sustain commitment over time.

Proximity

I want to add another parameter of reasoning to Young's suggestions, which is proximity. Being in the same or an adjacent location to a structural injustice flashpoint can be a reason to focus one's attention there. This aligns with the Global Justice movement's slogan of 'think global, act local'. There are a number of reasons why this is a valuable idea.

First, similar to having an interest in a particular structural injustice, proximity can provide inside knowledge. For instance, Indigenous defenders in Turtle

---

[106]bell hooks, *Feminist Theory: From Margin to Center* (Boston: South End Press, 1984), 64.

Island have drawn on their knowledge of the United National Declaration on the Rights of Indigenous Peoples (UNDRIP), which specifies the right to 'Free, Prior and Informed Consent (FPIC)', allowing Indigenous peoples the ability to grant or withhold consent for projects that affect them or their territories.[107] They have employed this to great effect in postponing or cancelling fossil fuel extraction projects across their territories.

Another advantage of proximity is generating numbers and boots on the ground. One example is the village of Balcombe in West Sussex, UK. Energy giant Cuadrilla proposed to start drilling for oil and fracking in the village, and residents united in protest across divides such as political affiliations, age, amount of protesting experience and so on.[108] The whole village came out in protest, along with seasoned anti-fracking campaigners from across the country, and they were successful in stopping the project. Local organizing against fracking is now widespread across the UK and Ireland.[109]

Local collective action can have the benefit of creating long-term networks of solidarity and mutual aid. For instance, after their successful campaign to stop fracking in their village, the residents of Balcombe decided to set up a local energy cooperative that provides solar energy to local schools.[110] In-person organizing can generate long-term friendships and collaborations and build community.

By fighting structural injustice in local communities, there is less risk of objectifying, patronizing or disrespecting victims of structural injustice in other places, with which individuals might be less familiar. It can be an act of solidarity with other people around the world, however, because by stopping new fossil fuel extraction in one location, this helps everyone around the world, particularly the most vulnerable who are most immediately affected by climate change. This does not mean disengaging with people from other parts of the world, however, and acting only on a local basis. Knowledge, expertise and experience of local organizing can be shared internationally. For instance, the knowledge that Balcombe residents have of Cuadrilla will be relevant to other communities across the world fighting this particular corporation. Indigenous activists fighting Shell, BP and other oil companies can share their knowledge of these corporations.

---

[107]Goldtooth, Saldamando and Gracey, 'Indigenous Resistance against Carbon', 3.

[108]Fiona Harvey, 'Anti-Fracking Protests in Balcombe Signal Major Shift in Public Awareness', *The Guardian*, 19 August 2013, https://www.theguardian.com/environment/2013/aug/19/fracking-prote sts-balcombe-cuadrilla-politics.

[109]Frack Off, 'Local Groups', accessed 7 January 2023, https://frack-off.org.uk/local-group-speci fic-pages/.

[110]Emily Wither, 'Can Local Communities Make a Difference in the Transition to Net Zero?' (UK: Channel4News, 2023); Repower Balcombe, 'Home', accessed 7 January 2023, https://www. repowerbalcombe.com/.

To act or not to act?

Challenging and repairing structural injustice is a never-ending project. Repairing one structural injustice, when these actions coalesce with the actions of other agents, can produce new unjust structural outcomes that no one intended. That is the nature of the relationship between structure and agency: structural elaboration that nobody could foresee might be the result. Such a dynamic is especially clear to see in the battle between currently existing jobs that are damaging to the climate and the need to mitigate climate change.[111] Mitigating climate change could create swathes of lay-offs and potentially long-term unemployment across the globe. Even if these jobs are replaced with green jobs, it takes time and investment (which is currently lacking) to retrain people. Similarly, adapting to climate change could benefit those who are already the beneficiaries of unjust structures, thereby entrenching existing structural injustice or creating new, unforeseen fault lines. Does this mean we shouldn't bother?

We tend to think of systems and corporate entities as static; they have always been this way and always will be. But this is a mistake. The capitalist economy is only two hundred years old. The fossil fuel economy is roughly the same age but accelerated significantly in the twentieth century and even more so over the last thirty years. The corporation as an instrument for exclusively maximizing private interests, rather than being a society-oriented entity, is a more recent phenomenon, emerging in the latter half of the twentieth century.[112] Or at least, early corporations portrayed themselves that way.[113] States are older, but the territories and constitutions of states have fluctuated ceaselessly, with new states emerging from changes in geo-politics like decolonization and the collapse of the Soviet Union, with ongoing territorial conflicts ever since these seismic shifts. The threat of climate change poses existential threats to the capitalist economic system, the fossil fuel industry, many powerful corporations and even some states.[114] Therefore, all these things can, do and will change. The question is, change into what?

The social ontology underlying this book is a critical realist one – that agents acting within pre-existing structures will generate new structures that may not resemble the intentions of any of the agents due to combined or clashing outcomes. Since we cannot know what future structural elaboration will look like, the battles are not about keeping things as they are but about shaping the

---

[111]See Robert Pollin, 'De-Growth vs A Green New Deal', *New Left Review* 112, no. July–August (2018): 5–25.
[112]Florian Wettstein, 'Corporate Responsibility in the Collective Age', 171.
[113]Roland Marchand, *Creating the Corporate Soul: The Rise of Public Relations and Corporate Imagery in American Big Business* (Berkeley: University of California Press, 1998).
[114]Jeff D. Colgan, Jessica F. Green and Thomas N. Hale, 'Asset Reevaluation and the Existential Politics of Climate Change', *International Organisation* 75 (2021): 586–610.

direction of change towards people and the planet rather than further towards the interests of rich and powerful individuals, states and corporations. This is obviously not an easy task, which is why mobilization on multiple fronts is necessary. Every steer in the right direction is worth fighting for.

We need only look at the recent past. This book wouldn't have been written if it hadn't been for feminist movements, disability rights activists and the civil rights movement in Northern Ireland. I can only write this book because many people before me challenged injustice in their own era. Certainly they didn't always get what they wanted. Often their efforts provoked backlash. In many cases, fighting injustice is a case of one step forward and two steps back. But that step forward is one step in the right direction; even if it makes an insignificant difference at the time, it could be the difference between someone in the future having a path laid for them or not. Making inroads and laying groundwork is what activism is all about. Mistakes are inevitable and good work being cancelled out by external forces or counter-revolution is common; but future generations can build on what has gone before and can also learn from those mistakes, missteps and counter-revolutionary tactics. As David S. Meyer puts it, 'activists make history, but they do not make it just as they please. In fighting one political battle, they shape the conditions of the next one.'[115] Fighting against structural injustice can result in structural elaboration, whereby the structures are improved for future generations. In other words, fighting against structural injustice now is what generates justice for future generations. Fighting structural injustice now is not merely a presentist project – it is necessarily forward-looking.

Apathy is not the appropriate response because apathy leads to total political collapse and paves the way for totalitarianism, as Arendt so astutely observed. That is why Arendt was so keen to preserve political responsibility as its own category of responsibility; a responsibility to uphold the public-political sphere where plural and dissenting voices can be heard.[116] Political responsibility for us means working to achieve solidarity with others and acting collectively to challenge structural injustice.

---

[115]David S. Meyer, 'How Social Movements Matter', in *The Social Movements Reader: Cases and Concepts*, 3rd edn (Chichester: Wiley Blackwell, 2015), 390.
[116]Hannah Arendt, 'Collective Responsibility', in *Responsibility and Judgment*, ed. Jerome Kohn (New York: Schocken Books, 2003), 147–58.

Bibliography

Abdel-Jaber, Hala. 'The Devil Wears Zara: Why the Lanham Act Must Be Amended in the Era of Fast Fashion'. *Ohio State Business Law Journal* 15 (2021): 234–65.

Accord, International. 'About Us', 2022. Accessed 2 September 2022. https://internat ionalaccord.org/about-us.

Ackerly, Brooke A. *Just Responsibility: A Human Rights Theory of Global Justice*. Oxford: Oxford University Press, 2018.

Afsar, Haleh, and Carolyne Dennis. *Women and Adjustment Policies in the Third World*. London: Palgrave Macmillan, 1992.

Ahmed, Sara. *Complaint!* Durham, NC: Duke University Press, 2021.

Aiyetoro, Adoja A. 'Formulating Reparations Litigation through the Eyes of the Movement'. *NYU Annual Survey of American Law* 58 (2001): 457–74.

Allen, Amy. 'Power and the Politics of Difference: Oppression, Empowerment, and Transnational Justice'. *Hypatia* 23, no. 3 (2008): 156–72.

Allen, Amy. *The Power of Feminist Theory: Domination, Resistance, Solidarity*. New York: Routledge, 1999.

Allen, Amy, Rainer Forst and Mark Haugaard. 'Power and Reason, Justice and Domination: A Conversation'. *Journal of Political Power* 7, no. 1 (2014): 7–33.

Amed, Imran, Achim Berg, Leonie Brantberg Saskia Hedrich, Johnattan Leon, and Robb Young. 'The State of Fashion 2017'. 2016. Accessed 29 August 2023. https:// www.mckinsey.com/~/media/McKinsey/Industries/Retail/Our%20Insights/The%20st ate%20of%20fashion/The-state-of-fashion-2017-McK-BoF-report.pdf.

Amed, Imran, Johanna Andersson, Anita Balchandani, Marco Beltrami, Achim Berg, Saskia Hedrich, Dale Kim, Felix Rölkens and Robb Young. 'The State of Fashion 2019: A Year of Awakening'. New York, 2018. Accessed 29 August 2023. https:// www.mckinsey.com/~/media/mckinsey/industries/retail/our%20insights/the%20st ate%20of%20fashion%202019%20a%20year%20of%20awakening/the-state-of-fash ion-2019-final.ashx.

Amed, Imran, Achim Berg, Anita Balchandani, Saskia Hedrich, Jakob Ekeløf Jensen, Michael Straub, Felix Rölkens, Robb Young, Pamela Brown, Leila Le Merle, Hannah Crump, and Amanda Dargan. 'The State of Fashion 2022'. New York, 2022. Accessed 29 August 2023. https://www.mckinsey.com/~/media/mckinsey/industries/ retail/our%20insights/state%20of%20fashion/2022/the-state-of-fashion-2022.pdf.

Anderson, Kevin. 'Why Carbon Prices Can't Deliver the 2oC Target'. kevinanderson.info, 2013. Accessed 4 October 2021. https://kevinanderson.info/blog/why-carbon-pri ces-cant-deliver-the-2c-target/.

Andonova, Liliana B. *Governance Entrepreneurs: International Organizations and the Rise of Global Public-Private Partnerships*. Cambridge: Cambridge University Press, 2019.

Annas, J. 'Being Virtuous and Doing the Right Thing'. *Proceedings and Addresses of the American Philosophical Association* 78, no. 2 (2004): 61–75.

Anner, Mark. 'Binding Power: The Sourcing Squeeze, Workers' Rights, and Building Safety in Bangladesh Since Rana Plaza', 2018. Accessed 20 January 2019. https://www.wiwiss.fu-berlin.de/forschung/Garments/Medien/2018-Anner-Research-Report-Binding-Power.pdf.

Anner, Mark, Jennifer Bair and Jeremy Blasi. 'Toward Joint Liability in Global Supply Chains: Addressing the Root Causes of Labor Violations in International Subcontracting Networks'. *Comparative Labour Law & Policy Journal* 35, no. 1 (2013): 1–44.

Anscombe, G. E. M. 'Modern Moral Philosophy'. *Philosophy* 33, no. 124 (1958): 1–19.

Aragon, Corwin, and Alison M. Jaggar. 'Agency, Complicity, and the Responsibility to Resist Structural Injustice'. *Journal of Social Philosophy* 49, no. 3 (2018): 439–60.

Archer, Margaret. *Realist Social Theory: The Morphogenetic Approach*. Cambridge: Cambridge University Press, 1995.

Arendt, Hannah. 'Collective Responsibility'. In *Responsibility and Judgment*, edited by Jerome Kohn, 147–58. New York: Schocken Books, 2003.

Arendt, Hannah. *On Violence*. London: Harcourt, 1970.

Arendt, Hannah. 'Personal Responsibility under Dictatorship'. In *Responsibility and Judgment*, edited by Jerome Kohn, 17–49. New York: Schocken Books, 2003.

Arendt, Hannah. 'Some Questions of Moral Philosophy'. In *Responsibility and Judgment*, edited by Jerome Kohn, 49–147. New York: Schocken Books, 2003.

Arendt, Hannah. *The Human Condition*. 2nd edn. Chicago: University of Chicago Press, 1998.

Arendt, Hannah. 'Thinking and Moral Considerations'. In *Responsibility and Judgment*, edited by Jerome Kohn, 159–93. New York: Schocken Books, 2003.

Aristotle. *The Nicomachean Ethics: Oxford World's Classics*. Oxford: Oxford University Press, 2009.

Armstrong, Andrea, and Ariel Colonomos. 'German Reparations to the Jews after World War II'. In *The Handbook of Reparations*, edited by Pablo de Greiff, 390–420. Oxford: Oxford University Press, 2006.

Arrington, Robert L. 'Advertising and Behavior Control'. *Journal of Business Ethics* 1, no. 1 (1982): 3–12.

Asbed, Greg, and Steve Hitov. 'Preventing Forced Labor in Corporate Supply Chains: The Fair Food Program and Worker-Driven Social Responsibility'. *Wake Forest Law Review* 52 (2017): 497–531.

Assembly, United Nations General. 'Declaration on the Establishment of a New International Economic Order'. Geneva, 1974. Accessed 22 October 2021. http://www.un-documents.net/s6r3201.htm.

Atkinson, Lucy. 'Buying in to Social Change: How Private Consumption Choices Engender Concern for the Collective'. *Annals of the American Academy of Political and Social Science* 644, no. 1 (2012): 191–206.

Aylsworth, Timothy. 'Autonomy and Manipulation: Refining the Argument against Persuasive Advertising'. *Journal of Business Ethics* 175, no. 4 (2022): 689–99.

Bachrach, Peter, and Morton S. Baratz. 'Two Faces of Power'. *American Political Science Review* 56, no. 4 (1962): 947–52.

Bair, Jennifer. 'Surveying the Post-MFA Landscape: What Prospects for the Global South Post-Quota?' *Competition & Change* 12, no. 1 (2008): 3–10.

Balchandani, Anita, and Achim Berg. 'The Postpandemic State of Fashion'. McKinsey, 2021. Accessed 15 April 2023. https://www.mckinsey.com/industries/retail/our-insig hts/the-postpandemic-state-of-fashion.

Balcombe, Repower. 'Home'. Accessed 7 January 2023. https://www.repowerbalco mbe.com/.

Banerjee, Abhijit V., and Esther Duflo. 'The Economic Lives of the Poor'. *Journal of Economic Perspectives* 21, no. 1 (2007): 141–67.

Bangladesh Accord Sectretariat. 'Quarterly Aggregate Report – on Remediation Progress at RGM Factories Covered by the Accord and Status of Workplace Programs'. Dhaka, Amsterdam, 2018. Accessed 20 January 2019. https://banglad esh.wpengine.com/wp-content/uploads/2018/12/Accord_Quarterly_Aggregate_ Report_October_2018.pdf. Accessed 21 December 2018.

Bank, The World. 'Reversals of Fortune'. Washington, DC, 2020. Accessed 10 September 2021. https://openknowledge.worldbank.org/server/api/core/bitstre ams/611fc6f2-140b-551e-9371-468eec64c552/content.

Bank, The World. 'World Bank Forecasts Global Poverty to Fall Below 10% for First Time; Major Hurdles Remain in Goal to End Poverty by 2030', 2015. Accessed 10 September 2021. https://www.worldbank.org/en/news/press-release/2015/10/04/ world-bank-forecasts-global-poverty-to-fall-below-10-for-first-time-major-hurdles-rem ain-in-goal-to-end-poverty-by-2030

Barkan, Elazar. *The Guilt of Nations: Restitution and Negotiating Historical Injustices*. New York: W. W. Norton, 2000.

Barnett, Clive, Philip Cafaro and Terry Newholm. 'Philosophy and Ethical Consumption'. In *The Ethical Consumer*, edited by Rob Harrison, Terry Newholm and Deirdre Shaw, 1–16. London: Sage, 2005.

Barry, Christian, and Kate Macdonald. 'How Should We Conceive of Individual Consumer Responsibility to Address Labour Injustices?' In *Global Justice and International Labour Rights*, edited by Faina Milman-Sivan, Yossi Dahan and Hanna Lerner, 92–118. Cambridge: Cambridge University Press, 2016.

Barry, Christian, and Scott Wisor. 'Global Poverty'. *International Encyclopedia of Ethics*, Oxford: Wiley-Blackwell, 2013.

Beckles, Hilary McD. *Britain's Black Debt: Reparations for Caribbean Slavery and Native Genocide*. Kingston: University of West Indies Press, 2013.

Begg, Bob, John Pickles and Adrian Smith. 'Cutting It: European Integration, Trade Regimes, and the Reconfiguration of East – Central European Apparel Production'. *Environment and Planning* 35 (2003): 2191–2207.

Beitz, Charles R. *Political Theory and International Relations*. 2nd edn. Princeton, NJ: Princeton University Press, 1999.

Bell, Alice. *Our Biggest Experiment: A History of the Climate Crisis*. London: Bloomsbury, 2021.

Benería, Lourdes, and Martha Roldan. *The Crossroads of Class and Gender: Industrial Homework, Subcontracting, and Household Dynamics in Mexico City*. Chicago: University of Chicago Press, 1987.

Bennett, W. Lance. 'The Personalization of Politics: Political Identity, Social Media, and Changing Patterns of Participation'. *Annals of the American Academy of Political and Social Science* 644, no. 644 (2012): 20–39.

Berenstain, Nora. 'Epistemic Exploitation'. *Ergo* 3, no. 22 (2016): 569–90.

Bierria, Alisa. 'Missing in Action: Violence, Power, and Discerning Agency'. *Hypatia* 29, no. 1 (2014): 129–45.

Bingham, John. 'Hijab-Wearing Muslim Women Being Passed over for Jobs in Last Form of "Acceptable" Discrimination – MPs'. *The Telegraph*. 11 August 2016. Accessed 12 July 2017. https://www.telegraph.co.uk/news/2016/08/11/hijab-wearing-muslim-women-being-passed-over-for-jobs-in-last-fo/.

Biskowski, Lawrence J. 'Practical Foundations for Political Judgment: Arendt on Action and World'. *Journal of Politics* 55, no. 4 (1993): 867–87.

Blake, Michael. 'Distributive Justice, State Coercion, and Autonomy'. *Philosophy & Public Affairs* 30, no. 3 (2001): 257–96.

Blau, Peter. *Inequality and Homogeneity: A Primitive Theory of Social Structure*. London: Collier Macmillan, 1977.

Boonin, David. *Should Race Matter? Unusual Answers to the Usual Questions*. Cambridge: Cambridge University Press, 2012.

Bosi, Lorenzo, 'The Dynamics of Social Movement Development: Northern Ireland's Civil Rights Movement in the 1960s'. *Mobilization: An International Journal* 11, no. 1 (2006): 81–100.

Bouwer, Kim, and Joana Setzer. 'Climate Litigation as Climate Activism: What Works?' London, 2020.

Bovens, Mark. *The Quest for Responsibility: Accountability and Citizenship in Complex Organisations*. Cambridge: Cambridge University Press, 1998.

Brock, Gillian. *Global Justice: A Cosmpolitan Account*. Oxford: Oxford University Press, 2009.

Brooks, Andrew. *Clothing Poverty: The Hidden World of Fast Fashion and Second-Hand Clothes*. London: Zed Books, 2015.

Bruckner, Benedikt, Klaus Hubacek, Yuli Shan, Honglin Zhong and Kuishuang Feng. 'Impacts of Poverty Alleviation on National and Global Carbon Emissions'. *Nature Sustainability* 5 (2022): 311–20.

Brulle, Robert. 'The Structure of Obstruction: Understanding Opposition to Climate Change Action in the United States', Climate Social Science Network (CSSN) Briefing, Providence: Brown, 2021. Accessed 20 November 2022. https://cssn.org/wp-content/uploads/2021/04/CSSN-Briefing_-Obstruction-2.pdf.

Brulle, Robert, and Carter Werthman. 'The Role of Public Relations Firms in Climate Change Politics'. *Climatic Change* 169, no. 8 (2021).

Butt, Daniel. 'On Benefiting from Injustice'. *Canadian Journal of Philosophy* 37, no. 1 (2007): 129–52.

Butt, Daniel. *Rectifying International Injustice: Principles of Compensation and Restitution Between Nations*. Oxford: Oxford University Press, 2008.

Butt, Daniel. 'What Structural Injustice Theory Leaves Out'. *Ethical Theory and Moral Practice* 24, no. 1 (2021): 1161–75.

Cairns, Ed, and G. W. Mercer. 'Social Identity in Northern Ireland'. *Human Relations* 37, no. 12 (1984): 1005–1107.

Caney, Simon. *Justice Beyond Borders: A Global Political Theory*. Oxford: Oxford University Press, 2005.

Canovan, Margaret. *Hannah Arendt: A Reinterpretation of Her Political Thought*. Cambridge: Cambridge University Press, 1994.

CARICOM. 'Ten Point Action Plan'. Institute of the Black World 21st Century, 2014. Accessed 9 June 2020. http://ibw21.org/commentary/caricom-reparati ons-ten-point-plan/.

Carrington, Michal J., Benjamin A. Neville and Gregory J. Whitwell. 'Why Ethical Consumers Don't Walk Their Talk: Towards a Framework for Understanding the Gap between the Ethical Purchase Intentions and Actual Buying Behaviour of Ethically Minded Consumers'. *Journal of Business Ethics* 97 (2010): 139–58.

Carroll, William K., and Colin Carson. 'The Network of Global Corporations and Elite Policy Groups: A Structure for Transnational Capitalist Class Formation?' *Global Networks* 3, no. 1 (2003): 29–57.

Carson, Andrea. 'Why Investigative Reporting in the Digital Age Is Waving, Not Drowning'. *The Conversation*, August 2019. Accessed 5 December 2022. https://theconversation.com/why-investigative-reporting-in-the-digital-age-is-waving-not-drowning-121045.

Chakravarty, Deepita. 'Docile Oriental Women's and Organised Labour: A Case Study of the Indian Garment Manufacturing Industry'. *Indian Journal of Gender Studies* 14, no. 3 (2007): 439–60.

Chant, Sylvia. 'Re-Thinking the "Feminization of Poverty" in Relation to Aggregate Gender Indices'. *Journal of Human Development* 7, no. 2 (2006): 201–20.

Chatterjee, Deen K. *The Ethics of Assistance: Morality and the Distant Needy*. Cambridge: Cambridge University Press, 2004.

Ciepley, David. 'Beyond Public and Private: Toward a Political Theory of the Corporation'. *American Political Science Review* 107, no. 1 (2013): 139–58.

'Civil Society Lampoon Exclusive "Green Rooms" in Protest Performance at the 12th Ministerial of the WTO'. *Our World Is Not for Sale*. 14 June 2022. Accessed 5 December 2022. https://ourworldisnotforsale.net/2022-06-14_R_protest.

Clarke, Blanaid, and Linn Anker-Sørensen. 'The EU as a Potential Norm Creator for Sustainable Corporate Groups'. In *Cambridge Handbook of Corporate Law, Corporate Governance and Sustainability*, edited by Beate Sjåfjell and Christopher M. Bruner, 190–203. Cambridge: Cambridge University Press, 2019.

Clean Clothes Campaign. 'Position Paper on Transparency'. Amsterdam, 2020.

Coalition, Media Reform. 'Media Ownership and Control'. Accessed 8 January 2023. https://www.mediareform.org.uk/key-issues/media-ownership-and-control.

Coalition, Media Reform. 'Our History'. Accessed 6 January 2023. https://www.mediaref orm.org.uk/about/our-history.

Cohen, Joshua, and Charles Sabel. 'Extra Rempublicam Nulla Justitia?' *Philosophy & Public Affairs* 34, no. 2 (2006): 147–75.

Colgan, Jeff D., Jessica F. Green and Thomas N. Hale. 'Asset Reevaluation and the Existential Politics of Climate Change'. *International Organisation* 75 (2021): 586–610.

Collins, Daryl, Jonathan Morduch, Stuart Rutherford and Orlanda Ruthven. *Portfolios of the Poor: How the World's Poor Live on $2 a Day*. Princeton, NJ: Princeton University Press, 2011.

Coote, Anna. 'Cameron's "Big Society" Will Leave the Poor and Powerless Behind'. *The Guardian*. 19 July 2010. Accessed 20 November 2022. https://www.theguardian.com/commentisfree/2010/jul/19/big-society-cameron-equal-opportunity.

Cordelli, Chiara. *The Privatized State*. Princeton, NJ: Princeton University Press, 2020.

Crary, Alice. 'Against "Effective Altruism"'. *Radical Philosophy* 2, no. 10 (2021): 33–43.

Creatives, Clean. 'The Future of Creativity Is Clean'. Accessed 6 January 2023. https://cleancreatives.org/.

Credit Suisse. 'Global Wealth Report 2021', Zurich, 2021. Accessed 7 October 2022. https://www.credit-suisse.com/about-us/en/reports-research/global-wealth-rep ort.html.

Dahl, Robert A. 'The Concept of Power'. *Behavioural Science* 2, no. 3 (1957): 201–15.

Data, CO. 'Volume and Consumption: How Much Does the World Buy?', 2018. Accessed 24 August 2022. https://www.commonobjective.co/article/volume-and-consumption-how-much-does-the-world-buy.

Database, Global Fossil Fuel Commitments. 'The Database of Fossil Fuel Divestment Commitments Made by Institutions Worldwide'. Accessed 6 January 2023. https:// divestmentdatabase.org/.

Davies, Robert. 'Social Responsibility and Corporate Values'. In *Making Globalization Good: The Moral Challenges of Global Capitalism*, edited by John Dunning, 301–20. Oxford: Oxford Scholarship Online, 2003.

Davis, Angela Y. *Freedom Is a Constant Struggle: Ferguson, Palestine, and the Foundations of a Movement*. Chicago: Haymarket Books, 2016.

Dawson, Bethany. 'Many in the UK Face a Grim Choice This Winter between Eating and Heating as a Cost-of-Living Crisis Grips the Nation'. *Business Insider*, 9 October 2022.

Dean, Jodi. *Solidarity of Strangers: Feminism after Identity Politics*. Berkeley: University of California Press, 1996.

Debter, Lauren. 'The World's Largest Apparel Companies 2019: Dior Remains on Top, Lululemon and Foot Locker Gain Ground'. *Forbes*, 5 May 2019. Accessed 21 June 2022. https://www.forbes.com/sites/laurendebter/2019/05/15/worlds-largest-appa rel-companies-2019/#24e6188390a2.

Dennett, Daniel C. *Elbow Room: The Varieties of Free Will Worth Wanting*. Oxford: Oxford University Press, 1984.

Derrida, Jacques. *The Politics of Friendship*. London: Verso, 2005.

Desmond, Matthew. *Evicted: Poverty and Profit in the American City*. London: Penguin Books, 2016.

Deveaux, Monique. 'Beyond the Redistributive Paradigm: What Philosophers Can Learn from Poor-Led Politics'. In *Ethical Issues in Poverty Alleviation*, edited by Helmut P. Gaisbauer Gottfried Schweiger and Clemens Sedmak, 225–45. Dordrecht: Springer Netherlands, 2016.

Dicken, Peter. *Global Shift: Mapping the Changing Contours of the World Economy*. 7th edn. London: Sage, 2014.

Douglass, Frederick. 'West India Emancipation: Speech Delivered an Canandaigua, New York'. Edited by University of Rochester Frederick Douglass Project, 1857 Accessed 16 November 2021. http://www.lib.rochester.edu/index. cfm?PAGE=4398.

Dreier, Peter. 'The Campus Anti-Sweatshop Movement'. *The American Prospect*, 19 December 2001. Accessed 31 August 2023. https://prospect.org/education/cam pus-anti-sweatshop-movement/.

Dunlap, Riley E., and Aaron M. McCright. 'Challenging Climate Change'. In *Climate Change and Society: Sociological Perspectives*, edited by Riley E. Dunlap and Robert J. Brulle, 300–32. Oxford: Oxford University Press, 2015.

Dworkin, Ronald. *Justice for Hedgehogs*. London: Belknap Press of Harvard University Press, 2011.

Edwards, Jess. 'We Spend Six Months of Our Working Lives Deciding What to Wear'. *Cosmopolitan*. London, June 2016. Accessed 12 July 2017. https://www.cosmopoli tan.com/uk/fashion/style/news/a43849/deciding-what-to-wear-six-months/.

Elder-Vass, David. *The Causal Power of Social Structures: Emergence, Structure and Agency*. Cambridge: Cambridge University Press, 2010.

Elson, Diane, and Ruth Pearson. ' "Nimble Fingers Make Cheap Workers": An Analysis of Women's Employment in Third World Export Manufacturing'. *Feminist Review* 7, no. 1 (1981): 87–107.

Elson, Diane, and Ruth Pearson. 'The Subordination of Women and the Internationalization of Factory Production'. In *The Women, Gender and Development Reader*, edited by Nalini Visvanathan, Lynn Duggan and Laurie Nisonoff, 2nd edn, 212–25. London: Zed Books, 2011.

Erskine, Toni. 'Assigning Responsibilities to Institutional Moral Agents: The Case of States and Quasi-States'. *Ethics and International Affairs* 15, no. 2 (2001): 67–85.

EU, Council of the. 'New Rules on Corporate Sustainability Reporting: Provisional Agreement between the Council and the European Parliament', 21 June 2022. https://www.consilium.europa.eu/en/press/press-releases/2022/06/21/new-rules-on-sustainability-disclosure-provisional-agreement-between-council-and-european-par liament/.

Extinction Rebellion. 'Free the Press'. Accessed 6 January 2023. https://extinctionrebell ion.uk/act-now/campaigns/free-the-press/.

Fanon, Frantz. *Black Skin, White Masks*. London: Pluto Press, 2008.

Fanon, Frantz. *The Wretched of the Earth*. London: Penguin Classics, 2001.

Feinberg, Joel. 'Collective Responsibility'. *Journal of Philosophy* 65, no. 21 (1968): 674–88.

Ferguson, Ann. 'Iris Young, Global Responsibility, and Solidarity'. In *Dancing with Iris: The Philosophy of Iris Marion Young*, edited by Ann Ferguson and Mechthild Nagel, 185–99. Oxford: Oxford University Press, 2009.

Fernandez-Kelly, Maria. 'Maquiladoras: The View from the Inside'. In *The Women, Gender and Development Reader*, edited by Nalini Visvanathan, Lynn Duggan, Nan Wiegersma and Laurie Nisonoff, 225–37. London: Zed Books, 2011.

Firchow, Pamina. 'Must Our Communities Bleed to Receive Social Services? Development Projects and Collective Reparations Schemes in Colombia'. *Journal of Peacebuilding and Development* 8, no. 3 (2013): 50–63.

Fischer, John Martin. 'Recent Work on Moral Responsibility'. *Ethics* 110, no. 1 (1999): 93–139.

Fischer, John Martin, and Mark Ravizza. *Responsibility and Control: A Theory of Moral Responsibility*. Cambridge: Cambridge University Press, 1998.

Fisher, Mark. *Capitalist Realism: Is There No Alternative?* Winchester: Zer0, 2009.

Fisher, Mark. 'Good for Nothing'. In *K-Punk: The Collected and Unpublished Writings of Mark Fisher*, edited by Darren Ambrose. London: Repeater Books, 2018.

Fisman, Ray. 'Did EBay Just Prove That Paid Search Ads Don't Work?' *Harvard Business Review*, March 2013. Accessed 15 August 2022. https://hbr.org/2013/03/did-ebay-just-prove-that-paid.

Florian, Wettstein. 'Corporate Responsibility in the Collective Age: Toward a Conception of Collaborative Responsibility'. *Business and Society Review* 117, no. 2 (2012): 155–84.

Forrester, Katrina. *In the Shadow of Justice: Postward Liberalism and the Remaking of Political Philosophy*. Princeton, NJ: Princeton University Press, 2019.

Fossielvrij, Reclame. 'Historical! Amsterdam First City World Wide That Wants to Ban Fossil Fuel Advertising', 2020. Accessed 22 November 2022. https://verbiedfossiele reclame.nl/amsterdam-wants-to-ban-fossil-fuel-ads/.

Fossil Fuel Treaty Campaign Hub. 'The Fossil Fuel Free Cities Toolkit'. Accessed 6 January 2023. https://campaign.fossilfueltreaty.org/cities/toolkit.

Foucault, Michel. *Power: Essential Works of Foucault 1954–1984 Volume 3*. Edited by James D. Faubion. London: Penguin, 2000.

Frack, Off. 'Local Groups'. Accessed 7 January 2023. https://frack-off.org.uk/ local-group-specific-pages/.

Frankfurt, Harry. 'Alternate Possibilities and Moral Responsibility'. *Journal of Philosophy* 66, no. 23 (1969): 829–39.

Fraser, Nancy. 'Climates of Capital: For a Trans-Environmental Eco-Socialism'. *New Left Review* 127, no. January–February (2021): 94–127.

Fraser, Nancy. *Scales of Justice: Reimagining Political Space in a Globalizing World*. Cambridge: Polity Press, 2010.

French, Peter A. *Collective and Corporate Responsibility*. Edited by Peter A French. New York: Columbia University Press, 1984.

French, Peter A. 'The Corporation as a Moral Person'. In *Collective Responsibility: Five Decades of Debate in Theoretical and Applied Ethics*, edited by Larry May and Stacey Hoffman, 133–51. Oxford: Rowman and Littlefield, 1991.

French, Peter A. 'The Responsibility of Inactive Fictive Groups for Great Social Problems'. In *Individual and Collective Responsibility*, edited by Peter A. French, 251–9. Rochester, Vermont: Schenkman Books, 1998.

Fröbel, Folker, Jürgen Heinrichs and Otto Kreye. *The New International Division of Labour*. Cambridge: Cambridge University Press, 1980.

Fuchs, Doris. *Business Power in Global Governance*. London: Lynne Reinner, 2007.

Galtung, Johan. 'Violence, Peace, and Peace Research'. *Journal of Peace Research* 6, no. 3 (1969): 167–91.

Gaztambide-Fernández, Rubén A. 'Decolonization and the Pedagogy of Solidarity'. *Decolonization: Indigeneity, Education & Society* 1, no. 1 (2021): 41–67.

Gereffi, Gary. 'The Organization of Buyer-Driven Global Commodity Chains: How U.S. Retailers Shape Overseas Production Networks'. In *Commodity Chains and Global Capitalism*, edited by Gary Gereffi and Miguel Korzeniewicz, 95–122. London: Praeger, 1994.

Gereffi, Gary, and Stacey Frederick. 'The Global Apparel Value Chain, Trade and the Crisis: Challenges and Opportunities for Developing Countries'. World Bank Policy Research Working Paper No. 5281. Washington, DC 2010.

Giddens, Anthony. *Central Problems in Social Theory: Action, Structure and Contradiction in Social Analysis*. London: Macmillan Press, 1979.

Glösel, Kathrin. 'Finland Ends Homelessness and Provides Shelter for All in Need'. *Scoop.Me*, 10 November 2020. Accessed 22 October 2021. https://scoop.me/ housing-first-finland-homelessness/.

Goldtooth, Dallas, Alberto Saldamando and Kyle Gracey. 'Indigenous Resistance Against Carbon'. Washington, DC, 2021. Accessed 6 January 2023. https://www.ienearth. org/indigenous-resistance-against-carbon/.

Goodin, Robert E. 'Responsibilities'. *Philosophical Quarterly* 36, no. 142 (1986): 50–6.

Goodin, Robert E., and Christian Barry. 'Benefiting from the Wrong-Doing of Others'. *Journal of Applied Philosophy* 31, no. 4 (2014): 363–76.

Gordon, Lewis R. 'Decolonizing Structural Justice and Political Responsibility'. In *What Is Structural Injustice?*, edited by Jude Browne and Maeve McKeown. Oxford: Oxford University Press, 2024.

Gordon, Lewis R. 'Iris Marion Young on Political Responsibility: A Reading through Jaspers and Fanon'. *Symposia on Gender, Race and Philosophy* 3, no. 1 (2007): 1–7.

Gould, Carol C. 'Transnational Solidarities'. *Journal of Social Philosophy* 38, no. 1 (2007): 148–64.

Gould, Carol C. 'Varieties of Global Responsibility: Social Connection, Human Rights, and Transnational Solidarity'. In *Dancing with Iris: The Philosophy of Iris Marion Young*, edited by Ann Ferguson and Mechthild Nagel, 199–213. Oxford: Oxford University Press, 2009.

Graeber, David. 'On the Phenomenology of Giant Puppets: Broken Windows, Imaginary Jars of Urine, and the Cosmological Role of the Police in American Culture'. In *Possibilities: Essays on Hierarchy, Rebellion, and Desire*, edited by David Graeber, 375–418. Edinburgh: AK Press, 2007.

Grealish, Rachael. 'NUS Calls for Unis to End Relationships with Fossil Fuel Companies'. *Freshered*, 2022. Accessed 6 January 2023. https://www.freshered.com/nus-calls-for-unis-to-end-relationships-with-fossil-fuel-companies/.

Green, Fergus. 'Anti-Fossil Fuel Norms'. *Climatic Change* 150 (2018): 103–16.

Gupta, Shirpa, and James W. Gentry. 'Evaluating Fast Fashion: Examining Its Micro and the Macro Perspective.' *In Eco-Friendly and Fair: Fast Fashion and Consumer Behaviour*, edited by Mark Heuer and Carolin Becker-Leifhold. London: Routledge, 2018.

Guthrie, Jonathan. 'Lex in Depth: Examining the Slave Trade – "Britain Has a Debt to Repay"'. *Financial Times*. 28 June 2020. Accessed 28 June 2020. https://www.ft.com/content/945c6136-0b92-41bf-bd80-a80d944bb0b8.

Hahn, Henning. 'The Global Consequence of Participatory Responsibility'. *Journal of Global Ethics* 5, no. 1 (2009): 43–56.

Hale, Angela. 'Organising and Networking in Support of Garment Workers: Why We Researched Subcontracting Chains'. In *Threads of Labour: Garment Industry Supply Chains from the Workers' Perspective*, edited by Angela Hale and Jane Wills, 40–69. Oxford: Blackwell, 2005.

Hale, Angela, and Maggie Burns. 'The Phase-Out of the Multi-Fibre Arrangement from the Perspective of Workers'. In *Threads of Labour: Garment Industry Supply Chains from the Workers' Perspective*, edited by Angela Hale and Jane Wills, 210–34. Oxford: Blackwell, 2005.

Hamber, Brandon, and Ingrid Palmary. 'Gender, Memorialization, and Symbolic Reparations'. In *The Gender of Reparations: Unsettling Sexual Hierarchies While Redressing Human Rights Violations*, edited by Ruth Rubio-Marin, 324–81. Cambridge: Cambridge University Press, 2009.

Hancox, Dan. 'No Logo at 20: Have We Lost the Battle against the Total Branding of Our Lives?' *The Guardian*. 19 August 2019. Accessed 15 August 2022. https://www.theguardian.com/books/2019/aug/11/no-logo-naomi-klein-20-years-on-interview.

Hansen, Suzy. 'How Zara Grew Into the World's Largest Fashion Retailer'. *New York Times Magazine*. New York, November 2012. Accessed 15 October 2022. https://www.nytimes.com/2012/11/11/magazine/how-zara-grew-into-the-worlds-largest-fashion-retailer.html.

Hart, H. L. A. *Punishment and Responsibility: Essays in the Philosophy of Law*. 2nd edn. Oxford: Oxford University Press, 2008.

Harvey, David. *The New Imperialism*. Oxford: Oxford University Press, 2005.

Harvey, Fiona. 'Anti-Fracking Protests in Balcombe Signal Major Shift in Public Awareness'. *The Guardian*. 19 August 2013. Accessed 6 January 2023. https://www.theguardian.com/environment/2013/aug/19/fracking-protests-balcombe-cuadrilla-politics.

Haslanger S, 'What Is a (Social) Structural Explanation?' *Philosophical Studies: An International Journal for Philosophy in the Analytic Tradition* 173, no. 1 (2016): 113–30.

Haslanger, Sally. 'Agency under Structural Constraints in Social Systems'. In *What is Structural Injustice?*, edited by Jude Browne and Maeve McKeown. (Oxford: Oxford University Press, 2024.

Hastings, Rob. 'Shein: Fast-Fashion Workers Paid 3p per Garment for 18-Hour Days, Undercover Filming in China Reveals'. *Inews*. 15 October 2022. Accessed 15 October 2022. https://inews.co.uk/news/consumer/shein-fast-fashion-workers-paid-3p-18-hour-days-undercover-filming-china-1909073.

Haugaard, Mark. 'Power: A "Family Resemblance" Concept'. *European Journal of Cultural Studies* 13, no. 4 (2010): 419–38.

Haugaard, Mark. 'Rethinking the Four Dimensions of Power: Domination and Empowerment'. *Journal of Political Power* 5, no. 1 (2012): 33–54.

Health, GBC. 'Our Partners'. Accessed 7 January 2023. https://www.gbchealth.org/partners.

Held, Virginia. 'Can a Random Collection of Individuals Be Morally Responsible?' *Journal of Philosophy* 67, no. 14 (1970): 471–81.

Hernández-Morales, Aitor. 'How Vienna Took the Stigma out of Social Housing'. *Politico*, 30 June 2022. Accessed 17 October 2022. https://www.politico.eu/article/vienna-social-housing-architecture-austria-stigma/.

Hertz, Noreena. 'Why We Must Defuse the Debt Threat'. *Contributions to Political Economy* 24 (2005): 123–33.

Heti, Sheila, Heidi Julavits and Leanne Shapton. *Women in Clothes*. London: Particular Books, 2014.

Hickel, Jason. *Less Is More: How Degrowth Will Save the World*. London: William Heinemann, 2020.

Hickel, Jason. 'Quantifying National Responsibility for Climate Breakdown: An Equality-Based Attribution Approach for Carbon Dioxide Emissions in Excess of the Planetary Boundary'. *Lancet Planetary Health* 4, no. September (2020): 399–404.

Hickel, Jason. *The Divide: A Brief Guide to Global Inequality and Its Solutions*. London: Windmill Books, 2017.

Hind, Dan. 'To Achieve Press Freedom, We Must Rewrite Journalism'. *Open Democracy*, 30 April 2021. Accessed 22 November 2022. https://www.opendemocracy.net/en/opendemocracyuk/achieve-press-freedom-we-must-rewrite-journalism/.

Hobbes, Thomas. *Leviathan*. 2018 edn. Open Road Integrated Media, Inc., 1651.

Honig, Bonnie. *Political Theory and the Displacement of Politics*. New York: Cornell University Press, 1993.

hooks, bell. *Feminist Theory: From Margin to Center*. Boston, MA: South End Press, 1984.

Hurley, Jennifer. 'Unravelling the Web: Supply Chains and Workers' Lives in the Garment Industry'. In *Threads of Labour: Garment Industry Supply Chains from the Workers' Perspective*, edited by Angela Hale and Jane Wills, 95–133. Oxford: Blackwell, 2005.

Hurley, Jennifer, and Doug Miller. 'The Changing Face of the Global Garment Industry'. In *Threads of Labour: Garment Industry Supply Chains from the Workers' Perspective*, edited by Angela Hale and Jane Wills, 16–40. Oxford: Blackwell, 2005.

Hursthouse, Rosalind, and Glen Pettigrove. 'Virtue Ethics'. *Stanford Encyclopedia of Philosophy*, Winter 2016 edition, edited by Edward N. Zalta. Accessed 28 May 2018. https://plato.stanford.edu/archives/win2016/entries/ethics-virtue/.

IMF. 'Press Release: Historic Quota and Governance Reforms Become Effective'. *International Monetary Fund*, 27 January 2016. Accessed 15 April 2023. https://www.imf.org/en/News/Articles/2015/09/14/01/49/pr1625a.

Insure Our Future. 'Our Best Insurance Is to Keep Fossil Fuels in the Ground'. Accessed 6 January 2023. https://global.insure-our-future.com/.

International, Oxfam. 'Richest 1% Bag Nearly Twice as Much Wealth as the Rest of the World Put Together over the Past Two Years'. *Oxfam International*, Accessed 16 January 2023. https://www.oxfam.org/en/press-releases/richest-1-bag-nearly-twice-much-wealth-rest-world-put-together-over-past-two-years#:~:text=According to Credit Suisse%2C individuals,record-smashing peak in 2021.

IPCC. '"Climate Change 2021: The Physical Science Basis". Contribution of Working Group I to the Sixth Assessment Report of the Intergovernmental Panel on Climate Change'. Masson-Delmotte, V., P. Zhai, A. Pirani, S.L. Connors, C. Péan, S. Berger, N. Caud, Y. Chen, L. Goldfarb, M. I. Gomis, M. Huang, K. Leitzell, E. Lonnoy, J. B. R. Matthews, T. K. Maycock, T. Waterfield, O. Yelekçi, R. Yu, and B. Zhou (eds.). Cambridge, United Kingdom and New York, NY, USA: Cambridge University Press.

Isaac, Jeffrey C. 'Beyond the Three Faces of Power: A Realist Critique'. In *Rethinking Power*, edited by Thomas E. Wartenberg, 32–56. Albany: State University of New York Press, 1992.

Jacobitti, Suzanne Duvall. 'The Public, the Private, the Moral: Hannah Arendt and Political Morality'. *International Political Science Review* 12, no. 4 (1991): 281–93.

Jaggar, Alison M. 'Measuring Gendered Poverty: Morality and Methodology'. Unpublished manuscript. In *British Philosophical Postgraduate Association*, 2018.

Jason A., Edwards, and Amber Luckie. 'British Prime Minister Tony Blair's Irish Potato Famine Apology'. *Journal of Conflictology* 5, no. 1 (2014): 43–51.

Jaspers, Karl. *The Question of German Guilt*. New York: Dial Press, 2000.

John C., Coffee, Jr. '"No Soul to Damn: No Body to Kick": An Unscandalized Inquiry into the Problem of Corporate Punishment'. *Michigan Law Review* 79 (1981): 386–459.

Jonas, Hans. *The Imperative of Responsibility: In Search of an Ethics for the Technological Age*. London: University of Chicago Press, 1985.

Jubb, Robert. 'Social Connection and Practice Dependence: Some Recent Developments in the Global Justice Literature: Iris Marion Young, *Responsibility for Justice*. Oxford: Oxford University Press, 2011; and Ayelet Banai, Miriam Ronzoni and Christian Schemmel, *Social Justice, Global Dynamics*. Oxford: Routledge, 2011'. *Critical Review of International Social and Political Philosophy* 16, no. 5 (2013): 698–713.

Kagan, Shelly. 'Do I Make a Difference?' *Philosophy & Public Affairs* 39, no. 2 (2011): 105–41.

Kang, Hye-Ryoung. 'Transnational Women's Collectivities and Global Justice'. In *Gender and Global Justice*, edited by Alison M. Jaggar, 40–62. Cambridge: Polity Press, 2014.

Kaplan, Rami. 'Who Has Been Regulating Whom, Business or Society? The Mid-20th-Century Institutionalization of "Corporate Responsibility" in the USA'. *Socio-Economic Review* 13, no. 1 (2015): 125–55.

King, Anthony. 'The Odd Couple: Margaret Archer, Anthony Giddens and British Social Theory'. *British Journal of Sociology* 61 (2010): 253–60.

Klein, Naomi. *Fences and Windows: Dispatches from the Front Lines of the Globalization Debate*. London: Flamingo, 2002.

Klein, Naomi. *No Logo*. 10th anniversary edn. London: HarperCollins, 2009.

Klein, Naomi. *On Fire: The Burning Case for a Green New Deal*. London: Penguin Books, 2020.

Knowles, Charlotte. 'Responsibility in Cases of Structural and Personal Complicity: A Phenomenological Analysis'. *The Monist* 104 (2021): 224–37.

Kohn, Margaret. *Brave New Neighborhoods: The Privatization of Public Space*. London: Routledge, 2004.

Korbin, Stephen J. 'Private Political Authority and Public Responsibility: Transnational Politics, Transnational Firms, and Human Rights'. *Business Ethics Quarterly* 19, no. 3 (2009): 349–74.

Kristof, Nicholas. 'Where Sweatshops Are a Dream'. *New York Times*. New York, January 2009. Accessed 2 September 2021. https://www.nytimes.com/2009/01/15/opinion/15kristof.html.

Kumar, Ashok. 'A Race from the Bottom? Lessons from a Workers' Struggle at a Bangalore Warehouse'. *Competition & Change* 23, no.4 (2018), 1–32.

Kumar, Ashok. *Monopsony Capitalism: Power and Production in the Twilight of the Sweatshop Age*. Cambridge: Cambridge University Press, 2020.

Kumar, Ashok, and Jack Mahoney. 'Stitching Together: How Workers Are Hemming Down Transnational Capital in the Hyper-Global Apparel Industry'. *Working USA* 17, no. 2 (2014): 187–210.

Kuruvilla, Sarosh. *Private Regulation of Labor Standards in Global Supply Chains*. Ithaca, NY: Cornell University Press, 2021.

Kutz, Christopher. *Complicity: Ethics and Law for a Collective Age*. Cambridge: Cambridge University Press, 2000.

Kutz, Christopher. 'Justice in Reparations: The Cost of Memory and the Value of Talk'. *Philosophy and Public Affairs* 32, no. 3 (2004): 277–312.

Ladd, John. 'Bhopal: An Essay on Moral Responsibiltiy and Civic Virtue'. *Journal of Social Philosophy* 22, no. 1 (1991): 73–91.

Lamb, William F., Giulio Mattioli, Sebastian Levi, J. Timmons Roberts, Stuart Capstick, Felix Creutzig, Jan C. Minx, Finn Müller-Hansen, Trevor Culhane and Julia K. Steinberger. 'Discourses of Climate Delay'. *Global Sustainability* 3, no. 17 (2020): 1–5.

Lambert, Rashaad. 'Exclusive: Lloyd's of London Responds to T.I'.s Open Letter Calling Out Its Ties to Trans-Atlantic Slave Trade'. *Forbes*, 14 August 2020. Accessed 8 November 2022. https://www.forbes.com/sites/forbestheculture/2020/08/14/exclusive-lloyds-of-london-responds-to-tis-open-letter-calling-out-its-ties-to-trans-atlantic-slave-trade/.

Lebron, Christopher. 'Equality from a Human Point of View'. *Critical Philosophy of Race* 2, no. 2 (2014): 125–59.

Lippke, Richard L. 'Advertising and the Social Conditions of Autonomy'. *Business & Professional Ethics* 8, no. 4 (1989): 35–58.

Lloyd's. 'Our History', n.d. Accessed 8 November 2022. https://www.lloyds.com/about-lloyds/history/.

Lloyd's. 'The Lloyd's Corporation', n.d. Accessed 8 November 2022. https://www.lloyds.com/about-lloyds/the-corporation.

Louie, Miriam Ching Yoon. *Sweatshop Warriors: Immigrant Women Workers Take on the Global Factory*. Cambridge, MA: South End Press, 2001.

Lu, Catherine. 'Colonialism as Structural Injustice: Historical Responsibility and Contemporary Redress'. *Journal of Political Philosophy* 19, no. 3 (2011): 261–81.

Lu, Catherine. *Justice and Reconciliation in World Politics*. Cambridge: Cambridge University Press, 2017.

Lukes, Steven. *Power: A Radical View*. 2nd edn. London: Palgrave Macmillan, 2005.

Macpherson, C. B. 'The Problems of a Non-Market Theory of Democracy'. In *Democratic Theory: Essays in Retrieval*, edited by C. B. Macpherson, 39–70. Oxford: Clarendon Press, 1973.

Mahony, Emma. 'Opening Spaces of Resistance in the Corporatized Cultural Institution: Liberate Tate and the Art Not Oil Coalition'. *Museum & Society* 15, no. 2 (2017): 126–41.

Manjapra, Kris. 'When Will Britain Face up to Its Crimes against Humanity?' *The Guardian*. 29 March 2018. Accessed 29 March 2018. https://www.theguardian.com/news/2018/mar/29/slavery-abolition-compensation-when-will-britain-face-up-to-its-crimes-against-humanity.

Manuel, Velasquez. 'Why Corporations Are Not Responsible for Anything They Do'. In *Collective Responsibility: Five Decades of Debate in Theoretical and Applied Ethics*, edited by Larry May and Stacey Hoffman. Oxford: Rowman and Littlefield, 1991.

Marchand, Roland. *Advertising the American Dream: Making Way for Modernity, 1920–1940*. Berkeley: University of California Press, 1985.

Marchand, Roland. *Creating the Corporate Soul: The Rise of Public Relations and Corporate Imagery in American Big Business*. Berkeley: University of California Press, 1998.

Marin, Mara. *Connected by Commitment: Oppression and Our Responsibility to Undermine It*. Oxford: Oxford University Press, 2017.

Marin, Mara. 'Transformative Action as Structural and Publicly-Constituted'. In *What Is Structural Injustice?*, edited by Jude Browne and Maeve McKeown. Oxford: Oxford University Press, 2024

Martí i Puig, Salvador. 'The Emergence of Indigenous Movements in Latin America and Their Impact on the Latin American Political Scene: Interpretive Tools at the Local and Global Levels'. *Latin American Perspectives* 37, no. 6 (2010): 74–92.

Marx, Karl, and Frederick Engels. *The Communist Manifesto*. New York: Pathfinder, [1848] 1987.

Mason, Paul. *Why It's Kicking Off Everywhere*. London: Verso, 2012.

May, Larry. *Sharing Responsibility*. London: University of Chicago Press, 1992.

Mayer, Robert. 'Sweatshops, Exploitation and Moral Responsibility'. *Journal of Social Philosophy* 38, no. 4 (2007): 605–19.

McCarthy, Thomas. *Race, Empire, and the Idea of Human Development*. Cambridge: Cambridge University Press, 2009.

McKeown, Maeve. 'Backward-Looking Reparations and Structural Injustice'. *Contemporary Political Theory* 20, no. 4 (2021): 771–94.

McKeown, Maeve. 'ETMP Discussion of Robin Zheng's "What Is My Role in Changing the System? A New Model of Responsibility for Structural Injustice"'. Pea Soup, 2018. http://peasoup.us/2018/06/etmp-discussion-of-robin-zhe ngs-what-is-my-role-in-changing-the-system-a-new-model-of-responsibility-for-str uctural-injustice/

McKeown, Maeve. 'Global Structural Exploitation: Towards an Intersectional Definition'. *Global Justice: Theory Practice Rhetoric* 9, no. 2 (2016): 155–77.

McKeown, Maeve. 'Iris Marion Young's "Social Connection Model" of Responsibility: Clarifying the Meaning of Connection'. *Journal of Social Philosophy* 49, no. 3 (2018): 484–502.

McKeown, Maeve. 'Structural Injustice'. *Philosophy Compass* 16, no. 7 (2021): e12757.

McKeown, Maeve. 'Sweatshop Labor as Global Structural Exploitation'. In *Exploitation: From Practice to Theory*, edited by Monique Deveaux and Vida Panitch, 35–57. London: Rowman and Littlefield, 2017.

McKeown, Maeve. 'Sweatshops and Shame'. Beauty Demands, 2017. http://beauty demands.blogspot.com/2017/08/sweatshops-and-shame_29.html

McKeown, Maeve. 'The Law's Contribution to Deliberate Structural Injustice'. In *Structural Injustice and the Law*, edited by Virginia Mantouvalou and Jonathan Wolff. London: UCL, 2024.

Medina, José. *The Epistemology of Resistance: Gender and Racial Oppression, Epistemic Injustice, and Resistant Imaginations*. Oxford: Oxford University Press, 2013.

Mehta, Pratap Bhanu. 'Cosmopolitanism and the Circle of Reason'. *Political Theory* 28, no. 5 (2000): 619–39.

Mele, Alfred. 'Free Will and Neuroscience'. *Philosophic Exchange* 43, no. 1 (2013): 1–16.

Merotto, Dino, Tihomir Stucka and Mark Roland Thomas. 'African Debt since HIPC: How Clean Is the Slate?' Washington, DC, 2015.

Meyer, David S. 'How Social Movements Matter'. In *The Social Movements Reader: Cases and Concepts*, 3rd edn, 386–91. Chichester: Wiley Blackwell, 2015.

Micheletti, Michele. *Political Virtue and Shopping*. New York: Palgrave Macmillan, 2003.

Micheletti, Michele, and Andreas Follesdal. 'Shopping for Human Rights. an Introduction to the Special Issue'. *Journal of Consumer Policy* 30, no. 3 (2007): 167–75.

Mies, Maria. *Patriarchy and Accumulation on a World Scale: Women in the International Division of Labour*. 3rd edn. London: Zed Books, 2014.

Mikler, John. *The Political Power of Global Corporations*. Cambridge: Polity Press, 2018.

Miller, David. *A Century of Spin: How Public Relations Became the Cutting Edge of Corporate Power*. London: Pluto Press, 2007.

Miller, David. *National Responsibility and Global Justice*. Oxford: Oxford University Press, 2007.

Miller, David. *On Nationality*. Oxford: Oxford University Press, 1995.

Mills, Charles W. 'Race and Global Justice'. In *Domination and Global Political Justice*, edited by Barbara Buckinx, Jonathan Trejo-Mathys and Timothy Waligore, 181–206. New York: Routledge, 2015.

Moellendorf, Darrel. *Global Inequality Matters*. Dordrecht: Springer, 2009.

Mohanty, Chandra. 'Under Western Eyes: Feminist Scholarship and Colonial Discourses'. *Feminist Review* 30, no. 1 (1988): 61–88.

Mohanty, Chandra Talpade. *Feminism without Borders: Decolonizing Theory, Practicing Solidarity*. Durham, NC: Duke University Press, 2003.

Mouffe, Chantal. *The Return of the Political*. 2nd edn. London: Verso, 2005.

Moyn, Samuel. *Not Enough: Human Rights in an Unequal World*. Cambridge, MA: Belknap Press, 2018.

Murphy, Simon. 'Factory That Supplied Tesco Compensated Abused Worker'. *The Guardian*. 22 January 2019. Accessed 22 January 2019. https://www.theguardian.com/world/2019/jan/22/bangladeshi-factory-that-supplied-tesco-and-marks-and-spencer-compensates-abused-worker.

Murray, Joshua. 'Interlock Globally, Act Domestically: Corporate Political Unity in the 21st Century'. *American Journal of Sociology* 122, no. 6 (2017): 1617–63.

Nadia, Khomami. 'Receptionist "Sent Home from PwC for Not Wearing High Heels"'. *The Guardian*. 11 May 2016. Accessed 11 May 2016. https://www.theguardian.com/uk-news/2016/may/11/receptionist-sent-home-pwc-not-wearing-high-heels-pwc-nicola-thorp.

Nagel, Thomas. 'The Problem of Global Justice'. *Philosophy & Public Affairs* 33, no. 2 (2005): 113–47.

Nathan, Clemens. 'The Value of Experience: What Post World War II Settlements Teach Us about Reparations'. In *Colonialism, Slavery, Reparations and Trade: Remedying the Past?*, edited by Fernne Brennan and John Packer, 209–20. Oxon: Routledge, 2012.

Neuhäuser, Christian. 'Structural Injustice and the Distribution of Forward-Looking Responsibility'. *Midwest Studies in Philosophy* 38 (2014): 232–51.

Newell, Peter, and Andrew Simms. 'Towards a Fossil Fuel Non-Proliferation Treaty'. *Climate Policy* 20, no. 8 (2020): 1043–54.

Noggle, Robert. 'The Ethics of Manipulation'. *Stanford Encyclopedia of Philosophy*, Summer 2022 edition, edited by Edward N. Zalta. Accessed 15 August 2022. https://plato.stanford.edu/entries/ethics-manipulation/.

Nolan, Peter, Dylan Sutherland and Jin Zhang. 'The Challenge of the Global Business Revolution'. *Contributions to Political Economy* 21 (2002): 91–110.

Norton, Ben. 'West Opposes Rest of World in UN Votes for Fairer Economic System, Equality, Sustainable Development'. *Multipolarista*, 22 December 2022. Accessed 22 December 2022. https://geopoliticaleconomy.com/2022/12/22/west-un-vote-economic-system-equality/

Nussbaum, Martha C. *Frontiers of Justice: Disability, Nationality, Species Membership*. Cambridge, MA: Belknap Press, 2006.

Nussbaum, Martha C. 'Foreword'. In *Responsibility for Justice*, edited by Iris Marion Young, ix–xxv. Oxford: Oxford University Press, 2011.

Nuti, Alasia. *Injustice and the Reproduction of History: Structural Inequalities, Gender and Redress*. Cambridge: Cambridge University Press, 2019.

O'Connor, James. 'Capitalism, Nature, Socialism: A Theoretical Introduction'. *Capitalism, Nature, Socialism* 1, no. 1 (1988): 11–38.

O'Neill, Onora. 'Global Justice: Whose Obligations?' In *The Ethics of Assitance: Morality and the Distant Needy*, edited by Deen K Chatterjee, 242–60. Cambridge: Cambridge University Press, 2004.

O'Neill, Onora. *Toward Justice and Virtue: A Constructive Account of Practical Reasoning*. Cambridge: Cambridge University Press, 2002.

OpenDemocracy. 'About Us'. Accessed 6 January 2023. https://www.opendemocracy.net/en/about/.

Oxfam International. 'The Inequality Virus'. Oxford, 2021. Accessed 20 September 2021. https://oxfamilibrary.openrepository.com/bitstream/handle/10546/621149/bp-the-inequality-virus-250121-en.pdf.

Parekh, Serena. 'Getting to the Root of Gender Inequality: Structural Injustice and Political Responsibility'. *Hypatia* 26, no. 4 (2011): 672–89.

Parrish, John M. 'Collective Responsibility and the State'. *International Theory* 1, no. 1 (2009): 119–54.

Pasternak, Avia. 'Limiting States' Corporate Responsibility'. *Journal of Political Philosophy* 21, no. 4 (2013): 361–81.

Pasternak, Avia. 'Voluntary benefits from wrongdoing', Journal of Applied Philosophy 31, no.4 (2014): 377-391.

Paton, Elizabeth. 'Fears for Bangladesh Accord'. *New York Times*. 28 May 2021. Accessed 28 May 2021. https://www.nytimes.com/2021/05/28/business/banglad esh-worker-safety-accord.html.

Peters, Greg, Mengyu Li and Manfred Lenzen. 'The Need to Decelerate Fast Fashion in a Hot Climate – A Global Sustainability Perspective on the Garment Industry'. *Journal of Cleaner Production* 295 (2021): 126390.

Pettifor, Ann. 'The Jubilee 2000 Campaign: A Brief Overview'. In *Sovereign Debt at the Crossroads: Challenges and Proposals for Resolving the Third World Debt Crisis*, edited by Chris Jochnick and Fraser A. Preston, 297–318. Oxford: Oxford University Press, 2006.

Pettit, Philip, and Christian List. *Group Agency: The Possibility, Design, and Status of Corporate Agents*. Oxford: Oxford University Press, 2011.

Pickard, Hanna. 'Responsibility without Blame: Therapy, Philosophy, Law'. *Prison Service Journal* 213 (2014): 10–18.

Pickrell, Emily. 'Oil and Gas Industry Must Get Serious About Climate Change to Compete for Millennial and Gen Z Workforce'. *Forbes*, 12 January 2021. Accessed 6 January 2023. https://www.forbes.com/sites/uhenergy/2021/01/12/ oil-and-gas-industry-must-get-serious-about-climate-change-to-compete-for-millenn ial-and-gen-z-workforce/

Pollin, Robert. 'De-Growth vs A Green New Deal'. *New Left Review* 112, no. July August (2018): 5–25.

Porpora, Douglas V. 'Four Concepts of Social Structure'. *Journal for the Theory of Social Behaviour* 19, no. 2 (1989): 195–211.

Powers, Madison, and Ruth Faden. *Structural Injustice: Power, Advantage, and Human Rights*. Oxford: Oxford University Press, 2019.

Prentice, Rebecca, and Geert De Neve. 'Five Years after Deadly Factory Fire, Bangladesh's Garment Workers Are Still Vulnerable'. *The Conversation*. London, November 2017. Accessed 6 September 2021. https://theconversation.com/ five-years-after-deadly-factory-fire-bangladeshs-garment-workers-are-still-vulnera ble-88027.

Rao, Rahul. *Third World Protest: Between Home and the World*. Oxford: Oxford University Press, 2010.

Rawlinson, Kevin. 'Lloyd's of London and Greene King to Make Slave Trade Reparations'. *The Guardian*. 18 June 2020. Accessed 18 June 2020. https://www.theguardian.com/world/2020/jun/18/lloyds-of-london-and-gre ene-king-to-make-slave-trade-reparations.

Rawls, John. *A Theory of Justice*. Revised edn. Cambridge, MA: Belknap Press of Harvard University Press, 1971.

Rawls, John. *The Law of Peoples*. Cambridge, MA: Harvard University Press, 1999.

Richards, Akilah S. 'How Blackgirl Natural Hair Is Shamed from Infancy to Adulthood'. *Everyday Feminism*, 2014. Accessed 15 November 2017. https://everydayfeminism. com/2014/08/how-natural-hair-is-shamed/.

Richardson, Henry S. 'Institutionally Divided Moral Responsibility'. *Social Philosophy and Policy* 16, no. 2 (1999): 218–49.

Risse, Mathias, and Gabriel Wollner. *On Trade Justice: A Philosophical Plea for a New Global Deal*. Oxford: Oxford University Press, 2019.

Robinson, Cedric J. *Black Marxism: The Making of the Black Radical Tradition*. 2020 edn. London: Penguin Classics, 1983.

Robinson, William I, and Jeb Sprague. 'The Transnational Capitalist Class'. In *The Oxford Handbook of Global Studies*, edited by Mark Juergensmeyer, Saskia Sassen, Manfred B. Steger and Victor Faessel, 309–28. Oxford: Oxford University Press, 2018.

Rorty, Richard. 'Human Rights, Rationality and Sentimentality'. In *On Human Rights*, edited by Stephen Shute and Susan Hurley, 111-135. New York: Basic Books, 1993.

Rossi, Arianna, Christian Viegelahn, and David Williams. 'The Post-COVID-19 Garment Industry in Asia'. Geneva: ILO, 2021. Accessed 22 August 2022. https://www.ilo.org/ wcmsp5/groups/public/---asia/---ro-bangkok/documents/briefingnote/wcms_814 510.pdf.

Rushe, Dominic. 'Unions Reach $2.3m Settlement on Bangladesh Textile Factory Safety'. *The Guardian*. 22 January 2018. Accessed 22 January 2018. https://www. theguardian.com/business/2018/jan/22/bandgladesh-textile-factory-safety-unions- settlement.

Rylko-Bauer, Barbara, and Paul Farmer. 'Structural Violence, Poverty, and Social Suffering'. In *The Oxford Handbook of the Social Science of Poverty*, edited by David Brady and Linda M. Burton, 47–74. Oxford: Oxford University Press, 2016.

Safi, Michael. 'Child Labour "Rampant" in Bangladesh Factories, Study Reveals'. *The Guardian*. 7 December 2016. Accessed 22 August 2022. https://www.theguardian. com/global-development/2016/dec/07/child-labour-bangladesh-factories-rampant- overseas-development-institute-study.

Salminen, Jaakko. 'The Accord on Fire and Building Safety in Bangladesh: A New Paradigm for Limiting Buyers' Liability in Global Supply Chains?' *American Journal of Comparative Law* 66, no. 2 (2018): 411–51.

Sangiovanni, Andrea. 'Global Justice, Reciprocity, and the State'. *Philosophy & Public Affairs* 35, no. 1 (2007): 3–39.

Sangiovanni, Andrea. 'Structural Injustice and Individual Responsibility'. *Journal of Social Philosophy* 49, no. 3 (2018): 461–83.

Saunders-Hastings, Emma. 'Plutocratic Philanthropy'. *Journal of Politics* 80, no. 1 (2018): 149–61.

Scanlon, T. M. *What We Owe to Each Other*. London: The Belknap Press of Harvard University Press, 1998.

Schefczyk, Michael. 'Modern Germany and the Annihilation of the Ottoman Armenians: A Note on the Political Avowal of Shame and Guilt'. In *Der Genozid an Den Armeniherlinnen: Beiträge Zur Wissenschaftlichen Aurfarbeitung Eines Historischen Verbrechens Gegen Die Menschlichkeit*, 85–111. Wiesbaden: Springer VS, 2018.

Schefczyk, Michael. "Moral Responsibility for Historical Injustice." In *The Routledge Handbook of Philosophy of Responsibility*, edited by Maximilian Kiener. London: Routledge, 2023.

Scheffler, Samuel. 'Individual Responsibility in a Global Age'. In *Boundaries and Allegiances: Problems of Justice and Responsibility in Liberal Thought*, edited by Samuel Scheffler. Oxford: Oxford University Press, 2001.

Schiff, Jade Larissa. *Burdens of Political Responsibility: Narrative and the Cultivation of Responsiveness*. Cambridge: Cambridge University Press, 2016.

Schmitz, Hans Peter, and Elena M. McCollim. 'Billionaires in Global Philanthropy: A Decade of the Giving Pledge'. *Society* 58 (2021): 120–30.

Scholz, Sally J. *Political Solidarity*. Pennsylvania: Penn State Press, 2008.

Scott, James C. *Weapons of the Weak: Everyday Forms of Peasant Resistance*. New Haven, CT: Yale University Press, 1987.

Scott, John. *Power*. Cambridge: Polity Press, 2001.

Seabrook, Jeremy. *The Song of the Shirt: The High Price of Cheap Garments, From Blackburn to Bangladesh*. London: C Hurst, 2015.

Sewell, William H. 'A Theory of Structure: Duality, Agency, and Transformation'. *American Journal of Sociology* 98, no. 1 (1992): 1–29.

Shapiro, Bradley, Hitsch Günter and Anna Tuchman. 'TV Advertising Effectiveness and Profitability: Generalizable Results from 288 Brands'. *Econometrica* 89, no. 4 (2021): 1855–79.

Shepherd, Verene A. 'Part Imperfect, Future Perfect? Reparations, Rehabilitation, Reconciliation'. *Journal of African American History* 103, no. 1 (2018): 19–43.

Shue, Henry. *Basic Rights: Subsistence, Affluence, and US Foreign Policy*. Princeton, NJ: Princeton University Press, 1980.

Silbey, Susan S. 'Ideology, Power, and Justice'. In *Justice and Power in Sociolegal Studies*, edited by Bryant G. Garth and Austin Sarat, 272–309. Illinois: Northwestern University Press, 1998.

Singer, Peter. 'Famine, Affluence and Morality'. In *The Global Justice Reader*, edited by Thom Brooks, 387–97. Oxford: Blackwell Publishing, 2008.

Singer, Peter. 'The Singer Solution to World Poverty'. *New York Times*. 1999. Accessed 22 October 2021. https://www.nytimes.com/1999/09/05/magazine/the-singer-solut ion-to-world-poverty.html.

Skorpen Claeson, Björn. 'Our Voices: Bangladeshi Garment Workers Speak'. Washington, DC: International Labor Rights Forum, 2015. Accessed 8 March 2019. https://laborrights.org/sites/default/files/publications/Our%20Voices,%20Our%20Saf ety%20Online_1.pdf.

Slote, Michael. *From Morality to Virtue*. Oxford: Oxford University Press, 1995.

Soper, Kate. 'Rethinking the 'Good Life': The Consumer as Citizen'. *Capitalism, Nature, Socialism* 15, no. 3 (2004): 111–16.

Spivack, Emily. *Worn Stories*. New York: Princeton Architectural Press, 2014.

Srinivasan, Amia. 'Stop the Robot Apocalypse'. *London Review of Books* 37, no. 18 (2015): 3–6.

Stangneth, Bettina. *Eichmann before Jerusalem: The unexamined life of a mass murderer*. New York: Vintage, 2014.

Statement, Civil society. 'Civil Society Statement on the Proposed EU Corporate Sustainability Due Diligence Directive', 2022. Accessed 23 August 2022. https:// corporatejustice.org/wp-content/uploads/2022/05/CSO_statement_CSDDD_EN.pdf.

Statista. 'Advertising Spending Worldwide from 2000 to 2024'. Statista, 2023. Accessed 14 April 2023. https://www.statista.com/statistics/1174981/advertising-expe nditure-worldwide/#:~:text=Global%20advertising%20spending%202000%2D2

024&text=Global%20advertising%20spending%20in%202022,by%20the%20 end%20of%202024.

Steinberger, Peter J. 'Hannah Arendt on Judgment'. *American Journal of Political Science* 34, no. 3 (1990): 803–21.

Stilz, Anna. 'Collective Responsibility and the State'. *Journal of Political Philosophy* 19, no. 2 (2011): 190–208.

Stoddard, Isak, Kevin Anderson, Stuart Capstick, Wim Carton, Joanna Depledge, Keri Facer, Clair Gough, et al. 'Three Decades of Climate Mitigation: Why Haven't We Bent the Global Emissions Curve?' *Annual Review of Environment and Resource* 46 (2021): 653–89.

Stones, Rob. *Structuration Theory*. Basingstoke: Palgrave Macmillan, 2005.

Stop Ecocide International. 'Activating a Law to Protect the Earth'. Accessed 6 January 2023. https://www.stopecocide.earth/.

Strawson, Peter F. 'Freedom and Resentment'. In *Freedom and Resentment and Other Essays*, 23–35. Oxon: Routledge, 2008.

Striker, Gisela. 'Aristotle's Ethics as Political Science'. In *The Virtuous Life in Greek Ethics*, edited by Burkhard Reis, 127–41. Cambridge: Cambridge University Press, 2006.

Thompson, Janna. *Taking Responsibility for the Past: Reparation and Historical Injustice*. Cambridge: Polity Press, 2002.

Thompson, John B. 'The Theory of Structurationism'. In *Social Theory of Modern Societies: Anthony Giddens and His Critics*, edited by David Held and John B. Thompson, 56–77. Cambridge: Cambridge University Press, 1989.

Trebilcock, Anne. 'The Rana Plaza Disaster Seven Years on: Transnational Experiments and Perhaps a New Treaty?' *International Labour Review* 159, no. 4 (2020): 545–68.

Trefis, Team, and Great Speculations. 'Trends in Global Advertising Industry: Winners and Losers Part 1'. Forbes, 2015. Accessed 7 October 2022. https://www.forbes. com/sites/greatspeculations/2015/09/28/trends-in-global-advertising-industry-winn ers-and-losers-part-1/#6334934250ac.

UCL. 'Legacies of British Slave-Ownership Project', 2020. Accessed 8 November 2022. https://www.ucl.ac.uk/lbs/project/project.

UN. 'UN Expert Warns of Dangerous Decline in Media Freedom'. United Nations Office of the High Commissioner, 2022. Accessed 6 January 2023. https://www.ohchr.org/ en/stories/2022/07/un-expert-warns-dangerous-decline-media-freedom.

UNHCR. 'Statelessness around the World'. United Nations High Commission for Refugees. Accessed 6 January 2023. https://www.unhcr.org/ibelong/statelessness- around-the-world/.

Valentini, Laura. 'Coercion and (Global) Justice'. *American Political Science Review* 105, no. 1 (2011): 205–20.

Vandenberghe, Frédéric. 'The Archers: A Tale of Folk (Final Episode?)'. *European Journal of Social Theory* 8, no. 2 (2005): 227–37.

Vargas, Manuel. 'The Trouble with Tracing'. *Midwest Studies in Philosophy* 24 (2005): 269–91.

Vasanthakumar, Ashwini. 'Recent Debates on Victims' Duties to Resist Their Oppression'. *Philosophy Compass* 15, no. 2 (2019): e12648.

Vergès, Françoise. *A Decolonial Feminism*. Edited by Ashley J. Bohrer. London: Pluto Press, 2021.

Vestergaard, Jakob, and Robert H. Wade. 'Still in the Woods: Gridlock in the IMF and the World Bank Puts Multilateralism at Risk'. *Global Policy* 6, no. 1 (2015): 1–12.

Vivian. 'I'm a Trans Woman and I'm Not Interested in Being One of the "Good Ones"'. *Autostraddle*, 15 May 2013. Accessed 12 July 2017. https://www.autostraddle.com/im-a-trans-woman-and-im-not-interested-in-being-one-of-the-good-ones-172570/

Vogel, David. 'Taming Globalization? Civil Regulation and Corporate Capitalism'. In *The Oxford Handbook of Business and Government*, 472–92. Oxford: Oxford Scholarship Online, 2010.

Vogler, Gisli. 'Power between Habitus and Reflexivity - Introducing Margaret Archer to the Power Debate'. *Journal of Political Power* 9, no. 1 (2016): 65–82.

Waldron, Jeremy. 'What Is Cosmopolitanism?' *Journal of Political Philosophy* 8, no. 2 (2000): 227–43.

Wallace, R. Jay. *Responsibility and the Moral Sentiments*. London: Harvard University Press, 1994.

Warren, Camille. 'Coming Undone: The Implications of Garment Industry Subcontracting for UK Workers'. In *Threads of Labour: Garment Industry Supply Chains from the Workers' Perspective*, edited by Angela Hale and Jane Wills, 133–61. Oxford: Blackwell Publishing, 2005.

Wartenberg, Thomas E. *The Forms of Power: From Domination to Transformation*. Philadelphia: Temple University Press, 1990.

Whyte, Kyle. 'Indigenous Climate Change Studies: Indigenizing Futures, Decolonizing the Anthropocene'. *English Language Notes* 55, nos. 1–2 (2017): 153–62.

Wicker, Alden. 'Fashion Has a Misinformation Problem. That's Bad for the Environment'. *Vox*, 31 January 2020. Accessed 26 August 2022. https://www.vox.com/the-goods/2020/1/27/21080107/fashion-environment-facts-statistics-impact

Williams, Matthew S. 'Global Solidarity, Global Worker Empowerment, and Global Strategy in the Anti-Sweatshop Movement'. *Labor Studies Journal* 45, no. 4 (2020): 394–420.

Williamson, John. 'A Short History of the Washington Consensus'. *Law and Business Review of the Americas* 15, no. 1 (2009): 7–26.

Williamson, John. 'Democracy and the Washington Consensus'. *World Development* 21, no. 8 (1993): 1329–36.

Wither, Emily. 'Can Local Communities Make a Difference in the Transition to Net Zero?' UK: Channel4News, 2023.

Wolff, Jonathan. 'Structural Harm, Structural Injustice, Structural Repair'. In *What Is Structural Injustice?*, edited by Jude Browne and Maeve McKeown. Oxford: Oxford University Press, 2024.

Wolgast, Elizabeth. *Ethics of an Artificial Person: Lost Responsibility in Professions and Organizations*. Stanford: Stanford University Press, 1992.

Woods, Ngaire. 'Making the IMF and World Bank More Accountable'. *International Affairs* 77, no. 1 (2001): 83–100.

Woods, Ngaire, and Amrita Narlikar. 'Governance and the Limits of Accountability: The WTO, the IMF, and the World Bank'. *International Social Science Journal* 53, no. 170 (2001): 569–83.

Young, Iris Marion. *Inclusion and Democracy*. Oxford: Oxford University Press, 2002.

Young, Iris Marion. *Justice and the Politics of Difference*. Princeton, NJ: Princeton University Press, 1990.

Young, Iris Marion. 'Political Responsibility and Structural Injustice'. *The Lindley Lecture*. University of Kansas, 2003.

Young, Iris Marion. 'Responsibility and Global Justice: A Social Connection Model'. *Social Philosophy and Policy* 23, no. 1 (2006): 102–30.

Young, Iris Marion. 'Responsibility and Global Labor Justice'. *Journal of Political Philosophy* 12, no. 4 (2004): 365–88.

Young, Iris Marion. *Responsibility for Justice*. Oxford: Oxford University Press, 2011.

Young, Iris Marion. 'Women Recovering Our Clothes'. In *On Female Body Experience: 'Throwing Like a Girl' and Other Essays*, edited by Iris Marion Young, 62–75. Oxford: Oxford University Press, 2005.

Yuval-Davis, Nira. *Gender and Nation*. London: Sage, 1997.

Zheng, Robin. 'Moral Criticism and Structural Injustice'. *Mind* 130, no. 518 (2021): 503–35.

Zheng, Robin. 'What Is My Role in Changing the System? A New Model of Responsibility for Structural Injustice'. *Ethical Theory and Moral Practice* 21 (2018): 869–85.

Zheng, Robin. 'What Kind of Responsibility Do We Have for Fighting Injustice? A Moral-Theoretic Perspective on the Social Connections Model'. *Critical Horizons* 20, no. 2 (2019): 109–26.

Zuboff, Shoshana. *The Age of Suveillance Capitalism*. London: Profile Books, 2019.

Zwolinski, Matt. 'Structural Exploitation'. *Social Philosophy and Policy* 29, no. 1 (2012): 154–79.

Zwolinski, Matt. 'Sweatshops, Choice and Exploitation'. *Business Ethics Quarterly* 17, no. 4 (2007): 689–727.

Index

Note: Figures are indicated by page number followed by "f". Endnotes are indicated by the page number followed by "n" and the endnote number e.g., 20 n.1 refers to endnote 1 on page 20.